IN THE
NAME
OF THE
FATHER

IN THE NAME OF THE NAME OF THE FATHER

FAMILY, FOOTBALL,
AND THE **MANNING DYNASTY**

MARK RIBOWSKY

LIVERIGHT PUBLISHING CORPORATION

A DIVISION OF W. W. NORTON & COMPANY

INDEPENDENT PUBLISHERS SINCE 1923

NEW YORK   LONDON

For information about permission to reproduce selections from this book,
write to Permissions, Liveright Publishing Corporation, a division of
W. W. Norton & Company, Inc., 500 Fifth Avenue, New York, NY 10110

For information about special discounts for bulk purchases, please contact
W. W. Norton Special Sales at specialsales@wwnorton.com or 800-233-4830

Manufacturing by LSC Communications, Harrisonburg
Book design by Daniel Lagin
Production manager: Anna Oler

Library of Congress Cataloging-in-Publication Data

Names: Ribowsky, Mark author.
Title: In the name of the father : family, football, and the Manning dynasty / Mark
Ribowsky.
Description: First edition. | New York : Liveright Publishing Corporation, A division
of W. W. Norton & Company Independent Publishers since 1923, [2018] | Includes
bibliographical references and index.
Identifiers: LCCN 2018008749 | ISBN 9781631493096 (hardcover)
Subjects: LCSH: Manning, Archie, 1949– | Manning, Cooper. | Manning, Peyton. |
Manning, Eli, 1981– | Manning family. | Quarterbacks (Football)—United States—
Biography. | Football players—United States—Biography. | Fathers and sons—
Mississippi—Biography.
Classification: LCC GV939.A1 R485 2018 | DDC 796.3320922 [B] —dc23
LC record available at https://lccn.loc.gov/2018008749

Liveright Publishing Corporation
500 Fifth Avenue, New York, N.Y. 10110
www.wwnorton.com

W. W. Norton & Company Ltd.
15 Carlisle Street, London W1D 3BS

1 2 3 4 5 6 7 8 9 0

For my own legatee, Jake Ribowsky

CONTENTS

INTRODUCTION

FAMILY MATTERS

"Has it ever struck you, Connie, that life is all memory, except for the one present moment that goes by you so quick you hardly catch it going?"

—MRS. GOFORTH TO THE WITCH, *THE MILK TRAIN DOESN'T STOP HERE ANYMORE* BY TENNESSEE WILLIAMS

Like the other famed Southern family dynasty of the last half century, the Bushes, who actually came by way of New England and not the Deep South, the three-headed Manning football dynasty, its roots in the Mississippi mud, seems never to go gentle into that good night. Witness the self-perpetuating saga of Eli Manning, the baby of the family, who still plays on Sundays, upholding the tradition built by his father, Archie, and updated by his brother Peyton—though Eli may have wished he too had retired before the 2017 season, when the weekly travails of the carnival act from hell known as the New York Giants won him three games and the kind of headlines no player with his achievement would want. Indeed, by the time this surreal nightmare was over, he found himself on a bad acid trip into the underbelly of his career, courtesy of a team without blocking, defense, or running, and a coach without a clue. The latter, a mustached mannequin known as Ben McAdoo, who had gotten to the playoffs the previous season with the same team almost solely on Manning's interception-prone but clutch arm. He then seemed to conspire with equally feckless team management and ownership to crucify their quarterback of distinction, keeping him from starting his 211th consecutive game, having bettered his brother's streak of 208 to trail only Brett Favre's record 297.

If this was meant as a power struggle that would climax with a Manning trade, it was the worst plot since the cork in the middle of the island in *Lost*. After one game, and in the midst of a backlash in the city not seen since a president told it to drop dead in the 1970s, the Giants brainless brahmins did an about-face, gave him his job back, and sent the coach packing, possibly to a gulag—but leaving open the question of whether the third Manning would stay or go, capping his career with a real team or, as his brother was prevented from doing, ending it with the one he began with so long ago.

By the new year, it was clear he would stay, less clear if he would be throwing to Odell Beckham Jr., a wildly talented receiver with the impulse control of a six-year-old, who surfaced over the last off-season in a video cavorting in bed, a funny looking cigarette in hand, with a woman holding a credit card in front of lines of white powder. That made it seem likely Beckham would be pawned to the highest bidder, leaving Eli's path back to the Super Bowl after five years in the woods even less likely. If so, his now long-ago victories over Tom Brady's New England Patriots in that event will always stand as Eli's only edge over Peyton, who lost to Brady 11 of 17 times, forever leaving his legacy unfairly damned by faint praise—as the best regular-season quarterback in history.

But give him props, Peyton Manning was great enough and charmed enough to beat Brady in their final clash, with a Super Bowl appearance as the reward and the chance to close out a fairy tale few believed was possible, retiring with his second NFL championship. Four seasons before, he too had been 36 and had undergone four neck surgeries that left the nerve endings in his right hand unable to feel the ball he was throwing. But, leaving the Indianapolis Colts for the Denver Broncos, his knees wobbling and joints groaning, he made it to his fourth Super Bowl, against the superior Carolina Panthers and their preening quarterback, Cam Newton, the avatar of a new generation of mobile, ultra-athletic quarterbacks. It was a generational settling of scores if ever there was one. And even if it was because he was lifted by his defense, the old boy sure did finish in style. The last pass of his career, the two-point conversion that made the final tally 24–10, put away his 200th career victory, a nice, round all-time record he held for less than a year before Brady bettered him (as he has in most metrics, including their head-to-head matches).

His 2007 championship ring from the Indianapolis Colts was now part of a matching set. Peyton could have gone on as a shell of himself, either in Denver or somewhere else, but a Manning has too much pride for that. And so, even though signed for another year at $19 million, he bowed out, battered and reduced, but on top. Of course, the last thing either Manning brother needed out of football anymore was capital, having socked away the kind of green that their old man—who in his day was the most celebrated college quarterback and the highest-paid NFL rookie ever—could only have imagined. Both sons have also eclipsed the on-field numbers Archie slaved to achieve. After playing 18 seasons, Peyton held 21 records, including: most MVP awards (5); consecutive seasons with 25 or more touchdowns (13); games with four or more touchdown passes (35); 4,000-yard seasons (14); touchdowns (539); passing yards (71,940); 300-yard games (93); seasons with 350 or more completions (10); comeback wins (45); game-winning drives (56); playoff appearances (15); Pro Bowl appearances (14); touchdowns in a single season (55); and passing yards in a season (5,477). Besides Brett Favre, he is the only other quarterback to have beaten all 32 NFL teams.*

As important, he positioned himself as a commodity, a man of prodigious talent and intellect—like his dad and brother, earning both Phi Beta Kappa and All-American honors. Not incidentally, he also won sympathy (as had his father) for failing—specifically, in big games (his playoff record was a tepid 14–13). Devastation humanized him, elevating his

---

* A feat made possible by not playing solely for one team. Tom Brady and Ben Roethlisberger have both beaten 31 teams—all but the clubs they've played on for their entire careers, the New England Patriots and Pittsburgh Steelers, respectively.

commercial appeal and neutralizing the old debates about Manning versus Brady, debates that were abjectly silly and are by now clearly settled: Brady is the better quarterback, but Manning is the better icon.

It matters not if Peyton doesn't use Nationwide as his insurance company or eats much pizza; only that every slice sold in 21 Papa John's franchises in Colorado delivers him a slice of the profits. After Peyton won that Super Bowl and his Broncos were feted at the White House, President Barack Obama stood right in front of him and riffed, "And then there's this guy from the commercials. It doesn't matter whether you need insurance, pizza, a Buick, you basically can stock your whole household with stuff this guy is selling."[1] Or, as a sportswriter put it, "The man sells everything from crappy pizza to Outlaw Country, and comes off the screen somehow not having cheapened himself."[2]

The Manning brothers know all about marketing themselves. They come from money, surround themselves with it, reek of it. Even Peyton's wife, Ashley, a Memphis native, bought into the ownership of the NBA's Memphis Grizzlies in 2012 with her own money. Both Mannings have hosted *Saturday Night Live*, their episodes the highest-rated of their respective seasons. Peyton has made $267.7 million from the game, and around $12 million or so outside of it in each of the last few years alone.[3] Even in a millennial-dominated culture that began to pass him by half a decade ago, he is a hip sort of dinosaur. And don't expect him to be extinct any time soon.

———

Blame Archie—who, despite thriving in more penurious times for athletes, has a net worth of around $10 million—for nurturing this national ubiquity. Though fewer fans each year seem to know it, for three years he *was* the Southeastern Conference (SEC), and beyond that, "the most fabulous athlete ever produced by the state of Mississippi," wrote the incomparable Paul Zimmerman in 1981. Directing the Ole Miss offense from 1968 through 1970, running and passing in a frenetic haze, he won the SEC Player of the Year award in '69—the same year he had to endure his father's suicide. On the Oxford campus, where he led teams onto the field carrying the Stars and Bars to racist chants from the stands, they set the speed limit at 18 miles per hour because Archie wore that number. They wrote songs about him, like "The Ballad of Archie Who." Sportswriters called him Ole Miss's "One Horseman." Fans named their children after him. He was deified as the SEC's Quarterback of the Quarter Century (1950–75). Expected to be a messiah with the New Orleans Saints when they drafted him in 1971, he instead became a symbol of neo-Southern failure. Through no fault of his own, the Saints were abysmal, and no one—not Archie Manning, not Robert E. Lee, not Jesus Christ himself—could save them. In both success and failure, Archie was a symbol of Southern manhood and white male privilege, or as one writer has put it, the South's "fusion of history and reality, of myth and memory."[4] His sons share some of that legacy.

Following Archie by a decade, Peyton made his name while the family name was still so familiar. When he had proven himself as a pro, in 1999, *Sports Illustrated* wrote that he was "more than living up to his pedigree."[5] Eli shared his brother's carnivorous competitive and mercenary instincts, and they took him to two championships—a remarkable achievement for a guy his own center once called "one of the most unathletic quarterbacks in the NFL."[6] More impressive was whom he beat to get them, both times taking down Brady's Patriots—the *unbeaten* Patriots—in the first meeting, Super Bowl XLII, when he made the play of the millennium, the long heave caught by David Tyree against his helmet. Both times, Eli came away as Super Bowl MVP. Less well remembered is that, to get there each time, he had to best the Green Bay Packers in the winter wonderland of Lambeau Field, against guys named Favre and Rodgers.

Eli is a hero and antihero at once. He is only the seventh quarterback in NFL history with at least 50,000 career passing yards, the sixth with at least 330 touchdowns. He's made four Pro Bowl appearances. He is also arguably the best fourth-quarter QB in the league, and one of the most durable of all time. He's currently working on a contract that guarantees him $67 million, second only to Andrew Luck's $87 million. His endorsements pull in $8 million more; his net worth is around $115 million. But no one can quite figure him out. During Peyton's farewell triumph, the Manning brood, gathered in a VIP box, celebrated. The beautiful and regal matriarch, Olivia Manning, clapped wildly. The forgotten Manning, Cooper—the eldest son, who was supposed to be the best athlete before he was felled by spinal stenosis, hoisted one of his children onto his shoulders. But Eli barely reacted. When Olivia tried to high-five him, she had to grab his hand. Some thought he looked "miserable."[7] But then, as Peyton says, his baby brother *always* looks like that. Or worse.

———

To be certain, Peyton was the only Manning who could have turned the family royal, his personality fine-tuned to please everyone despite either self-inflicted or concocted damage to his image. Indeed, he could not take his final bow without the scent of scandal, or maybe pseudo-scandal.

Even so, while New Orleans turned on Archie during his hellish years there, Peyton was Lancelot in the contrived pro football Camelot. This helps to explain why, even in his retirement, his orange Broncos jersey is still the second best-selling piece of NFL merchandise, outselling even the jersey of that other white knight, Brady. Eli perpetuates and accentuates the royal lineage, but the dynasty itself is bigger than either of them, because the Mannings' grip on the modern American sports id and popular culture was funneled through the American South, with football a conduit through the tides of still-incomplete social change. In the formative years of Archie Manning and, to a slightly lesser degree, his sons, each was the beau ideal of Southern manhood and its high-and-mighty traditions of arrogant grandeur, even though when Eli got to Ole Miss, the grandeur was more pitiful than powerful. From backwoods and dirt farms to blue skies and mansions, the lure of the gridiron has been irresistible.

For many of these reasons, football heroes from the South, like great novels from the South, seem to resonate more deeply than others. They transcend region and feel, instead, national. As with any great American success story, the story of the Mannings is at times complicated and dark, but it inexorably lurches forward, driven always by football and surrounded by the protective cloak of family.

PROLOGUE

MANNING INC.

A long journey through the byways and detours of America's modern football landscape led this time traveler to a clearing in the underbrush of the Deep South on a blistering hot afternoon in June 2016. Here, in a place called Thibodaux, Louisiana, could be seen the line of succession of the Manning royal family joined together on a football field—not a pro field, but one in the football backwoods, at a college out for the summer on the edge of town, Nicholls State University, where they have performed this ritual every year since 1995, when Archie began operating the Manning Passing Academy. The mission statement of the Academy is to provide four days of tutorials for high school and college quarterbacks, a vehicle Peyton and then Eli came aboard in the late '90s as co-directors of what has become a thriving operation, with a tab of $685 per attendee. As Archie proudly informed the visitor on the first day of the camp, his boys "have been here 100 percent of the time for 20 years; they've never left for an hour to go do something else."

For four days, in the pit of Guidry Stadium—named for Ron Guidry, the great New York Yankee pitcher known as "Louisiana Lightning"—on the campus where Archie used to attend training camp with the execrable Saints in the '70s, the Mannings would move over the grounds in baggy shorts and camp T-shirts, blowing whistles, dispensing instruction and gentle criticism, every word like gospel for the congregation. One of them, Dak Prescott, fresh out of Mississippi State, had no clue that he was weeks from suddenly finding himself the Dallas Cowboys' QB after Tony Romo was injured, about to ring up the best rookie season ever—19 years after one Peyton Manning did that himself. Another attendee was Cooper Kupp, an All-American from Eastern Washington University whose grandfather Jake once played left guard on Archie's Saints.

It was another year of dispensing such fragrant bromides—as Peyton would, in that nasal voice that comes out sounding higher than he wants it to—as "You've got to know what you're doing out there, because then you can get rid of the ball, and when you get rid of ball, you don't get hit" and "I try to throw the ball really quickly, before those big, ugly defensive linemen come tackle me." But because they're the Mannings, reporters will follow them here—one of whom, this time-traveling author, had long ago interviewed Peyton after his rookie season. The article that came out of it, titled "No. 1 with a Bullet," concluded that despite his Colts going 3–13, he was quite worthy of his $48 million contract.[1] He is not the sculpted specimen he was then, wear and tear leaving him looking every bit his age, the once cool-looking clamping of his jaws now something one might see when a middle-aged man leaves a proctologist's office.

Back in 2011, when he underwent the second and third of his neck operations and couldn't grip a football, much less a dumbbell, he texted someone a picture of himself from the college days, under which he wrote, "At one point I did look good."[2] Now, five years later, his growing forehead is a common punch line, one being that it "came from years of inbreeding."[3] Archie's showing his age, too. Nearing 70, the patriarch is long past the beatings he took in vain for the bottom-feeding Saints. Long ago, sporting freckles, red hair, and a nose for adventure, he was described as "Huck Finn"; even in 1981, at the end of his career, "He doesn't seem 32 years old," wrote Paul Zimmerman in *Sports Illustrated*.[4] A bit stooped but still trim, still running his mile every morning, Archie's face resembles that of another famous Southern man, Jimmy Carter. The eyes stare. There always was something sad in those eyes; betrayed by losing so much in his own career, the game can displease him. After the Broncos were blown out by the Seattle Seahawks in Super Bowl XLVIII, he stood alone outside the locker room and admitted, "That's why I hate football." He also will tell you he has actually rooted for only one team, Ole Miss; his son's teams have only rented his loyalty. "I'm beyond living and dying over football games" is a maxim of his.[5]

And Eli, the sole survivor? More than Peyton, he seems to have inherited the most from the old man. Tightly controlled, stoic to a fault—the "quiet one," they used to call him, as if he were a non-rocking George Harrison—Eli is also apt to seem, well, bewildered. In fact, his sideline reactions have regularly popped up on the internet, the most popular his dazed-eyed stupor (oh, and the one when his forehead was doused in blood). Fortunately, none of the Mannings take themselves too seriously off the field and have no objection to sending themselves up in TV commercials as arguably the three whitest dudes in sports. In one, they were cast in rappers' garb, chains around their neck, Eli in an Afro, striding through the streets of New Orleans, lip-syncing very bad white-boy rap. Archie, in a platinum-blond wig, sat perched, Elvis-like, on a velvet throne. They were so good that one rap purist implored, "Don't let the Manning brothers trick you into liking their rap video."[6] Consider, too, Peyton's mock-serious performance in a spoof for an ESPN awards show that turned the warmhearted football movie *The Blind Side* into a horror flick called *The Dark Side*, as an NFL star held prisoner and forced to play tackle. "I'm a quarterback!" he pleads at one point, in vain. (The funniest line was the "review" by New England Patriots coach Bill Belichick: "It's hilarious.")

Their acting abilities aside, very serious debates have occurred about which Manning brother was the better player. Eli couldn't hope to match Peyton's stats—except in the really big games. In 2013, *Washington Post* columnist Mike Wise, underscoring a certain segment of the media that was always rubbed wrong by Peyton, snarked that he was "simply a better Fantasy League quarterback, commercial pitchman and needy diva than his younger and more introverted brother. Eli can be an enigmatic wreck, but he is a more resourceful, money quarterback in the last two minutes of almost every game played in January or February [when] his brother . . . is usually hosting *Saturday Night Live*."[7] Never mind that Peyton got to those summit games five times to Eli's two. For his part, Eli is not the type to brag—or, for that matter, say much of anything. Asked about his brother's future on this day in Thibodeaux, he was his usual starchy self, making no eye contact, a half grin hiding his impatience to stop talking.

"He'll do what's best for him. He always has. And he's always succeeded."

The visitor tried a jokey question: Who knows more about quarterbacking, him or Peyton?

"Neither." He ran his hand through his damp hair. "My dad does. He *had* to be. Dad is also the only one of us that ever had a real job outside of football. He sold insurance, he's sold stocks, sold cars. He's more worldly than either of us will ever be. We've had it spoiled. Dad was my best quarterback coach. Peyton was already a huge star when I was still in high school. He had more to do than waste time with his kid brother. He didn't let me into his games much, and when he did, I would be stuck at center." The half grin returns. "That really pissed me off."

═══

Indeed, Eli consciously set out to be Not Peyton. Though both sons show traits of both Beaver Cleaver and Eddie Haskell, Peyton showed some real rebelliousness in not following Archie to Ole Miss, whereas Eli, the son who did, carries the school's nickname with more natural ease. He was indeed more of a rebel. Born to Generation X, Eli has a deeper grasp of the cultural diversions of the millennial crowd than Peyton, who was given a belated education in this regard in Denver, courtesy of what he coyly says were "some recent law changes,"[8] the results of which he could smell through his face mask playing in what aptly used to be called Mile High Stadium.

But just try to figure these Mannings out. They are devout Christians, though not without exceptions. They are Republicans, and after Donald Trump took power, Peyton came running to speak at a GOP function hosted by a man he'd shunned during the campaign in favor of Jeb Bush. And then there's Eli, who has hosted fundraisers for New Jersey Democrats and was voted the Democrats' favorite quarterback in a poll a few years ago (Tim Tebow was the Republicans' fave). The same Eli Manning who gave $2,700 to Jeb Bush in 2016.

If all this is confusing, one gets the idea that the three Mannings don't always know themselves who and what they are, only how they are supposed to look when the public is watching. Which explains why Peyton remains deep in the molecular structure of the game and the culture; the league's precipitous decline in TV ratings may even have had something to do with him not being seen *enough*. After all, the *Atlantic* once called him "a generational talent" who was "lab-built to fulfill the needs of the NFL, in regards to both the evolution of the sport itself and its family- and advertiser-friendly, corporate-synergistic sheen."[10]

─────

The stats don't lie. Peyton was a Pro Bowler 14 times, Eli four so far. Peyton's career yardage and touchdown numbers are beyond Eli's reach. Unless he wins a third ring, Eli will likely not be a Hall of Famer. Even winning his two, he is still the butt of the joke, caricatured as the bumpkin brother, though his IQ is the highest of them all. Indeed, one of his former Giant teammates swears that Eli's sometimes-inscrutable palaver is actually calculated. "That's all by design, not by default," said the player. "Eli's smart. He's playing chess while everybody's playing checkers."[11] Such qualities are hard to see in Eli, but he's been lucky, for sure: the only Manning to avoid major injury as he moved past Peyton's career-opening string of 208 consecutive games played (plus 19 more in the playoffs), the 10th-longest streak ever. That Peyton did that was no surprise; Eli, on the other hand, was dubbed "The NFL's Unexpected Iron Man" by *Sports Illustrated*, which ran a big photo of him, blood streaming from a cut on his forehead, and insisted, "Eli Manning is tougher than you."[12] Amen, brother. And in the end, when all that could be written about them has been, if Eli ends up with as many rings as Peyton, it will be his durability that separated them, and his most tangible advantage over the brother he followed into the center ring. Or maybe it was luck.

─────

As for the patriarch, Archie does not pretend he was the perfect father. "We had our problems," he says. "There were bumps in the road all along the way."[13] If asked which son is the better quarterback, his steel-gray eyes will bore a hole right through you—the exact look parodied in a commercial in which he reads a mock letter from Peyton, urging him to stop telling the media he loves all his sons the same, because "no one's buying it." During an ESPN show, Alec Baldwin asked Archie, "Peyton or Eli?"—meaning which was better. With rehearsed pique, Archie replied, "Let me ask a question: Alec or Billy?" Replied Alec, "Touché, Archie Manning." Truth be told, however, Eli is in fact the equivalent of Billy Baldwin.

But they are, as a whole, three sides of the same coin, which shines as the quintessential Southern family, loyal to each other to the end. Victory for one is victory for the family. That means everyone; when the ultimate pop culture gauge, *The Simpsons*, inevitably caricatured them in 2009, all three Manning brothers voiced their cartoon counterparts—including Cooper, the one cursed by bum luck, if making around $15 million as an energy trader can be called bum luck.

In his wing-tip shoes, he is, as much as his cleat-wearing brothers and father, part of the real family business—Manning Inc., the one that keeps the brand running. Eli did his part by making the 2017 NFL season the 20th in a row, and 33rd in the last 47 years, with a Manning playing quarterback. There was no third ring, yet, but there was the sort of reward clean-nosed veterans receive: he was co-winner, with the Arizona Cardinals' Hall of Fame–bound receiver Larry Fitzgerald, of the league's Walter Payton Award for his charity work, which included $2.5 million to open the Eli Manning Children's Clinic at the University of Mississippi Medical Center. Peyton, meanwhile, went about his uneasy second year of retirement, perpetuating the brand with a string of public and TV appearances. There is a reason the Manning Academy is still filled to the rafters. It is the same reason Peyton Manning still laces on his cleats and throws a football for only these few days every year. The kids who steam in need to see him. Archie and Eli Manning are royalty, but Peyton turns the key to Manning Inc. And even after two decades spent in incandescence, the simple validation of kids who dream of walking in his footsteps makes time stand still. If only it were that easy during the psychodramas of 20 years in that burning spotlight.

IN THE
NAME
OF THE
FATHER

CHAPTER 1

"THEY AIN'T STOPPIN' IN DREW"

The distance between the Manning clan and its roots can be measured in a newspaper headline from the January 26, 2008, *New Orleans Times-Picayune*. As if an elegy, it read, "The Hometown Archie Once Knew Is No More." That was more for dramatic effect than literal meaning. Save for football and gospel music, Mississippi has, over the last five decades, only gotten progressively moribund, earning its place as the poorest, least educated and most disenfranchised state.[1] But the town where Archie was born and raised—Drew, Mississippi—is still there, up in the northwest corridor of the Mississippi Delta—sometimes known as "the most Southern place on earth,"[2] all but swallowed up by miles and miles of cotton fields.

In the article, writer Billy Turner looked for traces Archie might've left behind nearly five decades ago. While the house where he lived and the fields where he played his way to fame were frozen in time, his connections to the town were invisible. At Drew High School, where he set records, few of the young black teenagers who make up the majority of the student body—the influx of whose families led white families to pull their kids out of the school and send them to another, whiter one in Sunflower County—had no idea who Archie Manning was, though they of course knew of his sons. There was still a school football team, and the stadium where he played still stood, but as Turner wrote, "It once was filled as Manning was rolling out right and either passing or galloping down the field. This season, the stands were nearly empty on Friday nights, and the team needs new equipment."[3] Drew High, which sits mere yards from the one-story house where Archie grew up (at 181 South Third Street, on the corner of Green Avenue), would itself empty out later that same year, its charter terminated, a victory for selective belt-tightening by the still-white county board of education that, not coincidentally around these parts, wanted to save money by closing a black school. As a result, for the last eight years, the abandoned skeleton of Drew High, its tan exterior and pinkish roof and empty classrooms, has sat forlornly vacant, weeds crawling up the walls.

The old Manning house still sits on the corner, its wood frame pale gray. In the backyard is the husk of a shack used once as a clubhouse, faded letters reading "No Girls Allowed" handwritten on the door, written by Archie before he knew better. Once, agents, managers, coaches, and fans would come calling here—"hundreds and hundreds," Archie's mother, Jane "Sis" Manning, once estimated. "People would call saying they wanted to represent him, telling him what subjects to major in. They'd show up at the door from all states of the Union. I had a ring stolen one time. One man walked in and took two pictures off the wall. 'I'll send them back,' he said. He never did."[4]

Not long after the *Times-Picayune* story ran, the state legislature suddenly decided to send to the governor House Bill 1480, designating a portion of US Highway 49W that runs through Drew as Manning Boulevard. They did this at the same time that another section of highway in Drew was designated the Van T. Barefoot Medal of Honor Highway, and yet another the George "Happy" Irby Parkway. The state senate also declared an Eli Manning Appreciation Day, 40 years after the town had a day for Archie Manning, as a reward for Eli not fleeing to Tennessee to play his college ball, unlike Peyton.[5] There was a time when Archie regularly returned to Drew over the summer to visit his mother and sister, but only until Sis Manning died in 2000. To some people around town, Archie turned his back on them. To be sure, Drew is not much on his mind.

"It's kind of sad up there, isn't it?" he told Turner. "I get back up there as much as I can but I don't make a big deal about it. I don't call ahead. I get up there when I'm nearby and I slip in and go to the cemetery or whatever . . . I just don't have time. When anyone asks me where I'm from, though, I say Drew. I don't even say New Orleans." He added, by rote, "Drew has been good to me and I say thank you each day for my life and being fortunate to spend the happiest part of my life here." But he also remembered what his father once told him, speaking of the state penitentiary just up the road in Parchman. Sometimes, prisoners would break out, making Archie wonder if they would make their way through town.

"Listen, they're over in Parchman," his dad would tell him. "If they come this way, they ain't stoppin' in Drew," just passin' through on the way to better places.

<hr />

The Manning ancestors who came to America looking for a better place came across the Atlantic from England and Scotland and settled in Virginia in 1745. One Elisha Manning, born in 1803 in Marion, South Carolina, would relocate his family to Crystal Springs, Mississippi, the heart of antebellum slaveholding society, nestled in the southwest corner of the state, bordered by the Mississippi River, just south of the Mississippi Delta. A year after the Civil War that cost Mississippi over eight thousand men, Elisha's grandson Elisha Archibald Manning had three sons, whose families had by the turn of the century found their way to Drew, a few hundred miles north up the Mississippi.

Named for the daughter of a slave owner, Drew was known mainly as a stop along the route of the Illinois Central Railroad. There, between the Sunflower and Tallahatchie Rivers, the Mannings lived on a homestead the census called the R. W. Manning Plantation, in the township known as Beat 5, Sunflower, which comprised Drew and Ruleville just to the south. The broiling-hot, tropically humid climate meant that the thousand or so farmers who wound up there could expect reasonably good profits when they took their cotton crops to be sold to the distributors. A new revenue stream opened up when soybeans and rice began to come into demand in the 1920s. In Drew, that was the definition of living the good life, though everything about it was humble. One neighbor of Archie Manning's granddaddy in the 1910s was a child named Thomas Lanier Williams. While this is not to suggest that Tennessee Williams was inspired by the Mannings of Mississippi, they were the sort of clan he spent a lifetime writing about in plays and novels as people more complicated than they looked, who existed in "an actual menagerie."

══════

African-Americans in Drew also pulled crops from the soil when not confined to their own neighborhoods. Not only were they neglected by the white town elders, but the Parchman prison was a convenient excuse for cops to believe—or pretend to believe—that black men seen in white neighborhoods were escapees and to exercise as much force as they wanted to subdue them. If they put up a fight, it was cause for putting innocent men in the slam, though any resistance—or sometimes none at all—was deemed strong enough to administer on-the-spot capital punishment. Southern culture author J. Todd Moye notes that Drew and its environs were "considered the most recalcitrant of Sunflower County and perhaps of the entire state," and "a dangerous place to be black." Within the walls of the prison, wrote Moye, black life "was worth next to nothing."[6]

To nobody's surprise, the Ku Klux Klan had a chapter in Drew. There is no evidence that any of the Mannings put on a white hood and robe, but neither is there any reason to believe they opposed the Klan. Rather, it seems they were simple cotton farmers trying to survive times that never got any easier. They worked, obeyed the law, and then put on their Sunday best and went to Drew's First Baptist Church.

Elisha Archibald Manning Jr., a short but barrel-chested man, was called Buddy. In 1927, his Drew High junior-year yearbook, the *Deltaneer*, shows him in a bow tie and sporty sweater, eyes round and staring as if for comic effect, hair cropped short, identifying him as "E. A. Manning, Wittiest Boy." In the senior yearbook, he is far more, well, mature, in a light suit, a wry but dashing smile. And he was as serious as a young man could be. Searching for more than a career as a planter, he went to Bowling Green Business College in Kentucky, then taught business at

Pachula High School and Northwest Mississippi Junior College in Sena-
tobia before moving back to Drew, ready to put his business principles to
good use within a profession he knew best. He got a job as manager of
Case Farm Supply, which sold sundry farm machinery such as mowers
and tractors.

Smart as he was, Buddy could read the economic trends, particularly
the slow death of King Cotton, and soon he was making enough to take a
wife, marrying in 1938 a girl from Humboldt, Tennessee, Jane Elizabeth
Nelson, nine years younger than he, whose own diminutive stature was
overcompensated for by a feisty but warm nature that led to her own
punchy nickname, Sis. They were inseparable, with Buddy freely admitting, only half in jest, that Sis wore the pants in the family. Their plans
for a family were put on hold when Buddy enlisted in the army after
Pearl Harbor was attacked. He served as a private, and then, in the flush
of the postwar burst of individualism and optimism, with the demands of
the newly booming economy increasing the value of his farm equipment,
he turned his attention toward growing a family.

In 1946, Sis became pregnant and gave birth to a son, Joe, who died
of complications in childbirth. A year later, they had a daughter, Pamela
Ann. Then, on May 19, 1949, eighty-five years to the day after the end of
a Civil War battle in Spotsylvania that Ulysses S. Grant would call the
bloodiest he ever saw, they had a son, Elisha Archibald Manning III. He
seemed small, but after they brought him home to the house a stone's
throw from the high school, he began to grow. Like Buddy, he had a less
stuffy identity—he was to be "Archie," a name the boy would long into
the future claim was the one on his birth certificate, though the city's
records show it as Archibald. He and Pam began school at A. W. James
Elementary, then Hunter Middle School—which were kept segregated
despite the Supreme Court's landmark *Brown vs. Board of Education*
ruling in 1954. In Drew, as all over the South, "freedom of choice" laws
funneled African-Americans into schools that were no more than shacks
without electricity or running water, such as the Drew Colored Consoli-
dated School.

But even white folks could only go so far in a town that called itself
"the waterfowl capital of the state" but was frequently hit by crippling

droughts. On that arid land, any lighthearted respite from work was welcome, something that united both ends of the racial divide. Yet, if not for Archie Manning, Drew might today be most famous for the achievements of its oppressed black residents, many of whom joined the great black migration from the Deep South. Two of them, Roebuck "Pops" Staples and his wife, Oceola, sang in gospel groups in Drew. After they moved to Chicago in 1935, they formed the Staple Singers. Others stayed put, turning to music as well for solace. In nearby Crystal Springs, Tommy Johnson wrote the classic "Canned Heat Blues." The white populace had its own musical cravings, many similar, such as their church choirs and the rising hillbilly beat taken from the black bluesmen, and later the rockabilly and nascent rock and roll of a truck-driving singer from Tupelo named Elvis Presley.

———

Life in Drew was an accretion of sleepy, dusty Delta days. But no one worked harder than Buddy Manning. When the census man came around to the house in 1940 and asked him how many weeks a year he worked, Buddy, calling himself a "sales clerk," answered "Fifty-two."[7] Years later, Archie Manning would have vivid memories of his father at Case Supply, holding court with salesmen and farmers, smoking, drinking nickel Cokes. It was, says Archie, "the place to go to bullshit."[8] Buddy was a tightly wound, anal man, almost obsessively focused on taking the family name higher, above the mundane picking and chopping of cotton and soybeans. He demanded the same kind of excellence and obedience from his own three sons. As Archie described him, "He was stubborn. He was tough. . . . He smoked, like everybody. Smoked Chesterfields. He wore to work, every day, a pair of khakis and a shirt. And he had to have two front pockets. . . . One pocket for his pens, and one for his Chesterfields."

To please Buddy, Archie hit the books hard and stayed out of trouble. Buddy had played some high school football, but his main contribution was as a guy who would stick his head into much bigger guys' chests and leave a mark during on-field fights. But Archie could not fail to see that Buddy was pushing his luck as he got older. He was, his son said, "never all that healthy. He smoked and didn't exercise, and was always struggling—with his health, with his job at Case, with life generally."

Pictures taken of Buddy, even when he was holding his son in his lap, are those of an unsmiling man, seemingly with the weight of the world on his broad shoulders. As Archie grew, he too played sports with an almost frightful competitive zeal and an eye for detail that was nearly obsessive-compulsive. As his sister, Pam, recalled, "Archie always worked very hard at everything he did, whether it was school or sports. I think he was just a good child. He did everything right." She recalled her brother proudly showing off a pin the Drew First Baptist Church gave him for perfect attendance at Sunday school. "It was like fourteen or fifteen years he didn't miss a day," she said, shaking her head still at that kind of dedication. "His friends poked fun at him for it, not that he cared."[9]

Why should he have? On the ball field or basketball court, he could eat them for lunch. His talent and coordination were obvious, but the clincher was his maniacal zeal to win. That, and his endless thirst for practice. With his leadership qualities, he was the ideal shortstop, barking out encouragement to his team and "No hitter, no hitter!" when the other team's kids stepped into the batter's box. Though he threw right-handed, he batted from the left side so as to see pitches from right-handed pitchers better. He recalled that "I was one of these ball-all-day type of kids," which enamored him to the school and Little League coaches. It may or may not be apocryphal, but Archie tells of building an actual full-sized baseball diamond, in the manner of *Field of Dreams*, in the backyard.[10]

As early as 1959, his name appeared in the papers—though not for sports, but rather something almost as important in these parts. The *Delta Democrat Times* of Greenville, Mississippi, listing the kids going to the Ki-Y summer camp, identified Archie and Pam. A year later, it told of Archie being in a 4-H Club meet meant for boys and girls who had "excelled in club work the past year and who have demonstrated good leadership." In '64, at a countywide talent and public-speaking contest on May 4, it was reported that "Archie Manning of Drew was first place in the junior boys' public speaking." At 14, he wrote an essay for school precociously titled "My Autobiography," in which he recognized that "I have been blessed with a healthy body and mind. I stand five feet six inches tall and weigh one hundred-twenty pounds. . . . I don't know what I intend to be but plan to enter some college. I hope to be someone my friends, teachers, and parents won't be ashamed of."[11]

Frank Crosthwait Jr., a lawyer and family friend who had gone to Ole Miss and became Sunflower County's top prosecutor, recalls Archie at First Baptist, wearing "a bright red jacket and white gloves. Listen, he always stood out, not because he wanted to but because he had that *look*, the red hair over his eyes, the strut, the confidence, not caring if anyone else ribbed him."[12] As Archie explained about the gloves, he had seen Pam wearing them and "fell in love with them." At 13, he began to attract notice for what would become a familiar reason. In '62, playing in the area's summertime Central Delta Babe Ruth League with older guys, he was chosen for an all-star team in a tournament in Columbus. Three players from each town were chosen, and on July 20 the *Delta Democrat Times* reported, "Drew's contributions to the team are Chuck Ford, Mike Brooks, and Archie Manning—the only 13-year-old on the team. Archie will be starting as the second baseman." Archie has fond memories of 1961, following the box scores and the *Game of the Week* as Mickey Mantle and Roger Maris got closer to Babe Ruth's home run record. The Yankees, he said, "were my team and I was a typical obnoxious Yankee fan,"[13] and he used to openly dream of playing shortstop for them. This too might have earned someone other than him a slap upside the head in Drew.

Drew High was the launching pad. He got there in 1964, a critical year both for him and the civil rights struggle. For Archie, the real world went only as far as his family, his only real refuge. People remember him not as shy so much as unwilling to trust anyone outside of Buddy, Sis, and Pam. When he would travel beyond Drew, people thought he had a touch of arrogance. But as Pam Manning explained it, he was simply a product of the town's tightly structured family ethos. "In a small town like that," she said, "all the families did things together. We had two or three churches, one school, and everyone knew everyone else." That meant pretty much always knowing where he was. It also meant that even the parents of other kids had a collective stake in his rising star. Wherever he went, it was with Drew on his back.

Buddy Manning—even his children called him Buddy, not Daddy—was, like most Southern gents, a big sports buff. His son recalls listening to Ole Miss games on the radio with him, his ear pressed to the radio on Halloween night 1959, when the Rebels played LSU in a battle of undefeated teams, a still-legendary game in those parts, and how he cried all night after Billy Cannon returned a late-game punt 89 yards, breaking seven tackles on the way, to put the Tigers ahead. The Rebels then marched all the way to the one-yard line before being stopped—by the ubiquitous Cannon, the Heisman Trophy winner that year. When the game was replayed on the radio at midnight, he listened again. "And when it was over I cried again."[14]

Buddy, who was built like a fireplug, had played and coached sandlot baseball and football. Besides Ole Miss, he rooted for the gridiron New York Giants in the then-ragtag NFL, mainly because of Charlie Conerly, their grizzled quarterback. In the late 1940s, "Chuckin' Charlie," born in Clarksdale, Mississippi, was the first great Ole Miss QB, though officially he was, in the terminology of the times, a tailback, taking the snap directly in the I formation and running the offense as the de facto QB (completing a then-record 133 passes in 1947). An ex-Marine who fought in Guam, the leathery-skinned Conerly was the very essence of postwar manhood—and, centrally, Southern manhood—later to grace billboards as the Marlboro Man. He owned several shoe stores in the Delta and had a glamorous wife, another reward for a prototypical football hero.

Of course, the idea that Archie, who to Chuck would surely have seemed like the choirboy he was, could have followed in his steps would have seemed preposterous. But Archie was intrigued at the élan of such sports heroes, and he and Buddy would be riveted to the gadget that was born just around the same time Archie was, when Giant games came on the tube in the South, again cashing in on Conerly's presence. However, life intruded on those father-and-son reveries when the cotton crop began to ebb and economic conditions worsened. The big old cotton farm ruled over by Elisha Manning Sr. out in the country was just one of many that lost their value. In town, Buddy had to put more hours into his work and could see fewer and fewer of his son's games, or even spend much time with him. As much pride as he had, he grew insular, depressed, unwilling to share his burdens with anyone. His son noticed, and in retrospect, subtly rebuked the irresponsible manner in which Buddy governed his life.

"[T]he farming was iffy and a lot of the farmers had a peculiar mentality about paying their bills. [They would] go right out and spend [their money]—buy a Cadillac, take a vacation in New Orleans, go to the Ole Miss games and party . . . never mind making the payments for the tractor they bought. [They] lived for the day." Buddy, he said, was both a perpetrator and a victim, since "many of his customers just flat-out didn't pay." Often, Sis would accompany him when he'd try to find the deadbeats and collect, an experience that for Buddy was "frustrating and embarrassing."[15] He was a bit of a dreamer; he wanted people to like him more than he wanted them to pay him.

"He wasn't the kind of person who thought a whole lot about money," Archie went on. "He was a funny combination, a rugged kind of man, but a scholar, too, a great Bible scholar. He loved poetry." Doing business conflicted with that. In time, he grew progressively unhappy. Of course, few Southern men let their soft side show, believing that a man shouldn't betray any real emotion. Archie recalls, "He didn't hug in those days like we do now." As for telling his children, even his wife, that he loved them, only the weakest of men went there. Archie's description of Buddy as a "tough guy" would have pleased him, as would his tribute that Buddy was "a good influence on my work ethic."

═══

Football wasn't Archie's preferred sport, yet he had no choice but to play it. In Southern towns like Drew, the best athletes had to prove themselves in the sacred group rituals of the gridiron. The rub was his size. Back in fifth grade, weighing all of 70 pounds and, as he put it, "scrawny and limby and [so] white-skinned that I was ashamed to take my shirt off, even to go swimming," he played in a pee wee league for older boys as a running back, given the ball only a couple times a game. But the next year, after filling out more, he was made quarterback despite not having a clue about how to play the position. The prospect was, he said, "as thrilling as it was daunting."

Because Buddy's personal travails were mounting, and he was less able or even moved to see Archie perform or throw the ball around with him, it was Buddy's brothers and sisters out at the old Manning farm who played surrogate. The sisters, Mamie and Lucy, were both unmarried schoolteachers who, said Archie, "were old maids when they died."[16] (By contrast, Sis's mother, Olivia Nelson, would marry three times.) His uncles, Peyton and Frank, also never stepped to the altar, but apparently not for lack of expertise—Uncle Peyton was a bit of a rounder. If Archie had an impish side, it was likely observed at close range when he would spend some time on the farm, or earning a little pocket change working on neighboring farms, chopping cotton for three bucks a day or cleaning bricks at half a cent per brick.

Usually, at sundown, Uncle Peyton would go into town in his Studebaker pickup, picking up four or five buddies, including a couple of naughty women, along the way. They'd alight at a redneck bar and drink until cross-eyed. Looking back, Archie would recall that, if he was around, they "might have limited their drinking and cussing some, but I had no qualms about that." Even for the underage, drinking was a rite of manhood in the Delta, and the barkeep would slip Archie a beer. But for the most part, he was a straight arrow and a late bloomer when it came to the opposite sex. Given a choice between a date or playing Ping-Pong, he said, "I played Ping-Pong."[17]

———

Even before he was a schoolboy star, Archie had an insatiable need to learn how to play the mental game along with the physical. His neighbor, James Hobson, three years older, had set records in school sports and on the sandlot and had been the starting quarterback wherever he played. Archie hung with him, taking his advice when he played quarterback in middle school. Sometimes, he would go right from a Saturday afternoon school game to a pee wee game on Beef Maxwell Field, the home turf of Drew High, named after a former local football hero who now owned the Western Auto parts store in town. Archie's frailty was a looming worry, compounded by the fact that the best athletes at Drew had to play both offense and defense, the student body of the school being so small that only around 25 kids came out for the rarely elite team.

During Archie's first year there, 1964, a rule barring freshmen from the varsity squad was bent so that he could back up Hobson, though he had never played a down. The next season, with Hobson gone to Delta State University in Cleveland, Mississippi, Archie eased into the starting job and would win his first citation in the papers—though not as he would have hoped. The November 1 *Delta Democrat Times* reported that, late in the first half against Leland High, "Leland end Paul Cuicchi... intercepted Archie Manning's pass seconds before the first half ended." Drew lost 27–6, not an uncommon sort of score, explaining why he had three coaches in four years.

As a sophomore, Archie broke his right arm against Indianola, ending his season early, which may have convinced him he should be a baseball player. That was still his game. He'd also run track as a sprinter and quarter-miler and was the captain and point guard on the basketball team, averaging 25 points a game. Still, as he continued to grow and become acclimated to the chores and demands of being the quarterback of the only high school team in Drew, it was nothing to sniff at. These games were big news in the area. The whole town was expected to show up for them, notwithstanding Buddy Manning's increasing absences.

Archie's last coach at Drew, Paul Pounds, was a neighbor of the Mannings and worked hard with him. Pounds saw a skinny, brittle kid who disregarded his safety when he ran like a mad bull. "He was tough. He'd done that bricklayin' all summer, his hands would be all callused, but he could throw like nobody's business. He didn't really know how to drop back and throw, so I just said, 'Listen, Redhead, get out around the end and go all the way.' Or he'd lower his head into a linebacker's chest. He had no fear."[18] That was not always wise. As a junior, Archie broke his *left* arm and went on playing with it in a cast. He was growing into his role, slowly. As a senior, he stood six foot two and a solid 170 pounds, still looking, as his school buddy Robert Khayat said, like "skin and bones and freckles," but bowing to no one, and paying for it. The *Delta Dem-*

ocrat Times reported that in a game against Winona, he was "knocked out of the game four times," but still won. A week later, he sizzled— "Indianola Is Victim of Drew's Manning" was the headline heralding the 27–21 victory, the game story calling him "the do-it-all kid" who "bomb[ed] a weak Indianola pass defense with everything but a worn-out pair of football shoes."

A common sight at a Drew game under the Friday night lights, one that would stir the crowd into a frenzy, was Archie breaking around end and threading his way down the field, sideline to sideline, hips swiveling like Elvis, as he eluded tacklers. As he recalled, "I wasn't fast but I was the fastest in Drew." He was also sneaky, hedging on a fake until a tackler had committed to an angle and got close to him. And when he broke clear, funny as he looked with those loose limbs, he ate up big chunks of turf.

But perhaps the most remarkable aspect of his senior year was not his combined 16 touchdowns, but that he led the Eagles to a 5–5 record. "Heck," says Pounds, "we were always overmatched. [Opponents would] have more seniors alone than we had players. Then they had to face Archie, and it would be 'good night.' One time, he told me he saw the middle linebacker cheating to the outside to stop him from getting around right end, because right-handed quarterbacks like to go right. We were behind, we needed a score, and Archie took a step right, turned around, and went left, all the way. I think he's still runnin'."

For moves like that, he was praised in the *Delta Democrat Times* as "one of the top quarterbacks in the [Delta Valley] conference." He was named to the first string of the all-county team. For a time, he even seemed to go Hollywood, bleaching his hair a weird facsimile of blond, saying later that it was a fad going around in school at the time. He had cause to strut. Nearing graduation, he was a 15-time letterman, too many to sew onto his school jacket. As soon as the football season was over, he was on the court with the basketball team, leading Drew to a win over Indianola by "scorch[ing] the sacks for 33 points." But, every bit as impressive, his academic average was 99.44, first in his class. Of course he was named Mr. Drew High and elected class president, to deliver the valedictory address on graduation day, something he says happened because he was the only one in the class who wanted to do it. His topic in the address was prophetic—as he recalled, "I just talked about how we were going to shape the future." If he only knew.

CHAPTER 2

MR. DREW

In 1966, an African-American man named Eddie James Stewart was beaten and shot to death in Crystal Springs, Mississippi, while in police custody, an incident the Southern Poverty Law Center has called racially motivated.[1] Some things have changed in the intervening 50 years, but a lot hasn't. In predominantly black Rueville today, there is a street named Barack Obama Avenue, but in 2012, Crystal Springs made news again when its own First Baptist Church denied a black couple permission to marry there.[2] Three years later, a Crystal Springs woman was one of eight white people convicted of federal hate crimes against African-Americans in Jackson.[3] Street signs can't wash away the bitter past, the most egregious moment burned into history on June 22, 1964, when black Meridian native James Earl Chaney and two white New York activists, Andrew Goodman and Michael Schwerner, were murdered in Philadelphia, Mississippi, a crime for which no one would be convicted for 40 years.

It was in this Philadelphia that a girl named Olivia Williams, soon to be Olivia Manning, was growing up. Her family and neighbors were the kind of good, churchgoing, very white folks Ronald Reagan had in mind when he announced his 1980 run for the White House in Philadelphia. Indeed, several of the Mannings were there that day, Olivia having taken her sons to the fair. When Archie, who was in training camp with the

Saints, saw the event on the news that night, he spotted Cooper, who was six, in the crowd, mugging for the camera.[4]

As Archie Manning was progressing through his teens, he lived among more than a few bigots. While the nation mourned the killing of its young president on November 22, 1963, in another Southern city, not everyone in Drew mourned the death of a liberal leader who had welcomed Martin Luther King to the White House. Only weeks after the murders in Philadelphia, Fannie Lou Hamer, vice-chair of the Mississippi Freedom Democratic Party, who had been beaten by cops while protesting Jim Crow laws, tried to relocate her organization from racially torn Rueville to Drew. The local white elders kept them out. The only concession the town made to racial progress was to grudgingly permit the children of longtime black resident Mae Bertha Carter to enter Drew High School while all others were relegated to dilapidated, segregated schools. The oldest Carter child, Ruth, was Archie's classmate, and she later taught at the same school, itself a signal moment in the town's evolution.

As Archie spun it, "There was no violence, no ugly incidents that made headlines. The people here aren't like that. The Carter children were simply ignored. . . . At noon they wouldn't eat lunch in the cafeteria, they'd eat on the gym steps. I think there was only one time I ever saw one of those Carter children smile."[5] That he could construe *ignoring* black people in defense of his town is revealing of a conditioned form of racism acceptance; moreover, only in the context of sports does Manning relate any positive examples of racial progress. For example, when the basketball team was competing to reach a district basketball tournament, some of the players' fathers said they wouldn't let the boys play against black players. But Buddy was not among them, and that was important, given that his boy was the star of the team.[6]

Buddy may not have been anything like a crusader, but he could read the trade winds. For Archie, the lesson may have been clear, but breaking with the Southern heritage of exclusion was not an easy step. He saw his hometown as neutral rather than racist. "Drew isn't redneck country; you have to go farther east in the state for that, to the hill country. It is primarily a community of struggling farmers."[7] That would have been news to old Joe Pullum, a black man lynched near Drew in the 1920s, legend being that he murdered thirteen men in the lynch party before they could slip a noose around his neck. And while the US Justice Department cracked down on "freedom of choice" laws designed to dodge the Constitution in 1968, for the next three years no more than a handful of black children were allowed into Drew High. In 1971, one who was, an 18-year-old girl named Jo Etha Collier, was killed in a drive-by shooting outside a grocery store near the school. By coincidence, that was the year Drew held Archie Manning Appreciation Day.

———

Archie's small-town struggles had mainly to do with exposure. As Paul Pounds says, "Reports of our games never even made it to Jackson, much less Memphis." Besides, his teams never finished above .500, and if Archie was known, it was for being, as he himself said, "tall, skinny, and injury prone." Only three schools *in total* were willing to offer him a scholarship: Ole Miss, Mississippi State, and one beyond the state line, Tulane. Even up in Oxford, the Rebels' flinty coach for the last 20 years, John Vaught, hardly believed he was mining for gold in Drew. But the timing would be providential. Quarterbacking was a sore spot for Vaught. At times in '66, three QBs had played in the same game. The Rebels still went 8–3, but that was good enough only for fourth place in the SEC, before they were hammered by Darrell Royal's Texas Longhorns 19–0 in the Bluebonnet Bowl. Back then, freshmen could only play on the junior varsity, but it was where the future was written. Not that Archie had any delusions that he could wind up like Charlie Conerly or Jake Gibbs. He was just thrilled that Vaught wanted him, given that his résumé "was loaded with risks."

Around Drew, his decision about where to go obsessed people, especially those with a parochial interest. In a scene right out of *Smokey and the Bandit*, the town sheriff, a Buford T. Justice type known as Snake Williford, called Archie one day and said he'd pick him up in his squad car. Archie had no idea why, but agreed. When he got into the cruiser, Snake's radio crackled with an urgent call about a man who had kidnapped two cops being on the loose and headed his way.

Snake had what looked like a machine gun in his lap and began rattling on about how, if need be, he would "show our force." Then, out of nowhere, he suddenly began to speak of his college days at Mississippi State, Ole Miss's traditional rival. He only stopped to apprehend the bad guy, no force necessary, handcuffing him and putting him in the back seat. Driving to the jailhouse, he went back to extolling Mississippi State to an incredulous Archie.[8]

State would invite Archie to visit their campus in Starkville. When they sent him a plane ticket, Archie got on a plane for the first time and went. However, the Bulldogs had fallen in the SEC, while Ole Miss, which was on a run of 10 straight years of bowl appearances and bore the lingering scent of national titles in 1959, '60, and '62 (if only unofficially, based not on the coaches' polls but on metrics determined by primordial sports-math geeks of the day—shockingly, Ole Miss has never won an *official* NCAA title). But Johnny Vaught was playing it coy with Archie. He sent a graduate assistant, Roy Stinnett, to Drew but didn't offer him a letter of intent. Then, days later, Vaught sent Tom Swayze, an Ole Miss star of the early 1930s who had spent the last 20 years signing players for Vaught. Swayze was, as Archie said, "a cocky kind of guy" who was playing hard to get. He kept asking how much Archie revered Ole Miss, but never said Ole Miss wanted Archie. Taking an active role, Frank Crosthwait, who was also an Ole Miss alumnus, drove Archie to Oxford and arranged for him to meet Vaught and the coaching staff. The offensive end coach, J. W. "Wobble" Davidson, who moonlighted as the freshman coach, took note of Archie's angular frame and called him "Ichabod Crane."

No offer was made until weeks later, when Archie and the Drew basketball team went to Clarksdale for a state tournament. One of the refs in those games happened to be Roy Stinnett, and he was quite generous to Ichabod Crane. As Archie remembered, whenever he had the ball, "if an opposing player got in my zip code he was called for a foul." In the first two rounds, he shot 43 foul shots alone and was the top scorer. Coming in as heavy underdogs, Drew got into the championship game. Moments before the opening tip-off, Stinnett came into the locker room and unfurled a letter of intent for a grant-in-aid football scholarship. Not knowing what else to do, Archie signed. Drew then won the tournament.

Archie looked back at this strange sequence of events insisting Stinnett was "totally fair and honest" in his refereeing, but then added, "If you want to jump to any conclusions . . . feel free."[9]

===

The grandstand at Beef Maxwell Field was always home to a congregation of Manning family members. But as time went on, the only one who missed his share of games was Buddy Manning, the man Archie most wanted to be proud of him. His son seemed to have learned to live without Buddy's guidance and strict codes. He could still be a choirboy, but more and more, also a bit of a rakehell. Another of his classmates, Georgeanne Clark, who went on to teach at Drew High, recalled, "On graduation night all the boys got kind of wild and woolly, and I guess Archie felt as president of the class he had to get the drunkest. My date had to leave me to go out and take care of him. The sight I'll never forget is Archie dancing around with a tambourine in his hand, saying, 'I'm the Drew High leader and I'm going to lead y'all to Slim's.' That was where we bought beer."[10]

Archie even now still held out some hope that he might get to play baseball, a dream that became a dilemma when he was drafted by the Atlanta Braves. Their general manager, Paul Richards, notified him that "our scout in your area will contact you shortly to discuss your baseball future with us. You will be a welcome addition to the Braves organization." But as heavenly as it seemed to someday play alongside Hank Aaron, a kid from the Delta had a higher authority to answer to: the great god of football. And at the altar of Ole Miss. As Pounds says, "If he didn't go there, his daddy woulda disowned him." On April 6, he traveled to Oxford to be honored by the Ole Miss chapter of the National Football Hall of Fame and was photographed standing with three other "scholar-athletes," two of them Ole Miss seniors. Also in the shot were Vaught, university chancellor Dr. John D. Williams, and athletic director C. M. "Tad" Smith. He hadn't even enrolled yet, and already he was in its Hall of Fame.

In his farewell to high school football, Archie played in the state high school all-star game in Jackson on July 31 and led his team to a 57–33 victory, throwing four touchdowns and running for another. He took home the MVP trophy. The next stop was Oxford, 60 miles northeast of Drew, the epicenter of a good bit of Southern mythology and college football royalty. Of course, the notion that Archie Manning might hold all that in his hands seemed preposterous. Not least of all to Archie Manning.

CHAPTER 3

"AIN'T YIELDING TO NOBODY"

Oxford, Mississippi, in Lafayette County, was built on lands bought cheaply from Chickasaw Indian tribes in the 1830s. It was named after England's most renowned college of higher learning, the legislature having determined in 1841 that the city would become the site of the first state university, which opened its doors in 1848, to 80 students. The campus sits squarely in the North Central Hills, a landscape of thick, leafy forests and red clay plains, a serene habitat that is anything but during football season. Oxford took its charter as an enlightened oasis seriously. Postwar, black freedmen were allowed to build homes, churches, and schools and to own their own businesses, even vote. The reductive "Ole Miss" itself derives from a "darky" term—"ol' missus," or a plantation's "old mistress."[1]

The culture of the town is rich. William Faulkner lived there as a child. John Grisham, a graduate of the Ole Miss Law School, and who in *The Pelican Brief* named a character—a Supreme Court justice, no less—after Archie Manning, has kept a home in the city. But like most of academia across the Deep South, Ole Miss also proudly venerates the Confederacy. For 20 years, the chancellor was a former Rebel general, A. P. Stewart. The original husk of the Lyceum, the august, pyramid-shaped, columned main building, still stands, its famous clock dead center above the portico. The Lyceum was also used as a hospital during the Battle of

Shiloh, and those who didn't make it are buried in a memorial graveyard on the grounds.

They started playing football at the school in 1893, when Ole Miss won four of five games, including the first-ever college game played in the state, on November 11: a 56–0 blowout of Southwestern Baptist University of Jackson, Tennessee. As the new century moved on, football gathered a raucous geographical resonance, as Southern college teams were picaresquely named for Longhorns, Bulldogs, Gamecocks, Tar Heels—and, of course, the ultimate panegyric, the Rebels. The first profound Southern team was the Alabama Crimson Tide in the '30s, followed by General Robert Neyland's Tennessee Volunteers. The winningest coaches became as iconic as their teams' names: Bud Wilkinson, Bear Bryant, Darrell Royal, Bobby Dodd. The longest-tenured, Bobby Bowden, coached Florida State for 40 years. Ole Miss was not yet that romanticized. When John Vaught was promoted from line coach to head coach in 1947, the school was regarded as backwoods. But his teams became a symbol of Old Confederacy pride. When the first college game was televised in 1948, the Rebels were on the field.

A starry-eyed Archie regarded Vaught as a kind of father figure, something not lost on his actual father. Indeed, Buddy Manning may have felt he was receding in his son's eyes as the man he had once revered. As proud as Buddy was, his boy's rise made him regard himself as more of a failure. The years had taken a hard toll on him. Still chain-smoking Chesterfields, the mounting stress of having to track down clients who owed him money was a losing grind. To help make ends meet, he had to do manual labor. Sis, too, pitched in, as a legal secretary. In 1964, Buddy suffered a mild stroke. Stubborn as he was, he refused to see a doctor. He recovered, but grew despondent. Archie recalled that Buddy "had a sister who'd been an invalid for some years, and my mother says he always had a horror of [himself being like] that."[2]

Whether he resented Archie for transcending him, only he knew. Southern men didn't feel any need to discuss such things, but even the Good Book didn't have any answers. At 56, seeing his son step into the Ole Miss glory factory, he may have felt his own life was over. In truth,

Archie could have used the old man's encouragement, believing his stardom was anything but a sure thing, with seven other freshman quarterbacks to beat out. That summer, Wobble Davidson, a gruff ex-Marine who played for and graduated from Ole Miss in 1942, ran a kind of boot camp—"a lot of fundamentals, a lot of hitting, a lot of tackling," as Archie recalled. He also had to submit to the old hazing rituals, his red hair shaved by the varsity guys. With a crush of schoolwork and football practices, he had little time for the cultural arising that was galvanizing his generation at the time, the so-called Summer of Love, nor did he have any interest in dropping acid and listening to *Sgt. Pepper*. He was more apt to tune his radio to stations playing Merle Haggard or George Jones. As the games approached, he had impressed Davidson and won the starting job in the opening JV game. Doing little right, he and the baby Rebels lost 28–0. But Wobble stayed with him, and with every snap he took, John Vaught was paying attention.

Vaught, a craggy, pug-faced good ol' boy who wore sharp suits, lizard-skin shoes, and a dashing fedora cocked just at the right angle, was born in Olney, Texas, in 1909. He would live 96 proud years and lead Ole Miss to its greatest heights. A former All-America guard at TCU, he won his first of six SEC titles right off the bat in 1947, when the Rebels made their first bowl appearance since 1936. In '54 and '55 they won the SEC again, losing the Sugar Bowl the first year, winning the Cotton Bowl the next. Then, in '59, led by All-America fullback Charlie Flowers, they went 10–1, the only loss the one that made the young Archie cry, that Halloween game clinched for LSU by Billy Cannon, though Vaught got revenge by beating the No. 1–ranked Tigers 21–0 in the Sugar Bowl on New Year's Day. Having notched eight shutouts that season, there was little doubt they had the best team in the land. But in those days the polls were released *before* the bowls, and the national title went to 11–0 Syracuse, leaving Ole Miss fans to claim the title using the conclusions of the era's math geeks (modern counterparts have agreed, not only about the 1959 team but the '60 and '62 squads that were stiffed in the pre-bowl polls, losing out to Minnesota and USC, respectively).

Overshadowing that 1962 season, Ole Miss became a flash point for the inevitable result of endless institutional racism and resistance to Supreme Court rulings. Predating by a year the sorry spectacle of George Wallace standing in the doorway at the University of Alabama, refusing entry to black students, Ole Miss did the same to James Meredith, who got through the door with the aid of 31,000 National Guard troops who clashed with student mobs, leaving two dead, hundreds wounded, and scores arrested. But did anything really change? In *The Last Season*, author Stuart Stevens wrote of being 10 at the time and, as a bonding communion with his father, indoctrinated by the mesmerizing rituals at Hemingway Stadium—Colonel Reb, the giant Confederate flag carried onto the field, the marching band's rendition of "Dixie," the crowd chanting, "The South shall rise again!" At one game, the segregationist governor Ross Barnett led the crowd in a pregame singalong that went:

> *We will not yield an inch of any field.*
> *Fix us another toddy, ain't yielding to nobody.*
> *Ross is standing like Gibraltar, he shall never falter.*
> *Ask us what we say, it's to hell with Bobby K.*
> *Never shall our emblem go*
> *From Colonel Rebel to Ole Black Joe.*

Wrote Stevens: "Twenty-four hours later, the Ole Miss campus was a war zone in the last battle of the Civil War, federal troops fighting southerners over integration. . . . But for me, 1962 will always be most remembered as the year my father and I cheered as Ole Miss went undefeated and won the national championship."[3]

Vaught liked to pretend that his all-white team actually saved the campus from civil war during the Meredith interlude. "When Ole Miss needed to survive and build a new image, as it sorely did in 1962," he later said, "a great football team [rose] as one of the most courageous in the history of the game." But Vaught admitted that he "dragged his feet" on recruiting black players, many of whom made sure to stay away from the school regardless.[4] Even today, one can still see the Stars and Bars smuggled into games. In 2014, a noose was hung around the neck of the statue of James Meredith, and alcohol and racial slurs were hurled at a black student as she walked near the campus. As one newspaper reported, "These two recent, racially charged incidents have some wondering if the school affectionately called Ole Miss is still stuck in the old days."[5] In 2017, as other old Confederate cities were taking down statues to their Civil War generals, Oxford stood firm, refusing to disturb the bronzed general looming over the town square.

Archie would soon carry that cursed flag out onto the field. He would never regret doing so. But he has agreed that he never looked at it from the perspective of black people. Ole Miss would be the last SEC team to integrate, not until 1971. While the SEC itself was known as the "final citadel of segregation,"[6] even Adolph Rupp, as unreconstructed a Southern racist as there was, had to start giving black kids scholarships to Kentucky to keep the basketball program winning when his Wildcats famously lost the national title to an obscure Texas Western team in 1966 that started five black players. The Kentucky football team was the first football program in the SEC to integrate, in 1967, followed by Tennessee a year later. But it was only when the federal government threatened to pull federal funding from schools not in compliance with the Civil Rights Act that the rest of the SEC got off its pale horse—the last rider being Ole Miss, after Archie was gone.

———

Archie has always laughed at the idea that Peyton thinks he was an "easy rider," his path to fame a breeze. It was not. His freshman season caromed from praise to skepticism. But he closed strong, wrecking the Mississippi State JV 49–7 in the season finale—he had to, since the varsity guys said they'd shave his head again if he didn't. For the short season, he put up nice numbers, completing 30 of 55 passes for 497 yards and seven touchdowns. And for good measure, playing both ways—as did most frosh—he intercepted four passes. But the real progress he made lay in winning the faith of Vaught, who thought he had found his next leader. The kid was skinny and bowlegged, but seemed to have antennae allowing him to sense when pass rushers were coming at him and get his feet moving to avoid them, and then bust it around end. One can imagine how flattered Archie was by that attention. When Vaught retired, only two coaches had a winning record against him: Bob Neyland and Bear Bryant, both by just one game. Even so, getting comfortable under Vaught's thumb was a task. The old coach was getting on in years and had coached so many players that at times he would reflexively call new ones by names from the past—even his potential savior he would call not Archie but Jake, as in Gibbs. But he was still a motivator, and for a legendary coach, he didn't shut out new ideas—if anything, he loved to steal them, lifting anything effective that other coaches were doing. Vaught would giggle at his thievery and say, "Coaches are great plagiarists."[7] He also listened—to his other coaches, even his young players. In their skull sessions, Archie told Vaught he didn't cotton to the Veer, which with its option plays left the quarterback with no cover. Vaught let Archie do what he had done for Paul Pounds: operate from the I formation and mostly sprint out, looking for a hole to run through or else fire a last-second pass to an open receiver. When Archie also said he'd like to get into pro-style drop-back pocket passing, the coach started working on that, too.

Although Vaught had never before started a sophomore at quarterback, in the March 29 *Delta Democrat Times*, assistant coach Jim "Buster" Poole, who had played for Ole Miss in the '30s and returned as an assistant coach after a pro career—he and two brothers played for the New York Giants—boldly said that, even with 45 sophomores and only seven seniors, "I am going to go out on the limb and say that in Archie Manning, they have the best freshman they have ever had at Ole Miss." The Rebels had gone 6–4 in '66 and 6–4–1 in '67, mired in fourth place in the SEC, and had become Alabama's favorite patsy as Bear Bryant's Tide rolled to two national titles. So here stood the freckle-faced kid from little Drew, on the gridiron, wearing No. 18. Though he still seemed skinny and frail, he had filled out some as a soph, up to around 200 sinewy pounds, and had come through Wobble Davidson's boot camp hardier, more mature. The timing of all this just seemed right, and in a larger cultural maw, far more significant than he could have possibly realized.

======

Archie stepped into a leadership role at Ole Miss as a scion of the baby boom generation, needing to find a sense of purpose even as all hell seemed to be breaking loose. Before spring practices began, first Dr. Martin Luther King and then Robert Kennedy were murdered as they campaigned for idealistic goals, the latter only a few hundred miles away, in Memphis. The body counts in Vietnam grew and the generals kept inflating the other side's losses. Old assumptions about patriotism and an infallible military were starting to wither. As practices under the broiling north Mississippi sun wore on, things were hotter in Chicago, where young people not unlike Archie were protesting in the streets and being beaten up by riot cops outside the Democratic convention. Americans were at war with Americans, a concept that was not unfamiliar to those in the South who revered their "heritage."

Now, in a highly ironic role reversal, Southern boys were, by and large, defenders of the Union their ancestors had fought and died trying to destroy, and which through federal legislation was trying to destroy the last vestiges of the Confederacy. However, while Archie had his draft deferment, others had to fight in his place. And heroism came at a price. A Drew resident, Robert Atkinson, won three Distinguished Flying Crosses flying P-4 fighter planes in the war, but too many would die alone in the steamy jungles a world away for reasons that were hazy at best, and dishonest at worst. But in 1968, patriotism was still used as a cudgel against reality, much to the advantage of that most amoral of politicians, Richard Nixon, who in midseason would ride an amoral "Southern strategy," stoking racial animus and fear, into the White House. As insular as Southern college football was, Ole Miss especially existed in splendid isolation, the only battleground that mattered being the grassy one for which Archie and his brethren prepared week after week.

In this cloistered world, Archie had also found his queen in Olivia Williams—who had the same given name as his maternal grandmother. In every way, she seemed out of his league. Growing up in Philadelphia, Mississippi, her father, Cooper Williams, owned a Standard Oil distributorship and was one of the wealthiest men in town. Her grandfather Sam and great-uncle Brown in 1907 founded the Williams Brothers store in Philadelphia, a country market that became famous for selling two tons of bacon a week, as well as such sundries as red-rind Wisconsin hoop cheese, mule collars, snuff, and chicken feed. Located on County Road 375, near the grounds of the Neshoba County Fair where Ronald Reagan made his brazen appeal to Southern white resentment in 1980, the store still stands proud, run by Olivia's brother Sid and their aunt, Peggy Dees.[8]

Olivia was something special: tall and graceful, swarthy, long-fingered, full-lipped. Bred on cotillion balls, she was pursued by military school cadets and high school Romeos alike. But she knew her sports, too, and like many in the Delta, she knew of Archie Manning. In his senior year, the Drew High basketball team played in a regional tournament at Philadelphia High. She was in the stands as he led the Eagles to an upset victory, impressed but also annoyed. He was, she thought, "as cocky-looking a player as I'd ever seen. . . . Long red hair. Tall and skinny. Dribbling the ball behind his back [m]aking shots from every angle." In the next game, for the tournament championship, Drew's strategy was to freeze the ball, Archie dribbling for as long as he could without shooting. They lost—4–2, believe it or not—and Olivia thought the redheaded guy had made a mockery of the game. "I told my friends I not only didn't like him. I despised him." And did so again when she watched the Drew football team win an all-star game. Seeing him given the game MVP trophy, she recalled, "I couldn't stand it."[9]

She was a legacy at Ole Miss. Cooper Williams had played football there, her brother Tommy was on the basketball team, her cousin Frank a linebacker on varsity. The first time she met Archie, he was walking on campus and she stopped in her spanking white Ford LTD and gave him a lift. He was stunned when she told him, "Oh, I know you. You're the one who beat Philadelphia our senior year." At first, they were like oil and water. Archie would crack to his buddies about how she never wore the same clothes twice and bragged about how she could get her rich daddy to buy her whatever she wanted. He seemed to her socially awkward, a goober. When his fraternity, Sigma Nu, had a mixer with hers, Delta Gamma, in the spring, he timidly asked her to dance. As they did, something meshed when she talked football. And when she learned he would be the varsity QB, he seemed no longer a gomer; if she was arm candy, he was a future star. "That was a big deal," she admitted. "I won't deny that. [It was] automatic status."[10] When she told her dad she was dating the new Rebels quarterback, he was as excited as she was. "When you gonna bring him home for dinner?" he asked. Soon they were growing closer, sneaking off together when they were supposed to be chaperoned. They were, to all who knew them, "a perfect couple," walking hand in hand about the campus. Fifty years on, they still are.

⸺

Archie's first game as first-string quarterback was on Saturday, September 21, 1968, against Memphis State, on the road before 51,046 at Memphis Memorial Stadium. The Tigers were John Vaught's biggest walkovers, his teams having gone 15–1–1 against them, but the Rebels trailed 7–0 at the half. Archie then threw a 19-yard touchdown strike to tailback Steve Hindman, and on the next drive rolled left and rumbled 44 yards to the 10. He found Hindman from the six to go ahead. In the fourth quarter, he ran one in from the two to ice it. His stats were efficient—8 of 14 for 116 yards, 8 rushes for 67 yards—and he earned SEC Back of the Week honors. It was how fables began. Two days later, Vaught rhapsodized that Manning was "the best quarterback prospect I ever saw." That was the prelude for their first home game—though not at Hemingway Stadium, the old concrete tureen having become too small to satisfy the demand for tickets; until 1981, the Rebels would play most big rivalry games in Jackson's Veterans Memorial Stadium. There, under the lights against Kentucky, Ole Miss again stumbled out of the gate, with Archie fumbling on a sweep from two yards out. He would pass 22 times and complete just seven. Going into the fourth quarter, the Wildcats led 14–10. Then Archie took off on a 20-yard touchdown. The Rebels went on to win 30–14, with Archie running 17 times.

Next was Alabama, also in Jackson, also under the lights, and carried nationally on ABC television. A crowd of 47,152 showed up, then the largest ever to see a game in Mississippi. "Ole Miss Rebels End Long 'Bama Drought" was the headline in the *Delta Democrat Times*. Grizzled old Bear Bryant said, "Ole Miss deserved to win. They had better coaching and better conditioning and wanted it more than we did." Not to mention a better quarterback. At 3–0, the Rebels sat atop the SEC and were ranked No. 15. The next game, in Athens against Vince Dooley's Georgia Bulldogs—the first meeting of those teams in Georgia since 1906—matched Archie against another sophomore sensation, Mike Cavan. Although the 'Dogs were ranked only 35th, Archie could do no better than a 7–0 lead at the half and had also sprained his thumb. Then Cavan got the lead with a fourth-quarter TD pass. Archie was picked off by Jake Scott, the future Miami Dolphin great, and Georgia won 21–7.

Now came the homecoming at Hemingway Stadium, fitted with those rancid tribal rites and echoes of the Old Confederacy. Men wore suits and ties to the games, women Sunday dresses and white gloves, corsages pinned to their jackets. The Rebels would parade through hordes of tailgaters and gawkers in the park outside the stadium called the Grove, which to Archie seemed less hallowed ground than a sanctuary for fans to drink themselves sloppy—by county law, he recalled, "you couldn't bring [inside the stadium] as much as a cold beer." To many, it seemed, this was more important than bowing to Southern football pretensions, given that thousands would forget about the game to remain out there, guzzling. Even his sister, Pam, he noted, preferred "socializing to the football."[11]

Clutching the Stars and Bars, Archie, his thumb taped, led his Rebels onto the field against Southern Mississippi, whom they had beaten eight straight times. After three quarters, though, they trailed 7–0. He then took them 72 yards down to the three and ran in the tying score. With four minutes left, the ball on the SM 49, Vaught sent in Studdard with the play. "Coach said to throw the ball to me," he said in the huddle. Archie did— for a touchdown. Ole Miss came out 21–13 winners, Archie going 21 of 39 for 255 yards, his 321 total yards breaking Charlie Conerly's school record. "I want to commend their boy Manning," said SM coach Pie Vann. "He's a fine runner and a good passer." The performance earned him another SEC offensive player of the week award. However, injuries were too steep a hill to surmount. With Archie suffering from groin and back injuries, the Rebels were blown out by the Houston Cougars, 29–7. But he hung in, and the next week, against LSU in Baton Rouge, he helped ignite a fireworks show for a screaming crowd of 69,337, as the teams piled up over 900 yards combined. The Rebels fell behind 17–3 before Archie gunned a 65-yard touchdown bolt to Floyd Franks, then ran another in from the two to tie it. The Tigers took back the lead with six minutes left, but Archie reeled off three key passes to the LSU nine and fired a dart to Hindman, who made a juggling catch for the winning score. When the smoke cleared, he had completed 24 of 40 for 345 yards, breaking his own yardage records, and making SEC player of the week for the third time.

But now he had bruised ribs, too, and Vaught chose to hold him out against Chattanooga. The Rebels won, and he returned for the Tennessee game on the road. Stiff-legged and in pain, he unleashed 40 passes but completed just 16 and was intercepted six times in a 31–0 shellacking. The best Ole Miss could manage the next week was a 17-all tie with Mississippi State on Thanksgiving, but any hope of winning the SEC was done. The consolation prize was a trip to the Liberty Bowl against Virginia Tech, where, after falling 17–0 in the first quarter, Archie pitched touchdowns to Hank Shows and Lon Felts. Hindman, the MVP of the game, ran 79 yards for the go-ahead touchdown in Ole Miss's 34–17 victory. It was a bittersweet end to a 7–3–1 season that had included wins over three highly ranked national teams. Archie's spin was that "maybe we had turned the tide." But Ole Miss put not a single player on the All-SEC team; even Archie, who had set Ole Miss records with 1,716 total yards and 13 touchdowns, was stiffed, losing out to Auburn senior QB Loran Carter.

As the season crumbled, he lost his usual affability and came close to wrecking things with Olivia. After the Mississippi State tie, they were supposed to go back to Philadelphia for Thanksgiving dinner with her parents. Instead, as she recalls, Archie was "in an ornery mood" and begged off. "You go ahead home," he told her. "I'm going back to Drew." But he knew he was blowing it with her and picked up the phone to apologize. He would make thousands of calls at the line of scrimmage, but none was ever as wise as that one.

CHAPTER 4

"I THINK BUDDY'S DEAD"

After a routine checkup in 1968, Buddy Manning was told that he had lung cancer. As his son flourished in Oxford, he adamantly told Sis not to break this news to him or Pam. Figuring he was a dying man, he became sentimental, crying the way Southern men weren't supposed to about his boy becoming the man he never had been. He tried to play the role of the hardworking husband and father, still chasing after deadbeat clients. But he began pondering what the future would be like for him, sick, bedridden, wasting away, a burden on his family. Apparently, he became convinced he wouldn't let it get that far. Archie, meanwhile, could have seen visions of his own future. After the football season ended, he played on the Ole Miss baseball team, which enjoyed more success than the football team had. As the Rebel shortstop for Tom Swayze, he hit only .260 but was a vital cog on a 27–15 team that won the SEC title in '69 and went to the College World Series in June, where the Rebels lost 14–1 to Texas in the semifinals and finished at No. 5 in the nation. With the spring semester over, Archie took a few summer classes. Then, in early August, Buddy went to Oxford to pick him up and drive him back to Drew for a two-week vacation, not disclosing anything about his cancer. But his boy could tell something was not right.

Archie would later describe Buddy as "an old 59" at the time, acting as if he had little to live for. On Saturday, August 16, 1969, while, thousands of miles away, half a million people of Archie's generation were rocking on at the Woodstock Music Festival, the Manning clan attended the wedding of a family friend. At the last minute, Buddy said he wasn't going, that he would stay at the house. "We'll cook steaks later," he told Archie. At the reception, a few of Archie's old high school chums wanted to go on a beer run, just up the road to Cleveland. But, tasting those steaks, he told Sis he was leaving early and drove back to the house. When he got there, he opened the door, tossed his keys on a table, and headed for the bathroom.

It was quiet in the house—no TV or radio was on—and he wondered if Buddy had gone out. His and Sis's bedroom was just before the john, and as Archie walked past it, out of the corner of his eye he could see his father lying on his back in bed. Figuring he was napping, Archie took another look. What he saw he would later call "a series of still shots, each one clear but incomplete. I see the gun on the floor, and the stick he used to fire it. And him lying there, face up, very still. And a big blood spot on his chest. 'Oh, God,' I thought. 'Oh, God, no.'"[1]

Buddy had meticulously planned his suicide. He had attached a stick to the trigger of the shotgun so that he could fire it at the correct angle into his chest. Archie, numbed by shock, did not scream in anguish. His legs didn't crumble and he didn't kneel down beside the corpse. Rather, he instinctively thought of Sis and Pam, and how much better it was that he found Buddy, not the women. Almost mechanically, he called the police, admitting rather incredibly in later years that "I wasn't sure of the gravity of it."

"I think Buddy's dead," he said.

Waiting for the cops to arrive, he began to clean up around his father's lifeless body, wiping blood off the bedspread and floor. He also called a family friend, Louie Campbell, asking him to go to the wedding reception, break the news to Sis and Pam, bring them to his house, and wait there until Archie could get there. When Buddy was removed to the morgue, Archie went to Campbell's house, where Pam kept crying out, "No!" Sis sobbed in his arms, but seemed not completely shocked; she had seen Buddy decline and may have been preparing herself for just such a prospect. If she blamed herself in any way for failing Buddy, she may also have believed Buddy had failed his children and especially his son, who would have to carry the mental scars of that day forever.

On August 18, a headline in the *Delta Democrat Times* read, "Archie Manning Finds Father Shot to Death." But it was not the big news one might have expected. As if not overplaying the tragedy out of deference to the family, or shame to the town, the paper ran it on page 12, along with such news as "Fire Damages House Trailer." An astonishing coincidence was that, only a day later, the paper reported that "Sunflower County farmer-businessman R. W. Manning, 67, drowned Monday night when he apparently fell into a giant air conditioning system at the cotton gin he operates." It added, "Manning was a cousin of Ole Miss star quarterback Archie Manning's father, Buddy Manning, who shot himself to death this past weekend at his Drew home."

Around Drew, Buddy's suicide was a mystery and a tragedy best left unexamined out of respect. The funeral was at First Baptist Church, the burial at Drew Cemetery in a grave alongside his father and among the plots of several Manning generations, under swaying magnolia trees. At the funeral, says Frank Crosthwait, who helped make the arrangements, Archie "held the family together. Archie was so darn brave. He felt he owed it to Buddy to carry the family name with dignity. It was like he grew up right there."[2] During the mourning period, someone from Case Farm Supply came by the house and gave Sis a check for the equivalent of what Buddy would have made that year—$6,000. In the end, that was how Buddy Manning's life and worth were quantified: tipping money in the future for his son and the grandsons he never saw.

Within the family, there was almost no discussion of why it happened. His mother's succinct explanation was that Buddy "just didn't feel good anymore." Their grief was balanced by either shame or Southern stoicism. Archie would admit, "I never talked to my mother about it in any depth. I don't talk to my kids about it. Olivia and I have gone over it from every angle without any real conclusions. But I still *think* about it," especially every August 16. Never, though, has he shed a tear in grief. His way of dealing with it, he swore, was to make sure he would be "a lot closer" to his own children someday.

=====

Archie at first wanted to quit school and go to work as the family bread-winner. As Pam Manning observed, "He grew up in a matter of two minutes. Any decision made in our household after that, Archie was the one to make it."[3] However, Sis talked him down. Buddy, she said, would have beaten him black and blue if he dropped out. Sis assured him that her work as a legal secretary, combined with Buddy's death benefit from the Veterans Administration, would suffice. And it was certainly easy to envision Archie's future income as a pro football player in terms of how it would help the family. So he went back to Oxford, a scab on his soul. But he would not be hounded by the press about it. In an era long before tabloid journalism, prying social media, and 24-hour TV news, the story of Archie Manning's father was either not well known or kept quiet by his teams' public relations people, lest it complicate the carefully stoked fable of the South's perfect native son. The sportswriters who had heard it through the grapevine viewed it as off-limits or a brief aside. Many of his coaches and teammates, when told of his father's suicide, came to Drew for the funeral. But that was the last time the subject was mentioned as Archie pursued that great goal Buddy had always had for him, through the game Buddy revered.

Already, he had earned high marks from the pro scouts; one of them, New Orleans Saints chief scout Henry Lee Parker, said after Archie rallied Ole Miss to beat LSU the year before, "I'll take him right now."[4] There would be 16 holdover starters on the roster, and some preseason polls ranked the Rebels No. 1 in the SEC, a tall order given the competition; as Vaught predicted, "I can't see anyone going through the season unbeaten."[5] The opening game against Memphis State at Hemingway Stadium was believed to be a tune-up, even if the Tigers were defending Missouri Valley Conference champs. And it was, as Ole Miss stomped them 28–3, with Archie running in two touchdowns. However, in a recurring sign that the Rebels were heartbreak kids, they next played Kentucky in Lexington, another seeming walkover. They lost, dropping Ole Miss from No. 8 to No. 20.

It was no way to approach their first big hurdle, against Alabama in

Birmingham, but Archie was the last thing any opposing coach wanted to have to play against. Indeed, Bear Bryant found it nearly impossible to prepare for him. Not even his own teammates knew what he'd do, since so much of the Rebel attack happened on the fly. Archie would sometimes improvise in the huddle, scratching out a play on a whim and diagramming it on the turf with his finger. The Alabama game, on October 4, 1969, would be one of the first college games to be televised at night for a prime-time national TV audience, pushed back to 8:30 because ABC wouldn't preempt *The Lawrence Welk Show*.[6] It was a contest not just for SEC supremacy but for the braggin' rights of the whole South, even if neither team ranked in the top 10 nationally. After the pomp of the pregame, pseudo-Confederate rituals, the teams exchanged first-quarter touchdowns. But the Rebels' blunders cost them. On a 70-yard drive, Archie hit Riley Myers, who fumbled at the 'Bama four. Down 14–7, he led them to the nine, but the Rebels missed a field goal.

In the third quarter, Archie tied the game with an 11-yard pass to Jim Poole, then put the Rebels ahead on a 17-yard touchdown run. However, early in the fourth quarter the Tide quarterback, Scott Hunter, brought them back and took the lead, whereupon Archie came back, ending a drive with a touchdown on a sneak. So now it was 32–27 Rebels, with seven minutes left. On fourth-and-goal, Hunter called time and came to the sideline next to the Bear, a man of few words. "Run the best you got," he drawled. That turned out to be a touchdown pass for a 33–32 Alabama lead, and with 1:48 left, Archie took over for a last shot, all the craziness having left the crowd damp and hoarse. As Hunter recalled, just the sight of No. 18 was daunting. "Every time I looked up," he said, "we were behind. . . . Archie kept scoring points." And again he had the Rebels on the go, but could only get as far as the 'Bama 49. Only eight seconds remained, with no time-outs. Eschewing a Hail Mary, Archie threw short to Franks, who was tackled on the 42 as the clock died, leaving Ole Miss in agony.

Yet in heartbreaking defeat, Archie gained more attention—and empathy. As he will tell you, "It put me on the map." As he trod off the field with his head down, players from both teams and fans who leaped from the stands wanted to shake his hand or tap his shoulder pad. When

Hunter shook his hand, he noticed that Archie "had tears in his eyes. What could you say? Here's a guy who just played the greatest game any college football player ever had and lost by a point." In the locker room, he slumped onto a stool and, without peeling off his uniform, put his head in his hands and quietly sobbed. The Rebels' assistant coach, Bruiser Kinard, came over and put his arm around Archie's shoulder.

"Tough one to lose," he said, "but you did yourself proud out there."

Archie looked up. "Shoulda won, Coach," he said. "Shoulda won."[7]

Never before that night had a college quarterback passed for 300 yards and run for 100. He completed 33 of 52 for 436 yards—beating the old SEC record by 126 yards and falling just 59 short of the NCAA record at the time—and rang up 540 total yards, a record that would stand for 40 years. The Rebels had 30 first downs and 606 total yards, both new Ole Miss records. The 55 completions by both quarterbacks set a new NCAA record; in all, 24 school, SEC, and NCAA marks were set. And if Archie's passing wasn't enough, at the time he was second in the SEC in rushing. Having survived by one point, Bryant—who, contrary to public opinion, called it "the worst football game I ever saw"—nonetheless frothed over Archie, who, he said, "dominates a college game better than Joe Namath."[8]

———

Despite the fact that the Alabama loss killed the Rebels' chances for an SEC title, the school's athletic department began getting around 5,000 pieces of fan mail each week for Archie, a budding legend. Against No. 6 Georgia, he hurt his neck in the second quarter. He repaired to the locker room, immersing himself in ice in a trough used to store Coca-Cola. Then, in the third quarter, he sprinted back onto the field to a great roar and took the Rebels to a 25–17 win. They next destroyed Southern Miss 69–7, but then did a complete reversal, decimated in Houston 25–11. Down 23–12 against unbeaten, third-ranked LSU, Archie made up the deficit and fired a 30-yard touchdown pass to Studdard for a 26–23 win—another thriller, and one that prompted a lawsuit, filed in federal district court by a Baton Rouge lawyer seeking, apparently not in jest, an injunction to keep Archie from committing "further harassment" of LSU.

After they blanked Chattanooga 21–0, the Rebels faced another unbeaten team, No. 3 Tennessee, in Jackson. The Vols were 11-point favorites and acted like it. Their All-American linebacker, Steve Kiner, ran his mouth to *Sports Illustrated* during the week, slagging the backwoods team with the goober quarterback. When asked if he agreed that Ole Miss had "some horses," he smirked, "Hee-haw, them's not horses, them's mules." Of the quarterback, he asked, "Archie who?" That prompted the writer, Pat Putnam, to add to the story line: "You can guess how gracefully that was received in Oxford and Biloxi and Vicksburg, where they hang pictures of Archie Manning . . . on the living room wall, right next to the ones of Robert E. Lee. . . . In Tennessee . . . they laughed and started handing out Archie Who? buttons. And, baby, that really tore it."[9] The game, much like the 'Bama contest, would thus find its way into history as the Mule Game—or, as it turned out to be, the "Jackson Massacre," given the Rebels' 38–0 wipeout, the Vols' worst defeat since 1923.

———

The season closed with a 48–22 rout of Mississippi State on Thanksgiving, sending the Rebels, ranked No. 13, to a Sugar Bowl victory on New Year's Day against Frank Broyles's third-ranked Arkansas Razorbacks. It had been a strange dichotomy of a season, their final ranking at No. 8 earned by beating three nationally-ranked teams, but they also lost to three doormats. There was no downside for Archie. Lamont Wilson, a postal clerk in Magnolia, rewrote Johnny Cash's "Folsom Prison Blues" as "The Ballad of Archie Who," its lyrics a paean to "the best dad-burned quarterback to ever play the game." Recorded by a local group called the Rebel Rousers (not the '50s and '60s British R&B band) on a label called Hoddy Toddy, one verse went:

> *The ball is on the 50, the down is third-and-10,*
> *He runs it down the sidelines; yes, Archie takes it in.*

It became a regional hit, selling over 35,000 copies, mostly in Mississippi. One was apt to hear it on the radio while cruising through Drew beside signs reading "Home of Archie Manning" or under the marquee of a movie theater reading "Wow That Manning Boy." A Jackson motel put up a sign reading "Archie Slept Here." The Firestone department store ran an ad promoting an "Archie Manning Special Price" for its TVs. He made appearances such as one at the MediSav drugstore. The artificial turf at Hemingway Stadium was called the Archie Manning Memorial Carpet. Buttons around campus read, "Archie for Heisman Trophy" and "Archie's Army." Posters, dolls, T-shirts, they all made money for the school. A joke went around about a man about to jump off a bridge. His friend begged him to think about his family and religion.

"Don't have any family, and I don't believe in religion."

"Well, then, think about Archie."

"Archie who?"

"Jump, you SOB, jump."[10]

In November, when *Time* evaluated the Heisman Trophy race, it dubbed him "Heismanning" and "Huck Finn in hip pads." However, outside the South, his numbers didn't move the sportswriters. That year, San Diego State's Dennis Shaw, under pass-obsessed coach Don "Air" Coryell, racked up 3,185 yards to Archie's 1,762. Archie did win first-team All-America and first-team All-SEC, was named SEC Player of the Year, and won the Walter Camp Memorial Award, given by the Washington Touchdown Club to the outstanding college back in America. But Heismanning finished a distant fourth in the Heisman vote, won by Oklahoma fullback Steve Owens. No matter. Archie, now the patriarch of the family and face of the SEC, owned the South.

CHAPTER 5

"HE HAS MADE PEOPLE FORGET JAMES MEREDITH"

The new decade began better than it would end for Archie Manning. After another baseball season—winning All-SEC honors on a 25–8 Rebels team—and a summer at home spent still trying to come to grips with being the man of the family, he began his third and final season as Ole Miss's field general. When the *Sports Illustrated* college football preview came out, he was on the cover, ball locked in his hand, looking downfield. That season would be, the magazine pointed out, a "Red-Letter Year for Quarterbacks," the cream of the crop being Stanford's Jim Plunkett and Ohio State's Rex Kern, though writer William F. Reed posited that "the best of them all is ARCHIE," who he said "hardly resembles Mr. Good-Looking All-America Cover Boy Quarterback... [and] seems to reflect a certain quality of sadness and rural innocence." His father's suicide was briefly mentioned, as a "tragic footnote." Reed could "envision Manning back home in rustic little Drew, Miss., ... sailing down the river on a raft or sneaking off to some secret shady fishing hole." Yet the reality was that Archie could not escape his fame, and the "fever" surrounding him, which included a dozen writers dying to coauthor his autobiography, a fast-food chain planning to sell "Archie Burgers," and a Memphis company wanting to put out a line of Archie products, one of them a life-sized Archie balloon.

"I've never seen anything like it," said Vaught of the fuss. "I guess it's the times, the desire to glorify athletes, like the Namath thing. Thank goodness Archie is a smart man, a sensible man, and he hasn't let any of it go to his head. Why, I don't think he even thinks about it."[1] Archie himself couldn't understand it. "The only thing I can figure out is that Archie is a different name," he mused. "Maybe if it were Bill or something, none of this would have started."[2] He was also aware that he had to be careful. Prohibited from accepting compensation from merchants, he first agreed to, then canceled an appearance at the MediSav, writing in an open letter published in the *Delta Democrat Times*, "It has been pointed out to me that my appearance at a commercial function of this sort could seriously jeopardise my amateur standing."[3]

Another byproduct of the attention was the ragging his teammates gave him about it. Jim Poole recalled the players calling him Archie Who, or Archie What, or Archie Why, and taking the practice field singing "The Ballad of Archie Who." Archie could deal with that, even take it as a sign of respect. But, he admitted, "sometimes my patience gets short. Like when I'm introduced to somebody, especially women, and they say, 'Archie who?' and then laugh and laugh like they're the first person to ever say that. And sometimes when I sign an autograph I'll only sign my first name, not to be cocky, just to get through them all. Then people come back griping, wanting me to sign my last name, too, and that kind of hacks me off."[4] To keep from seeming cocky, he forbade his mother and sister from wearing "Archie Who" buttons at games and refused to run for class president, knowing it would be a too-easy victory. He decided to live off campus in an apartment with Billy Van Devender, to avoid being mobbed all the time. He did put on one of those buttons at a Sigma Nu frat party, to poke fun at himself. That may have been the only time he actually *enjoyed* himself the past few years. And did he ever. Poole, cracking up, has indelible memories of lugging a soused Archie over his shoulders and Archie singing, badly. At all other times, he had to watch what he did and said.

One exception was his uncharacteristic response to campus static about the team's inconsistencies. "I get real disgusted with some students," he said. "I've always gone along with whoever is running the show, like a coach. I might not think he's right sometimes—I get hacked off at Coach

Vaught every now and then—but he's the one running things."[5] That was certainly to be expected of a team man, but also a son of the South who was conditioned to regimentation and was not comfortable with dissent on or off the field. As other campuses exploded in student protests, leading to the horror of Kent State in May 1970, when "tin soldiers and Nixon coming" resulted in four students killed by National Guard troops, many colleges subsequently shut down during a moratorium period, but few did so in the South. Archie was content with the establishment crushing dissent. As for the war in the jungle, his deferment kept him safely distant from it, and he didn't see any hypocrisy in taking a dim view of draft dodgers and expatriates streaming to Canada. Wrote Reed, "Although he wears his hair so long that it curls out from beneath his helmet, the only way Archie likes his rebels is as a nickname for the football team." Rather than being impatient with the lack of racial progress on his campus, he said, "I'm kind of proud of Ole Miss. We've had a few incidents, but it's all been minor," such antiwar and civil rights demonstrations being "minor" matters not pertinent to his world or world view.

During the summer of 1970, he had traveled to Washington, D.C., where marches of that kind were common, for the Touchdown Club award dinner. Wearing black tie, he was seated between liberal Supreme Court justices William O. Douglas and Tom Clark, looking quite uncomfortable. As Reed noted, it was "an awkward spot for a Southerner to find himself in these days." But he kept himself on safe ground, a natural diplomat smart enough not to lurch into politics. When one media story dissected another famous Archie—the fictitious one named Bunker, whose satiric, white working-class racist bellowing had been cheered, not derided, by real working-class whites—the title was "Archie Who? Not Manning for Sure."[6] But while politicians of all stripes tried in vain to woo him, he was simply, by dint of his background and color, taken by some as a defender of the Southern heritage of hate. At the Rebels' homecoming game against Houston in 1970, some Ole Miss students shouted at black Cougar players, "Kill that nigger!" and "Tree that coon!" Some black Rebel fans sequestered in the south end zone displayed signs calling Manning a "redneck."[7]

Trying to walk down the middle, the school tried to present the quarterback as a unifier. Archie, wrote the campus paper the *Daily Mississippian*, "has been the best thing to happen to this university and this state in many, many years. He has made people forget James Meredith, [Ole Miss] Dean [Joshua] Stanford, and Fulton Chapel," the last the site of black campus demonstrations. That was hooey, given Ole Miss's stalling on full integration, with not even a black fraternity allowed on campus until 1977, a year after the first black vice-chancellor was hired. But a certain resident of Washington, D.C., knew it was good politics to mention the Manning name, if he could remember it. When President Nixon took a trip to the Mediterranean that fall, he made small talk with sailors aboard the USS *Saratoga* by talking football. Texas looked pretty good, he said, "But watch out for Mississippi and that . . . ah . . . ah . . . ah . . . that Archie Manning."[8]

———

John Vaught, looking ahead to the 1970 season, was again raving about his leader. "I have now reached the point with Archie that anything he wants to do from any place on the field at any time is all right with me." The Rebels, ranked fifth in the preseason polls, began the season with a 47–13 thumping of Memphis State, Archie throwing one touchdown and running for two. They beat Kentucky 20–17 in the SEC opener, though Archie sustained a recurrence of his groin injury. That was when he learned how capricious stardom can be. Lying in bed in his room that week, he told Billy Van Devender with a cynical grin, "Boy, the mail sure dropped off this week." Perhaps attempting to reduce expectations, he also said his numbers might dip, being that "there are not too many games you play like the one we had with Alabama last year."[9]

But with Alabama next, again on prime-time TV, there was zero chance he'd sit out. The game, in Jackson, was sold out for months, and at the kickoff, *Sports Illustrated* said, "the 46,000 seats were overflowing with bourbon-sipping, flag-waving zealots, and the flags were not designed by Betsy Ross." With intended cheek and irony, the magazine billed the clash as "Archie and the War Between the States." On campus, Rebel fans were so stoked they put up mocking signs on the athletic dorm reading "The Bryant Hilton." Archie himself was so zoned in on the game that he nearly forgot Olivia's birthday, sending her belated flowers. And she was a tad worried about him. "Even before the Tennessee game last year he wasn't this fired up," she said. "Why, I think he wants to hurt somebody, and that's not like Archie." Although the game was devalued by Crimson Tide QB Scott Hunter being out with a separated shoulder and Archie hobbled by the groin pull, he threw for two touchdowns and ran for another. Vaught had begun to work option plays, the kind Archie once dreaded, into the offense, though now that he was up to around 200 pounds he could withstand open-field hits better; as *SI* observed, "Manning worked the option play about as well as a quarterback can." And he walked off a winner, 48–23, only the second Ole Miss win over Alabama in 60 years. Still sizzling, he cranked three more touchdowns the next week, including passes of 66 and 52 yards to Studdard, to beat Georgia 31–21.

But now came this season's rattlesnake bite. With a "breather" scheduled against Southern Mississippi, whom they'd stomped in nine straight games, Ole Miss, a 35-point favorite, fell behind early and Archie had to throw a school-record 56 passes to try to catch up, completing 30 for 341 yards. Not enough, as they fell 30–14. They did right themselves against Vanderbilt, 26–16, but now came disaster. While leading the Rebels to a 24–13 win over Houston, a hard hit broke Archie's right forearm. With Manning out, Ole Miss beat Chattanooga but went down 19–14 to Mississippi State. Their dreams of a national title were over. Still, an Orange Bowl berth was at stake when they played LSU in the season finale, and Archie tried to play with his arm encased from hand to shoulder in a protective plastic sleeve. He passed to Poole for a first-quarter TD, but the day belonged to Tigers quarterback Bert Jones. As LSU pulled away, Archie retired to the bench. Final score: 61–17.

Coming into the game ranked at No. 16, they emerged unranked, their season record 7–3. As consolation, they were invited to play in the Gator Bowl against No. 11 Auburn, led by junior quarterback Pat Sullivan, who led the nation in total offense and would win the Heisman a year later. This made for an obvious story line: Archie, in his farewell to college football, fighting for his reputation against a new top dog. Though Ole Miss fans wore "Pat Who?" buttons, Sullivan quickly put the Tigers up 21–0. Archie, who had missed practices while he had surgery to insert a metal plate in his forearm, again wore that bulky cast/sleeve, but kept scrambling around and throwing. He ran one touchdown in from the two, then hit Floyd Franks for a 34-yard touchdown. But Auburn had him running for his life, and after a 42-yard run in the third quarter he was so spent he had to come out. He returned, but after another long run, when he reversed field twice, he was done. So was Ole Miss, losing 35–28. "My wind left me," Archie said afterward. "That old hospital bed never got off my back. . . . That baby [on my arm] got kinda heavy."[10]

In the final coaches' poll, Ole Miss crept back to No. 20. Archie, though, had lost altitude. The feverish hype of autumn having cooled considerably, he was omitted from the All-America teams. Plunkett and Notre Dame's Joe Theismann came in ahead of him in the Heisman vote. His college career had produced 4,753 passing yards and 31 touchdowns, yet among the many school records he had set, only that single-game onslaught against Alabama would withstand the test of time; the others would be fair game for dashing quarterbacks, including his youngest son. Today, he ranks no higher among Ole Miss quarterbacks than eighth in passing yardage. And yet, throughout the South, his legend would far outlive his heralded career, the topic of endless stories told by aging Rebel fans at dinner tables and family picnics.

What's more, the Gator Bowl was also the end of the line for Vaught. In ill health, he suffered a mild heart attack after the season and quit, replaced by Billy Kinard. He would be healthy enough to return for a last roundup in '73, after Kinard was fired, then retire permanently to run the school's athletic department. His record was 190–61–12, with six SEC titles and the production of 18 All-Americans to his credit.

When Archie and Vaught walked off the field after the Gator Bowl, the first black player was due to walk onto the Ole Miss varsity the following season. Much of the grandeur and delusional mythology of the Ole Miss tradition went with them, though not everyone on campus was ready to deify Archie. Rebels basketball star Johnny Neumann, who would lead the nation with an average of 40.1 points per game in 1970–71 and sign a $2 million contract with the Memphis Pros of the American Basketball Association, lamented, "Archie sure did hog the headlines. Why, I could score 60 points one night and the next day's lead story would say, 'Archie Says Broken Arm Hurts Golf Game' or 'Archie Plans to Watch TV and Turn in Early.'" On Neumann's car was a bumper sticker with his opinion. It read, "Archie Is a Saint . . . But Johnny's a Pro."[11]

==========

Relying on their own methods of evaluating college talent, NFL scouts had lost none of their ardor for Archie, who was assumed to be among the top three picks in the upcoming draft—all of them quarterbacks—along with Plunkett and Santa Clara's Dante Pastorini. Accordingly, agents came streaming to the house on Third Street, some showing up unannounced during the season, meaning that their offers were, as Archie would put it, "illegal solicitations."[12] He had Frank Crosthwait politely send them on their way, as he did with the agents who dropped in after the season, when it was legal. One, Herb Rudoy out of Chicago, hung around the house for hours, waiting for him to come home. As Archie recalled, "After a while he got tired of waiting and he got up to go, but before he left, Sis gave him a jar of her homemade peach preserves and another jar of pickle relish. I could just picture him going back to Chicago with those two bottles and people asking him, 'Well, did you get Archie Manning?' and him saying, 'Nope, but I got these.'"[13]

There was no scouting combine then, and the IQ tests given to college players were rudimentary. Neither were the cream of the crop brought to New York for the draft, which was not yet televised and took place in the morning. The 1971 edition was held on January 28 and 29 in a small, airless room in Manhattan's Belmont Plaza Hotel. On that day, Archie sat by the phone in the office of the Ole Miss athletic department, awaiting word on what was a remarkable milestone in NFL history. The first pick was owned by the Boston Patriots (who became the New England Patriots in March), the second by the New Orleans Saints, the third by the Houston Oilers. Plunkett, who had played in a pro-style drop-back scheme at Stanford, was expected to go first. The next two teams in line, being from the South, lusted for Archie, especially the Saints, who had come into the league only in 1967 and were dreadful. The league's second Deep South team, after the Atlanta Falcons, they played in the 19th-largest city in the country—the biggest after Indianapolis, San Antonio, and Memphis not to have a franchise—and, with a large surrounding regional market area, could sell a lot of tickets and advertising with a top-rated attraction. Anticipating that Archie was the ideal get, the team cleared roster and salary space by trading the creaky veteran quarterback Billy Kilmer to the Washington Redskins, which for Kilmer was the sort of liberation that Archie Manning, in time, would only be able to wish for.

═══

As Johnny Neumann suggested, Archie was already a saint in Oxford. And his gal, Olivia Williams, was royalty, having been named homecoming queen during the season. When Archie played in the Hula Bowl college all-star game, he invited Olivia and her family to come along with Sis and Pam to Honolulu, where it was played. When they got back, they tied the knot, on January 21. Perhaps not coincidentally, at the draft lottery for men his age in July 1969, his birth date had been drawn 75th, a low number that would normally have sent him to Vietnam. With that number still hanging over his head as graduation neared, getting hitched won him a marriage deferment.

The wedding was at Philadelphia's First Baptist Church, the reception at the National Guard armory, the country club being too small to hold the groom's teammates and the bride's high-society family and friends. The local cops helped out, too. When Archie and some buddies tarried before the service at a honky-tonk called Ed's Beer Joint, Archie and his best man, Billy Van Devender, were given a lift to the church in a squad car. Incredibly, the public was invited, and at the reception some strangers made off with napkins, champagne bottles, tablecloths, whatever, as souvenirs. The next day, Archie and Olivia were off to Acapulco for a honeymoon, where Archie forgot he was a redhead and got a terrible sunburn. Returning home, they rented an off-campus apartment and went back to their studies.

As expected, a week later the Saints made him their No. 1 pick. At Ole Miss, Archie received calls from Saints general manager Vic Schwenk, coach J. D. Roberts, and owner John Mecom. But he wasn't going to come cheap. He had by now enlisted Frank Crosthwait to handle negotiations for him, as a family lawyer. As for an agent, he and Frank chose Ed Keating, an eager 34-year-old underling at the biggest sports agency of all, Mark McCormack's International Management Group, which handled the fabulously wealthy golf troika of Arnold Palmer, Jack Nicklaus, and Gary Player. Archie, meanwhile, did the banquet circuit, feted by the Mississippi Economic Council, and autograph signings, collecting around $800 a week for appearances. He also had his "day" in Drew in early February, honored at a ceremony at City Hall emceed by the mayor— who was now none other than Snake Williford. Archie, Olivia, and his mother and sister rode down Main Street, where all 20 stores festooned their windows with pictures of Archie. An automobile dealer presented him with a new Lincoln, another a ski boat. His Ole Miss teammates came in for the day, as did J. D. Roberts from New Orleans. Baseball Hall of Famer Dizzy Dean and Mississippi senator Jim Eastland also grabbed some face time.

It was the biggest event ever held in Drew, and at the time was a welcome relief from the realities the town had tried so hard to resist. Even as late as Archie's senior year, Drew High had admitted only four black students, all from the Carter family. The rising racial tension encroached on Archie's big day. One of the bands was to be an all-black unit, but the oldest of the Carter daughters approached the band's director, saying Archie had been "ugly" to her during their time at the school, which led the band to drop out. Archie would leave town upset about it. Decades later, he still was. "There was no truth in it," he insisted, adding that it was "the polar opposite of what I would have done." In his memoir with Peyton years later, he reserved nine pages for his halting path to racial acceptance. But while he tried hard to be sincere, his innate Southern conditioning was obvious in his downplaying of the tensions in Drew during his formative years. He noted that his uncle had rented homes on the farm to black folks, and that blacks had cheered him at Ole Miss. But he also drew an unfortunate, even jarring tautology with the Trumpian-sounding bromide that "the stereotyping is repulsive . . . both ways. All black men aren't noble, all white men aren't swine."[14]

The negative vibe with the black band did nothing to make Archie want to rush back to Drew. On the other hand, Sis had spent her whole life there and had no intention of ever leaving. And Pam had married

Vernon Shelton, a native of the city who had also gone to Ole Miss and then taken a job teaching history classes to inmates at the Parchman prison. Archie didn't begrudge them for remaining on the family's long-time soil. Pam, he said, "won't live anywhere else. Must be in the genes."

———

Crosthwait and Keating played hardball with the Saints for months, something the multimillionaire Mecom and his front-office people did not expect from a supposed hick. Archie was asking for a five-year, $1 million deal, spread out over 10 years for tax abatement. He had leverage, too. During his college years he'd been drafted twice more by big-league baseball teams, the Kansas City Royals and the Chicago White Sox. In May 1971, when he and Olivia collected their degrees and she took a job as a teacher in Batesville, he still had not signed with the Saints. In those months, John Vaught had acted as a surrogate as well, playing bad cop by hinting that Archie might just go play in the Canadian Football League. "I'm a little disappointed with the Saints' attitude," the former coach said. "The Saints don't seem to realize Archie is a unique talent . . . [H]e would have no trouble getting a one-year contract for at least $125,000 [in Canada]."[15]

On July 9, Crosthwait said Archie might skip the July 30 College All-Star Game, a preseason event played in Chicago that pitted the top collegians against the NFL champions. As an unsigned player, Manning was not yet covered by the Saints' insurance. So Crosthwait said he would only play if the team paid the premium for coverage above the $24,000 the organizers of the game provided. Crosthwait got the idea from the Patriots, who paid on behalf of their still-unsigned quarterback, Jim Plunkett. What's more, Plunkett ticked Archie off when he made a remark that he was "honored" to play in the game, which Archie construed as a slap at him for holding out. Nerves were clearly beginning to fray all around.

Neither would Manning attend the Saints' preseason camp in Hattiesburg, Mississippi. He did visit the camp and meet with Vic Schwenk, but Crosthwait couldn't be there because he had more pressing business, the kind that really did change things in the South. As prosecuting attorney for Sunflower County, he had indicted three white men for murder in the shooting death of that Drew High School student, Jo Etha Collier, on the eve of her graduation in May. Her murder came during what was called a "wave of senseless killing in Mississippi of black citizens by white citizens"[16] and led to black marches through the town. Although the case was a landmark, in the end the only man convicted was sentenced to a mere five years and set free after three. In the Delta, civil rights remained stuck in neutral.

Archie, meanwhile, was becoming frustrated with the pace of contract talks. So was Vaught, who after the Saints made one offer was either joking—or worse, wasn't, since the NCAA would not have laughed—that "Archie made more than that playing here!"[17] Mecom, too, was now getting impatient. The 31-year-old son of Texas oil baron John Mecom Sr. had been the team's majority stockholder since its creation. A pudgy-cheeked guy with a rich-brat reputation, he had not involved himself in the negotiations at first. Now he did, biting the bullet to make Archie the highest offer ever made to an NFL rookie, though Archie had to come down from his original asking price. On Friday, July 23, Archie drove his big Lincoln back to the Saints' training-camp base in Hattiesburg with Crosthwait. They went up to Mecom's suite at the Holiday Inn, where the owner and his lawyer, Glen Magnuson, presented the team's offer: $100,000 plus escalating bonuses, for five years. It was a deal.

Though the yearly salaries—$30,000, $40,000, up to a maximum of $70,000—seem like small change next to his sons', back then they were about average for league quarterbacks—except Joe Namath—and more than the average salary of all but four teams. The Saints' average salary, by contrast, was a meager $21,700.[18] Archie was also given a $160,000 signing bonus, and a $250,000 insurance policy, bringing the price tag to $410,000, the most ever lavished on an NFL rookie, and slightly more than Plunkett, the No. 1 pick. It was not quite the three-year, $427,000 windfall the New York Jets of the American Football League had given Namath in 1965 to put the upstart loop on par with the NFL in the public consciousness. But if Delta Archie was no Broadway Joe in terms of self-promoting, skirt-chasing, drama-queen rebelliousness, if there was a city in which he could create a stir, it was certainly *N'awlins*. And he had two good knees.

The Sunday *Delta Democrat Times* ran a three-quarter-page headline reading, "Archie Signs with Saints." Now he was free to make a hasty trip to the College All-Star Game, though all he would do was stand on the sidelines, in no condition to play, and pose for photographers with the other rookie quarterbacks. Having lived in the SEC bubble, he recalled, "I had no idea what style Dan [Pastorini] played. I didn't know where the hell Santa Clara was. It could have been in Egypt as far as I knew. I don't think I'd ever heard of Dan before the draft."[19] Then it was off to the Saints' camp, where J. D. Roberts, tasting imaginary sugar plums, awaited the commodity of an unproven player he stirringly called "the best young quarterback in the country."

CHAPTER 6

MUDBUGGERS

The New Orleans Saints were born in 1966 as a condition the NFL had to meet to be allowed to merge with the AFL. In June 1966 the leagues, which had been competing with each other since 1960, agreed to begin fully-interlocking play in 1970, with a new championship game, later dubbed the Super Bowl, to begin after the '66 season. However, this was all contingent on Congress granting an exemption from antitrust laws designed to prevent such an obvious monopoly. That was the cue for Louisiana's powerful Democratic congressman Hale Boggs, the House majority leader and an old hand at horse trading, to demand a new franchise in his backyard in exchange for moving the antitrust exemption along. On November 1, 1966—All Saints' Day—Commissioner Pete Rozelle made the announcement of the franchise at the Pontchartrain Hotel, a proud moment indeed for the city and an ownership group led by John Mecom that had cobbled together the $8.5 million franchise fee (the value of the Saints today is $1.52 billion). The team was named after the gospel hymn "When the Saints Go Marching In," a choice that beat out such suggestions as the Deltas, Jazz Kings, Ramparts, Crawfish, Mudbuggers, and Stevedores.

The Saints, whose first signed player was by chance an Ole Miss alumnus, kicker Paige Cothren, would play in the rapidly aging Tulane Stadium, where Archie had beaten Arkansas in the 1970 Sugar Bowl.

Before going down in a plane crash, Boggs lived long enough to see John Gilliam return the first kickoff the Saints ever fielded, for a 94-yard touchdown. A long, cold winter then set in. The Saints won no more than five games in any of their first four seasons. During one extravagant halftime show reenacting the Battle of New Orleans, a real cannon backfired, blowing three fingers off one of the actors' hands. Their original coach, Tom Fears, was replaced midway through the '70 season by John David "J. D." Roberts, a former Marine and All-America guard on Bud Wilkinson's 1953 Oklahoma Sooners, but Roberts's only win that season came on a then-record 63-yard field goal by club-footed Tom Dempsey, after which they lost 12 straight. And now Archie Manning came marching in, sparking delusions of glory.

When he got to the team's summer camp in Hattiesburg, Mississippi, TV cameras recorded every moment of his workouts. But the long-suffering veterans on this moribund team hardly genuflected before him. As in college, he was hazed, forced to stand on tables in the cafeteria and sing the Ole Miss fight song, though he was allowed to keep his hair. Curiosity ran high when, after just a week of practice, the Saints played their first preseason game, against the Buffalo Bills. Roberts, who had told Archie he wouldn't play, shocked him when, with five minutes to go, down by seven, he turned to him and barked, "Get in there." He did, and promptly threw four passes, completing none.

That was par for the course with Roberts, who was at times as addled as John Vaught. During games, he would mumble non sequiturs. Surveying the field during that opening preseason game, he said, "I don't know who that No. 32 is, but he's a damn good-looking running back"—referring to one O. J. Simpson, the most famous player in the country. Still, Roberts knew what he had in Archie. Even with three other quarterbacks ahead of him on the depth chart, after Archie threw a touchdown and ran for 30 yards in another exhibition against the Dallas Cowboys, he was named the starter. The season opener, against the Los Angeles Rams, sold out Tulane Stadium on September 19, fed by headlines in the *New Orleans Times-Picayune* like "All New Orleans Hopes on Rookie QB Archie Manning." The paper, going all in on the new kid in town, offered fans a 16-page booklet called *The Making of a Saint* for half a buck.

Remarkably comfortable in the glare of the spotlight, wearing a new number—8, because 18 was taken—he wore dashing white shoes à la Namath, but those shoes could not dance away fast enough from the constant pressure of the Rams' Fearsome Foursome defensive line, which sacked him six times in the first half alone, thrice by the always-terrorizing Deacon Jones. Even so, at halftime the score was 3–3. And in the third quarter, he led a drive that ended with a six-yard touchdown pass to Dave Parks, then another with a two-yard plunge by fullback Bob Gresham, making it 17–3. There was a Mardi Gras atmosphere in the old stadium. However, the Rams roared back with 17 straight points and took the lead, 20–17. With the clock running down, Archie indeed marched the Saints, 70 yards in eight plays. He then hit Danny Abramowicz with a 12-yard pass to the L.A. 13. An interference call put the ball on the 1. Two plays failed, and it was third-and-goal, with time for just one play. Roberts, wanting it all, dismissed a tying field goal. "We're going for it!" he shouted to Archie. But he was befuddled about what play to call. When Archie got into the huddle, Abramowicz asked him what the play was.

"Damned if I know," he said. "They never told me."[1]

He didn't get cute with it. He took the snap, cut left against the grain, saw a hole, and dove over the goal line, winning his debut 24–20, whereupon he nearly needed a security detail to get off the field amid the rapturous fans. He had gone 16 of 29 for 218 yards, a modest total, but had kept his head and was only intercepted once. The fan base was convinced. The *Baton Rouge State-Times and Morning Advocate*'s sports editor, Bernell Ballard, wrote, "Archie Manning has done it. . . . Worth a half-million [sic] to sign? Brother, at $1 million, Manning would be the biggest bargain pro football ever found." The *Times-Picayune*'s sports editor, Bob Roesler, seemed to break into song: "Archie Manning, Archie Manning, Archie Manning. That's all you could hear Monday. At the service station, the cigar counter, butcher shop, laundry, lunch counter. . . . With Archie alive and well, who knows, maybe the Saints will go 14–0." Roesler noted that, late in the game, after Jones had crashed in but missed the sack, Archie "walked over and offered to help Deacon to his feet. Manning is that sort of person."

The *Advocate*'s Saints beat man, Bud Montet, even had biblical visions. "Archie Manning," he wrote, "put the 'halo' back on the Saints when he rolled over the goal line."

═════

The euphoria lasted all week. Then the San Francisco 49ers came in and skated to a 38–20 win, sacking Archie eight times on the hard artificial turf. He scrambled to a 13–13 tie in Houston a week later. In Chicago, the Saints fell behind the Bears 35–0 at the half and lost 35–14, a game in which Archie pulled a thigh muscle and was benched. But he was a tough nut to crack. At home against the Cowboys, he put the Saints up with a 29-yard pass to halfback Tony Baker, then made it 17–0 on a 13-yard rush. The defense held tough, and his two-yard run capped the game, a 24–14 win—one so traumatic to Dallas coach Tom Landry that he junked his two-QB shuttle system and went solely with Roger Staubach; a few months later, the Cowboys would win the Super Bowl on this very turf.

Archie's thigh remained a problem, and he missed some or all of the remaining games. When he was in the lineup, he was battered on nearly every drop back or scramble. Over the season, he was sacked 40 times and could only shake loose enough to run the ball 33 times, picking up 173 yards and four touchdowns. Toward the end, the fuddled Roberts tried a wishbone-type option play, which only made Archie more of a sitting duck. Abramowicz felt for him. "Archie, you're living on borrowed time," he told him in the huddle. "You'd better forget that damn thing," meaning the wishbone.

"What can I do?" Archie said. "They keep sending [the play] in."[2]

It could have been worse. Abramowicz swears he saw some very big and mean linemen pull back when they had Archie in their sights. The Rams' great defensive end Jack Youngblood, he said, told him, "I can't do it to that boy. So many times I've had a straight shot on him when his back was turned, but I just can't do it." Archie appreciated that. Youngblood, he said, "was nice enough to pick me up every time he knocked my ass off."[3]

The Saints ended the season at 4–8–2, last in the NFC West Division, and Archie would have to get used to this. His own numbers were entirely anemic: 1,164 passing yards, a 48 percent completion rate, six touchdowns, seven fumbles, the last an all-time team worst. The NFL's quarterback rating wasn't adopted until 1973; calculated retroactively, it put him at 60.1 on a scale from 0 to 158.3.

There were other transitions he had to make, *off* the field. In the heart of New Orleans, there were dozens of African-Americans on the field and thousands on the streets of the city. Suddenly, it was he who felt like the outsider. "When I first came to the Saints I was concerned with how the black players would accept me," he recalled.[4]

Indeed, he had arrived in style, in his big, white Lincoln Continental, wondering "how black players might think of the rookie white guy from Ole Miss with the newfound 'wealth.'"[5] He even tried to hide the car, parking it on the street instead of in the players' lot. In fact, many of the black Saints *were* wary of him. But defensive lineman Richard Neal, who would tragically die young at age 35 from a heart attack, was, Archie said, "kind of a leader among the black players, knew what I was going through." Neal took the Mannings to dinner, the sight of two high-profile couples of different color more than a little symbolic.[6] Archie's new world also included the presence of a gay man, spare running back Dave Kopay, who wouldn't come out until after his career but whose secret was quietly known. If Archie was "late coming" to such things, he was game to accept social change, even if uneasily. In his memoir with Peyton, he recalled—in perhaps a bit too much detail—the moment when he shared a locker room with a black man and his mind was fixed on a particular stereotype. Describing USC linebacker Charlie Weaver—the Detroit Lions' first-round pick in '71, whom he practiced against at the College All-Star Game—he wrote that Weaver was "the blackest man I'd ever seen," adding with remarkable obtuseness that when he saw Weaver in the shower, "there he was, full view, and I have to say it startled me. The thought of showering with blacks—integration down to the bare essentials—had never occurred to me."

He also cited one unnamed black receiver who had a racial chip on his shoulder pad, once telling him in the huddle, "We all been talking and we think you're throwing more passes to the white guys." That, he wrote, made him "see red," and he nearly fought it out with the guy. His parting shot to this "knucklehead" was to slime him as someone who "couldn't lay off the drugs," no doubt hoping the object of the insult would know exactly who he meant. He then leaped into a self-congratulatory paean. "The 'black community,' if you will, has been wonderful to me. No, they're not all people I see every day, but . . . I consider them blessings in my life." He added, "For my boys, race has never been much of a concern either way."[7]

<hr />

New Orleans itself was going through a painful transition, aided in no small way by a biracial football franchise. Maurice "Moon" Landrieu, who was elected mayor in 1970, a rare liberal in the town, remembered, "We had a race issue back then. If you remember people sat in segregated seating at [the minor league baseball] Pelicans games. Now, all of a sudden we had NFL games and blacks and whites were seated together. I can recall very vividly John Gilliam's return of the first kickoff. The stadium went wild, and I'm sitting here watching all of these white people cheering for a black player. That was unheard of before. In terms of race relations, the Saints were a tremendous gift to the fans and the people of New Orleans."[8] The Saints made an effort at optics; three of the team's cheerleaders were black.

But any signs of progress came with lingering stubbornness, and they still do. Integration didn't follow white fans or players out the stadium exits. Archie and Olivia's first digs outside of Oxford were an apartment near the Saints' training grounds in Metairie, a suburban cradle on the edge of Lake Pontchartrain where, in 1990, ex-Klan leader David Duke was elected to the state legislature. Racial divisions in New Orleans seemed to carry over to front-office decisions. Where Mecom *père* was a remarkable exception as a liberal oilman, Mecom *fils* was not. And the NFL had little to say about the segregated housing for black players and the separate hotels during the preseason in places like Birmingham. There was suspicion among black players and fans when the Saints traded Ken Burrough, the team's No. 1 pick in 1970, to the Oilers for a draft pick and three ineffectual players—all because, it was said, J. D. Roberts thought Burrough, a black man, was "goldbricking."[9] Burrough, whose skills Archie could have used, would play 10 more years and make the Pro Bowl twice.

Richard Neal, too, was traded—in 1973, to the Jets. These kinds of strong, outspoken black men were by rote labeled "troublemakers." Playing within these old shibboleths, Archie's identity was carved by white privilege. The spoils of Southern football stardom were his. In 1973, he was made the grand marshal of the Peach Parade, on the eve of the Peach Bowl in Atlanta. In the Deep South, gigs like that were reserved for men of honor and distinction, as long as they were white. Like Drew, New Orleans would inevitably morph into a near-opposite image, to be defined by its black mayor in 2006 as a "chocolate" city. And even by the time Archie and Olivia arrived, the interracial vibe was strong within an overall stew of different cultures. Once, the couple thought they might move back to Mississippi after the season's end, but that changed once they became addicted to the eateries in the French Quarter, on Basin Street, wherever the scent of gumbo led them—their favorite being Commander's Palace in the Garden District, down by the Mississippi River, where they filled up on bread pudding soufflé and crawfish étouffée. Even now, Peyton says he will eat crawfish only in New Orleans.

The town would never be fueled by football the way Dallas was in the early 1960s on its way to wealth and arrogance. But whatever the city is, the Saints made football a part of the equation, for better and worse. In the cynical words of one resident commenting on a story about the Saints on the *Times-Picayune* website in 2016, "Before the Saints, [New Orleans] was a party city with a corrupt administration, few major private sector employers. Now it's a party city with a corrupt administration, few major private sector employers and a football team."[10]

———

While John Vaught had said Archie would "revolutionize" pro football,[11] he never quite got there. But neither was he alone in the game of busted expectations. Jim Plunkett and Dan Pastorini would have almost as hard a time as Archie. Instead, Terry Bradshaw, helped to no end by the Pittsburgh Steelers' Steel Curtain defense and talented playmakers, was headed for four Super Bowl wins in the '70s. Roger Staubach was doing with his arm and legs in Dallas what Archie was supposed to do, albeit with the kind of coach Archie never had. Staubach, taking note of this, said, "You know, there are a lot of people who think that if Archie and I had been drafted by opposite teams, we would have had opposite careers. And they might be right."[12]

During the 1972 season, Archie would work twice as hard for literally half as much. After a 34–14 loss on opening day to the Rams, the Saints made it close before losing to the Kansas City Chiefs, but lost the next three games badly. Then came two weeks of false hope. Playing the 49ers on the road, they were down all game until Archie hit Parks with a 30-yard TD pass for a late 20–17 lead, though the 49ers were able to ease their embarrassment with a late field goal. Next, at home against the Philadelphia Eagles, the Saints romped 21–3, Archie throwing for 295 yards. But six losses in the last seven games restored the usual order. They finished 2–11–1, with Archie needing to pass a league-high 449 times, completing 230 for 2,781 yards (second only to Joe Namath), 18 touchdowns (one off the league high), and 21 interceptions (fewer than Plunkett's 25). He also led the league again in times sacked: 43. The Saints scored only five rushing touchdowns.

When it was over, Roberts's offensive coordinator, Ken Shipp, a bright football man, jumped in a heartbeat to the Jets. The GM, Vic Schwenk, was fired and replaced—in what still seems like a practical joke—by *Apollo 12* astronaut Richard "Dick" Gordon Jr., Mecom apparently believing that if Gordon could go to the moon, he could deliver something equally improbable: a winning Saints team. Gordon wasn't so sure. "I have a great deal to learn," he said.[13] His first move was to can Roberts—not before the next season so that another coach could have some time to prepare, but after the fourth and final exhibition game. The new head coach—Roberts's backfield coach, John North—was, like his predecessor, an ex-Marine, a Purple Heart recipient who was wounded so gravely in the Pacific Theater in World War II that his parents were told he had died. That sort of grit was needed by the Saints, and a player who had it, Oklahoma defensive tackle Derland Moore, was a second-round draft pick starting a 13-year career in New Orleans. Still, Archie had no chance in '73.

On opening day, the Falcons wiped the Saints out, 62–7. The next week was an improvement—they lost 40–3 to the Cowboys. They played tough in Baltimore, losing 14–10, before finally winning, at home against the Bears, 21–16, with Archie running in two touchdowns. The Saints then won two in a row for the first time with Archie. They finished the season at 5–9, which could be measured as improvement, good enough for a tie for third place in their division. Gordon insisted the team was just three players away from winning the Super Bowl. That prompted local sportscaster Buddy Diliberto to say, "Only if those three players are God the Father, God the Son and God the Holy Ghost." Gordon wasn't amused. Diliberto was banned from the team plane, as the edict went, "for life plus ten years," which Diliberto snarked might not be long enough for the team to win. Indeed, Danny Abramowicz was overjoyed to be traded to the 49ers after the second game of that season. Before he cleared out, he had some advice for the beleaguered quarterback.

"Archie," he said, "you'd better get out of this place. They're going to kill you here."[14]

CHAPTER 7

"STRANGLED BY THE TRAUMA"

As Richard Nixon became consumed and then subsumed by the Watergate scandal in August 1974, Archie came to summer training camp with no way out. Three seasons of sluggish progress had taken a toll, physically and on his pride and ego. All he could really do was sink his roots further into the Louisiana clay and take advantage of his saintly status to grab as much as he could off the field. He was making $70,000 a year, but almost all of his salary was deferred for tax purposes, and there were no playoff or Pro Bowl perks. What's more, on March 6, 1974, Olivia gave birth for the first time, meaning he had a new expense. It was a son, Cooper, named after her father. He came into the world with a ruckus, Olivia wondering how she got through delivering a 12-pound, three-ounce bruiser.

Although Archie's contract would not expire until after the '75 season, leverage was on his mind—and Ed Keating's. By chance, it was in even greater supply in 1974, as the NFL again found itself with competition after a coterie of millionaires put together a 12-team circuit, the World Football League. At the same time, in the spring of '74, the NFL players' union went out on strike, hoping for a better result than it had obtained from two previous labor disputes. But with teams threatening to use rookies and scab replacements, most veterans crossed the picket line. Others eagerly heard out fat offers to commit to the new league, the

Memphis team striking gold by signing Miami Dolphins running backs Larry Csonka and Jim Kiick and receiver Paul Warfield—all represented by Keating, who wrangled for them a combined $3.5 million deal scheduled to begin in '75, after their NFL contracts expired.

The WFL began its inaugural season on July 10, to big crowds and loud headlines. Archie, playing it coy, said the new league "intrigued" him and that Memphis was "the only team I would consider playing for." He half-joked, "Do you think they have enough money to pay me?" while insisting, "I'm happy in New Orleans."[1] In truth, he was torn. And he despised playing on the concrete-like artificial turf at Tulane Stadium; having shattered his arm on similar turf at Ole Miss, he even blamed swollen wisdom teeth on his head smashing into that surface. No matter. When plans were revealed for the construction of a properly futuristic, decadent new downtown home, the Louisiana Superdome, set to open in time for the 1975 season, there would be artificial turf there, too.

What's more, he and Olivia didn't feel comfortable with a good many other players and their wives or girlfriends. This no doubt had to do with jealousy about his contract, but neither were the Mannings much into socializing. At games, sitting with the other women, Olivia would endure petty gossip-mongering. Sometimes they would say something unkind about Archie, prompting Olivia to say, politely, "Please don't talk about my husband like that." At the same time, Archie was soldered to the town and the team, popular beyond the win-loss records. In '74, the US Postal Service reported that Archie had received 20,800 fan letters in the past year, behind only Hank Aaron, Dinah Shore, Johnny Carson, Joe Namath, and Bart Starr among sports and entertainment figures.[2] Indeed, the hints he dropped about jumping leagues, and headlines such as "WFL Teams Seek Archie Manning," rightly made John Mecom nervous.[3]

This was no accident. Archie wanted a restructuring of his contract, with more cash freed up. And Crosthwait annoyed Mecom even more when he called the players' union to make sure that the owner's threats to withhold promised bonus money from striking players would not be legal. Indeed, seeing Archie leading the strikers seemed to make the owner snap. "We've had a difficult time developing a leader on the field, and that includes Mr. Archie Manning," Mecom groused, adding that he was "disappointed in some of his actions the last few weeks. I hope he tries as hard on the field to be a leader as much as he is off the field." Burning, Archie responded, "If he wants to get into a debate on leaders, I don't see what ground he has to walk on. He, Mecom, has been the leader for seven years now. If I'm to blame for the last three years, who's to blame for the other four? . . . This has really upset me that he would say that about me. It's not my way to get into controversial situations. That's not the way to run a successful franchise. But I'm not going to sit here and take it."[4]

Mecom, as if playing a game of chicken with his star, implied that he could replace Archie easily enough with his backup, Bobby Scott. When Archie and Keating met with Saints brass in late July, the agent recalled, "Archie couldn't believe it. For the first time in his adult life, he was faced with a situation where [Saints officials] had their backs to the wall and said some things they may live to regret."[5] Mecom didn't know how close he came to losing Archie, nor Memphis Southmen owner Johnny Bassett how close *he* came to landing him. But Bassett roiled the pot by offering Archie a $1.5 million deal for three years once his Saints deal ran its course in a year. All Gordon offered was to extend Archie's contract, with no money boost, which Crosthwait called unacceptable. Archie, he said, wanted Mecom to pony up a league-record $170,000-a-year salary. But when the stalemate continued past the end of the strike on August 10, Mecom seemed to believe that Archie was bluffing and had no stomach to leave the Saints. On September 10, Crosthwait blustered to the press that Archie had rejected the Saints' "final offer" and had "cut the string" with the Saints. But there was no longer any talk of defecting to the WFL.

Mecom had it right. As the '74 season wore on, he continued stalling on a new Manning pact, merely assuring Archie that he would offer an extension and a raise at some point before the contract ran out. The bluster from the Manning camp ended, especially when it was clear the WFL would be a failure—it would limp into a second season in '75 with the NFL stars it had raided, but collapse two-thirds of the way into the schedule, sending the expatriates back to their old or other teams, many at higher salaries (and, for the three Dolphins, with their guaranteed WFL contracts still honored, giving them *two* salaries). Archie, happy he had been boxed in, expressed relief that he had not signed a future contract with the WFL, because "my family would get a lot of harassment" around town.[6] He could also be relieved that he was not part of yet another magnificent failure.

———

Needing a house now that they were parents, Archie and Olivia bought a quaint, pale-yellow-and-white camelback cottage at 1316 Seventh Street. Even today, the value of the property is modest, around $700,000, but it sits in the historic Garden District, a neighborhood created a century and a half ago as a refuge for whites who didn't want to live in proximity to Creoles in the French Quarter. They had swallowed hard before deciding to become city folk. But once ensconced, they assimilated easily, and why not? Without calling for reservations, Archie could get right through the door anywhere, whether Pascal's Manale restaurant for the barbecued shrimp, or to listen to jazz in Al Hirt or Pete Fountain's clubs in the Quarter. On the street, the usual rules of conduct seemed lifted for him. Driving his new red Corvette one day, a perk for endorsing an auto dealer, he braked late at a stop sign, causing a fender bender with a car in front of him. The guy at the wheel of the other car bolted out and came looking for a confrontation, but when he recognized who was at the wheel, he froze and smiled. "Hey, Arch!" he woofed. "Go Saints!" then drove off.[7]

Archie told of another, scarier time, when he and Saint linebacker Rick Kingrea headed for the French Quarter to rustle up some Lucky Dogs, the famous hot dogs legendarily sold from wiener-shaped pushcarts on the street. When Kingrea got out to buy them, traffic backed up and people began banging on the car. Plainclothes cops pulled Archie out of the driver's seat. "[They] had [us] against the wall and were searching us," he recalled. "One of them recognized me. He said, 'Oh, it's you, Archie. Sorry,' and they drove away."[8] The Mannings were never seen as distant from the masses. As Cooper pointed out, Archie wasn't really a red Corvette kind of guy. "My mom drove a station wagon, my dad [usually] drove an Oldsmobile. We were around fame but we weren't entrenched in it. We weren't going to Europe on private planes."[9]

Favoritism, however, came with pitfalls. Somewhere in every crowd was a guy just itching for him to blow off an autograph request so that they could complain about how big a jerk he was. However, it was good for his bottom line that the team's PR people went on presenting him as a humble throwback to happy '50s family values, never mind Buddy's suicide. All around town, Archie's face was popping up in ads and at appearances. In a typical example, an ad in the *Times-Picayune* read, "You are invited to meet ARCHIE MANNING and view the beautiful new Breckshire Apt. Tuesday, Oct. 19 from 2 to 4 p.m. Children must be accompanied by an adult."[10] Gigs like that multiplied endlessly—banquets, bank and supermarket openings, state fairs, business conferences, art festivals, whatever, wherever—earning him more than six figures a year. In a still-prehistoric era, when money from jerseys, footballs, and the like bearing players' numbers and names went mainly to the teams and not the players, Archie was given a cut of the proceeds from posters of him, which were often prizes offered in newspaper contests and sweepstakes. Kids feverishly joined "official" Archie Manning Fan Clubs, for which he hired a PR man to send out certificates fake-signed with a rubber stamp. Making the scene wherever he could, Archie was reported during the winter of '74 to be at a charity banquet downtown, where the guests of honor were "Louis Prima, the Dick Stabile orchestra, and Archie Manning."[11] For the era, that was the big time.

=====

In 1974, Dick "Moonbeam" Gordon used his first-round pick on Ohio State linebacker Rick Middleton, when all the scouts were raving about his Buckeye teammate, two-time All-America Randy Gradishar. He did this because Gradishar had some knee issues, which would do nothing to prevent him from becoming a seven-time Pro Bowler and a Defensive Player of the Year—for the Denver Broncos. And Middleton? He played two seasons as a Saint, then was traded to the 49ers and was out of football in four years.

Always in the crosshairs, meanwhile, Archie was an even more harassed target. Through the first five games, four of them losses, he threw three touchdowns and seven interceptions. Ominously, he hurt his knee early on and also had soreness in his arm all season, which was diagnosed as bicipital tendinitis. He missed three games—though he did beat the Eagles and Rams—but never quit. The Saints won five games, again finishing third, but his stats were an eyesore—1,429 yards, six touchdowns, 16 picks, a 49.8 QB rating.

Proving that unmet expectations will erode idolatry, despite his immense popularity there now could be heard scattered booing after a killer interception or scramble that went nowhere. Some catcalls were even being directed at Olivia as she sat in the stands, forcing her to sit in the owner's box instead, where, thankfully, they served booze. In time, she said, Saints games stopped being fun and instead cast a pall over the whole city. "I remember how we'd feel on Monday mornings when Archie was playing. You know, life goes on, you still had to get the kids up, and I'd feel almost like somebody just died, which is ridiculous, but you were so down and the whole city's mood was like that." Cooper, who was too young to know better, thought it would be fun to join in the chorus, which drew dirty looks from the other VIPs in the box. He remembered his mother during those days as almost forlorn. "One minute, she'd say, 'What you did was not appropriate,' and in the next breath it would be 'Please put some ice in my margarita.'"[12]

———

Archie went in for knee surgery over the off-season, but it didn't keep Mecom from making good on his promise. On July 9, 1975, he finally gave Archie his extension, tacking on four more years at what Archie sheepishly described as "a handsome sum of money," which turned out to be $600,000 and a $65,000 bonus. Mecom half-gloated, half-rued that Archie was the only one in town who would be able to afford a suite in the new Superdome, since "I can't afford one anymore."[13] Keating had lain low at the signing, letting Crosthwait take the bow. Mecom, who never thought he'd be paying players much when he bought the team, lamented, "Don't tell me about country lawyers."[14] Crosthwait, Archie would say late in his career, "is the reason why I've slept better for the last ten years."

That is, when he could sleep at all. The '75 season would be the nadir of his career, though it began hopefully enough in the bourgeois splendor of the Superdome (called now, with even more élan, the Mercedes-Benz Superdome). Eight years in the making, costing $134 million, it sat on 70 acres in downtown New Orleans, in a formerly rough neighborhood a couple miles from the Garden District. Built by private funds and public bonds, with the Saints signing annual leases, it was modeled on the Houston Astrodome, resembling a giant tiered mushroom. It was then the largest domed structure in the world, seating over 73,000, with dozens of private luxury boxes for the idle rich, the newest prerequisite of NFL high society. Prophetically, the stadium was built over a cemetery, and one day in the future a deadly hurricane would turn the place into a morgue.

Held out of preseason games and practices for fear he'd strain or even break something, Archie hobbled through games, still hell-bent and pushing his luck on every down, but in vain as usual. Dick Gordon even gave him a target, using his first-round draft pick in 1975 on Larry Burton, a blindingly fast All–Big Ten receiver and sprinter from Purdue who had run fourth in the 200-meter finals at the 1972 Olympics. But the Saints lost five of their first six, their first at the Dome a 21–0 loss to the Cincinnati Bengals. That was lights out for John North. Mecom canned him and elevated the team's 60-year-old personnel director, Ernie Hefferle, as interim coach. Hefferle won his first game when Archie hooked up with Burton on four long passes, but could only watch helplessly as the Saints lost their last seven and ended at 2–12. Archie made it into 13 games, his shoulder and knee aching, his arm deadening with each start. He finished with his worst completion rate (47 percent), seven touchdowns, 20 interceptions. In the carnage, he was sacked 49 times, the most of his career.

"Dear God, it was awful," said Derland Moore, wincing. "For as long as he was a Saint, the offensive philosophy was simple: Archie hauling ass. And that was before quarterbacks took the snap five yards back of the line, with some room. He was under center, and as soon as he took the snap, he was runnin' for his damn life. You seriously had to wonder when he went down if he would ever get up again."[15]

Looking back, Archie said, "I played in the games in '75 without being able to practice. Then, I'd just finished watching the Super Bowl on TV when I got a call from the league office. Roger Staubach couldn't play in the Pro Bowl. He was injured. Fran Tarkenton had already said he couldn't play. The game was a week away and they needed an NFC quarterback. "I said, 'Hold on a minute,' and I got a ball out of the trophy case and went outside with Olivia and tried throwing to her in the dark. I couldn't get the ball to her. All I could do was lob it."[16] He stayed home, and before long, determined that he had no recourse during that off-season but to undergo an operation—two, as it turned out.

As Moore recalled, "They did an experimental surgery and then he began rehabbing. You don't ever want shoulder surgery. When you wake up, you gotta keep the razor blades out of your reach, it's that bad. And it didn't work, so they had to go back in and redo it. Most people would have been destroyed by that. But I never heard him bitch, not one time." A laugh. "I'll tell you what, everything I saw in Peyton and Eli, I saw in Archie. Playing in pain, making unbelievable throws, all that. That crazy pass to Tyree in the Super Bowl? Archie made plays like that all the time. He was always running for his life, get away, and boom, the pass was right there. It just didn't happen in a Super Bowl, and there was no ESPN so nobody outside of New Orleans saw it. And they didn't give a shit because we'd lose the game, anyway."

======

Archie would lose a season—the healing process for his shoulder stretched through 1976—but gain another son. On March 24 of that year, Peyton Williams Manning was born on his uncle Peyton's 75th birthday and was named after him. Like Cooper, he was a big'un, 10 pounds, with that big old head people would come to joke about. "Peytie Pie," as Olivia called him, shared the upstairs room with the big brother, both of them fed and diapered by the glamorous first couple of New Orleans.

Archie also had a new coach, and not just any coach. Mecom lured Hank Stram, the dwarfish, manic fellow the world had come to know from his bravura performance as coach of the AFL's Kansas City Chiefs when they beat the heavily favored Vikings in Super Bowl IV. Miked up for the game, he was seen and heard in the film of the game yapping, adjusting his hairpiece, and merrily mocking helpless Viking defenders. Stram would only take the job if he also was made general manager, ending Dick Gordon's mission to nowhere. Stram's multiple offensive sets and moving pockets were ahead of his time, as were his training methods, which included weight lifting. He put Archie on a rehab and conditioning program that included tossing a medicine ball to an equipment man named Silky Powell, who threw so many balls back to the quarterback that he blew out *his* shoulder.

Two quarterbacks filled in for Archie that season, both of them doomed. The first, Bobby Scott, floundered, then tripped over a TV cable on the sideline and tore up his knee. The job then went to mediocre veteran Bobby Douglass. Between Bobby A and Bobby B, the team went 4–10, and rather than wondering how much better Archie might have made the team, the Saints' brass—a year after giving Archie his extension—fretted that he might never be able to throw again. "There were so many rumors floating around," recalled Derland Moore, who swears "they had Archie traded to San Francisco before Scott went down. It wasn't talked about, but believe me, it happened. If Bobby hadn't gotten hurt, he would have been a 49er—they may not have had to draft Joe Montana. History would have changed but for that TV cable."

Archie was able to make his comeback in '77, the year that a grinning Southern Democrat was sworn in as president. The first game of the season was against the Packers at the Superdome, and Manning went 18 of 30 for 225 yards. His fourth-quarter 59-yard TD pass to tight end Henry Childs narrowed the score to 24–20. The Pack held on, but there seemed to be reason to believe this would finally be the season of deliverance. Archie's load had been relieved by Stram's first- and second-round picks in the '76 draft, Chuck Muncie and Tony Galbreath. They rumbled for a combined 1,455 yards and nine touchdowns and caught 62 passes. Still, the defense was a leaky boat, mistakes came at the worst moments, and losses continued piling up. The fans, in no mood for another season of shame, now booed Archie without mercy. Up in the stands, Olivia wore dark glasses, her head covered by a scarf so she wouldn't be recognized. "It was just horrible," said Moore. "They were like animals. You'd hear it everywhere, on the street, wherever you went. I'd go out somewhere to get relief drunk and I'd wind up in a fight with somebody. It was a nightmare."

Few fans sympathized with Archie's latest round of injuries—by late season he was playing with a broken jaw and a sprained ankle. Nor did Mecom have any patience with Stram. The season's penultimate game was against the second-year Tampa Bay Buccaneers, who had lost 26 consecutive games, turning a great college coach, John McKay, into a national joke. But the Saints lost 33–14, with Archie benched in the second half for his own protection. Afterward, Mecom was apoplectic. "There is dissension on the defensive team," he said. "I've told [Stram] that and he doesn't believe me. Now it's infecting the offense. . . . I have not interfered with him. I've given him everything he's asked for, everything. I've been crucified by the press for some things I've done, but you don't criticize him." Stram, a man rarely at a loss for words, could only respond, "I would rather not make any comment," but said, "We are all very ashamed of what happened today," calling it "my worst coaching experience. We got strangled by the trauma. The harder we tried, the worse we got."[17]

The Saints limped in at 3–11–1, one game better than Tampa Bay, and Stram knew he was a goner. Still, his axing right after the new year hit Archie hard. Saying he was "crushed," he equated it to the deepest scar of his life. "I got a big lump in my throat," he said, "kind of like when my daddy died. . . . We haven't even scratched the surface, and it's over."[18]

═══

Stram's linebacker coach, Dick Nolan, inherited the job, his second go-around as a head coach. An underrated defensive back on the great New York Giants teams of the 1950s, where he learned from defensive coach Tom Landry, he applied Landry's "flex" defense as defensive coordinator in Dallas and then as head coach of the 49ers for eight years, twice coming up one game short of the Super Bowl. Assessing the Saints, the chain-smoking, dour-looking Nolan drafted for offense—the top pick Wes Chandler, Florida's All-American receiver—and made key trades for receiver Ike Harris and guard Conrad Dobler. This was meant to benefit Archie, around whom Nolan's offensive coordinator (and brother-in-law)

Ed Hughes built a low-risk, run-heavy attack, softening defenses with Muncie and Galbreath—"Thunder and Lightning," as they were dubbed. Muncie, said Archie, was "the fastest back out of the I formation I've ever seen. Toes in, kind of hunched over, then boom! Gone."[19]

It seemed promising indeed when the Saints won the '78 opener against the Vikings, 31–24, with Archie throwing only 22 times, completing 15 for 193 yards, while Fran Tarkenton filled the sky with 49 passes, four of them intercepted. The formula, however, broke down when the defense faltered. In the second game, falling behind against the Packers, Archie had to go up top, throwing 53 times, completing 33 for 303 yards and a touchdown in a 28–17 defeat. And then Muncie broke down. He suffered a string of injuries and could only play in 13 games. Archie would rack up 3,416 yards—third behind Tarkenton and Jim Hart—and completed a career-best 62 percent of his passes, garnering 17 touchdowns but also 26 interceptions, though his passer rating was still a robust 87.1, fifth-best in the NFL. The Saints, 5–4 at midseason, concluded at 7–9, again in third place. But for his hard labor, Archie finally won his All-Pro stripes, the only Saint player who did that year, and was named the NFC's Offensive Player of the Year. By the terms of his contact, that was worth a bundle—his salary zoomed up to $370,000, the most of any quarterback. On the Saints, the feeling was that it was the least he was owed.

"I was thrilled to death for Archie, but at the same time I was pissed," said Derland Moore. "With the shit he went through, anyone else would have just said, 'Just get me out of here.' And I wish he would have, I really do. Because in New Orleans they took him so much for granted. They never knew what they had in him. I heard them booing him and I wanted to go up into the stands after 'em. That was what it was like to play for the New Orleans Saints. It was like being in a nightmare and not being able to wake up."

CHAPTER 8

GOOD LORD, I FEEL LIKE I'M DYING

The Saints were screwy enough to make a punter their No. 1 draft pick in 1979: Russ Erxleben of Texas. But they were becoming enough of a big-time operation to hire a conditioning coach, an executive vice-president, and a vice-president of player personnel. That season, after losing their first three games, they hit their stride and only lost two in a row once. With three weeks to go, they looked up and were tied with the Rams atop the NFC West at 7–6. They then went cross-country to play the always-scabrous Raiders on a Monday night, the biggest game the Saints had yet played. They came out on fire. Galbreath and Muncie each ran for a touchdown, and Archie threw two more, to Galbreath and Henry Childs, to take a 28–14 lead at the half. That grew to 35–14 after an interception was returned for a touchdown. But these were the Saints, a team seemingly doomed to suffer. And before they knew what hit them, Ken Stabler had passed for three touchdowns, leaving the Saints dazed and 42–35 losers. They still had an outside shot at the playoffs when the Chargers came in for the season finale and left them for dead, winning 35–0.

The Saints finished 8–8, which glass-half-full optimists could appreciate as the team's first non-losing season. They jumped up to second place in the division, a game behind the Rams, who went to the Super Bowl. They were fourth in yards, first in rushing touchdowns, and scored 370 points, one behind the NFC-leading Cowboys. Archie passed for 3,169 yards and 15 touchdowns and ran for 186 yards. He, Muncie (the first Saint runner to clear 1,000 yards), Chandler, and Childs made the Pro Bowl. However, if they had found a degree of stability, leave it to John Mecom to mess even that up. Never cut out for hands-on, daily team chores, he handed over the GM duties he had tried his hand at after the season to a fellow much like him, Steve Rosenbloom. The 34-year-old son of L.A. Rams owner Carroll Rosenbloom, he had run that team until his father died in a drowning accident, after which he was fired by his stepmother, Georgia Frontiere, who took control of the Rams. Rosenbloom arrived even as he was being implicated in a ticket-scalping scandal.[1] While not directly involved, Steve was said to have known about his father's plan to scalp Rams tickets.[2] Although Al Davis got a lot of mileage from this matter in his legal warfare with the NFL, which ended with him winning the right to take his Raiders to Los Angeles, no one was ever punished in the scandal. Yet, as omens went, it didn't seem to be the ideal move for a team seeking legitimacy and credibility.

With the new front-office alignment in place, the 1980 season opened against the 49ers, a bitterly contested game in which the Saints went down on a field goal. Promising as the close defeat was, though, the following week they were mauled by the Bears 22–3. And then they just kept losing. And losing. To teams good and teams lousy. Four games in, they also lost Muncie, not to injury but to his own inner devils. The most troubled player the Saints ever had, Muncie could never coexist in the racist crucible of the Deep South. Having grown up in rural Pennsylvania and gone to ultra-liberal Berkeley, he once said, "After Berkeley's tolerant atmosphere, it was quite a culture shock coming to New Orleans. I lived in a very nice neighborhood, but my house and car were routinely vandalized by racists."[3]

Muncie was known to be using cocaine, and in time he became withdrawn, coming in late for meetings and practices, missing flights, and generally trying Nolan's patience. Archie was understandably torn. "It was amazing how he performed [but] he basically slept through every meeting," he said. "I very seldom called a play where I didn't stop and tell Muncie what he was doing. He gained like 1,200 yards one year on one engine. I don't know what he was doing during the week but he wasn't thinking about football."[4] With the Saints in a tailspin, Rosenbloom traded Muncie to the Chargers for a second-round draft pick. Muncie would play for four more years, on three division champs, twice as an All-Pro, but his life was a mess. Upon being traded to the Vikings in '85, blood tests revealed traces of cocaine and he was suspended, then he quit. Four years later, he was convicted of selling cocaine and jailed for 18 months; he died in 2013, at age 60, working as a drug counselor.

As with the sacking of Stram, Archie never forgave the brass for letting Muncie go. In his home, he had kept on the wall a large picture of the big man smashing through the line. Though Rosenbloom vowed that "we will be more productive without him,"[5] in his absence the Saints' top rusher that season ranked 48th in the league. With their record 0–10, Buddy Diliberto, who was still banned from the Saints' team plane, came up with an inspired idea. Cribbing from the self-billed "Unknown Comic," who appeared regularly on *The Gong Show*, the radio host wrote "Ain'ts" on a brown paper bag, cut holes for the eyes and nose, and wore it over his face to the next game. Though to some it bore a mild resemblance to a Klan hood, the gag immediately caught on, with fans showing up to the remaining games so bagged,[6] sometimes embellished with things like "Ain't It a Shame," repurposing New Orleans native Fats Domino's '50s rock-and-roll anthem into a '70s lament. The next week, during the Saints' Monday night game against the Rams, Howard Cosell, seeing hordes of bags in the crowd, mused, "They really have a sense of humor here."[7]

That included Archie's first son. Now six, Cooper put a bag over his head at one game as well, and also slipped one on his baby brother Peyton's noggin. This was not funny at all to Olivia. After she reprimanded him, Cooper refrained from putting it on again, but it just seemed like the thing to do at the Superdome. Which would explain why, when she became pregnant again, she decided not to subject herself to the games at all. She stayed at home, not even eager to listen on the radio.

As for Dick Nolan, he may have wished he had one of those bags, too, without holes cut out for his eyes—or nose. By that Rams game, the already cadaverous Nolan looked bloodless. Smoking six packs a day now, he was dealing not only with the team's ills but Rosenbloom's meddling, which he believed was intended to turn players the GM favored against him. He was right. According to Derland Moore, "half the guys had an allegiance to Nolan, half to Rosenbloom."[8] After the Saints lost to the Rams 27–7, Nolan got a break—he was fired. Watching him go down, Archie commiserated with him. "No one took [losing] harder than Dick Nolan," he said. "His face got to me, his eyes all red. I knew he wasn't sleeping at night. He was just dying."[9] Nolan landed on his feet, hired again by Tom Landry as an assistant coach with the Cowboys. But for the Saints, more trouble was coming. First, defensive end Don Reese hurt his knee, then he called his teammates "sorry bastards." Moore responded by telling Reese he had "quit on the team." Reese then jumped him and they fought it out. Moore rolls his eyes about this incident now, leaving Reese's own history—he'd come to the Saints after being let go by the Dolphins after he and a teammate were busted in a drug sting for which he served prison time—and the trouble he would soon find himself in to speak for itself.

Rosenbloom promoted as interim coach Nolan's longtime offensive coordinator, Dick Stanfel, who had never been a head coach before and never would be again. The Saints lost two more games, the latter in which they led the 49ers 35–7 before collapsing in a heap and losing 38–35, still the greatest blown lead in a regular-season game in NFL history. That defeat put them at 0–14, tying the '76 Tampa Bay Buccaneers' record for futility. The Saints did get it together for one Sunday, nipping the Jets 21–20 before losing to the Patriots to end up at 1–15, then the second-worst season ever by an NFL team. For Archie, nothing would ever wash away the taste of that season of putrefaction, which he called "the most miserable thing I've ever gone through."

The irony was that he actually racked up his career high in touchdowns, 23, his 20 picks not so terrible given that his rate of 3.9 interceptions per 100 pass attempts was the second-lowest of his career, and he had his best completion percentage, 60.7. Still, Cooper Manning would never feel compelled to apologize for his seditious booing that year. "Everyone else was doing it and you know, it's a copycat league," he would say. "I mean, 1–15 is 1–15!"[10]

Archie almost didn't survive it, and wouldn't have if Steve Rosenbloom had gotten his way. A bottom-line type with scant empathy for any player, he wanted to trade a 32-year-old quarterback who had taken a career-long beating. When Nolan was still the coach, Rosenbloom had tried to get him to bench Archie in favor of backup Guy Benjamin. Rebuffed, his next aim was to renegotiate Archie's contract on insulting terms. He sent the assistant he had brought with him from the Rams, Harold Guiver, to meet with Archie, armed with a poison pill disguised as a contract extension. "It was an extension with an insignificant raise," Archie recalled. "I told him, 'Look, I was born at night, but not last night.'"[11]

In truth, Crosthwait had broached the subject of him moving on to a team where he could do some winning, and not, as Archie said, "agree[ing] to man an oar on a slave ship."[12] As a model, it seemed pertinent that Jim Plunkett flourished after getting out of New England, leading the Raiders to the championship in '80. But Archie opted again for loyalty and cockeyed optimism—and a gigantic new contract—when Mecom overruled Rosenbloom and gave him five years and $600,000, by far the most of any quarterback in the league. Mecom then took the logical next step, unceremoniously firing Rosenbloom, explaining, "Steve was vehement about Archie's going," but adding, "the only problem with Archie here is that everyone else can't measure up to the standards he has set."[13]

Mecom again made big changes. His next coach was the inimitable Oail Andrew "Bum" Phillips, a human comic-book character in a crew cut, 10-gallon hat and cowboy boots. The 57-year-old native Texan, once Bear Bryant's assistant at Texas A&M and Sid Gillman's defensive coordinator with the Houston Oilers before succeeding Gillman as head coach, had gotten to the AFC title game twice in five years before wearing out his welcome. In mid-January, he and his assistant coaches, including his son Wade, were hired en masse by the Saints, whereupon Bum threw his considerable weight around, making changes. One of the first was to release Reese, who signed with San Diego. Phillips then drafted South Carolina's All-American running back George Rogers, the Heisman Trophy winner, and All-American linebacker Rickey Jackson of Pitt. The dismissals of Muncie and Reese were explained by Mecom assistant Fred Williams's admission that "we undoubtedly had problems in 1980," coded language for drugs.

Phillips also snatched redshirted Illinois quarterback Dave Wilson—who had once thrown for 621 yards in a game—in the supplemental draft, a move that struck observers as odd, what with Manning's new contract. Asked if replacing Archie was in his plans to remake the team, Phillips denied it and spent much of training camp slavishly praising him. Was Archie's age a worry? "Not the way that guy takes care of himself," he said. But Archie would soon come to learn that when it came to the truth, he couldn't take anything Bum Phillips said to the bank.

———

Olivia gave birth to their third son, Elisha Nelson Manning, on January 3, 1981. Needing more room for the boys to roam, she and Archie looked around for new digs. For a time, they considered the suburbs. Then Olivia told Archie, "There's a million suburbs—there's only one Uptown." Inured to the sights, sounds, tastes, and aromas of the Garden District, they settled nearby in a large, white, two-story, four-bedroom Victorian at 1420 First Street, surrounded by a brass gate, Old French columns, and turrets up and down the front of the house. Just down the street lived novelist Anne Rice. What they couldn't have known was that Archie's tenure as a Saint was growing short. Indeed, at 31, it felt as if the glory days at Ole Miss were as distant as the Confederacy. That year, *Sports Illustrated* ran a sympathetic profile of him with the title "The Patience of a Saint," casting him as a fallen idol, a golden calf now with arthritis. With not much in his pro career to hang a hat on, Archie was reduced to saying, "Success, you know, is a relative thing," as close to self-pity as he would allow himself. "I've enjoyed so little success as a professional player. I've sat around with [Terry] Bradshaw and [Bob] Griese and [Ken] Stabler, and I couldn't open my mouth. They'd be saying, 'Remember the '75 playoffs?' or 'Remember that pass I threw in the Super Bowl?' and I'd be thinking about our 8–8 season, or our wins over Minnesota in '78 or Tampa Bay in '79. It's all relative. Those things stick out to me, but what am I going to say?"[14]

As a kind of epitaph, and cautionary tale, author Paul Zimmerman wrote: "[W]hen you mention Manning's name around the league you strike an uncharacteristic vein of compassion. Or worse . . . an object lesson, a textbook argument against rushing a baby quarterback into combat: 'You think your kid ought to play right away? Well, look at that Manning with the Saints. They turned him into a basket case down there.'"

For many fans around the country, the brief mention of Buddy's suicide in the article was the first they'd heard of it. The photos in the story were also the first time his sons were seen by a national audience, five-year-old Peyton captured throwing a baseball in one photo, Archie cradling the infant Eli in another, a seeming sneer on the little guy's face. In the neighborhood, it would become a familiar sight to see Archie on the balcony of the house, tossing passes to all three of his boys in the yard below. Archie would obsessively make home movies of the boys, a self-conscious effort to preserve personal memories of the days when he attempted to be a better father than Buddy had been to him. Because the boys predictably took to sports, he kept the living room free of bulky furniture so they could play indoor football. Archie had Saints uniforms made in their sizes, their names and the number 8 on the back. They made up their own game that Cooper called 'Mazing Catches, wherein each son would try to top the others. As Eli recalled, "If it was a little wet and you could dive and slide, that was the big play," though because he was so much younger than Cooper and Peyton, he was often a spectator as his brothers and their buddies gathered for rounds of touch football. This might help explain why Eli was the least impressed with himself—and even his dad.

"We were probably a little spoiled having a professional quarterback throwing to us," he said. "That was just what my dad did. It was normal, like—O.K., so, should I go up and ask my friends' dads for their autographs, too?"[15]

The most competitive son was the middle one. Peyton behaved like someone had died and left him boss, even when his own father was there.

Archie remembered the time he agreed to coach a neighborhood basket-ball team. "I couldn't go to the tryout, so I just drafted all my friends' kids because I thought that would be nice for everyone to play together. Well, we were terrible. We were very bad. And Peyton got really mad at me. 'Why did you draft these guys? What's wrong with you?' He was really competitive. And so that's when I quit being a head coach." He made sure the boys did their schoolwork and studied their Cub Scout manu-als, and he went hunting and fishing with them when he could. But that could not stop him from feeling guilty about not being with them for long periods during the season. Mindful of how Buddy had pulled away from him, he began taking Cooper and little Peytie Pie to Saints practices and games. They became fixtures on the field during warm-ups and around the locker room, even getting wrapped with tape to feel like real players. Archie resolved not to let them be smartasses, something Cooper seemed to have a natural propensity for. "My personality was very different from my dad's," Cooper said years later. "I can remember early on when I'd do something, he'd say they found me on the doorstep, they didn't know where I came from." Archie's word for him was "renegade."[16]

Indeed, Cooper was growing up with a distinctly broad view of the world beyond his own family. When he was seven, he told a sports-writer that his favorite team was the Chargers. His three favorite play-ers were Lance Alworth, John Jefferson, and Lynn Swann—all receivers. His favorite Saint was Wes Chandler, though he did say Archie Manning was "my second favorite [and] my favorite quarterback." Cooper looked back at his relationship with Peyton as contentious. They were, he said, "always butting heads," and Peyton was "kind of a tattletale, a study guy, a mama's boy—and a daddy's boy, too. . . . He was so neat, and I was a slob."[17] They would fight and scrap and cuss each other, earning a slap on the butt from Archie, which they accepted as the price of establishing their turf. He had just one rule for them as they grew: "Whatever you do, finish what you start."

When Archie went to Honolulu for the '79 Pro Bowl, he took the family. Looking around one day, he couldn't find Peyton. He began fran-tically searching for him. Then a catamaran came into shore. There he was, sitting in the little boat with Walter Payton, having decided on his own to go sailing with the great running back.[18] He was three at the time. There was also the day when Archie took him to the weight room and Peyton fell and hit his head, spurting blood. Archie rushed him to the emergency room, but not once did Peyton cry. "It doesn't hurt," he kept saying. If it did, Archie knew, he just wouldn't let it show. Years later, he still wouldn't. As Archie put it, "He refuses to give the other side the satisfaction."[19] The boy had an attitude, and a mouth. At 12, playing basketball, he sassed his coach, telling him he didn't know what he was doing. Archie, in the stands, was aghast and dragged him to the coach's house later to apologize.

Peyton was fortunate that was all Archie did. Usually, exercising some old-school paternal discipline, he would tan his boys' hides with "No. 8," the thick belt that had his uniform number etched into it, warning them, "No. 8's comin' out!" But even with that risk, Peyton and Cooper would go on with their fussin' and fightin'. Eli, in his bedroom down the hall, would hear them "slamming each other against the wall and all the pictures crashing to the floor." Oh, they loved each other plenty. Each of them wouldn't have hesitated going upside someone's head who had a nasty word for the other. But, for Peyton, keeping up with and even humbling his big brother were all that mattered.

─────

In 1981, Bum Phillips's offensive coordinator, King Hill, one of the most accomplished men in the game, devised a powerful attack. It relied heavily on the tank-like George Rogers, who made people forget Muncie, running for a team record (and then-rookie NFL record) 1,674 yards and 13 touchdowns en route to the Pro Bowl. On the other side of the ball, under Wade Phillips, Rickey Jackson would begin a 15-year career in which he was a Pro Bowler six times before being elected to the Hall of Fame. But the Saints still reeked of failure. They lost six of their first seven games, five in a row, and by November were also-rans. Hobbled by sundry physical ills all season, Archie missed four games. The Saints went 4–12. Saints fans, now tired of booing, began to stay home in large numbers.

When the '82 season rolled around, Archie learned how phony Bum

Phillips was. The previous year, before the Saints played his old Oilers team, led by the aging Ken "Snake" Stabler, Bum had given his men a fiery pep talk. "Fellas, I been tellin' you all week this is just another game. *Bull . . . shit!* This is life or death! My life—or your death!"[20] When the Saints won 27–24, Archie figured he'd earned some goodwill. But now, during preseason, Oilers coach Ed Biles cut Stabler, who at 37, with gimpy knees and a belly frequently filled with beer, seemed done. Phillips quickly signed his old quarterback to a $450,000 contract and named the Snake his starter, over Archie. In the season opener at home against the St. Louis Cardinals, Stabler looked reborn. He completed 19 of 27 passes for 221 yards and a touchdown, though the Cards won 21–7. To say Archie felt sandbagged would be a gross understatement. His only appearance in that game was as mop-up man, one with the highest salary in the league.

The good news—for Archie—was that it would be the last New Orleans would see of him as a Saint. Not singing rhapsodies to him anymore, Phillips traded him. Archie knew it was coming. A hasty deal was worked out with the Oilers to exchange the biggest star the Saints ever had for 30-year-old, three-time former All-Pro tackle Leon Gray, who was recovering from Achilles' heel surgery. Biles and Houston's general manager, Ladd Herzeg, demanded that the Saints pick up half of Archie's contract, and Phillips agreed. This time, John Mecom didn't stand in the way, not incidentally because he was close to selling the team and making a windfall profit from the pitiful franchise. The trade was made on Friday, September 17. When Archie was told, it had to sting that he had come so cheap. Years later, he was still miffed, recalling that Gray was on the "downside of his career . . . to put it politely." Somewhat irrationally, he came to believe that Phillips "wanted me gone because I had a lock on the endorsements in town, and he liked to do endorsements." More plausible was that Phillips yearned to re-create his old Oiler team. Some began to call the Saints "Houston East."

—

Tarnished or not, Archie Manning was still a saint to many in New Orleans, and the trade was a delicate matter, though not to the buzz-cut coach. As it was, Bum barely said goodbye. The decision, he conceded, was "tough," given that Archie had done "many good things for this city" and had been "a loyal and good quarterback." But he justified the move by pimping Gray the way he had Archie only a year before, as an ageless player who was vital for the Saints to build an offense. A good many Saint players, though, regarded Stabler as a short-term solution at best, and a train wreck at worst. Archie stayed on the high road but was so broken up that when Phillips asked him to address the team one last time, he refused. "I just couldn't do it,' he said at a farewell press conference. "I'm having trouble just talking."[21]

Once the shock had worn off, he could see the move as others did, as a benefit, being able to escape the Saints for his own sanity. After 10 seasons in Purgatory, he had left pieces of himself on fields all around the league, sacked 340 times, his 115 touchdowns submerged by a 35–91–3 record. Peter Finney, in an elegy titled "Requiem for Saints No. 8," likened him to Terry Molloy, Marlon Brando's tragically exploited antihero in *On the Waterfront*, who lamented that, but for the manipulations of others, he "coulda been a contender." At the same time, there were those in the city who hailed the trade as "long overdue."[22] Olivia, no doubt saying what Archie couldn't, admitted, "I sort of feel relieved. I just didn't think I could go back to the Superdome and sit there anymore. I had just gotten where I didn't look forward to it anymore."[23] Cooper, for his part, was miffed—not that his dad was traded, but that he wasn't traded to Dallas or Pittsburgh.

To be sure, Archie could not have been relieved about going to Houston. As Finney wrote, "The Oilers have the look of an unmade bed, wandering aimlessly in the NFL jungle, with a coach, Ed Biles, whose days may be numbered. Of one thing you may be sure. Diminished physical skills aside, Archie will give it his best shot."[24] Archie saw himself less heroically. He would cynically say the deal had made him "a full-fledged mercenary."[25] But the timing was fortuitous. Ripping the veil off the festering drug problem on the Saints just months before, in June 1981, *Sports Illustrated* published a bylined confessional by Don Reese, indicting the league as a whole and in particular the "horror show in New Orleans," where he said players "snorted coke in the locker room before games and again at halftime, and stayed up all hours of the night roaming the streets to get more stuff." He laid blame on Chuck Muncie for getting him hooked on freebasing cocaine, and claimed that Nolan and Mecom "must have suspected that we were on the stuff."[26] That same year, former Saints running back Mike Strachan was sent to federal prison for dealing coke.[27]

Archie, in his memoir with Peyton, dealt with the drug issue as he had the team's racial tensions—guardedly, writing that "cocaine raised its ugly head in the NFL" during those years, and, "taking into account New Orleans's tendencies toward over-the-edge lifestyles, it was a sure place for it to find expression." But, he insisted, "Me, I knew nothing about it. . . . I suppose I was too straight, too naïve, too removed from the element involved."[28] All the same, a Saint no more, he could justifiably say with some hope that he was getting "a fresh start." And Ed Biles seemed ecstatic to have him. "I've been wanting this guy since I got the job," he said. "We were discussing trading for him a year ago." Cold comfort for a man who knew he was swapping one horror show for another.

CHAPTER 9

"A DOGGONE GOOD TRIP"

Archie arrived in Houston two days before the second game of the season. He went alone, Olivia and the boys remaining home, both relieved and disoriented by the sudden turn of events. The Oilers, quarterbacked by Gifford Nielsen, had been beaten by the Cincinnati Bengals in their opener. Now, in the mausoleum-like Astrodome, Archie, wearing the team's baby-blue-and-white uniform, watched from the bench as Nielsen beat the Seattle Seahawks. And then, everything stopped dead. There had been rumors during summer camp that the NFL Players Association would go on strike. Now the union decided it was time, negotiations with the league having broken down. As the strike dragged on, some players made money by playing in exhibitions. CBS replayed old Super Bowls and low-level college games. The new cable sports network, ESPN, as well as NBC, showed Canadian Football League games. Archie, hunkered down in New Orleans, was honored by the town on October 7, when the city council proclaimed Archie Manning Day, with Mayor Ernest "Dutch" Morial—the first black mayor of the city—presenting him with a certificate at City Hall.

The strike ground on. But predictably, the players began to buckle. Only willing to sit out so long, many turned on the union, forcing its executive director, Ed Garvey, to resign. Finally, after 57 days, they capitulated, accepting a new five-year collective bargaining agreement with modest gains. The league then patched together a nine-game schedule with a 16-team playoff tournament scheme. The season resumed on November 21, the Oilers playing the Steelers at home. With no practice time with the team, Archie still hadn't learned much of Biles's run-and-shoot offense, one of the looser systems that came into vogue in the '70s—the most heralded, of course, being Bill Walsh's West Coast offense. Biles went again with Nielsen, who threw three interceptions in the Oilers' 24–10 loss. Archie's first action in Houston was again as a mop-up man, going one of five for 23 yards. With a full week of practice, though, he started the next week in New England, hitting 19 of 23 passes for 231 yards and fourth-quarter TD passes to veteran tight end Dave Casper and receiver Mike Renfro, cutting the Patriots' lead to 29–21, which was the final score. Impressive as it was, Archie came away from another painful Sunday. With running back Earl Campbell now a shell of his old self, battered from years of having to carry far too many times, and a porous offensive line, Archie was swamped and sacked six times. The next week, he was sacked five more times by the Giants in a 17–14 defeat.

The Cowboys then came to Houston for a Monday night game. During the week, columnist Sam Blair of the *Dallas Morning News* penned a splendid encomium to Archie titled "Manning's Optimism," tracing his grit to Buddy's suicide, which Archie said he thought about every day.[1] But his determination was no match for the Oilers' flaws. That night, he threw a 54-yard bomb to Renfro to put the Oilers up 7–0—then lost 37–7, going down another six times and fumbling on a handoff. Next came a 35–14 stinker against the Eagles, in which he ate turf seven times. After tearing his hamstring, Archie missed the last two games. The Oilers finished 1–8, last or near last in every category but two: fumbles lost and sacks.

Living in a cramped garage apartment near the Oilers' practice facility, Archie had fled as much as he could, often using off days to fly to New Orleans. During school breaks, Olivia put Cooper or Peyton on a plane to be with him in Houston for a few days. If Archie couldn't usher them around the practice grounds, he'd turn them over to the third-string quarterback, Oliver Luck—who also would sire a son, Andrew, who would far surpass him, as the quarterback who allowed the Indianapolis Colts to perfunctorily dismiss Peyton Manning after 13 years spent becoming the best quarterback in history.

=====

The Houston press didn't make him much of a story out of Archie. Mainly, he was treated as a highly paid—yes, mercenary—gunslinger passing through, sure to be unloaded. After that disconnected season, when a quarterback his age might consider retiring, Archie actually looked forward to being back in the crucible in '83, even if, as he recalled, the Oilers' offensive line was "a sieve." He played well, but the Oilers lost the first two games of the season.

But Biles now turned on him as suddenly as Bum Phillips had, another quarterback's misfortune giving Biles the opening to send him on his way. When the Vikings' Tommy Kramer tore up his knee, coach Bud Grant and general manager Mike Lynn approached the Oilers about dealing Archie. Within two days, it was done. Biles and Herzeg agreed to trade Manning and Dave Casper for two 1984 draft picks. It wasn't so easy for the Oilers to dump Archie, however, since they were splitting his salary with the Saints. In the end, he would be paid for that season by all three teams, surely an NFL first. As coldly as Phillips had, Biles informed Archie by calling him late on a Wednesday night, after Archie got back from a rodeo. When the quarterback picked up the phone, the personality-challenged coach asked, "Where the hell have you been?"

"I don't have to tell you where I've been," Archie told him. Then he found out he was traded.

Casper, who Archie said "detested" Biles, was delighted to go. But Archie was ambivalent. Believing he might play out his career in Houston, he had bought an apartment downtown and Olivia had decorated it. Accustomed as he was to feeling like no more than chattel, he packed up again, putting the furniture in storage, where it sat for years. He and Casper then waited at the airport to be picked up by Viking officials in a private jet and flown to Minneapolis. When they landed, Archie was put up at the Radisson Hotel. The offensive coordinator, Jerry Burns, handed him the team playbooks and told him he had two weeks to learn Bud Grant's arcane system, the one that had gotten the team to four Super

Bowls in the '70s, where they lost all four convincingly. Archie called it "a mass of cross-wiring" that required players to read their own patterns *and* everyone else's.[2]

He was on the sideline in his new purple uniform as the Vikings beat the Buccaneers in overtime in Tampa Bay. (In his memoir, Archie misremembered this game being played against the Packers in Green Bay, where they won another overtime game in Week 8.) The Vikings, who had moved indoors to the capacious Hubert H. Humphrey Metrodome—the third such dome Archie had called home within a year—were anchored by running backs Darrin Nelson, Ted Brown, and Tony Galbreath, who had won his liberation from the Saints in '81. Grant, who'd missed the playoffs only three times in his 16 years on the job, wanted Archie to loosen things up. Needing to work harder under the stone-faced, authoritarian coach, his body wasn't cooperative. He was sore, winded, and unable to lift his usual weight in the gym.

He and Casper were due to undergo a physical when they arrived, but Grant told the team trainer, "They look okay to me." Only when Archie's hands started shaking did they give him the physical. It indicated a thyroid condition, which the trainer believed could be cured with rest. However, the team's octogenarian owner, Max Winter, who was still a near daily presence in the locker room, suggested he get checked out at the Mayo Clinic down in Rochester, Minnesota. There, he was diagnosed with Graves' disease, a hereditary autoimmune condition related to hyperthyroidism, one potentially fatal if left untreated. He began treatment with radioactive iodine pills, which would continue on an outpatient basis. Because one effect of the condition was bulging eyes, when he saw himself in the mirror he panicked, until he was told it was to be expected, as were the heart palpitations that also scared him. Another effect was weight loss, and he dropped 15 pounds. For three weeks, he was on injured reserve. When he was reactivated, looking like a schoolkid in an oversized helmet, Grant sent him in to mop up for quarterback Steve Dils in a 34–14 Viking blowout of the Oilers—who, as it happened, had fired Ed Biles the week before and would go 2–14 that season. But Archie never got in for another down the rest of the way as the Vikings closed out at 8–8, fourth in the NFC Central. Somehow still remaining optimistic, he told Grant he would return, possibly for two more seasons. Pertinently, he was due to be paid around $600,000 for each of those years.

―――

When he came north for training camp in '84, something was missing on the Vikings: Bud Grant. With no warning or explanation, the aging coach had quit over the off-season. Winter replaced him with Les Steckel, the 38-year-old receivers coach, who had been a colonel in the Marines and seen combat in Vietnam. He was one smart fellow, holding degrees in social work, human relations, and political science, and he had been a top hand in Bobby Kennedy's 1968 presidential campaign. But Steckel coached with little sense; as Archie said, he was "not what you call a by-the-book planner. His practices might last one or three hours . . . until he feels you've done it enough."[3] He also had his players compete in an "iron-man" competition, having them do things like rope climbing and swinging across jungle-gym bars, leaving several with pulled hamstrings and other assorted strains.

Archie was so unimpressed with Steckel that he would call his elevation "an insult to the other coaches."[4] To be sure, Steckel was in over his head. Tommy Kramer came back from knee surgery, but had drug and alcohol addictions[5] and was sacked four times and intercepted three times in a 42–13 opening day rout by the Chargers. When the Vikings fell to 2–5, Archie was given his first serious action, coming in against the Detroit Lions after Kramer left with a shoulder injury. He went just 5 of 13 for 40 yards, but hung tough, putting the Vikings up 14–13 in the fourth quarter. After the Lions kicked a field goal to go ahead, Archie tried to move into winning field-goal range, but threw a killer interception. He got his first start two games later, with pitiless timing against Mike Ditka's Bears, who owned perhaps the best defense ever seen in football, one that would propel them to a championship the following season. They feasted on Archie, sacking him 11 times, one shy of the NFL record—leaving him feeling, as he put it, "whacked." Somehow, he kept the Vikings in the game even as the Bears ground out 229 yards rushing, but down 16–0 entering the final quarter, Steckel showed mercy, sending in Wade Wilson. Archie came out of the 16–7 defeat with a pulled hamstring. He missed four games, and then played sporadically the rest of the season. The Vikings finished 3–13. He was sacked 18 times. All in all, it was as if he never left the Saints.

———

Archie had rented a furnished house in suburban Minnetonka. Olivia and the boys flew up to live with him, the kids going to school in the neighborhood. Archie broke his own rule about such things and coached Cooper's fifth-grade football team. But the cold and snow were too much. Archie tells of the day snow piled up and Olivia kept staring at a pond in the backyard. "What happened to all the ducks?" she asked. Told they flew south, she replied, "Sounds like a good idea to me."[6] She and the boys returned to New Orleans. If Archie returned to Minnesota next year, she told him, he would go alone. And he did go back—he had to, with all that money on the table—saying in advance that it would be "my last season. There's not much of a market for a 36-year-old quarterback."[7] There was one hopeful sign: Les Steckel was fired over the winter and Bud Grant returned for one final year. Archie gloated over Steckel being dumped, pointing out in his memoir that "he hasn't been a head coach since"[8]—a dig that willfully omitted that Steckel was later an assistant coach with four NFL teams and two college teams, and is now president of the Fellowship of Christian Athletes.

But Grant did Archie no favors. His arm weak, still battling the thyroid condition, Archie played in one preseason game before Grant called him into his office. Grant was typically terse and blunt. "You know, Archie, you're not very fast anymore," he said. Then, "You ever think of retiring?" Archie was caught by surprise.

"Not until now," he said.

"I think you should," Grant made clear.

The coach eased his mind a bit, telling Archie he wouldn't be cut, but he would be the third-string quarterback the rest of the season. Archie had one last question.

"What about the money?"

Assured that he would be paid in full, Archie agreed to the humiliation. He could have asked about being traded again, but with his salary he knew there would be no takers. If he harbored any notion of perhaps playing his final downs in New Orleans, there was no sign that anyone on that team wanted to accommodate him now that John Mecom had completed his sale of the franchise to Tom Benson, a bonanza for Mecom at $72 million, nine times the original price tag of the expansion Saints.

Once the new order was in place, everything old was swept away. And so Archie would wrap up his career as a nomad, a long way from home. When it was over, he would have to live as easily as he could with a 35–101–3 record, having never played for a winning team. In recognition of how the deck had been stacked against him, and the blood he had spilled so valiantly for them, the Saints retired his No. 8 jersey.

Entrenched as a figure of great sympathy and pity, he had done more for the team and the sport than most people knew, as a ligature between football eras *and* cultural ones. During his career, old societal conceits died a hard death, along with many leaders and the naïve belief that presidents were noble and that American wars would never end in defeat. In Archie's Deep South, life had come to require acceptance of young black men as the biggest football stars in once-alabaster college kingdoms. And yet the case could be made that, as the overall culture seemed to retrench through the '70s in recoil from the tumultuous '60s, so did the South on its own terms. And if Jim Crow was pronounced dead, its intent remained alive in the neglect of black neighborhoods and laws that disproportionately punished black offenders. There was even a whiff of antebellum hubris when Ronald Reagan reached the White House, his legacy representing, wrote *Washington Post* columnist William Raspberry in 2004, a "bitter symbolism for black Americans."[9]

Yet in Archie's insulated world, his glory and agony wrote their own epitaph. As he summed it up, "It's been a doggone good trip, the whole thing." His retirement was not big news in most places, though in New Orleans, page one of the August 27 *Times-Picayune* was headlined "Archie Quits Football; Elbow Pointed the Way," a photo of him scrambling in a Saints uniform beside it. But if the good trip was done, his DNA would soon enough be back in the NFL again.

CHAPTER 10

"WE'RE NOT AVERAGE. WE'RE COOP AND PEYT."

C ooper was the first to show that sort of promise. He began attending the Isidore Newman School, a private prep academy on Jefferson Avenue, not far from the Manning home in New Orleans. Running from kindergarten through high school, Newman's most famous graduates had been musician Harry Connick Jr. and authors Michael Lewis and Christopher Rice, but its gonfalon would come to be football. In 2010, ESPN ranked the school as the best incubator of NFL talent of any high school in America—having spawned not only the Manning brothers but two future NFL receivers: Omar Douglas, who played with the Giants in the '90s, and Odell Beckham Jr. Cooper had athletic skill and a mind for detail, handed down by the father who calls himself "an organization nut."

"[He's] just like me," Archie once said. "He can't open gifts at Christmas without having a garbage can so he can throw out the wrapping paper right away."[1]

But Cooper was also a scamp, a class clown, and when he insisted to his father that he wanted to play football in school, Archie says, "My first reaction was to try to scare him out of it. I really didn't think he could." Still, due to his pedigree, he was assumed to be a natural quarterback. When he started high school, he made the team as the second-stringer—reluctantly, given that he never had a yen to play the position.

Tony Reginelli, the Newman football coach, remembered Cooper telling him he wanted to play receiver. "He told me, 'Coach, Peyton's gonna be here next year, anyway.' And he was right, he wouldn't have had a chance."[2] Indeed, while neither Peyton nor Cooper had played organized football, word was that Peyton was Archie's heir apparent. However, it was Cooper who would feel the pressure of being the No. 1 son. During his freshman season at Newman, game stories in the papers habitually identified him as the "son of former Saints quarterback Archie Manning." It was hard to avoid the glare, since he was wearing Archie's Ole Miss number, 18, above MANNING on the back. At first, Reginelli played him only in spots. On September 17, 1989, the Newman Green Wave—the Greenies, who played in the Class AA division of the prep school league—met Ecole Classique in a non-division game. As the *Times-Picayune* reported, "Perry Eastman threw two touchdown passes each to Tyler Whann and Omar Douglas, and Cooper Manning completed his first varsity attempt for a touchdown to lead Newman to a 36–14 victory."

The next week was a division game against district rival Redeemer. In the fourth quarter, says Frank Gendusa, the offensive coordinator, "The guys ahead of him got hurt so we sent Coop in. We were on our own one-yard line and I told Coop to fake a bootleg and heave one for Omar [later a Big Ten sprint champion]. He did, and Omar ran all the way for a 99-yard touchdown." The play, the longest in Newman history, won the game. That was the good news. The bad was that, as Gendusa adds, "We had to start Coop the next week against Belle Chase—and he threw five interceptions."[3] During that game, Cooper said later, "I was crying to myself in the huddle."[4] As Archie recalled, "I waited up for him to come home. I thought he might need consoling. I can remember games when I had five interceptions—at least three times in my career—and I wanted to jump off a bridge afterward. When Coop came in the door, I said, 'You didn't beat me. I threw six against Tennessee in Knoxville one afternoon.'" Cooper had a ready excuse. "They weren't my fault, Dad. I'm a receiver, anyway."

And, according to Reginelli, he was one hell of a receiver. "He had great hands," Reginelli said. "He didn't have Omar's speed, but he could get open." As a junior, switched to the position he wanted, he made the Class AA all-state team with 37 receptions for 783 yards, a 21.2 yards-per-catch average, and 11 touchdowns. Still, Archie was not convinced Coop had what it took to be a serious player. Early in that season, when he scored a touchdown in practice one day, he went into a jiggling end-zone victory dance. Such celebratory excesses had become common in the NFL, but the schoolboy league prohibited them. "Do that again, Manning," Reginelli barked, "and you'll never get off the bench."

There was also the fact that, like Archie, Cooper was a basketball star as well, the shooting guard and captain of coach Billy Fitzgerald's state title–winning teams (the point guard on which was Randy Livingston, a future two-time All-America at LSU), and in the spring was on Fitzgerald's baseball teams. There would need to be some factor that determined which way he went. That factor would come walking onto the football field and take over, just as Cooper had said he would.

═══

When Peyton was a sophomore and eligible for the team, Reginelli saw enough of his skills in early practices to hand him the starting quarterback job. And Peyton was ready for it, having gorged himself on the art and science of the position since he was a toddler. Watching game film with Archie in the den, he'd want to know about formations, tendencies, defenses, where the seams were. He would ask Archie to pull out his dusty Ole Miss films, even his Drew High films, not for nostalgia but as instruction for a teenager on throwing a football either soft or hard, on faking a handoff, on when to scramble out of the pocket. Watching the legendary Alabama game or the Sugar Bowl, he would tell Archie what he had done wrong. To this day, Peyton can announce from memory the Ole Miss lineup: "Jernigan from Jackson, McClure from Hattiesburg . . ."

Archie could find his immersion irksome. Peyton, he says, "watched film every day. I'd say, 'Son, go get a girlfriend. Go to a movie. You need to get out more.'" But, like Archie himself in his teenage days, his boy had little time for anything else. He played basketball and baseball, but his world was football—in particular, quarterbacking. Reginelli was taken aback at how much energy he put into practice and study, while Cooper, well, didn't. The differences between them were obvious. Cooper was always far more popular than the overwound Peyton. His report cards would be littered with C's, but teachers would scribble on them what a delight he was, whereas Peyton would get A's, with no further comment. Peyton only dreamed he could be popular. "I'm a serious person by nature—sometimes too serious," he said years later. "Cooper and I always had this deal: His job was to help me stay loose, and mine was to help him be more serious. 'Peyton, loosen up a little bit,' he'd say. I've helped him, too, because now he understands how inappropriate it is to make fun of a guy just because he's wearing an ugly sport coat."[5]

They found their happy medium on the field, where they could anticipate each other's moves. On a subconscious level, they were still competing for their father's approval, which is why Cooper kept going in football. And Archie could seem more like a coach than a dad. On weekends, he'd put on sweats and take them to the school field and hone their skills. He'd fire passes to Cooper from 10 yards away, at varying angles, at different speeds and difficulty level—Ten Balls, he called the game. If Cooper flubbed any, they'd start over and keep going until he cleanly caught 10 in a row. But Archie would sometimes think about his presence and pull back, fearing he was sending the wrong message to them, that they had to excel in football as the price of his love. "You can become a man in every form and fashion without becoming an athlete," he once said. "I think sports are good, but I don't think they're necessary."[6] It was easy for him to say, but it was an article of faith to the boys that when they began to play football in earnest, they never felt they had an option to turn back.

———

Fatherhood was no easy chore for Archie. He figured he'd done well with his first two sons, in no small part because of Olivia, who was the soft side, the "velvet glove," as he put it, providing the hugs and kisses, cutting them slack while he cracked the whip. But Eli was a different matter altogether. For all their differences, Cooper and Peyton were strong, even bullheaded in their own way, and fed off each other. Eli, though, as the third son, came of age as a loner with no chance to do anything better than his brothers. Archie remembers him as a happy infant, that his first spoken word was—he swears—"ball," and that he would sleep with either a basketball or football in the crib. But, too young to be taken into Cooper and Peyton's circle of friends, he kept to his room, "so laid-back and reserved that half the time you weren't even sure he was in the house," Archie said.[7]

As Cooper recalled, Peyton wasn't like Eli's older brother, but more like "a second father." And for a time, Eli was so insular that Archie wondered "if I lost Eli." Archie and Olivia fretted about him. Seeing how much trouble he was having reading, they took him for an evaluation at a special language-arts school, which if he attended would have necessitated repeating a grade. The evaluation indicated he should be given extra tutoring, which in itself can be traumatic for kids wearing the "special ed" label. He spent much of his preteen years behind Olivia's skirt, and as a result took on many of his mother's traits. In time, he would try to find a niche somewhere between Cooper's class clown and Peyton's class geek. It was a small middle lane, but he had no intention of leaving it to get where he wanted to go.

━━━━

In the fall of 1991, Peyton Manning was the starting quarterback for the Newman High team, still skinny and a bit gawky, though he was tall and could throw a ball true and long. Cooper Manning had made all-state and was the team captain. They were on a storied path, and Peyton was not prepared to take a back seat to anyone. If you screwed up on the field, you'd hear from him, even if you were a senior. As arrogant as a 16-year-old could be, he even had a tiff with Billy Fitzgerald when the basketball coach, he claimed, reneged on a promise to make him a starter. Fitzgerald, whose tough treatment of players led some parents to complain to the school, apparently didn't appreciate that Peyton, like Cooper, waltzed onto the team when football season ended. Peyton let him know he felt it was unfair. "We got into each other's face pretty good," he recalled, "and used words you'd never hear in Sunday school. It almost got physical."

Archie was livid. Amending his usual wisdom, he told Peyton, "I know I've always told you never to quit something you've started, but this might be a time that you should." By mutual agreement, Peyton dropped off the team and apologized to Fitzgerald, though years later he would only allow that "I was more wrong than Fitz." He went on playing baseball for him, hitting .400 the next season as a shortstop. Fitzgerald, on his part, put the episode in a positive light. "It was typical of Peyton the competitor," he reasoned. "I don't fault him for it. It was a privilege to coach him." Returning the favor, Peyton would look back fondly at Fitzgerald, who he said "taught me about toughness."[8]

Even back then, Peyton was clearly his own man. As if wanting to delineate his talent from his father's, when he came to the varsity he wore No. 14—nothing with an 8. People could easily see that football really wasn't fun for him, but rather, serious business. Tony Reginelli often had to pull him aside and admonish him for getting in the faces of teammates who blew assignments or, in Peyton's eyes, didn't give their all. As with Archie in high school, Peyton made it known he was not going to be a sitting duck in the backfield. "Coach, we're not gonna run the option, are we?" he asked Reginelli early on. As the coach recalled, "He *did* run the option—one time, and he ran it around 60 yards. He had to prove he could do it; then that was the end of it."[9]

In Cooper, he had a target with a psychic connection. The first time they played a game together was on September 7, 1991. As the *Times-Picayune* covered it, "Cooper and Peyton Manning—sons of former Saints quarterback Archie Manning—connected on two touchdown passes Friday night to lead Newman to a 14–6 victory over Riverside. Peyton Manning threw a 20-yard scoring pass to his brother Cooper late in the first quarter, then threw an 18-yard TD pass in the second quarter."

Archie and Olivia, of course, were there watching, with 10-year-old Eli, who had also discovered he could throw a good spiral. Seeing them playing in their bright green uniforms was just an extension of their living-room and front-yard football skirmishes—complete with the petty spats. Neither seemed to have any patience for the other. When Peyton would overthrow him downfield, Cooper would mope back to the huddle, glaring at him, and vice versa, Peyton figuring Coop should have been where he threw it. If Coop was wide open when he made a catch but was caught from behind, he'd hear about it for days. "Cooper could let a bad play go. Peyton couldn't," said Gendusa. "When Peyton got too wound up, I'd tell Cooper to call time-out, tell a joke, pass gas, anything to calm Peyton down."[10] But Peyton believed Coop needed to chill, the flak he'd give him for throwing a bad pass "a royal pain." When their teammates would hear them sniping at each other like that, they got excited, because whenever those two wanted to prove to the other who was right, the next play might be the game-buster.

———

Needless to say, that happened a lot. The coach's son, Reggie, who also played on that team, said, "I'll never forget a throw [Peyton] made at St. Martin's. He threw a dart to Cooper, who was streaking across the middle of the field, and it was right where it needed to be. It was a major college throw as a high school sophomore. Cooper took it for about a 50- or 60-yard touchdown, and I remember thinking, 'Wow, my father has something special here.'"[11] Another teammate, defensive tackle Nelson Stewart, said, "Here was a kid running a pro-style passing attack and hitting a third read which was a 25-yard post. We would line guys up in some unique formation and then—[with] his own verbiage—he'd break them out of it into the real play just so he could see how the defenses aligned." Indeed, way before an older Peyton Manning ever started moving people around before the snap and barking "Omaha!" and other mystifying semiotics, he was doing something like that with slightly less sophistication at Newman.

By late September, he had found Cooper 13 times, five for touchdowns. However, unknown to anyone but Cooper was that something was wrong with his right hand. The first time Peyton dropped back in that Riverside game, Cooper ran one of his smoothly intricate routes, faking the cornerback out and making a beeline for the end zone. The pass landed in his hands—and fell between them, incomplete, a shocking moment for a guy who almost never dropped one. "He just missed it," Archie remembered. "We all sat there stunned."[12] Cooper had not even told Archie that the fingers of his hand felt numb, about the worst thing a receiver could experience. He was able to adapt. When it got cold and he could barely grip the ball, he tucked it under his left arm to keep from having it stripped. He even began tossing the ball with his left hand; when he held for the kicker on field goals and extra points, he put the ball down with that hand. Somehow, he got away with it, telling his brother and his coach that he had a mild sprain, and was as productive as ever. Which meant college recruiters were regular attendees at his games. Both Archie and Peyton kept on him to get in the gym, pound weights, and work endlessly on his footwork on pass routes. Too often, they thought, he was a goofball, a lounge comic. But during his senior year, he became a ringleader for the cause of extended practicing.

"Cooper and his group of seniors were like Bolsheviks," Peyton recalled, also calling them "reactionaries," which is something akin to comparing Lenin and Marx to the czars. Clearly not a history or poli sci major, he apparently meant they were insurrectionists, rabble-rousers, because "they wanted to change things, mainly Newman's laissez-faire attitude toward football." Indeed, with its emphasis on academics, Newman had a modest athletic scope until Billy Fitzgerald's championship basketball teams elevated its profile. But unlike the intense Fitzgerald— who, when he was given the runner-up trophy in a tournament, smashed the thing to pieces—Reginelli was laid-back. Cooper, prodded by his brother, began getting teammates together for unsanctioned practices, joined by Peyton when he got to the varsity.

That season, Peyton likes to say, was the happiest of his life. Cooper went on tearing up the prep school circuit and again made all-state. When they played Episcopal High in the Superdome—most of the high schools played one game a year under the roof—they lost 35–14, but much was made of Episcopal quarterback/defensive back Van Hiles holding Cooper to one catch, as rare as that was.[13] On the other hand, Peyton, despite his poise and long-ball dramatics, was prone to mistakes and interceptions, 13 in all. But he fed Cooper 76 balls for 1,250 yards. In the district quarter-finals, Cooper was double-teamed the whole game, yet Peyton still found him 12 times. Next came Haynesville in the semifinals, and a real nail-biter. Newman was behind all game, but as the clock wound down, Peyton was driving them upfield for the winning score. Trying to hit the tight end, he was picked off—the kind of killer interception that all quarterbacks dread. Walking off the field, head down, he felt an arm around his shoulder and a familiar voice in his ear, the voice that had always scolded him when he threw to someone else.

"Don't worry about it, Peyt," Cooper told him. "It was a great year."[14]

Completing 60 percent of his throws, Peyton had compiled 2,142 yards and 23 touchdowns, and he ran seven more in. Cooper left behind career school records with 125 catches, 26 touchdowns, and over 2,000 yards. That spring, as he finished his last semester playing baseball again for Fitzgerald, the recruiters descended on him. However, there was little doubt he would retrace Archie's path to Ole Miss, and he made it official in March. By then, however, he had grown nearly despondent about his hand. Just like on the gridiron, he adapted, doing his shooting and dribbling with his left hand. No one knew why. "I kept it a secret," he remembered, "because I thought if word got out, players for other teams would figure out how to defend me."[15] Newman won the state roundball title again, but Cooper had a confession for his brother. "My ball's gone dead. I can't spin it," he said, meaning he couldn't balance the ball on the index finger of that hand, because he couldn't feel it.

He also told this to Archie, who took him to the Saints' orthopedic surgeon for an MRI. The diagnosis was a "nerve condition," specifically of the ulnar nerve that runs through the arm and fingers. This was not an uncommon injury among athletes, and in late spring he underwent routine surgery to relieve pressure on the nerve. Over the summer, before leaving for Oxford, he played in the Louisiana high school all-star game in Baton Rouge. He made his usual array of catches, even though the numbness was still there. Assuming it would eventually subside, and with a world of optimism, before he left New Orleans he scratched out a message in Peyton's junior yearbook.

"Peyt," he wrote, "We had our fun times and our serious times (watch out world, you ain't seen nothin' yet)."

=====

For Cooper, this was not his father's Ole Miss. Although the speed limit on campus was still 18 miles an hour, an odd sort of tribute to the man who'd worn that number, the Rebels had lost that old-time religion. Attendance had fallen and the old rituals involving Colonel

Reb and the odious Stars and Bars before games at Vaught-Hemingway Stadium were now a wheezing parody as the reality took hold that black athletes were eclipsing Dixie's white sons. Rebels coach Billy Brewer, a hot-wired guy who had played for John Vaught in the late '50s, had revived the team when hired in '83. However, Ole Miss was found to have committed recruiting violations in 1987, then again in '93, taking them off TV for a year. Nonetheless, Brewer pushed on, filling players' heads with promises of SEC glory. Arriving in Oxford, Cooper moved into a dorm not far from where his father had lived. He went through the same initiations, his head shaved bald. Brewer, who had planned on redshirting him, instead put him on the squad as a freshman. Archie and Olivia had already checked the schedule, planning to attend as many games as they could, sometimes bringing their luggage to Peyton's Friday night games so they could get right on the road afterward.

However, it became clear that the surgery had done Cooper little good. Feeling pain and numbness still, he could no longer hide his lame hand from the coaches and trainers. Archie and Peyton drove up for the second Ole Miss game, though all Cooper did for those first two games was ride the bench. Afterward, the team doctor, Ed Field, found Archie. "I don't feel right about Cooper's arm . . . we don't like what we see," he said, advising Archie to get his boy checked out by an orthopedist and neurosurgeon. The next week, he was at the Baylor Medical Center in Dallas. Archie also flew with him to the Mayo Clinic, a place he knew well. The process was rougher on him than it was on Cooper, who he said "kept things loose."

It was also rough on Peyton. He was already in his junior year, planning to follow his brother to Ole Miss. A week after the trip to the Mayo Clinic, with Ole Miss on a break, Cooper came home to watch Peyton play. That day, Archie got the call from Baylor. The doctors had concluded, and the ones at Mayo concurred, that Cooper had spinal stenosis, a narrowing of the vertebral canal, which can be hereditary, congenital, or caused by continual trauma, such as on football fields. Indeed, slender as he was, Cooper had been lucky so far; one more hit might have left him paralyzed. The doctors laid it out: not only were his football days over, but he was not to engage in *any* sports, period, with friends or, in the future, his own children. Archie bit his lip hard when he heard it, knowing that for Cooper this would be something like a death sentence, requiring a complete change in lifestyle. What's more, living a regular life was not assured; he would need delicate spinal surgery. With all the pounding Archie had taken, it was his oldest son who would suffer the most; if he could have traded places with him, he would have.

The worst of it was having to tell Cooper—and Peyton. He and Olivia put it off all that day, though if they wanted Peyton to keep his bearings for his game, he was on edge waiting for the doctors' report. Against Fisher High, in a downpour, he went 8 for 32 for 35 yards, Newman losing 8–3. Then, while Cooper hung with friends, Archie and Olivia went to meet Peyton outside the locker room and told him the terrible news. He was shaken, nearly unable to speak. Archie asked if he wanted to be there when they broke it to Cooper. "I can't," he said, jaw tight, eyes welling up. "I'm sorry, but I just can't do it."[16]

Archie and Olivia still couldn't, either. They kept stalling until, alone with him in the house that night, they gave Cooper the news, emphasizing that he could have been crippled already, and he'd be able to live a healthy life. But as they knew, it would be small solace. "Cooper cried when we told him," Archie said, "but for the most part he was a trouper. It was Peyton we really worried about. He was near depression . . . he didn't think life was fair at all." Peyton stayed out late, avoiding coming home. When he finally did, everyone was asleep. Still unable to face Cooper, who would be leaving early Saturday morning for Oxford, he went into his room and wrote a long letter.

What I'd do to have you back again as a receiver I don't know. But this is all part of growing up—learning to cope with change. I'll be seeing you plenty, I know, but things will be different. I know other people have gone through losing their older brother or sister before, but I think me and you are different. We're not average. We're Coop and Peyt. We always have been and we always will be, thank God.

Your bro and pal, Peyt.[17]

As Peyton says now, speaking for the family, "Nothing . . . has ever been as devastating," with one exception. "I know Dad has always said that he hadn't had those kind of awful feelings since his father's suicide." The family did a lot of crying during those days. And for Peyton, the worst of it was when Cooper, his fate decided, told him, "Peyt, I'll be playing my dreams through you."

————

On September 29, the Ole Miss athletic department released the news that the little-known son of Archie Manning would not play again due to a "congenital problem and a bulging disk in his neck." Reached for comment by the press, Archie said, "What hurts the most is knowing how happy he's been the last two months being in the Ole Miss family." The shock of it was traumatic for the family and for people around town. Peyton had to somehow suck it up and get his head into football, and he did so by wearing his tribute to Cooper on his back—changing his number to 18. He went out and threw for 2,335 yards, 30 touchdowns, and—incredibly—just four interceptions, earning Louisiana High School Player of the Year honors for 1992.

Cooper remained in school, his scholarship honored because of a medical stipulation, and, as if in semi-denial, kept coming to football practice, to hang out and schmooze with the players. During games, he was allowed on the sideline. Then, before a practice, defensive end Jack Muirhead wondered, "What the hell are you doing here? You should be out fishing, you should go play golf or something, go chase some girls." At that moment, Cooper said, he realized he had no reason to be there, and from then on wasn't. In June of '93, he had the spinal operation at a New Orleans hospital, a procedure that stretched three hours, the first of three such operations. Peyton had a baseball game that day and Archie told him to play, but his mind was elsewhere and in the third inning he left, driven by Billy Fitzgerald's wife to the hospital. There, he joined Archie, Olivia, Peyton, and Eli, who were in a waiting room with a chaplain. "We prayed, we prayed a lot," Peyton recalled. Seeing Archie ashen and sobbing was especially unnerving. "He doesn't [cry], not very often, but then he couldn't seem to stop. It was just so scary."[18]

The surgery done, Cooper awoke, groggy but sentient enough to be alarmed that his whole body was numb, his left leg tingling. As Eli remembered, "The back of his head was shaved, and there was a big, long incision. . . . He needed a wheelchair and then a walker and a cane to get around. I try to picture myself in his situation—and to picture Peyton in his situation—and I'm telling you he dealt with it a thousand times better than either of us would have." Cooper turned to a difficult rehab. When he went back to Ole Miss for his sophomore year, he had to use a cane to walk, though the worst part was being pitied around campus. Unable to feel his legs at times, he would buckle. Hearing people around him speculate that he was drunk, he didn't correct them. Being smashed was easier to live with than being infirm.

He would stop feeling sorry for himself, work hard in therapy, and go about his studies. He conditioned himself not to roughhouse with his brothers. If there was one consolation, it was his hope that, just as at Newman, his brother would enter Ole Miss triumphantly as the scion of Archie Manning. But as the Manning family tree grew, at least one of the branches would grow in a different direction.

CHAPTER 11

EVERYTHING'S COMING UP ORANGE

A lingering aspect of Cooper's football denouement was that Peyton, too, could have potential spinal problems. He and Eli were also tested by orthopedic surgeons, and while they were cleared to keep playing, Peyton later revealed that they "checked my neck and found that it isn't completely normal." Accordingly, he said, when on the field, it was with the knowledge that every down might very well be his last.[1]

After all, he knew no other way. While Cooper had done his "Bolshevik" training at Newman High hard but with a grin, Peyton did it with a scowl. As Tony Reginelli remembered, "He was always looking for ways to get better, no matter what. He was always in my office, lookin' at film. Peyton would come in on a Saturday morning. He'd beat all the assistant coaches in. After games, we'd have dinners with alumni and all the families would be there. But I'd look around and Peyton wasn't anywhere. He'd be with some of the other guys, working on their plays. I didn't care, but the school people didn't like that. All the players were supposed to be there. So he'd come by for a few minutes, then disappear."[2]

Frank Gendusa remembered the time he heard something going on in the dark, long after practice, in one end zone. He got a flashlight, went out to the field, and came upon Peyton. "He was wearing these strange shoes, like on platforms. He said he was trying to build up his calves, hoppin' around on these shoes."[3] Over the summer, Peyton would arrange to work out with Saints players at their camp, working with quarterback Jim Everett. When word got back to Newman, Reginelli again had to put his foot down. "See, working out at the Saints' camp was against the rules. I put an end to that, so Peyton and Jim Everett just went over to the Tulane campus, which also wasn't supposed to be allowed, but . . . hell, I wasn't gonna tell on him."

Not all Peyton's extracurricular time was consumed by football or studies. After practice, some of his teammates would blow off steam doing other drills. There are stories of him, and Cooper before him, fake IDs in hand, heading for the French Quarter, a lot like the way Archie had tanked up at the beer halls in Drew. And of course, being the football hero had dividends with the coeds—as well as run-ins with lesser jocks. At a team party, one of the linebackers, whose girlfriend dumped him for Peyton, clocked him with a sucker punch to the face. The next day at practice, Peyton sought to even the score. "Okay, let's go," he challenged the guy, who begged off.[4] Even if he had been beaten to a pulp, he had to defend his honor. He was a *Manning*, damn it.

Peyton's senior year of '93 was implicitly a preview for college recruiters. At 18, he was a robust six foot five and 200 pounds, still with filling out to do but no weakling, his swagger just this side of arrogant. Newman again cruised to the II-A regional state quarter-finals, to play Northeast High. And it was no small event. Reginelli scheduled the game in Baton Rouge, the night before Ole Miss's season finale against LSU, specifically so that Rebel recruiters could make their pitches to Peyton after the game, which was as eagerly watched as the next day's college tilt. "The stands were so packed, the coaches could hardly move," said Reginelli. "There was no room for any of our assistants upstairs. It was a miserable day, it just poured and it was bitter cold, but recruiters came in from all over the country. We were trailing in the fourth quarter, but we blocked a punt and recovered on their six-yard line, but there was so much chaos, the guy who was supposed to count [the players] did not. We had 12 men on the field, so the block didn't count. And then Northeast drove the length of the field and scored. We lost 39–28. I was so distraught, I never once looked at the film. Still haven't."

Peyton left the field in defeat having passed for 2,703 yards that year with a jaw-dropping 39 touchdowns and nine picks, and with school career records of 92 touchdowns and 7,528 passing yards while compiling a 35–4 record. "When he came off the field," Gendusa said, "I looked up at him and I said, 'That was a helluva run.' He was composed, he never showed a lot of emotion, but he was hurtin', they all were. You couldn't get those kids on the bus or to take their uniforms off. They wore 'em all the way home." For Peyton, there were honors to be had, including being named the Gatorade National High School Football Player of the Year. The press release noted that he had a 3.3 grade point average, was a school tutor, and was a Special Olympics volunteer. Reginelli was quoted that he was "a once in a lifetime player" and "a chip off the old block."[5] Figuring he had come as close as he ever would, Reginelli called it quits as a coach. But for the kid who gave him a ride on his ascent up the ladder, life as he would come to know it was just beginning.

Peyton's choice of a college would have been a foregone conclusion if not for Cooper's aborted career at Ole Miss. No longer was there a dream scenario of them playing together at Archie's old duchy. There were also the school's mounting woes with the NCAA—which now included how it went after him that night in Baton Rouge. The next day, Billy Brewer let slip that he was close to signing Peyton, violating a rule against such public statements by coaches. Brewer was reprimanded, but his recruiting scandals were soon out of control, involving gifts to recruits such as cash, cars, and visits to strip clubs. In July, athletic director Warner Alford resigned, and a day later Brewer was fired. The new man, interim coach Joe Lee Dunn, would have a demoralized team that would go 4–7, including defeats by scores of 59–3 and 38–0. Perhaps foreseeing this, Peyton decided early on not to be involved in that mess. On some level, as well, he had reservations about being treated as something special just because of his surname. That seemed too easy to him. But also too much of a ghost to compete with, unable to live up to his own legacy. "I kind of had the feeling if I went to Ole Miss, I'd be an instant celebrity without doing anything," he said. "Mississippi people think I'm a quarterback, but I could never live up to how good they think I am."[6]

Archie couldn't pretend he didn't have a dog in the hunt. He and Olivia both assumed Peyton would not break the chain. They would get calls from alumni they had known, or not known, urging Archie especially to lay down the law to his boy. But he never lobbied his son as he went about deciding, meticulously weighing the pros and cons of each school. When invited to visit schools, Peyton would have long discussions with their players, coaches, school officials, students, maybe even the janitor. In a bull run Archie knew well, recruiters streamed to the house or to Newman by the bunch—head coaches like Gary Moeller from Michigan or Lou Holtz from Notre Dame. A day after the Sugar Bowl, Florida's Steve Spurrier dropped by. Billy Brewer, before he was canned, tried to curry favor with the family by promising *Eli* would be the starting QB, too, when his time came.

Said Reginelli, "He had every school from A to Z after him. I didn't even show him all the mail he got, it was so much. I didn't know where he was gonna go. I think he was turned off by Billy [Brewer], who bad-mouthed LSU. To Peyton, that was playing dirty." Neither did Brewer read him right. He promised to unretire Archie's No. 18 so Peyton could wear it—which was the last thing he wanted. Another Ole Miss recruiter, Keith Daniels, brought along a David Letterman–style Top 10 list of reasons why he should pick Ole Miss—No. 1 being "We have the best-looking women in America." It would have meant more to Peyton if he claimed to have the best football program in America.

————

Playing a shrewd game of media titillation, Peyton let it be known that he had narrowed his choice down to Ole Miss, Florida, Notre Dame, Michigan, and Tennessee. After weighing every factor, Peyton was sure that the Tennessee Volunteers made the most sense for him—not without irony, given that one of Archie's landmark moments, shoving Steve Kiner's "mules" crack down their throats, came at the Vols' expense. As with Ole Miss, Tennessee had a history; unlike Ole Miss, it had a string of championships, all six of them bred by the legendary General Robert

Neyland. There were also celebrated reigns by Doug Dickey, Bill Battle, and Johnny Majors, who won three SEC titles before giving way in 1993 to his offensive coordinator, Phil Fulmer, who went 10–2 but lost to Penn State in the Citrus Bowl.

While Smokey the dog, the Pride of the Southland marching band's rendition of "Rocky Top," and the Vol Walk weren't exactly Colonel Reb, "Dixie," and the procession through the Grove, the overtones were just as steeped in the Confederacy. The stadium named after the old General held over 95,000, and the team's orange uniforms and checkerboard end zones made for stirring imagery on autumn Saturdays. Under Fulmer, who played guard on the Vol teams that beat Archie—the Mule Game aside—they weren't a big passing team but did employ a pro-style offense, and had a big back in James Stewart, a future first-round NFL pick, as well as superb receivers in Billy Williams and Joey Kent. Perhaps clinching it, Fulmer's offensive coordinator, David Cutcliffe, hit it off with Peyton when he came recruiting. Cutcliffe didn't give him any false hope of starting right away; the Vols' starting quarterback, senior Craig Colquitt, was about to take over for Heath Shuler, who had finished second in the Heisman voting in '93. His backup was junior Todd Helton. And another top recruit, Branndon Stewart, would also be ahead of Manning on the depth chart.

With a week left until the deadline to declare his choice, however, he was still playing it coy, and with the phone ringing off the hook, Archie got him away from the madding crowds by staying with him at the downtown Hilton, where he could make his decision in Garbo-like seclusion. Peyton stayed up all night, rerunning the data in his head. Then, at around 6 a.m. on a Monday, he awakened Archie and said it was Tennessee. But he felt he owed it to his father to give him one last veto. He told Archie he'd go to Ole Miss if he wanted him to.

"Don't even think about it," Archie told him. "You go where you want to go."[7]

═══

He began to make a round of phone calls, waking up people who would be the most let down. Olivia and Cooper came first, then his grandparents still living in the Delta. He rang up Tony Reginelli with the words "Everything just came up orange." Then he called Fulmer, who, when he got the good news, said he felt like turning cartwheels in his pajamas. Not as ebullient was Keith Daniels. When Peyton gave him the obligatory soft soap about how much he enjoyed meeting him, the silence was stony.

"I don't think he bought it," Peyton would say.

Neither, seemingly, would the entire state of Mississippi, which took the decision as a betrayal—one many blamed on Archie, not only for not delivering his son to Ole Miss, but worse, letting him go to a bitter rival. Over the next months, even years, he would endure vituperative letters and calls. Peyton felt guilty about it, repeating the truism that "he didn't deserve [it]." Indeed, Archie had maintained strong ties with his alma mater and chaired fundraising drives that fetched $10 million. He was a season ticket holder for decades, holding the same six seats, even though he almost never used them. But to self-appointed Rebel gatekeepers, it wasn't good enough. The worst was John Vaught, who had detested Tennessee going back to the Neyland days. "Archie," he said on the phone, "you have to talk Peyton out of this. He's making a big mistake." As much as Archie tried to explain that his son was a grown man who could think for himself, the old coach didn't give in. He was on the board of a corporate celebrity golf tournament Archie regularly competed in; from then on, Archie was told, he was no longer invited.[8] Peyton, too, felt the heat. He recalls his own poison-pen letters. "I hope you break your leg" was one of the *nicer* ones.

A Tuesday afternoon press conference was arranged at the Hilton, where he signed his letter of intent. The next day's papers carried the news, with headlines that cut all of Mississippi to the quick, such as "Archie's Son Spurns Ole Miss for Tennessee." As aggrieved Mississippians groused and groaned, Cooper, after initial disappointment, showed solidarity by wearing a Tennessee cap around the Ole Miss campus, willing to fight if anybody gave him grief about it. No one did; mostly, it was met with a shrug. On a campus that now liberally enrolled students of all races from all over the country, and as hoary native pride was adjusting to a new kind of South, the only ones who really gave a hang about the

Peyton Manning college derby were those who hadn't been on that campus for years, if at all. In cultural terms, that was a sign of progress.

=====

Peyton put in one final baseball season for Billy Fitzgerald, finished up at Newman, and with scant time to enjoy the summer flew to Knoxville for Fulmer's training camp. He was already getting star treatment, even as a headline read, "Manning Happy to Wait for His Turn as Vols' QB."[9] He began putting in long hours studying for classes and football, rarely leaving his dorm room, not even to get something going with a pretty, toothy, long-haired brunette named Ashley Thompson, whom he met on a trip to Memphis with a new teammate. Ashley, who was about to leave for her sophomore year at Virginia, was much like the girl who married dear old dad. She came from money, her father an investment banker and real estate developer. She also knew her football; her granddad, Van, had played on the Vols' title teams of '39 and '40, and her brother, Will, was on the Virginia varsity. She was always impeccably dressed, and when they met, Peyton wasn't. "He was wearing this really ugly pastel shirt," she recalled, "and I had a feeling he was going to be a nerd."[10] They did spend some quality time together, but when she went back to school, and he did the same, it seemed a quick summer fling.

Meanwhile, Vol business consumed him. A cautious Fulmer was on record that Peyton would sit on the bench, perhaps the entire season—as would, he said, Branndon Stewart. Still, Peyton was his usual know-it-all self. At quarterback meetings with Cutcliffe, when questions would be asked of the coach, Peyton would beat him to an answer. Once, Todd Helton barked at him, "Peyton, don't answer my questions!" He could also be a bit of a phony, not above some treachery. When Stewart asked him if he wanted to study game film together, Peyton declined, saying he had an exam the next day—then watched the film alone, his notes reserved only for himself. Years later, he would called such behavior "sneaky" but vital to get "an edge," explained as "a sudden response to a competitive urge." Another time, he "accidentally" locked Stewart out of the film room.[11]

He couldn't help himself; in many ways, he was programmed for success at any price. He developed a strained relationship with Helton, despite the fact that they were never really competitors, as Helton was in his final year at Tennessee, on his way not to a pro football career but a Hall of Fame–worthy one in baseball, drafted in the first round of that spring's major league draft. His crime, in Peyton's mind, was to playfully call him "R2D2," more machine than man. Remembering the jab, Peyton would write years later in his and Archie's memoir that Helton "didn't have a quarterback's mentality. He had a baseball player's mentality. You don't study in baseball the way you do in football. He thought he could get by on ability alone."

At the same time, Peyton could be melted by the romance of college football. When he mined Cutcliffe—"Coach Cut," he called him—for old war stories from his days with Bear Bryant, Cutcliffe said, "you [could] see him just light up. . . . Peyton has a true love of college football. He knows the way Saturday afternoons are supposed to smell in the South." Of course, that smell had become less acrid since Archie's heyday. As Peyton said, referring euphemistically to the racial composition of his team and the SEC, "I'm trying to get the whole experience, but the game has changed a lot. We've got guys on our team from all over the country. They're all great guys, but everybody does his own thing. It's different, that's all."[12]

Not that Knoxville was paradise. Brooklyn-born Bernard King, as an All-American Vols forward from 1974 to '77 preparatory to a 14-year NBA career, told ESPN in 2013 that he had encountered constant racially profiled stops, and that his coach, Ray Mears, warned him that the cops would "do anything to get him."[13] Even two decades later, a campus watchdog group, combing through online posts, branded UT a "cesspool of anti-Semitism and racism," going as far as to say, "We have never seen such a like-minded group of bigots. . . . In the case of the University of Tennessee, there is no veil, just raw bigotry."[14]

<hr>

Peyton was getting bigger all the time. Like Archie, lifting weights had beefed him up to around 210 pounds. He could take a hit and bounce up. His release was quick and sure, and he could shimmy his way out of traffic, slow feet and all. He recognized defensive patterns and tendencies and could change a play at the line, something Cutcliffe encouraged. Little wonder that Fulmer, echoing what John Vaught once said of Archie, observed, "You can talk about Peyton for hours, and it sounds like some fairy tale."[15] But Fulmer had to make a choice. Either Manning or Stewart would likely start in their sophomore year. The coach wanted both to get experience as freshmen, but if he kept one or both out completely, they could be redshirted—that is, eligible to play as a fifth-year senior. The issue was still to be answered when the Vols began the season on September 3 against UCLA at the cavernous Rose Bowl, a game broadcast nationally in prime time on ABC. The preseason polls had the Vols ranked 13th, the Bruins 14th, and Fulmer had high hopes. But before anyone had worked up a sweat, Colquitt ran an option, was hit, and shattered his knee, suddenly ending both his season and his college career.

This meant that Fulmer's plans to redshirt his two freshmen quarterbacks were dependent on Helton's ability to stay healthy. He went in but was unable to get anything going, so Fulmer made a bold move, apparently at the behest of Cutcliffe, who called down from the upstairs coaching booth and had the phone handed to Peyton. "You're up," he told him. "Get us going." In the sea of humanity in the Rose Bowl, Archie and Olivia sat, having made the long trip even though Peyton was thought unlikely to play. As their son put on his helmet, Olivia poked Archie and said Peyton was going in. "Naw," he said, "ain't gonna happen." But it did. Peyton, wearing No. 16, jogged onto the field into a game his team was losing 18–0. When he got to the huddle, greeted by in some cases 22-year-old men, he went all rah-rah, clapping his hands and insisting, "I know I'm a freshman but we're gonna take it down the field and score, and then—"

"Just shut the fuck up," one of the linemen cut him off, "and call the play!"[16]

Actually, the plays were being called by Cutcliffe, and he wasn't about to let the kid throw. Manning handed it off twice, then, on third-and-short, the Bruins were late sending in short-yardage guys and some of the Vols were shouting, "Snap it! Snap it!" before the defense was set. He did, but before he could do anything else he was swarmed and tackled for a loss. Flustered, Fulmer now turned to Stewart, but he too was in over his head and Fulmer went back to *Helton*. That, finally, was the right move. Catching fire, he led the Vols to 23 fourth-quarter points, though the Bruins escaped with a 25–23 win. Afterward, Fulmer was heavily criticized for using both Manning and Stewart and thus losing the chance to redshirt one or both of them, one columnist writing that he "must have suffered a mental block."[17] It seemed worse when the Vols were next crushed by No. 1–ranked Florida 31–0 in a much-hyped contest that drew a rabid 96,656 fans to Neyland Stadium, with Peyton getting in for only a few plays, throwing five passes, completing three for 27 yards, with a touchdown pass called back by a penalty. Tennessee then went to Starkville to play Mississippi State, and on a first-quarter scramble, Helton sprained *his* knee. He too was done for the season.

His head spinning because of his volatile quarterback situation, Fulmer now turned again to Coach Cut's pet—appropriately, within the borders of Mississippi. Now, though, Peyton was more at ease. The restraints on him lifted, he dropped back with the mechanical fluidity of a pro, eyes scanning receivers, narrowing the field into zones of opportunity. Cranking up, he fired frozen ropes through the wind, completing 14 of 23 for 250 yards, including a lightning-like 76-yard bomb that receiver Kendrick Jones snared in full stride. But Fulmer was still not ready to fully trust him. When the game seesawed back and forth, he tried Stewart again, but an interception brought Manning back in, later to admit that he was not entirely upset that Stewart's failure "made a good situation even better for me."

Midway through the fourth quarter, the Vols were up 21–17. But when he could have put it out of reach, he too threw a pick. This turnover, one of six by the Vols—one on each of their last four possessions—set the Bulldogs up for a 52-yard drive that featured a fourth-and-12 conversion just before a two-yard touchdown pass with 36 seconds left to win it 24–21. It was the first time since 1988 the Vols had lost three in a row in September, and while Peyton told reporters he had "felt good out there," Fulmer was more tempered. Manning, he said, "made a few freshman mistakes" and was only "a little bit ahead [of Stewart] from a mental standpoint, handling the huddle, audibles, that sort of thing."[18]

The following week, October 1, was the homecoming game against 3–0 Washington State, the best defensive team in the nation. Playing coy, Fulmer didn't announce Peyton as the starter until Friday. And when he sent him out on the field, it was under orders not to challenge that defense but to take what he was given. The result was a tense battle in which he threw only 14 passes for a mere 79 yards. But Tennessee broke the big ones—a 62-yard reverse by receiver Nilo Silvan, a Manning sneak on fourth-and-one to keep a critical drive going, and a clutch 41-yard pass to Jones. Peyton was also wily enough to sell a key roughing-the-passer call while throwing from his own end zone, leaving Cougar players moaning that they'd been hosed by the refs. It took all of that for the Vols to prevail 10–9, a win that established Peyton as the permanent starter.

Stewart believed the deck was stacked. "Peyton was a lot more into football than I was," he acknowledged a few years later. "He grew up with the game. I grew up in a family that never even watched football."[19]

There was no doubt that a wily Peyton skillfully courted Cutcliffe. Indeed, he never passed up a chance to bathe the coach in heavy syrup, calling him his "father away from home." Even early on, when an equally wily Cutcliffe had visited the Mannings' home, he asked Archie to sit in on the meetings. For Stewart, beating out Peyton was one thing; beating out *Archie Manning* was another. And so, after the season, seeing his career wasting away, Stewart would transfer to Texas A&M. That should have been enough for Peyton to allow Stewart to recede into his shadow. Yet it stuck in his craw that some concluded he had steamrolled Stewart. Long past this interlude, when he was an NFL megastar, he still went after Stewart in his and Archie's memoir, suggesting with a seeming low blow that Stewart had been undone by *his own* family; that his mother "had a reputation for being 'involved,' to put it politely," apparently meaning she was far more demanding than Archie ever was, and recalled her wildly applauding in the stands whenever he threw an interception.[20] He did, however, easily slide into nice-guy noblesse, noting that he and Stewart had "kept in touch" and even attended a jazz festival together in New Orleans.

As he gained more and more altitude, he needed to be the last man standing. That was more than competitive fire; it was Manning law.

———

Still, Fulmer was not quite ready to commit to him. Midway through that freshman season, the Vols were 3–4 and Peyton had not played well, sacked three times by Alabama and hurried into two interceptions. The coach had even put Stewart in for one series of downs. Not in the mood to aggrandize his starter, Fulmer pointed out to the press that Manning had thrown a key pass to the wrong side of the field. When reporters relayed this to him, Peyton got his back up.

"I threw to the side I was coached to throw to!" he replied, his neck reddening.

Fulmer couldn't let such impudence slide. Though he would cut the kid much slack for impudence—"Peyton lives to be better," he said during that season. "He's like the coach's little son who's 5' 9" and can't break an egg when he throws, except Peyton is 6' 5" with a world of talent"[21]—he called Peyton into his office for what the latter would call a "little contretemps," insisting that he stood up for himself, explaining his mouthing off as "another manifestation of my stubbornness," or "that little mean streak" that arose "when I feel wronged."[22]

Things were dicey for the Vols. They had fallen from the national rankings in the last week of September—the first time in 84 weeks they were off the list. An Associated Press dispatch after the Alabama game was headlined "Frustrations Mounting at Tennessee" and second-guessed that "Monday morning quarterbacks may be wondering why there's not more playing time for Branndon Stewart." Though the team kept it quiet, halfback Jay Graham had a locker-room fight with a teammate and sustained a broken jaw. Even with the last four games of the regular season against mainly mediocre teams, Peyton was up, then down. When he went 5 for 12 for a paltry 32 yards and a pick against South Carolina—earning him boos from the home crowd for the first time—he took a seat on the bench, watching Stewart play well, winning the game 24–13. But the following week he led the Vols to a 65–0 nuking of poor Vanderbilt, which allowed them to finish the regular season a respectable 7–4 and earn an invite to the Gator Bowl against another also-ran, from the Big East, No. 17 Virginia Tech.

There was a symmetry about the matchup, since Archie had beaten the Hokies in the 1968 Liberty Bowl in Jacksonville, and the only real interest in this renewal was the hype around his son. The Vols were favored, but hurting. Aaron Hayden, their second-best runner, had broken his leg in the Vanderbilt game. The Vols still had weapons, mainly James Stewart, who had rushed for 1,028 yards and 11 touchdowns, but Peyton had never fully been unleashed, not throwing more than 23 passes in any game; his leading receiver, Joey Kent, had only four touchdowns. Half-back Nilo Silvan broke his ankle. With the second-best defense in the SEC and the 13th-best rushing team in the nation giving him field position, he could pick his spots, completing 61.9 percent of his passes for 1,141 yards, 11 touchdowns, and just six interceptions; accordingly, his passer rating, though deceptive, was a sky-high 145.2. (That he was not Archie was evident in his rushing stats—21 carries for *minus*-26 yards.)

By the end of the first quarter, Peyton had his team up 14–0, the second drive kept alive by passes of 43 yards to Kent and 35 yards to wide-out Marcus Nash for the score. In the second quarter, an end-around run by Kendrick Jones broke for 76 yards, setting up another touchdown, and the game was essentially over. It ended at 45–23 and Manning, whose passing the AP account called "near-perfect," completed an economical 12 of 19 for 189 yards. Stewart, the game MVP, ripped out 85 yards and three touchdowns, and Kent had six catches.

With the win, the Vols closed out the season 8–4, not too shabby for a team led by a freshman quarterback whose knack for drama and completing the crucial pass won him the SEC Freshman Player of the Year award. They also gained back a national ranking, at No. 22. Given the pothole his team had fallen into early in the season, things had turned out rather well for Fulmer, who was given a contract extension through 1999 and now had the quarterback who would let him mount a serious run at a national championship. In the purview of the quarterback, that *had* to happen. Fate had cheated his daddy, but there was no place in his life for failure.

CHAPTER 12

JUST RIGHT

I n July 1995, when Phil Fulmer called his team together for their summer practices, he acknowledged that Peyton probably would not stay for four years. He was cruising through his courses ahead of schedule and, given his pedigree and good-enough freshman season, would surely be able to write his own check with the NFL when and if he came out after his junior year. The pro scouts knew he was a pro in waiting. His receivers, brushing off his headlines, had been dubbed Wide Receiver U. One of them, Marcus Nash, recalls Peyton's instinct for knowing how to attack shifting defenses, from man-to-man to zone. "These were mainly pro coverage strategies, but the colleges started using them and he was on top of it."[1]

Nash was himself absorbing an immense amount of detail from Peyton, saying, "Our coaches didn't have to do that much coaching." Dave Cutcliffe pretty much left Manning on his own, to call or change plays on the spot, performing his traffic-cop rituals to move people around. Nash likes to wax about the time against Georgia when, on a third-and-inches from the Bulldog 10, Peyton took the snap and plunged ahead on a sneak, but as he was about to be stopped, he regained his footing and began to roll right, floating back to the 20. Nash assumed he would throw the ball away, but instead saw Peyton make a subtle hand gesture directing him to go to the end zone. He got there just as the pass did and snared it for a touchdown as he tumbled almost out of bounds. When Manning reached the sideline, Fulmer and quarterbacks coach Randy Sanders congratulated him for a "good call." "Nine times out of ten, Peyton's gonna throw the ball if he can," Nash said. "As a receiver, you had to be aware. If you got an inch open, he'd put it right in your hands."

⸻

The Vols had 17 starters returning in his sophomore season, awaiting only their natural-born leader to take them over the top. He expected no less. Over the summer, his maniacal training habits took on a renewed fervor. Up at 5 a.m., he would call slumbering receivers and defensive backs and they'd go to work on seven-on-seven drills in the broiling sun. "We all went to work—hard—that summer," said Nash. "The seniors had never done anything like that before, and I think they resented us for it. But they had to admit it made them better." The other standout at Wide Receiver U, Joey Kent, recalled the incongruity. "It was tough for me, adjusting to his work ethic. He was so young."[2] A native of Birmingham, Alabama, whose father had played QB at the small black school Alabama A&M, he never had reason to doubt his own work ethic until he heard from Peyton's roommates about how he made them crazy. For one thing, he commandeered a VCR they had put in the living room. One early roomie, linebacker Greg Johnson, recalled, "We figured maybe we could bring dates over and watch movies. That lasted maybe a month." At which point they moved the VCR into Peyton's room, freeing up the living room. Because he so rarely came out, they took to calling him Caveman, his bedroom the Cave, where he could be found on Saturday night, barely hours after a game, watching tape of it.

Early on Monday mornings, he would hit the gym for a two-hour workout before class, and while many of the Vol athletes stayed as far as possible from the section of the campus called the Hill, where the classrooms were clustered, he was usually the first one in his seat. Once, because he always did his assignments, two girls in a literature class asked him for a quick summary of *The Awakening*, the 1899 Kate Chopin novel about women finding their place in the paternal South. Hardly something a Southern man of privilege might be expected to understand, but Peyton went on for 20 minutes about it and the women had to beg him to stop.

Already having made the cover of 13 football magazines over the off-season and summer, his gift for drama led Archie to remark, with a little worry, "It's like Peyton went from a freshman to a media darling. He's not getting his in-between."[3] He was named to the preseason All-SEC team, and the Vols were picked to fight it out with Florida for the SEC East title, perhaps even be a dark horse for the national crown. As the season neared, however, trouble started coming in bunches. Over the summer, 27 Vol players were busted in a telephone credit card scam, resulting in safety Jason Parker and defensive tackle Leland Taylor being suspended, most being sentenced to community service, and all dunned for repayment of dorm fees and game passes. Then, tailback Travis Cozart pleaded guilty to assault and was cut, soon to be arrested for selling crack, and five others were busted on various related charges.[4]

Peyton kept out of trouble—so far—and was pulling rank like he owned the place. Once again pushing the envelope with unauthorized workouts, he put a sign up on the field reading, "Throwing at 5:30, Seven-on-Seven, Mandatory." The other players, especially the older ones, sneered at the notion of the sophomore deciding what was mandatory, and the coaches took the sign down, admonishing him that there were no mandatory workouts in summer. Unfazed, he put up another one, cheekily reading: "Mandatory Voluntary Workout." They tore that one down, too. Years later, he was still seething about it. If he had put up one reading, "Keg Party, 5:30. Bring Your Cleats," he surmised, everyone would have shown up.[5] Not surprisingly, he was rarely invited to a keg party.

Fulmer seldom got in the way of Manning's workouts with Cutcliffe. At practice, they would work apart from the rest of the squad. Cutcliffe had him perform one continuous stop-and-start drill, tossing him the ball at varying intervals as he kept on the move, counting out "one-two" in his thick Southern drawl, with different cadences and emphases, with Peyton never stopping his feet either before or after throwing on the two count. Cutcliffe intuitively programmed Peyton's mind, feet, and arm to react in unison. Another had him throwing from one fixed spot, but at dozens of angles. To Cutcliffe, the best players are slaves to repetition, and few were as willing a slave as Peyton Manning. He was nowhere near as tight with Fulmer; at times they seemed like strangers to each other. And he was still the old Bolshevik, chary of the power structure of the school. Soon, he had another of his "little contretemps" with authority, when he tried to chase the Vols baseball team off a practice field. Bawled out by athletic director Doug Dickey, the former Vol quarterback from back in Archie's college days, he got in Dickey's face. Dickey let it slide, establishing the common law that when Peyton Manning fought authority, authority didn't always win.

═══

Fulmer wasn't happy when the Vols began scrimmaging over the summer. Peyton threw four touchdowns in the last of these preseason sessions, but Fulmer believed he had missed some keys and that "we didn't have very much emotion."[6] Peyton agreed, citing the "off-the-field problems" the team had been through. Even so, the Vols were ranked eighth when the season began at home against East Carolina and romped to a 27–7 win. Peyton hit on 17 of 29 for 178 yards, finding Nilo Silvan with a 31-yard touchdown. Then, in their first real test, they played Georgia, and he completed his first six passes and 13 of his first 15, hitting Kent with a 45-yard pass, then bootlegging eight yards for one score and rolling right and zipping one to Ronnie Pillow from the one for another. He would notch another touchdown to Kent. In all, he racked up 349 yards, going 26 of 38, and Graham plowed out 137 yards. The 30–27 win preserved the Vols' No. 8 ranking.

Now came the fourth-ranked Gators, in Gainesville's Ben Hill Griffin Stadium—known as the Swamp—one of the top games of the early season, a must-see on national TV. That week, Peyton holed up, monk-like, in his room, watching game tapes. He also gave his first interview with *Sports Illustrated*, the editors having planned to run a cover story of him after the game. "I can't wait to get out there," he told writer Tim Layden. "I want to run through the tunnel for warmups and hear people yell, 'Manning, you suck!' and 'Tennessee sucks.' I want to hear that. I came to Tennessee to play in this kind of game."[7] The two-time defending SEC champs also couldn't wait. Their junior quarterback, Danny Wuerffel, a

Heisman finalist the year before, had thrown 49 touchdowns in his 17 college games and led the Gators to wins in their first two games this season by outscoring their opponents 87–28.

Game day brought typical Florida conditions: rain and oppressive humidity, but Peyton took advantage early on. On his first offensive play, he zipped a pass to Kent that broke for 72 yards. He then sent a nine-yard spiral to Nash for a 7–0 lead—15 seconds into the game. *That* had visiting Vol fans delirious, more so when Peyton hooked up with Nash on a 20-yard touchdown that made it 23–7 at the end of the first quarter. But Steve Spurrier kept his head and his game plan intact. Over the next three quarters, his team conducted one of the most astounding turn-abouts in SEC history. Wuerffel threw one touchdown after another—six in all, a conference record, and four to Ike Hilliard alone—and ran in another. As *Sports Illustrated* noted, "The noise from beneath the umbrellas and ponchos beg[an] to sound like the ceaseless roar of traffic." On the sideline, a helpless Manning "sat on a metal bench, hair matted to his forehead, anger fixed on his soft face." After the surreal 62–37 carnage—the most points ever surrendered by Tennessee—Peyton, wrote Layden, "walked from the floor of the stadium and paused in the tunnel outside the locker room. There, he embraced his father, who whispered to him, 'We're proud of you.' "

As humiliating as the loss was, Tennessee only slid to No. 15 in the polls; the cold reality was that Spurrier's team had lost at the Swamp just twice in five years. And none of the collapse was Peyton's fault. He had toyed with Spurrier's defense, putting up 326 passing yards. In between the Gators' ridiculous 48 straight points, Jay Graham fumbled twice, Kent once, and Hall missed a chip-shot field goal. Even so, the calamity was a lesson learned; like a jilted lover, Peyton was shoved aside by *SI*, his cover story given to Wuerffel and the Gators. The lesson: fate could be fickle, fame fleeting, if you gave them a chance to be.

The stupefying defeat was only one blow for Fulmer. Two days later, Nilo Silvan, the team captain, was arrested and charged with raping a 17-year-old who happened to be Joey Kent's girlfriend. Although a grand jury declined to indict him and the charges were dropped, Silvan was immediately cut from the squad, amid headlines like "Trouble in Tennessee Volunteer Football—Program Racked by Scandals," the story asking, "Is the Volunteer program out of control?" and wondering whether Fulmer was "producing thugs."[8] As in '94, the Vols desperately needed a midseason resurrection, with Peyton saying they needed to "pull a little closer together."[9] Luckily, the next game was at home against SEC doormat Mississippi State. Cutcliffe called some well-timed trick plays, or as Fulmer would call them later, "neat little thoughts." It was 31–0 at the half and ended 52–14, Peyton racking up 235 yards before being allowed to end his day.

The Vols would not lose a single game the rest of the season. They trampled Oklahoma State 31–0 and No. 18 Arkansas 49–31, Peyton going a jaw-dropping 35 of 46 and amassing 384 yards, setting a school record for completions and earning SEC Offensive Player of the Week honors. Ranked 10th now, they met No. 12 Alabama at Birmingham's Legion Field before 84,000 fans. The AP's pregame story read, "The Alabama–Tennessee rivalry, dominated by the Crimson Tide in recent years, has a new, dangerous variable—Peyton Manning . . . a poised leader whose zip, savvy, and quarterback smarts seem to have caught up with his family." 'Bama coach Gene Stallings also framed him in terms of his kin: "I think he's proud of the fact that his daddy was a good player, but he wants to be a good one, too. Some hide from [family comparisons] a little bit, but obviously he doesn't."[10]

On the first snap, he sent one long downfield for Kent, a step ahead of the cornerback. It dropped into the receiver's arms, and he just kept on running, 80 yards, for a touchdown. Peyton, seemingly with X-ray vision, completed passes in the teeth of the Tide's coverage, with two more touchdowns to Nash and a one-yard rushing TD. His numbers: 20 of 29 for 301 yards. Fulmer, now greatly relieved, said, "The frustration is off my back." His boys moved up to No. 6, then decimated Carolina 56–21. Their only close call was against Kentucky, barely surviving 34–31. Finishing at 10–1 and ranked fifth in the nation, they had a date in the Citrus Bowl on New Year's Day against No. 4 Ohio State. Far more than in the previous year's Gator Bowl, Peyton would be under the microscope in a game of real significance, his Vols matched with a Buckeyes team powered by quicksilver running back Eddie George, whose 1,826 yards rushing and 23 touchdowns had just won him the Heisman Trophy—Peyton came in sixth.

Fulmer and Cutcliffe played this one conservatively, beating the Buckeyes at their own game, with Jay Graham rumbling for 154 yards and a 69-yard TD to George's 101 yards. Peyton again was dead-on, his 47-yard touchdown pass to Kent in the second quarter tying the game at 7–7. He threw 35 times, completing 20, mainly short ones that amounted to only 180 yards but kept drives rolling. The Vol defense forced three late-game fumbles. Tennessee came away 20–14 winners. So now he was two for two in games that, for his purposes, counted the most: high-rated bowls. And if he wasn't quite flashy enough—or perhaps too *entitled*—for the Heisman electorate, he had indisputably stamped a national power in his image. The Vols made it to No. 3 in the final Associated Press poll, a tribute to their grit. And it was with delight that they watched Florida play for the national title and get dismantled by Nebraska 62–24.

Over the season, Manning had thrown 380 passes and had just four intercepted, the fewest of any quarterback in the nation, and set yet another school record, 132 passes without a pick. His 2,954 passing yards, 22 touchdowns, and 146.5 rating were modest next to Wuerffel's 2,266 yards, 35 TDs, and 178.4 rating, but overall Peyton ranked higher—ninth versus 14th, the only sophomore among the 14 highest-rated college quarterbacks. Joe Lee Dunn, who after his inevitable firing by Ole Miss had become Mississippi State's defensive coordinator, had the best explanation: "Here's the way I look at it. Danny Wuerffel is a good college quarterback. Peyton is a good pro quarterback. Right now."[11] The pro crowd agreed. At off-season banquets, when Peyton would sit beside scouts and coaches, he would discuss not the grilled salmon but the nuts and bolts of formations and theories. Chargers quarterbacks coach Dwain Painter was so impressed that he began asking *Peyton* to explain certain plays and strategies. Painter, used to college kids asking about things like meal money and road curfews after they would get to the pros, said of Manning, "After talking to him it's obvious he's way ahead of most young quarterbacks."[12]

A savant, a wunderkind, a gift from the gods, whatever one called him seemed to be inarguable. Numerous accounts pointed out that he not only took his studies seriously but would complete all his required credits in his major—communications, a skill he correctly figured he would need to master—early, after his junior year. On the assumption that this year on the field would have to be his last, *Sports Illustrated* this time didn't hedge its bet. Even before the season began, the editors put him on the cover, with the headline "In His Father's Image" and the ghostly specter of a young Archie right under him. Tim Layden, all but genuflecting, wrote in the story, "Peyton Manning is the player of the year before the first ball is snapped. He holds in his 20-year-old hands the dreams of Tennessee football fans, who desperately want an SEC title and the Volunteers' first national championship since 1951, and who want to see Manning become the school's first Heisman Trophy winner. He is also some NFL team's living fantasy, a 6' 5½", 223-pound once-in-a-decade catch who might enter the draft after this, his junior season."

Peyton would keep everyone in suspense about that. But he was clearly thinking beyond college. That year, Ashley Thompson would graduate from Virginia, and she went to work in Knoxville in the marketing department of Eagle Distributing, a beer distributor. She and Peyton had seen each other infrequently but had gotten more serious. Her apartment was their love nest, with no shortage of suds in the fridge. She had to get used to being put in reserve during the season. Included in that *Sports Illustrated* piece, she confirmed that he normally would be holed up in his room, studying schoolbooks or playbooks, rather than taking her out somewhere, even after winning a game. With a sigh, she said, "I'm guessing most college players are out celebrating on Saturday night." Archie, who had also been a bookworm in college but would jump at the chance to be with Olivia, wished Peyton would—or *could*—enjoy himself more.

Archie thought he was to blame for not preparing Peyton for the downside of early fame. "I think sometimes I talked too much," he told

Layden. "I never knew he was setting it in his mind that just because things were a certain way for me, they would be the same way for him. Something is missing for Peyton. He's on top of college football, and it's different from what he expected."[13] The fame had perks, however. Before home games, Peyton would stroll with Ashley, arm in arm, on the procession into the stadium through the walkway later to be named Peyton's Pass, waving and blowing kisses as fans went *aahh*. Not quite believing it himself, he said at the time, "I walk in and there's George and Barbara [Bush] and the governor. . . . Next thing I know we're all posing for pictures together." At moments like that, angst took a back seat to ego. And it felt pretty damn good.

But ego could also override his better judgment, with consequences he would regret but never seem to leave behind.

=====

On February 29, 1996, Peyton had an off-season physical therapy session with the Vols' assistant trainer, Jamie Ann Naughright Whited. The married, 26-year-old Whited, a former Tennessee student, had him on the table and was examining his foot when, she would say, he began "asking me several personal questions," including whether she "hang[s] out with people she works with" and what she did on weekends, questions that "she felt were inappropriate."[14] She said she then "looked up to see his exposed rear end." He had bared "the gluteus maximus, the rectum, the testicles and the area in between the testicles. And all that was on my face when I pushed him up. To get leverage, I took my head out to push him up and off." She also said she told him, "You're an ass."[15]

Sickened, Whited went to the head trainer, Mike Rollo, who listened but took the issue no further. Sensing a whitewash from the athletic department, Whited herself went to Doug Dickey. It is unclear what action, if any, he took, but on May 2, the *Knoxville News Sentinel*, getting wind of the story, ran a story headlined "UT's Manning Tries to Apologize for 'Clowning Around' Incident." It quoted Peyton as saying it was all a "misunderstanding," that he had "half-mooned" another student when Whited "happened to see it," and that "it was nothing more than a joke toward somebody else." He said he left a phone message on Whited's answering machine and sent her a registered letter of apology, without response. He then pledged, "My practical jokes have come to an end."

Among the laughably weak disciplinary measures taken by the school was the revocation of his dining room privileges at the training facility for two weeks, and having him run laps at 6 a.m., which he might have done regardless. Whited, feeling stigmatized and mocked, requested and was given a medical leave of absence. Then she was summarily fired. Three months later, in August, she filed a 33-point complaint with the City of Knoxville, alleging sexual harassment, denial of benefits and promotions, and illegal termination. She listed similar incidents going back to her days as a student, such as being called "Bumpers" by athletes and coaches referring to her breasts. They had, she said, shown pornographic movies while she rode the bus with them, sang songs about her having fictitious sex with the janitor, and run drills naked in front of her. She also was peppered with AIDS jokes, a hurtful attack on her brother, who had the disease. While working on Fulmer's big toe, she claimed, he came on to her, saying, "Jamie, you like big men, don't you?"

While she didn't file specific charges against anyone, and his name was X-ed out when the complaint was released to the public, it was clear who she meant when she recounted the episode. Now taking her seriously, the university commenced hushed negotiations led by a court-ordered mediator. On August 15, 1997, it was announced that the school would pay her a $300,000 settlement, after which Archie was compelled to say, "Neither Peyton nor anyone in our family was privy to the mediation nor were we involved. I read about it in the paper like millions of other people."[16] This was entirely plausible, given that he paid not a cent of the settlement, nor did the school, whose insurance against lawsuits—with premiums paid by the taxpayers of Tennessee—covered it. And Peyton was relieved of the need to address the subject ever again, as the case was subject to a confidentiality agreement precluding any of the parties from speaking about the matter.

News of the settlement hit the wires and TV sports shows, mainly with a winking, poke-in-the-ribs tone describing how Manning had "flashed his backside." One paper ran a story with the headline "Manning Mooning Expensive."[17] Rush Limbaugh, seeing a chance to slut-shame one more woman on the radio, predictably insisted that Whited had accused Manning just to "extort" money.[18] With supporters like that, it was fortunate for Peyton that the story had a short shelf life, a temporary diversion from the ongoing boy-king narrative that resumed in full force when Peyton arrived in camp for the '96 season. By then, the divorced Jamie Naughright had found work elsewhere, first as a trainer for the Olympic track trials, with a letter of recommendation from Dickey as "an asset to the athletics program" and a "well-qualified athletic trainer." Tidbits of the case had come to light in the interim, such as the possibility that Peyton had retribution in mind that day in the trainer's room—perhaps for Naughright having accused him of cheating in a class two years before the incident. If so, it would explain why, the gag order notwithstanding, he just could not let it go and was waiting for what he saw as the right time to get even with the woman whose life he had nearly destroyed.

———

In what many assumed would be Peyton's last college season, the Vols were ranked No. 2 in the preseason polls, with Peyton a sure All-America pick and Heisman favorite. They opened by clocking UNLV 62–3 and UCLA 35–20. However, they had lost three starting offensive linemen to the pros, and this loomed as a potential bugaboo against the better teams, one of which was next in line: the dreaded Gators, ranked fourth. The match was in Knoxville this time, and the party atmosphere would be larger, with Neyland Stadium having been expanded to hold 102,544. On game day, even as rain pounded the city, students screaming, "Beat Florida!" filed in, the authorities admitting 5,000 more people than the official limit, swelling the crowd to 107,608, a sea of heaving, orange-draped humanity. There were also more press credentials issued than for any game in Tennessee history. "It's going to be fun," Manning promised.

But it wasn't. Trying to unnerve him, Gator defensive end Tim Beauchamp said Peyton could be "rattled." Steve Spurrier's team was, as always, a bunch of strutting cocks on the field, with cause. Danny Wuerffel, a senior now, had taken the team to 55–21 and 62–14 wins.

And the ultimate strutting cock, Spurrier, set the tone early, going for it on fourth-and-10 on the game's first drive, whereupon Wuerffel threw a 35-yard touchdown. Peyton on *his* first drive threw a pick, Wuerffel threw another touchdown, and just like that, the game was effectively over. After two more Wuerffel touchdown passes, three more Manning interceptions, and a fumble return for a Gator touchdown, it was 35–6 at the half.

As the rain turned the field into a mud puddle, Peyton had to try to foment the same kind of comeback the Gators had made a year ago in the Swamp. Spurrier helped him out. In the second half, he took his foot off the Vols' neck and just tried to run out the clock. Meanwhile, Peyton loaded up. He tossed a 24-yard scoring pass to wideout Andy McCullough and a three-yarder to running back Eric Lane, cutting it to 35–22 with seven minutes left. Then he fired a 14-yard scoring strike to McCullough with 10 seconds left, cutting the lead to 35–29. A successful onside kick would have made a miracle possible, but the Gators recovered, ending the game. Leaving everyone breathless, Peyton had cranked up 65 times, more than he ever had or ever would again, completing 37 of them for 492 yards—all school records—along with the four touchdowns. The Vols outgained the Gators, 501 yards to 304. But once more, Manning had to walk off the field a loser to Florida.

Even with the frenzied comeback, which made Peyton proud that "no one quit," the Manning hype slowed. The press was brutal, with headlines like "Gators Put Tennessee, Peyton in Their Place" and snarky observations such as "If only Tennessee had a little more time to prepare. Obviously, 369 days . . . weren't enough. Nor was (former?) Heisman Trophy candidate Peyton Manning. . . . Maybe the Volunteers needed Archie Manning."[19] Wuerffel, who had outplayed him, practically clinched the Heisman that day. Meanwhile, among pro teams, games like this only reinforced that Peyton was wasting his talent in college; by contrast, Wuerffel wasn't in the same galaxy. Indeed, the very next day, up in New York, a game between the lowly Giants and Jets was being called "the Manning Bowl," with the loser gaining more leverage to draft Peyton should he turn pro early. The Jets brass admitted they were ready to trade quarterback Neil O'Donnell and his $25 million contract to make room for him. "He's the first pick," said the crosstown Giants' director of college scouting, Tom Boisture. "Last year, this year, next year, whenever he wants."[20]

=====

Knocked down to No. 8 in the polls, the Vols would have appreciated a pushover game. Instead, the next one was another hurdle, if only for Peyton, as it was against Ole Miss. Fulmer had put the match off for two years, knowing how awkward it would be for the Manning family. But a game between the schools was such a natural attraction for Ole Miss that the school went to great lengths to get it on the schedule, making Tennessee an offer it couldn't refuse. First, the Rebels were able to move the game to the spacious Liberty Bowl in Memphis, which would also relieve some of Peyton's angst about playing on the same turf that Archie had, almost literally in his shadow. They then secured a promise from the Liberty Bowl to pay $1 million to host the game, which they would split with Tennessee. When ESPN committed to televising the game, it would bring in more cash.

For Archie, the game still revived the deep-seated issues of his son breaking the chain of succession. Rebel linebacker Walker Jones, who was a friend of the family, said on the eve of the game, "Archie gave the better part of his life to [Ole Miss], and his own flesh and blood is going to be competing against it. Both have mixed emotions, especially Archie."[21] Playing against Ole Miss also forced Peyton to again address turning his back on the old man's legacy, and insist all over again that there was "nothing negative about Ole Miss as far as why I didn't go there. It was really a case where I couldn't go to two schools."

It also shed attention on the forgotten son, who would sit with his parents and John Grisham in the stands and try to be neutral. This would be a difficult task for Cooper, who still had a hard time being cut out of what had essentially become the family business. And because he looked enough like Peyton to fool people, he could exact some playful revenge. Once, as he was walking around with a beer can in his hand, someone called out to him, "Peyton, what are you doing?" As sloppily as he could, he replied, "Just drinkin' whiskey and chasin' women is all."[22]

Cooper would graduate that same year and go out into the business world. His trade was another pressure-filled game, selling high and buying low, dealing in gas and oil stocks for the brokerage firm Howard, Weil, Labouisse, Friedrichs, working out of a plush office with a panoramic view of New Orleans on the 35th floor of the Energy Centre, a couple of blocks from the Superdome. Not that he didn't still carry the sense that no matter how successful he was, Archie would never be able to see him in the same light as his other sons. His boss, Bill Walker, said in 2003, "I've talked to Archie and Olivia about Cooper. I wanted them to know how good he is at his job. While they can clearly see Peyton's and Eli's success, I'm not sure they fully understand Cooper's."[23]

In 1999, he married New Orleans insurance lawyer Ellen Heidingsfelder, four years his senior. She accompanied him on his doctor visits, learning not to panic whenever he would have a relapse, go numb, and have to sit motionless until the feeling returned to his limbs, and worrying herself sick when Cooper had to have another surgery, a cervical fusion. His doctors also assured that his stenosis was not hereditary but rather congenital, meaning he would not pass it on to his own children. Archie and Olivia became grandparents when May was born in 2003, and then Archibald—called Arch—in 2004, and Heid in 2006. The kids took communion according to the rites of the Catholic Church, Cooper having converted to Ellen's religion after they married. "I just decided that if we got married and had children, it would probably be best to be all on the same team," he said.[24] He bought a three-story home in the Uptown section, lived in semi-fame, and practiced one-liners about being the "other brother" while insisting, as he did in 2004, "I've always had this desire just to be normal."[25] He didn't need to add that was one thing his brothers would never do.

———

The Rebels had climbed out of the Billy Brewer mess under Tommy Tuberville, who came into the game 3–1, but they were easy meat for Peyton. Exorcising any demons, he went 18 of 22 for 242 yards and a touchdown to Nash, needing to play only three quarters of the 41–3 romp that put the Vols back on track. "Now we're the hunters, not the hunted," he insisted, even if he would, for some on his ancestral turf, always wear the scarlet letter of betrayal. He also took from the game an indelible memory of one play. In 2013, after Peyton had signed with the Broncos, Vols video coordinator Joey Harrington answered a call in his office. "I pick up the phone and I go in the corner where it's quiet, and he says, 'In 1996, Tennessee played Ole Miss in Memphis, in the third quarter we ran a play called Flip Right Duo, X Motion, Fake Roll 98 Block Pass Special. I need you to find that play, I need you to digitize it and I need you to send it to me at Denver, in my email.' Exactly where he said it would be [on the tape] is what he said would happen. He wanted to use the play as part of the Denver playbook."[26]

The Vols swept past Georgia on the way to Alabama, who came to Neyland Stadium ranked seventh, Tennessee sixth. For most of the game, it was the Vols who were the hunted. Never getting loose, Peyton would complete just 12 of 25 passes for 176 yards, throw a touchdown and a pick, and be sacked four times. The Tide went ahead 13–0 in the third quarter, running back Dennis Riddle en route to 184 rushing yards. But now the Vols awakened. A Manning scoring pass and a Graham run tied it. Then, with 2:17 left, Graham burst through a hole and just kept chugging, 79 yards, to the end zone. The Tide made a last-ditch drive that got them to the 11 when time ran out on the 20–13 Tennessee win, arguably Peyton's most important yet, as it kept the Vols in the hunt for the SEC title, at the least.

The following week seemed a steal against unranked Memphis, who had lost 15 straight to the Vols and were 26-point underdogs. However, they were surprisingly gritty, and Peyton surprisingly ineffective. He threw for 296 yards and a touchdown, but also threw two interceptions and was sacked three times. In the fourth quarter, the Tigers' Kevin Cobb fielded a punt, hurdled a tackle, and, landing on one foot and elbow, took it all the way back, 95 yards, to tie it at 14–14. The Vols went up on a field goal. But, looking for more, Peyton launched an off-target pass that was intercepted and run back 77 yards, and Qadry Anderson tossed a three-yard touchdown to Chris Powers with 34 seconds left, touching off a wild scene as Memphis students poured onto the field, tore down the goal posts, and paraded around the field with the pieces. This was the first loss by Tennessee to anyone other than Florida in over two years, and it cost them dearly. They sank to No. 12, and even though they won the next three games, it only got them to No. 9 when the regular season ended. Having been close to playing for the national title, their reward was another consolation bowl, the Citrus, against No. 11 Northwestern. Worse, Florida had rebounded and would win another national title. The Citrus Bowl, meanwhile, was hyped as perhaps Peyton's final college game, and he obliged by throwing early touchdowns to Peerless Price and Joey Kent, running in another for a 21–0 lead. The Wildcats stormed back to a tie, but Manning then hit Kent with a 67-yard heave and put it out of reach with his fourth touchdown, to Dustin Moore. Final score: 48–28. Final ranking: ninth.

If it was his valediction, it was a memorable one—27 of 39 for 408 yards. And now the clock began to tick. Most football people were sure he would go pro. He had all the cred he needed, even though his touchdown-to-interception ratio of 20–12 put the Heisman out of reach. Riding the crest of the Gator season, Wuerffel won it as expected, Manning coming in a distant eighth. Though he got his All-America honor, it was on the third team. The more trenchant numbers to the pro crowd were his career highs of 3,287 yards and 147.7 rating. With this disconnect in mind, he saw Heisman voters as superficial, even dim. A year later, he said, "I learned about individual awards last year. I had one off half [against Florida] and I went off the books, finished eighth."[27]

Peyton clearly had a hint of a Peck's bad boy about him, a guy who could believably duck out of church to get a beer or, say, drop his pants at the wrong time. By contrast, the pious Wuerffel said he prayed for touchdowns and refused to accept being honored on the *Playboy* All-America team in '96, saying, "That's not the type of person I am."[28] Self-serving treacle like that made him a safe choice, numbers aside. Nevertheless, to NFL scouts, Manning was the safe choice, just mean and devious enough to be a leader of men. Which explains why so many expected him to do just that after the '96 season.

But because you just can never quite figure out a Manning, he made everyone wait again as he played out the newest guessing game: Would he stay or would he go?

CHAPTER 13

"I'LL WIN FOR YOU"

A s early as October of '97, *Sports Illustrated* was writing that Tennessee "may well be looking for a replacement for Peyton Manning, the predicted No. 1 pick in the 1997 NFL draft."[1] The Atlanta Falcons, on the chance that they'd be so bad they would have the first pick in the draft, traded journeyman quarterback Jeff George and his $3.64 million contract after the season. Such maneuvering was part of what writers called the "Peyton Manning sweepstakes." Even George's own agent, Leigh Steinberg, acknowledged that "there's a quarterback shortage" in the NFL and that "you can't split Peyton Manning into 30 pieces."[2] Not a soul would have blamed Manning if he had left Tennessee to cash in. But he regarded his three years as unfinished business, and he felt part of a family in Knoxville. Though never the most gregarious of guys, and often one who prickled the others with his attitude, they had grown together, black and white, going through hell sometimes. The year before, when Joey Kent was married, Peyton attended the wedding in a black church, joining in on gospel songs sung by the choir.

These moments, as with Archie being taken to dinner in the black part of town by Richard Neal, were small but important road signs for a Manning clan bred and conditioned to accept black exclusion. And the idea of wading into a pro clubhouse was a daunting one for a 20-year-old who had lived a cloistered life. Then, too, wasn't he a disciple at the altar of college football? Even if it wasn't all he dreamed it would be, why not wring the last drop from that fantasia? This was a deeper wish than the one assumed by those who figured that if he turned down the pros, it was "to have one more year of studying, parties and the roar of college crowds."[3] In truth, his studies were done, completed in three years, and the parties meant nothing to him. But the college crowds? The pomp? The smell of the air on Saturday mornings? The damp afterglow of victory? You bet.

In the end, he just had to give it one more go-around in a blinding orange uniform, even if it meant risking an injury that would devalue him by millions. This was not a small matter; wisely, Archie took out a very pricey $7 million insurance policy with Lloyd's of London, the most ever for a college player, to be paid if his son's career was ended by injury.[4]

As the early-March deadline approached for his decision, he spent typically long hours on the phone, calling other athletes for advice. These included quarterbacks past and present—Roger Staubach, Troy Aikman, Bernie Kosar, Phil Simms, and Drew Bledsoe, who had come out early in '93—and even the most famous early pro leaper of all, Michael Jordan, who told him to take the money and "don't look back."[5] That indeed may have helped make his decision for him—in reverse. He wasn't ready to *not* look back. By March 6, with more college life left in him, he opted for the womb of the Vol family. He called Archie, who came up to Knoxville with Olivia for the announcement. When he called Phil Fulmer, it was 1 a.m. and the coach was again in his pajamas. "I'm staying, Coach," he told him. Fulmer burbled back, "I love you, man!"[6]

Speaking in the athletic complex, wearing a suit, two-toned shirt, and tie, his teammates gathered around him, he said, "I don't wanna expect to ever look back. I'm staying at Tennessee." The pro crowd was shocked, not to mention disappointed, given the thin crop of quarterbacks eligible for the '97 draft. As soon as the news went out, Bill Parcells, who had been named coach and general manager of the Jets and had been holding off on trading the first pick, quickly dealt it to the St. Louis Rams, there being no one on draft day worth keeping it for. Indeed, God's pick, Wuerffel, wasn't taken until the fourth round, when he was plucked with the 99th pick by the Saints, to play three mediocre seasons for them and three more as a journeyman.

For Peyton, the prospect of playing in New York might well have helped him make his decision. The prickly *New York Daily News* columnist Mike Lupica wrote, "You know what I really heard from Peyton Manning [at the announcement]? That he did not want to play for the Jets. This was a business decision, and a lifestyle decision. New York/New Jersey lost."[7] If so, Manning had thought about the business angle beyond a superficial level—that playing in the Big Apple might kill his marketability if he was a quick failure and Parcells lost faith in him. New York was too big for him to be Peyton Manning; he'd have to be another Joe Namath. That was a bridge too far. He acted like a courtly Southern man and good Southern scion, one with an old-world value system, notwithstanding his sly deviation from the image. Parcells, who had lost the most by the decision, praised him the most, drawing a broad perspective that "the common feeling in this country today is that everybody sells out for the money and opportunity. In Peyton's case, I admire his decision and think that it took courage to make it . . . I think it's refreshing, really." NFL vice-president Joe Browne also called it "the right thing to do," no matter that the league had made it almost too easy for underclassmen to go pro.[8]

How much did the Jets lose? Consider that Parcells, who had left coaching the Patriots to take the job, brought with him his defensive-backs coach, a cryptic fellow named Bill Belichick. What-if is a fun game to play. Had Peyton Manning come to New York, not only might Parcells—who immediately turned the team's fortunes around—have won a title, but when he moved on, Belichick might not have had to go to New England to coach a mighty team. He might have had one coaching Peyton Manning—against Tom Brady.

———

Coming back to Tennessee only heightened his regional appeal as a favorite son. Over his years at the school, there would be 68 children named Peyton born at the University of Tennessee Medical Center, and when he left it would be the 51st most popular infant boy's name in the state, prompting Archie to lament, "I only had dogs and cats named after me."[9] In the fall of 1997, Peyton was technically a student but on campus only to play football. In fact, he looks back somewhat sheepishly at the free time he had as everyone else studied and toddled to and from classes. Living with Ashley in an off-campus apartment, before the '97 season he'd bide his time hunting and fishing. They went on getaways, to Cancun, to Las Vegas, paid for by her salary. Although suspicious-minded writers wondered if there had been some sort of under-the-table "arrangement" for him to stay, the only perk he could legally partake of, he said, was to drive around in Phil Fulmer's Lexus.[10] Metaphorically, to be sure, he was the driver of Fulmer's team, his éclat such that even now the NFL's Falcons were *still* pining away for him, with open talk not particularly refuted by the team that if they were to "tank it" in '97, they could draft him after all.[11]

For the Vols, losing was not an option. The mainspring would be powered by the Manning–Marcus Nash battery. With Joey Kent gone, Nash, a senior who had already snared 101 passes and seven touchdowns from him, would be his go-to guy, though Peerless Price and Jeremaine Copeland would also prosper, and tailback Jamal Lewis was a reliable ground presence. Rated No. 5 preseason, the Vols waded in against Texas Tech, blowing them away 52–17. The first major test was next, a trip to the Rose Bowl to play UCLA, a nationally televised game on ABC. This, of course, was where Manning had made his shaky debut, a distant memory now. This time, he barely had to break a sweat in taking the Vols to a 27–6 lead, hurling two touchdown passes. Bruins quarterback Cade McNown outpassed Manning 400 yards to 341 and led a comeback, but the Vol defense held them off in the 30–24 win.

The schedule makers had laid a trap for them, though, placing the Florida game on September 20, though the Vols had a two-week layoff to prepare. The Gators had tuned up by decimating poor Central Michigan 82–6, a wipeout that Steve Spurrier smugly called "a confidence builder" for his No. 3–ranked team. Worse for the No. 4 Vols, it was their third straight road game, and in the Swamp. That Manning was the focus was evident when *Sports Illustrated* pimped the game with a story titled "Putting Peyton in His Place," the title feeding off Spurrier's verbal jabs at him. "I know why Peyton came back for his senior year," went one. "He wanted to be a three-time star of the Citrus Bowl." These sorts of lines had a hard edge, as Spurrier was genuinely irked by the big talk coming from Vols fans and Fulmer. He also couldn't abide the unrelenting star treatment afforded to Manning, who hadn't won anything. Indeed, Tim Layden, who had been a virtual PR man for Manning, wrote of him now as a paladin who "signs autographs, speaks to school-children, visits hospitals and throws the deep sideline route. Last week when Tennessee students camped out waiting for fewer than 800 tickets to go on sale for [the] game, Manning bought 20 pizzas for those at the back of the line." And "His talent is so surpassing that he alone is capable of deciding the game on the strength of his own work, and it would surely be the single, heroic performance that would cement his place in college football history."[12]

Peyton was politic. Asked if he came back expressly to beat Florida, he said, "It's hard for anybody to beat Florida. I came back to be a senior.... I just want to win so badly. Football is all about team and all about winning.... I want to win this year more than anybody else in the country. I guarantee you that." Still, it was plausible that he did want to wipe away that Gator stain, which he took personally, admitting that this "isn't just another game, it's huge. It's different from every other game."

Spurrier surely felt that way. The too-tanned former quarterback could only take satisfaction by making Peyton leave the field again in defeat. His task was to figure out how to do it without Wuerffel and his two pro-bound receivers, Reidel Anthony and Ike Hilliard, though the swarming bump-and-run defense coached by Bob Stoops was intact. The new QB, sophomore Doug Johnson, a walk-on who had been playing baseball in a rookie league, was green but had thrown for 460 yards in the tune-up games. One thing the Gators had not lost was their ability to trash talk. Manning, said tackle Mo Collins, "is highly overrated. He's a good player, but I don't know if he deserves all the exposure he's getting. I just want to know what the big thing is [about him]."[13] Spurrier said it was an "important" game, but nothing like, say, Georgia or LSU.

This was the sort of loose-lipped talk that Fulmer had clamped down on, lest it be bulletin-board fodder. Dave Cutcliffe went no further than to say, "Our attitude is, 'If we don't beat them, nobody else will.'" Peyton's boldest statement was: "They're the champs, they can talk all they want. Until we change the trend around here all we can do is take it." He only wished he could say what he wanted to, and did years later—that Spurrier "didn't show much class."[14]

———

The prospect of humbling the big shot brought a then-record 85,714 people to the Swamp, nearly every one of them prepared to shower abuse on Peyton. As one report observed, "There was an undertone of ugliness at the Swamp."[15] It only got uglier. Down 7–0 near the end of the first half Peyton, under severe pressure, threw an errant pass that was intercepted by safety Tony George, who ran it all the way back 89 yards. That was basically the game. Johnson would wind up with a middling 14 of 32 with two interceptions, but also 261 yards and three touchdowns. Peyton had to air it 51 times, completing 29 for 353 yards and three scores, but the 33–20 Gator win stung. Crossing paths with Spurrier after the gun, he would recall, they shook hands, "but he didn't look me in the eye."[16] Salting the wound further, Spurrier said he was surprised his offense played so badly and still won so easily.

His chance to beat the Gators now gone, Peyton could still make it a season to remember. Shrugging off the defeat, he was back in the saddle. He would strafe Ole Miss 31–17—this time with no demons anywhere around—and then faced undefeated, No. 15 Georgia, a make-or-break moment for the season. This was not only a personal vindication for him, it was the coming-out party for Jamal Lewis, the future Baltimore Ravens mainstay, who as a freshman broke out big, running for a breath-stealing 232 yards, propelling him to what would be a 1,364-yard windfall season. Yet such was the Vols' dominance that Peyton also threw 40 times, completing 31, with four touchdowns—so effortlessly that when he couldn't help but throw his final scoring pass late in the no-contest game, Georgia coach Jim Donnan grew beet red and later tore into Fulmer for running up the score, which ended at 38–13.

Next to fall were Alabama, South Carolina, Southern Mississippi, and Arkansas. Then came a date with Kentucky, a middling team but a meaningful match in that it pitted Peyton against a new flavor, sophomore sensation Tim Couch, a real gunner who was breaking school records and winning favor as an early contender for the Heisman. But this was a Manning stunner. The game was never a contest, as Peyton was money all day, only 10 of his 35 throws not caught, five going for touchdowns, no picks, and when the 59–31 rout was done, he had collected 523 yards—his career high, college or pro, and a Tennessee record until Tyler Bray broke it by seven yards in 2012. Stat freaks by rote call this Peyton Manning's best game ever, in particular for his 14.9 yards per attempt, still a Vol record. "Above all others, including Manning's own performances," wrote one such analyst, "this day against Kentucky stands out as the best we've ever seen."[17]

On November 29, he bid adieu to Neyland Stadium, beating Vanderbilt to clinch the SEC East title and move the Vols up to No. 3, rarefied air indeed. Sweeter yet, in parallel time, Spurrier and his Gator blowhards had withered, losing to the very teams Spurrier had said he feared most, Georgia and LSU, dropping them to No 13. That put Manning in his first SEC title game—and the Vols' first ever—facing the SEC West champs, the 9–2, eleventh-ranked Auburn Tigers. Played in the massive, cacophonous Georgia Dome on December 6 in what one scribe has called "the single best environment I've ever seen for a college football or any sporting event,"[18] it drew a record crowd of 74,896 and was a prime-time must-see. In a natural clash of styles, the game showcased Manning against Dameyune Craig, a highly dangerous run-and-gun QB. An added incentive for Tigers coach Terry Bowden was that his more famous father, Bobby, coach of the Florida State Seminoles, had his team ranked fourth, and if Auburn knocked out Tennessee, Bobby Bowden would get a shot at the national title in the Orange Bowl against Nebraska. Manning and Craig had become friendly on the banquet circuit, but Peyton took the field with blood in his eyes. In short order, he threw a 40-yard touchdown to Price. However, the Vols would stumble through much of the game, Peyton contributing to their six-turnover parade with two interceptions.

Ominously, Auburn took the lead on a 24-yard fumble recovery for a touchdown and led 20–10 at halftime; it looked like Tennessee was "seemingly determined to ruin Manning's league finale with a Pop Warner–level display of bumbling."[19] With 30 minutes left to right the ship, Peyton got seven back with a five-yard pass to Copeland. Craig matched that with his second scoring pass, going up 27–17. Peyton, hot now, bombed one away to Price for a 46-yard touchdown—though on the conversion attempt, Auburn blocked the kick and ran it all the way back for two points. So it was 29–23. A minute into the fourth quarter, Manning had a second-and-10 on his 27-yard line. He took a two-step drop, swiveled to his right, and threw a short one to Nash, five yards downfield. Finding himself in man-to-man coverage, Nash spun to the outside, put a hip fake on a defender, and cruised down the sideline to the house, a 73-yard streak.

That made Peyton, who racked up 373 yards and four touchdowns, the SEC's all-time leader in passing yards and touched off a semi-crazed reaction by the team, and a more controlled one by him. He ran down the field, pumping his fist, then pushed guys toward the bench so as to avoid a flag for excessive celebration before Jeff Hall kicked the winning point of the 30–29 death match. This, wrote one reporter, was "classic Manning. Understated. Intelligent. Selfless. And, well, OK, boring. No . . . poses. No finger-pointing smack talk. Not even one of those Danny Wuerffel praying-hand jobs."[20] True indeed was that Peyton saw such displays as "pandering to the individual."[21] At least until the game was over. Then, named the game's MVP, he tarried on the field with jubilant Vol players and students, before grabbing the baton from the bandleader and leading repeated renditions of "Rocky Top."

⸻

SEC crown in hand, ranked third in the country, the Vols now would go up against Tom Osborne's frightful Nebraska Cornhuskers in the January 2 Orange Bowl—Peyton's last call. In the interim, he would savor the spoils of the miraculously revived season, receiving the Maxwell Trophy and a number of other honors. When he journeyed to New York as one of the top candidates for the Heisman, he went on David Letterman's *Late Show* to amiably engage the host in a competition, tossing footballs across 52nd Street toward an open window. But he would not get the Heisman, beaten out by Michigan's terrific defensive back Charles Woodson. Even if it did seem trivial in the broader, cosmic scope of his rising star, not winning the Heisman bugged him. He showed as much in his memoir with Archie when he wrote, "I didn't cry over it," and then did just that. He called the Heisman committee "rude" and "poorly organized," adding that he had been at banquets with past Heisman winners who were "drunk as skunks." Woodson had won, he ventured almost comically, because he would be playing in the Rose Bowl and ABC wanted the Heisman winner in it.[22]

For the Vols, there was a dollop of schadenfreude, too—Spurrier's acrid joke about Peyton being relegated to the Citrus Bowl became a delicious irony when the Gators ended up exactly there themselves, while the Vols played for consideration as national champs. Few, however, gave Tennessee much of a chance against the undefeated 'Huskers, who had annihilated Texas A&M 54–15 in the Big 12 title game. Moreover, the Orange Bowl would be Tom Osborne's finale before retiring. With Michigan ranked No. 1, Osborne needed to run up the score to make his case for the national title. The Vols, of course, needed to win and hope for an equally unlikely loss by Michigan to No. 7 Washington State in the Rose Bowl. The 'Huskers were the Vols' polar opposite, a plundering herd that rarely passed, and Fulmer knew he had no way to stop them. Worse, the still-fickle-fingered Vols had two early fumbles and trailed 14–3 at the half, then 28–3 late in the third when Peyton, who could only muster 134 yards, finally connected with Price.

That was the last TD he would throw in college, and Fulmer mercifully let him come out early. The 'Huskers won going away, 42–17, and Ahman Green broke the Orange Bowl record with 197 rushing yards. In the end, "UT was nothing more than a prop for Nebraska's big show."[23] Afterward, Peyton, with Archie, journeyed into the winners' locker room to congratulate Osborne, who returned the favor with nothing but praise for the losing quarterback. Just minutes after removing his uniform, Peyton was in a different time frame, his Vol records—including 7,382 passing yards, 53 touchdowns, 576 completions, 904 attempts, and a 63.7 completion percentage—a thing of the past. His biggest beneficiary, Nash, caught 76 passes and 13 touchdowns that season, for 1,170 yards, and both made first-team All-America, solidifying Nash's status as a first-round draft pick—by the reigning NFL champ Denver Broncos, with whom he would win a ring as a rookie as a part-time target of John Elway.

"How's that for a dream come true?" Nash said. "I caught passes from maybe the two best quarterbacks of all time. How many guys can say that?"

=====

The whole world assumed Peyton would be taken with the first pick by the Indianapolis Colts, who had won the Manning lottery by going 3–13, one more loss than the San Diego Chargers, Arizona Cardinals, and Chicago Bears—the Atlanta Falcons had the bad timing to approach mediocrity at 7–9. The Colts fired coach Lindy Infante and dumped the 34-year-old incumbent quarterback, Jim Harbaugh. The new coach, Jim Mora, had coached the Saints for 10½ seasons, and as such was tight with Archie, who had spent most of those years as the team's radio color analyst. Mora coyly said when he got the job, "I know [Peyton] well. He spent a lot of time around our organization. He's an excellent young prospect."[24] Also playing it close to the vest was the Colts' new GM, Bill Polian. At the league's March scouting combine in Indianapolis, Polian spoke of "weighing all our alternatives."[25] In fact there was only one alternative: Washington State's Ryan Leaf, who had turned pro after his junior season, in which he led the school to its first Rose Bowl appearance in 67 years. Leaf, who came in third in the Heisman vote, had more passing yardage than Manning on 60 fewer completions. About as tall, he also outweighed him by 25 pounds, and he could move.

A football writer who polled 20 general managers wrote, "The overwhelming consensus [is] Manning may have the more recognizable name, but Leaf clearly is the preferred quarterback among league executives. Fourteen of the 20 polled said they would draft Leaf . . . citing [his] stronger arm, better mobility and more promising long-term prospect as a franchise-caliber player." Less noticed was the cautionary report by another scout who said Leaf was "self-confident to the point where some people view him as being arrogant and almost obnoxious,"[26] though these adjectives were not uncommon in relation to Manning, either.

A Manning slight was not implausible. Gauged outside of actual game conditions, he could only demonstrate skill level, not the instinctive "third eye" developed through endless study. He could seem awkward, slow. And a new wrinkle had arisen. Lusting for Leaf, who had dazzled the West Coast as much as Manning had the South, the San Diego Chargers were in a bind. They had the No. 3 pick and would be shut out of landing either QB. So they swapped their position with the Arizona Cardinals, who sat at No. 2, trading two first-round picks and two starters. This development made Leaf want to avoid the Colts any which way he could. Years later, his agent, Leigh Steinberg, maintained that he devised a plan to irritate Mora, thus turning the Colts off to him.

Such an attempt at manipulating the draft was not without precedent—the most famous example being John Elway, who in 1983 was similarly repulsed at the prospect of being chosen No. 1 by the then-Baltimore Colts. Elway's agent, Marvin Demoff, threatened that Elway would sit out of football for a year and play baseball to avoid playing on a perennial loser and becoming "the next Archie Manning." The Colts still took Elway, and wound up trading him to Denver a few days later.

As the Steinberg plan transpired, Leaf stood Mora up when the two were to meet, on a pretext of having an MRI. Steinberg later said he knew this would make Mora go "berserk."[27]

Even so, as late as mid-April, Chargers GM Bobby Beathard was projecting that the Colts would go for Leaf. But Polian was suggesting otherwise. Leaf, he said, didn't have that much better an arm than Manning, and Manning had a quicker release. He was also projected to play right away, whereas Leaf needed more seasoning. During the ebb and flow, *Sports Illustrated* defined the issue as a hard choice between the "safe" Manning and Leaf as "the potential mother lode."[28] With so much at stake, Polian watched tape of every one of the two quarterbacks' passes—1,505 for Manning, 880 for Leaf—compiling their success rates in different game situations. Mora and the Colts' new quarterbacks coach, Bruce Arians, did the same to compare notes. Polian also paid $5,000 to the former 49ers coach Bill Walsh, who had groomed Joe Montana into a Hall of Fame quarterback, to watch the tapes and provide his opinion. At one of the combine workouts, Polian stood just feet away as both young men went through drills; one of his conclusions was that Leaf had thrown 60 yards without striding, Manning 58. Polian estimated he spent 14 hours a day over four weeks making these comparisons. "Did we overanalyze?" he said later. "Absolutely."[29]

———

Peyton was unsure whether the beaches and smog and mellow-rot vibe of Southern California could ever be to his liking. He saw Indianapolis as an unpretentious heartland outpost—even if, in reality, it was no small town but the 13th-largest city in America. He remembered how awed he had been when he visited Notre Dame in South Bend, and likened himself to the "hick from French Lick," Larry Bird—who, after his Hall of Fame career with the Boston Celtics, was now coaching the Pacers not far from where the Colts played. Unlike Leaf, he was in no hurry to flaunt an agent. Archie's man, Ed Keating, had died in 1996 from cancer, though the family's old lawyer, Frank Crosthwait, was still on a loose retainer. Archie and Peyton planned to interview a number of agents when they went to New York for the draft. Meanwhile, Mora and Polian, along with offensive coordinator Tom Moore and Arians, journeyed to Knoxville and gave him a last once-over on April 1, for which Peyton enlisted Marcus Nash to catch his passes during drills. They would do the same with Leaf on the coast. Just before Easter, the Colts' owner, Jim Irsay, who had taken over the team when his father, Robert, died in 1996, met with Peyton in Miami at the Surf Club, which Irsay owned.

"I'll win for you," the kid told him, a promise that, Irsay would recall, "sent shivers up my spine."[30]

When Polian brought him to Indianapolis for another meeting, Peyton was even ballsier.

"If you don't draft me," he said, "I'm gonna kick your ass for the next fifteen years."[31]

Peyton wanted someone from the Colts to confirm they were going to take him, but it didn't happen. As the days ticked down, rumor had it that the Colts were shopping the top pick to other teams for a king's bounty. Annoyed, Peyton told Archie he wasn't going to New York for the draft.

Archie laid down the law, saying how unprofessional that would look. And so, a few days before the draft, they arrived, booked into the same hotel where the other top picks and their families were put up, including Leaf, who arrived with 30 members of his family. The two rivals spent time together that week giving interviews, and they grew friendly. That week, as well, Peyton and Archie interviewed two dozen agents. One, 45-year-old Tom Condon, a stocky former guard for Boston College who went on to play 12 seasons for the Kansas City Chiefs, had also served as president of the players' association before turning agent in '91 with the IMG mega-agency, which of course Keating had helped build into a corporate titan. Condon showed up at the hotel looking much unlike the usual crowd of Brooks Brothers–suited, Gucci loafer–wearing super-agents. As Archie remembered, "He knocked on the door and he was standing there and he had on a pinstripe suit coat, shirt, tie . . . and blue jeans."[32] Condon's explanation for that was simple. "I was supposed to meet [the Mannings] at 9 or 10 o'clock. So I end up running around that morning, trying to find some dress pants somewhere. Of course, nothing was open."

Peyton and Archie had a gut feeling about him, that he would do his work removed from the spotlight. Neither did he have a problem having Crosthwait sign off on deals. Before walking out of the room, Condon was part of Manning Inc.

———

That Friday night, Leaf had dinner with Steinberg and Chargers owner Alex Spanos. At the next table were Peyton and Archie. The draft would commence at 11:45 a.m. on Saturday, a far cry from the prime-time spectacle of today, and even now the Colts were dawdling. As Peyton tells it, he learned his fate later that night on a media cruise around Manhattan with the top players. He was standing with Condon, he said, when the agent's cell phone rang. On the other end, Polian said, "We're taking Peyton." Condon handed him the phone.

"You ready to lead the Colts to the Super Bowl?" Peyton said Polian oozed.

"Yessir, I'm ready."[33]

If this happened, then Polian put the others in the Colt brain trust through unnecessary hell the rest of that night and into the morning—or else, had second thoughts himself. Because, according to insiders, they stayed up all that night going back and forth between the two quarterbacks, during which "there was arguing going on . . . it was intense."[34] Peyton and Archie cabbed it to Madison Square Garden on Saturday morning and stood in a backstage area, casually munching from a bag of potato chips. Peyton then took his seat in the front row alongside other top draftees to be, with Leaf a few feet away on a couch.

Insiders say the absolute final decision was only made 15 minutes before the draft, when Irsay notified Steinberg that his client was not going first, whereupon Leaf, whose stomach was nervous, let out a loud hoot and got up and went to the bathroom. Commissioner Paul Tagliabue made it official moments later, intoning in a lawyerly monotone, "With the first pick in the 1998 NFL draft, the Indianapolis Colts select Peyton Manning, quarterback, University of Tennessee." Peyton then rose to the stage, to be glad-handed by the commissioner and Irsay as he donned a blue and white jersey that had been made with his name on the back. Taken to an interview area, he uttered his first words as a pro, polished as could be. "I realize the pressure," he said, "but I think it's exciting to be part of going in and trying to make a turnaround. I'm going in humble, but I'm going in to compete."[35]

Flashbulbs went off around him, and then he had to clear out for Leaf, taken by the Chargers. The Mannings then caught a flight to Knoxville, where the Vols were retiring his jersey at halftime of the team's spring scrimmage and naming a street on campus after him. The day was eventful, historic in terms of a father-and-son dynasty, with appropriate rewards, although *New York Times* football writer Mike Freeman opined, "Most N.F.L. observers feel that Leaf is walking into a better situation than Manning. The Chargers' staff is composed of quarterback-friendly coaches like the head coach, Kevin Gilbride, and the offensive coordinator, June Jones."[36] And Spanos had big visions, or fantasies. "Son," he told Leaf, "I'm looking to you for the next fifteen years."[37] Polian was more tempered—"He fit best for us"—reminding everyone that general managers' decisions go wrong a good half the time. "History," he said, "tells us that sometimes fate intervenes."

Polian was prepared to hold some sort of salary line, though Freeman figured Peyton would put to shame his old man's now-emaciated salary history. "Look for Manning to receive a signing bonus worth $8 million to $10 million, with his total contract in the tens of millions of dollars," Freeman wrote. "That is an amazing number when you consider the contract his father received. . . . These days, a quarterback might spend that much on shoes."[38]

CHAPTER 14

"A GOLDEN STAIRCASE FROM HEAVEN"

Fate is indeed fickle. In Tennessee's first season without Peyton Manning, they would go undefeated, beat Florida, take the SEC, and at last win the national title. It was a glorious day for the school's record holder in every passing category, but there had to be thoughts of why it had happened not with him but his former backup, Tee Martin, Tennessee's first black quarterback. Martin was deferential. "I like being the guy to follow behind Peyton Manning," he said, writing his epitaph.[1] Down in the Swamp, they would still gloat about those four wins over Peyton, one fan site in 2012 giddily reminding the world that "Peyton Manning Never Beat Florida."[2] But nothing could dent the Manning brand, which now would prop up not just a young man but a corporate entity.

The culture that had bred Archie's son had undergone serious changes, carving another fleeting alliance between North and South when, in 1992, another Democratic president from Dixie charmed his way into the White House with a thumbs-up sign and the cunning to claim the mantle of "the first black president." Since Archie's rookie season two decades before, black players had won the majority of Heisman Trophies. The first African-American on Bear Bryant's Crimson Tide, John Mitchell, became Bryant's first black assistant coach. But even as almost half the players in the NFL were black by decade's end, Division I colleges employed just 12 African-Americans as assistant coaches, just

four as head coaches. (Sylvester Croom was the first in the SEC, at Mississippi State.)[3] Peyton Manning had no material effect on any of this, nor on
any other pressing issue, except that on an ethereal level he was a rising
leader of men in a corporate complex coated in pseudo-militaristic and
pseudo-religious imagery, incidentally, as a proud white Southern son.
That meant, independent of anything he said or did, the pride and preju-
dices of his home turf—and faint hopes of enlightened progress beyond
the gridiron—could be channeled through him.

And now, just as he punched his ticket to the pros, another son
named Manning was peeking through the window. Barely a ripple in his
brother's eddy of headlines, dramas, and dollar signs, 16-year-old Elisha
Nelson Manning, known only as Eli, appeared quietly in 1997 as another
prototypical long-legged, lean-as-a-two-by-four teenager blessed with
an elastic arm. He made the Newman varsity in 1996, like his brother
never having played a down of tackle football but ready to take his place
in the family line of succession. Frank Gendusa had taken over as the
Newman High coach by then and could barely distinguish him from
Peyton. "Same size, same arm strength, same work ethic. Peyton did
have better personnel around him, and he was more assertive while Eli
was laid-back—we nicknamed him 'Easy.' But when he had to make a
critical play, he'd get that look in his eye that would scare you."[4]

He was still insular, keeping to himself more than not. But when
puberty hit full force, his isolationist tendencies merged with a rebellious
streak. All the Manning brothers were independent in their own way,
and Eli owned a wanderlust not found in Cooper's class clowning or Peyton's "smartass" tendencies. For Eli, the game had almost nothing to do
with Peyton, but rather offered an avenue to expand his cloistered life.
When he took control of the Green Wave offense, he and his own circle
of buddies would find their way to Bourbon Street for a night of whatever. Archie, occupied as he was with trying to guide Peyton into the
pros, didn't keep a close eye on his youngest boy. Olivia would tell him
what Eli was doing during those forays, and he would either yawn or lay
down the law to a smirking Eli.

In an example of the latter, Archie and Olivia were supposed to go
out of town and leave Eli, who promised to behave, alone in the house,

whereupon he threw a wild pool party for half his class—not realizing that his parents had decided *not* to go and were in their bedroom upstairs. When Archie looked down from his window, the yarn goes, the party animals scattered. When Archie brought it up, the kid snarked about being given the third degree by "the Secret Service."[5] Getting away with stuff like this had to make his brothers envy him. But to his parents, his late-blooming manhood was a relief, given his mama's boy childhood. Besides, he knew how to play the Manning stereotype; he could "yes, sir" and "no, sir" like a pro. He was smart, even if in a devious way. Smart enough to know football was going to take him to where he wanted to go.

Indeed, he was making people at Newman forget Cooper and Peyton. Four times each he would letter in football and basketball, twice in baseball. College recruiters began to make their way to the same field where many of them had seen Peyton star. The Friday night lights that burned bright for his brothers now shone on him. In that bright light, he looked much like Peyton, but he could run a bit faster—4.8 in the 40, a tenth faster than Peyton—and jump higher. Eli hit it hard in the gym and he took direction well. But he was not the demon of film-room preoccupation; more like Cooper in this respect, he just wanted to go out there on game day and cut loose. Where Peyton and Cooper knew enough about the NFL as kids to have their own favorite players who were not named Archie Manning, Eli didn't bother to follow pro games. "He's just not overly impressed about things," said Cooper. "He doesn't care, one way or the other, about stuff other people care about."[6] That sophomore season, he threw five touchdowns in a game against Fisher High. Afterward, Archie told him he was getting ready for "the next level" of big-time college ball.

"Aw, I was just having fun," his boy said.

Archie never had to shoo Eli away from watching old game film to go out and chase girls. All Eli ever said about those grainy old films, or perusing his dad's stats, was, with future irony, "Geez, Dad, you threw a lot of interceptions, a *lot* of interceptions." Rather than bubblegum cards, he collected Metallica and Nirvana tapes. On Super Bowl Sundays or during a big college game—even Peyton's—he'd get bored and put on headphones and blast "Lithium" or "Wherever I May Roam," or play

Grand Theft Auto on the GameCube. One day he was a metalhead, the next a straight arrow and straight-A student. Probably, *he* didn't know what he was. Most of all, says Gendusa, "It didn't seem to me that he was trying to outdo what Peyton had, or that he resented being in his shadow." Nor, for that matter, his father. Eli was an '80s kid; by that time, Archie's day was over. Archie tried to be there for every game, but the next morning he'd be on his way to Peyton's games, leaving Eli to his own routines, which were less about white privilege than selfish conceits. In his senior yearbook, he chose as the quote under his photo not a biblical or historical citation, but a facetious one from the *Saturday Night Live* "Deep Thoughts" segment that went, "Broken promises don't upset me. I just think, why did they believe me?"[7]—a shape-shifting of moral responsibility and reversing of blame that perfectly codified Generation X's amorality and cynicism.

The first time his name made the papers—beyond the local high school scores—during that junior season was in a small AP item that noted, "With Tennessee idle this weekend, quarterback Peyton Manning had a chance to come back home and cheer his kid brother and alma mater to victory. Wearing a green Newman High School baseball cap and a big button with brother Eli Manning's picture on it, Peyton watched Eli throw for 341 yards and two touchdowns to beat St. Bernard 45–14 Friday night."[8] Already six foot four and a sinewy 190 pounds, he was a monster that night. In the first half alone, he hit 13 of 18 passes for 257 yards, one a nine-yard touchdown to tailback Justin Seale. He then lofted a 51-yard TD pass in the third quarter to receiver Devin Wakeman, finishing 16 of 25. Gendusa, as Tony Reginelli had done with Peyton, let him throw freely and he went 139 of 245 for 2,340 yards, with 24 touchdowns and seven interceptions as a sophomore—beating Peyton's first year at Newman in all but completion percentage. Freed up even more as a junior, he went 142 of 235 for 2,547 yards—again, more yardage than Peyton—with 23 TDs and nine INTs.

Because Eli seemed not to have to turn his head from side to side while reading the defense at the line, while still seeing the entire field, Gendusa deduced that he had a "slow" eye, the left one, which moved a minuscule one degree behind the right. Gendusa recalled the time when "Eli looked like he'd be sacked; this guy swung him around and [Eli] threw a little sidearm pass to the running back. I don't know how, sometimes, they see people. It's an uncanny knack good quarterbacks have, [and] he has it."[9]

Archie was pleased with Eli's progress. During the week, he sometimes came to shoot the breeze with the coach. "With Archie, he doesn't say anything unless you ask him," said Gendusa. "I asked him one time how we could get it to the tight end more. He showed me a couple things they did back in the day and we tried some stuff, but it was really a matter of Eli getting more confident. And Archie just wanted to be there for him. That was his favorite place, sitting in the bleachers at our stadium. One of our assistant coaches' father and his brothers were Ole Miss alumni from Archie's days there. They knew him, how much his dad's suicide hurt him. It didn't matter what the boys did. If he could watch Cooper's business meetings, I'm sure he would."

———

Tom Condon and Frank Crosthwait, springing into action after the draft, hit a brick wall with the Colts. Naïvely, Peyton thought the contract would be dispensed with quickly. Instead, just as with Archie in his time, negotiations stretched on. This was standard procedure in football, but Peyton was drafted just as the NFL's new TV contract increased the salary cap by nearly $13 million, to $54.4 million, and all players were demanding higher contracts, with even linemen upped to an average of $4 million a year, receivers $3 million. Peyton was miffed when he went to the Colts' spring camp, still unsigned. When he put on his jersey, it was with a new number—18, as if he had at last accepted the insignia worn by his heroic, if failed, father and then, abortively, by Cooper.

Even before he threw a pro pass, he was being mass-marketed. Condon had set up a corporation for him, and he gave motivational speeches—which he downplayed as "basically, 20 minutes' worth of ways to say, 'Work hard.'"[10] They also began a charitable foundation called PeyBack, its charter to aid underprivileged youth. He unveiled a website, PeytonManning.com, at a time when few athletes believed this was necessary. Condon signed him to an endorsement deal with Adidas.

He made appearances with country singer Kenny Chesney, singing—to be generous—a duet they recorded on a CD called *NFL Country*, while slinging an unplugged guitar he had no idea how to play. His image was as calculated as Joe Namath's, his polar opposite. He had, after all, studied communications, and it was no accident that he spoke in measured, humbled tones, at least for public consumption. Of course, no fans were allowed to see the Manning who had sat on Jamie Whited's head. Even in private, he had learned to keep the heat off of himself. As a friend of his said, "He might tell you to do something stupid, but he's not going to be the one to get nailed for it." The image he laid down demanded that he say things like "I've tried to keep myself out of bad situations, and if that means I'm a Goody Two-Shoes, so be it."[11]

═════

The Colts, who in an earlier life rode Johnny Unitas's arm into the modern age of pro football, and Earl Morrall's to their last title in 1970, had not featured a prominent quarterback since the last years in Baltimore, when Bert Jones was the league MVP in '76. The resulting lack of success, and dwindling crowds, sent Bob Irsay to Indianapolis, where poor Jeff George spent five seasons in the early '90s scraping himself off the turf. While Jim Harbaugh quarterbacked them to the playoffs twice, and to the AFC title game in '95—blessed with a receiver like Marvin Harrison, the team's first-round pick out of Syracuse in '94—the ream relapsed the next year to 3–13, and that was the seed that developed into Peyton Manning.

Based just on what he saw of him in the spring workouts, Jim Mora was sold. "You're my starting quarterback, no matter what," he told him.[12] That put immediate pressure on Peyton. Mora, an ex-Marine, was very hard on all the players.[13] At 61, gaunt and crazy-eyed, the salt-and-pepper-haired former NFL tight end began his coaching career in the mid-'80s in the USFL, winning two titles in that upstart league's fleeting three-year existence. Mora then turned the Saints around, taking them to their first playoff appearance in '87. But he became legendary mainly for some all-time sports meltdowns, scolding sportswriters, calling fans "disgusting" and "shameful." He made the playoffs four times with the

Saints, winning the team's first division title but not a single playoff game, finally quitting midway through the '96 season after a profanity-filled tirade.

Mora did have sound ideas, and his players appreciated that he could foam at the mouth in defending them. The rub for Manning was that he was more of a ground-and-pound coach, and he brought with him from the Saints Tom Moore, who had coached in the NFL for two decades, as offensive coordinator. Bruce Arians, his quarterbacks coach, had overseen a big running game under head coach Mike DuBose at Alabama before that program was wrecked by recruiting violations. Peyton recalled hearing that Arians wasn't a passing coach, which he later said was "unfair" and "all wrong. It just goes to show what people think they know when they don't."[14]

The new Colts regime was committed to tailoring the team to Manning, drafting fleet receivers like Washington's Jerome Pathon and Florida State's E. G. Green. They already had a headliner in running back Marshall Faulk, who in his first four seasons cleared 1,000 yards thrice and had added value as a receiver. And best of all, there was Harrison, a sphinx of a man who did all his talking with his hands and feet. Slender and shifty, Harrison was an All-America running down Donovan McNabb's passes at Syracuse. Terribly shy but with a hunger for practicing the same minutely precise pass routes, he was clearly the kind of player Peyton longed for. At the minicamp, the veterans were impressed with Manning's command, his grasp of the system. Faulk raved, "He's picking up the offense so quickly. He's getting his reads, making quick decisions. He's not back there indecisive. . . . I'm expecting a lot from him."[15]

He had a lot to learn. The Rubik's Cube of plays, checkoffs at the line based on formations and keys, and down-and-distance probabilities in a typical NFL playbook made the Vol system seem like a *Sesame Street* lesson. Green, who held the Florida record with 29 touchdowns, said, "I'm really struggling with the plays. If I know what route to run, it's great. But I'm confused and I have to adjust to it."[16] And Peyton, appearances to the contrary, confessed, "My head is kind of swirling. I'm thinking about a whole lot of things. I probably am getting a little too impatient, trying to get my reads too fast. I didn't call the plays right a couple of times. I know I can do better."

When the Colts opened training camp in July, Manning still was unsigned, the team's offer $10 million less than Condon and Crosthwait were willing to accept. As uncomfortable as Peyton was that he was one of those guys he'd hated when he was a kid reading about player holdouts, Crosthwait said Peyton actually wanted to take the deal—prompting Archie to scold him, saying the first deal he signed would determine the value of all future ones.[17] That was the cold reality of sports capitalism. Nor were rookie holdouts anything new. In 1986, Marvin Demoff held out Rod Woodson, the Steelers' first-round pick, for 95 days, during which Woodson ran in track meets in Europe. In the end, he signed a four-year, $1.98 million contract, at the time the largest rookie deal in the team's history.

What's more, Ryan Leaf was also a holdout, as was the No. 3 pick, Florida State defensive end Andre Wadsworth, taken by the Arizona Cardinals. Unlike Manning, the latter two were leaving a trail of hard feelings with their teams, especially Leaf, who had flown to Las Vegas on Alex Spanos's private jet and partied into the night. During the negotiations, he said things like "I didn't leave college early so I could sit on the bench for a year." He missed the first six days of camp and was fined $10,000 for each day he was out. Then Steinberg raked in a deal for $31.25 million over five years with an $11.25 million signing bonus. The bonus and his $6.25 million salary set rookie records. When camp opened without Manning, Robin Miller, in the *Indianapolis Star*, reflected the front office's spin that Manning was at fault, since the team had "gone out of its way to promote a new spirit and a fresh start when its central character isn't on the payroll."[18] They had also made promotional deals based on him being there, one of them with Coca-Cola. Sticking up for the young QB, Joe Montana blamed the team, saying, "They've already put Peyton in a tough situation by making him the starter, so don't compound the problem and cost him valuable time" by pinching pennies.[19]

On Tuesday, July 28, after four days, they shook on the contract—six years, $38 million in base salary, an $8.4 million signing bonus (spread out over three years to lessen the tax burden), with incentive bonuses that could boost the total to $48 million. That worked out to 96 times Archie's then-record rookie deal, and it gave him bragging rights over Leaf by a slight margin, as well as the same salary as three-time MVP Brett Favre. Naturally, Peyton had a deft one-liner. "People ask me what I plan to do with my money. I plan to earn it," he said in a statement, passing up a press conference to hurry to camp at Anderson University in eastern Indiana.[20] Numbers like those would go a long way in establishing the new football order, and Condon would be the most rewarded. Manning "changed the landscape for me. I knew after that everything would be different."[21] By 2006, he would be named by *Sporting News* as the most powerful agent in sports; today, his client list of NFL players and coaches is arm-length, including Drew Brees, Matt Ryan, Tony Romo, Matthew Stafford, Sam Bradford . . . and Eli Manning.

Peyton arrived right on time. The top echelon of NFL quarterbacks was thinning out. John Elway was 38 and facing his final season— eventually retiring as MVP of the Super Bowl. A year later would be it for Steve Young and Dan Marino; two years later, Troy Aikman. Warren Moon was a 42-year-old backup. Favre, who won a Super Bowl in '96 having beaten a serious addiction to painkillers, was pushing 30, and while he would be given a 10-year, $100 million contract extension in 2001 and amass records, he would age fast and hard. Tom Brady, meanwhile, was a junior at Michigan, still battling Drew Henson for the starting job, two years from being a ho-hum sixth-round pick by the Patriots. The leftover QB crowd was a mélange of good but not great (Drew Bledsoe, Vinny Testaverde) and just not great (Scott Mitchell, Tony Banks, Todd Collins, Gus Frerotte, Elvis Grbac). It seemed like the field was being cleared for the next really great one, and the question remained: Manning or Leaf? A closer look would have revealed the answer immediately. While Leaf partied, Manning was launching a brand. When Leaf ended his holdout, he had ballooned to 260 flabby pounds and was grousing about the workload. Peyton was lean and hungry, burying his nose in homework. And the buzz around Colts was instant; as the *Star* put it, "Manning-Mania Hits Colts' Camp" and "Fans Flock for Brush with $48 Million Man."

Not that there weren't vipers lying in wait. During Peyton's holdout, he, Archie, and Olivia had dinner in New Orleans at Mosca's Restaurant, where Peyton was seen chugging beer. The next day in the paper, there was a giddy blurb about how, while his team labored in the heat, their first pick was knocking back cold ones. When he made his entry at camp, the *Star*'s Bill Benner wrote with a smirk, "Let the record show that Manning officially joined his teammates at 10:30 a.m. Wednesday, arriving not in a Brinks truck, a silver Rolls or even on a golden staircase from heaven."[22] Despite trying to tone down some natural instincts, Peyton couldn't hide his displeasure with pro-style showboating and laziness in practices, which he said was "worthy of an ass-chewing." Media observers referred to his "throwback brashness," not all of it sitting well. When he made known another of his pet peeves—how players from both sides fraternized after games on the turf they'd fought over, saying, "Just get the hell off the field. You just lost; what are you smiling about?"—the veterans laughed, knowing he would be expected to be the first one out there to congratulate or be congratulated by the opposing quarterback.[23]

Student of the game that he was, he knew the tides of history he was challenging; rookie quarterbacks were almost always duds, stuck as they were on bad teams. Of the 10 QBs among the top picks in the regular or supplemental draft during the 1990s, only Bledsoe had made the Pro Bowl. The eldest, Jeff George, had won neither a playoff game nor made All-Pro. But Manning seemed to stand apart from that sorry litany.

Getting into the role of a savior, he would work the rope line after practices, signing autographs, sweating in the sun. He fulfilled constant requests for interviews. On the field, he quickly adapted to Moore and Arians's mid-to-deep passing game, meshing with jumbo tight ends Ken Dilger and Marcus Pollard over the middle, something he'd rarely done with his tight ends at UT, and Harrison, a ticking time bomb on long throws. But the offensive line was patchwork, and he tried hard to forge a symbiosis by insisting that his locker be in the same block as theirs. He wasn't reluctant to admit, "I've put a lot of thought into being a leader."[24]

The preseason games offered the cynics more opportunity to prick him. Against the Seahawks in Seattle, his first pass soared into the hands of Marvin Harrison for a 48-yard touchdown. But after three more sloppy series—it didn't help that the telemetry system in his helmet carrying the plays from Moore upstairs shorted out—yielded a fumble and an interception and he came out trailing 24–7, the angle of the game story was, as one reported, "Manning looked like an ordinary NFL rookie," outshone by middling Seahawk QB Jon Kitna.[25] Moreover, Leaf did better in his debut, prompting the headline "Early QB Edge to Leaf," with the observation that "Manning looked more like a backup than the No. 1 draft pick," while Leaf "looked like he's ready to step right in."[26] That apparently went right to Leaf's head. He began dissing Manning openly, mocking "Perfect Peyton" and boasting that he was "more marketable than the Golden Boy on the endorsement end of things; I got personality."[27]

Originally, Mora thought rooming Manning with veteran quarterback Bill Musgrave would aid his education, but then he cut Musgrave, realizing that the best thing for Peyton was just to let him alone with his film and playbook. Manning moved into a room at the preppy Indianapolis Athletic Club on North Meridian Street, which he rarely left. When he did, he would flit over to the posh St. Elmo Steak House on South Illinois Street, a few blocks from the RCA Dome, and wolf down shrimp cocktails saturated with the house-special horseradish, and then talk with Archie on the phone, as he did each night. When Musgrave left, to be hired as the Carolina Panthers' quarterbacks coach, it was with the impression that Peyton was a rare superstar in waiting, in that "he comes across as being very mortal."[28] Polian was cautious about presenting him as a savior. The team hung murals outside the Dome pimping Faulk and defensive back Jason Belser, not Peyton. There was some grumbling when Peyton—who, like all quarterbacks, was not to be hit during practice—pushed for and got more full-contact scrimmage time for the offense, meaning contact for everyone else.[29]

More serious rumblings were coming from San Diego, where Leaf's bluster ate at his teammates—one of whom, All-Pro linebacker Junior

Seau, laid Leaf out during a scrimmage. One writer began a column by calling Leaf "the punk."[30] As if on cue, the Colts' third preseason game was against the Chargers, a match that filled the RCA Dome. Not that it mattered, but both were awful, though Leaf could massage his ego when the Chargers won 33–3, inspiring headlines like "Leaf Outshines Manning." Manning's final prep, against the Lions, was tantalizing; he threw two long touchdowns to Harrison.

Now the games were for real. One player from Archie's era remained in the NFL: 36-year-old journeyman quarterback Steve Bono. Meeting Peyton before a game, the Rams quarterback, like many with long memories, said, "Man, this makes me feel old."[31] Yet for Archie—who, with Eli, Olivia, and her parents, came to Indianapolis for the season opener against the Miami Dolphins—it must have seemed like only yesterday that he had thrown passes from the veranda to the son whose debut was the biggest story in the NFL.

═══

The late Sunday game, aired on national television, was a stern test. Jimmy Johnson, in his third season as the Dolphins' coach, had built a defense that would give up the fewest points in the league that year, and he smugly warned the kid he was in the big leagues now. Sold out for weeks, the game drew 60,587, the first opening-day sellout at the RCA Dome since 1989. Bettors, believing the hype, made the Colts only a three-point underdog. The *Star* headline on that morning read, "Colts Ready for New Journey." The fans, many of whom lined the downtown streets the day before for a parade for the team, were in full throat as the offense was introduced and the savior jogged out of the tunnel across the field. After the kickoff, the excitement crackling, he stuck his hands under center Jay Leeuwenburg, took the snap, dropped back three steps, and floated a soft pass to Faulk for a 15-yard gain. The fans had a shared thought: *Super Bowl, here we come.*

But it was a tease. The Dolphins fed Peyton a blizzard of defensive looks and blitzes. And while he hung in, the besieged offensive line crumbled, leaving him sacked four times and hurrying way too many passes, three of which were intercepted—all of which, it was reported, led Archie to "hang his head." The ugliest, from his own three with 1:32 left, was forced over the middle to Harrison, but was picked and run back for a touchdown. Not until the Colts were down 24–9 did he complete a drive, finding Harrison with a six-yard touchdown pass to close it out at 24–15. The stats weren't bad—21 of 37 for 302 yards—leading one *Star* writer to insist Manning was "impressive" and showed "considerable progress."[32] But even though Marino was a modest 13 of 24 for 135 yards, the consensus was that the veteran and future Hall of Famer had given him a lesson.

Sports Illustrated's Marty Burns wrote sympathetically of Peyton leaving the field, his jersey soaked with sweat and his eyes moist with tears: "[He] didn't seem to hear the cheers raining down on him from the stands, and he barely noticed when Colts coach Jim Mora gently patted him on the back as they walked together to the locker room. . . . After he had changed out of his uniform and into a pair of brown slacks and a white golf shirt, he met his father outside the Colts' locker room. Peyton wore a look of disappointment on his face, and it remained there even as Archie put an arm around his shoulder and they walked out of the building together."[33]

Burns noted accurately that he had "displayed poise, confidence and a passing touch seldom seen in a young quarterback." Marino agreed, saying, "He's going to be a good quarterback for a long time. He showed a lot of guts. He hung in there against a lot of pass rush in tough situations." And yet, Peyton looked back at the game with a wince. "I didn't realize how out of sync I was," he said. "Very seldom do I make a throw where the ball comes off my hand and I immediately think, 'Interception!' Most of the time I feel like I've made a good decision, and when something bad happens, it happens. But everything I did . . . was too fast. My footwork, my passing, even my demeanor."[34]

His rookie season was going to be a trial. The second game, against the Patriots in Foxborough, was a 29–6 defeat, with Peyton going 21 of 33 for only 188 yards, a late touchdown pass to Torrance Small, three more picks, and a fumble. Said Pats safety Willie Clay, "He's a rookie quarterback, and that's exactly how he played." The press was snarky—"If Peyton Manning wants to learn from his mistakes, he has plenty of material to cover," wrote one reporter.[35] Another posited that, in a league where quarterbacks were "falling like flies," Manning was Exhibit A in terms of "youngsters [being] thrown in too early and tak[ing] a beating,"[36] exactly what had been written about Archie.

Next came a 44–6 crushing by the Jets, which reportedly left Polian "furious," mainly at his sievelike defense.[37] Then there was a sentimental journey to play the Saints in New Orleans, his family and dozens of relatives in the stands. He seemed poised for his first win as a pro, a flare pass to Faulk breaking open for a 78-yard touchdown in the fourth quarter, putting the Colts up 13–6. But then Danny Wuerffel, again getting the best of him, threw a touchdown with the clock running out to tie it, and the Saints won in overtime with a field goal. The pattern was holding, as Peyton's 309 passing yards were nullified by three interceptions. Then, in a harbinger of things to come for both men, in the first official clash with Ryan Leaf, again in the Dome, he got some satisfaction. Leaf had played marginally better than him in the early weeks, but Peyton's 19-yard touchdown toss to Faulk set the mood. Neither he nor Leaf was impressive, but in a field goal–dominated affair, the Colts prevailed 17–12.

The season played out with more nice numbers but precious few victories, prompting the headline "Manning Growing, but, Oh, the Pain of Learning on Job."[38] The offensive line did begin to congeal along with him, the sacks trailing off—by season's end, he had gone down only 22 times—and he was becoming more nimble, dancing away from pressure. Accordingly, games became, well, *games*. There were close losses, one a 34–31 squeaker against the haughty 49ers in San Francisco, lost on a field goal with eight seconds left, and the Jets disaster was avenged when they met again. Down 23–10 after the Jets' Aaron Glenn returned a missed field goal 104 yards, Peyton hit Harrison with a 38-yard touchdown, then, with 30 seconds to go, Marcus Pollard from the 14 to eke it out, 24–23. However, the Buffalo Bills demolished them 34–11, followed by two more close defeats to the Ravens (despite 357 yards by Manning) and the Super Bowl–bound Falcons. In a 39–26 win over the Bengals, he went 17 of 26 for 210 yards and three touchdowns, breaking the NFL rookie record for TD passes—held for decades by none other than Chuckin' Charlie Conerly, an honor Peyton called "special." The season closed with two more close defeats, the last 27–19 to the Carolina Panthers after the Colts lost a double-digit lead for the fifth time over the season.

For all the excitement, hype, hyperbole, and money, the Colts' season ended as it had the year before: 3–13. The only quarterback in the league to take all of his team's snaps, Manning's numbers were nifty. He led the NFL in attempts, with 575, was second to Favre with 326 completions, third with 3,739 yards (the first Colts quarterback with 3,000 yards since Bert Jones in '81), fifth with 26 touchdowns—but first with 28 interceptions, his passer rating a tepid 71.2. On the plus side, almost every rookie passing record was now his, though all but the TDs (tied by Russell Wilson in 2012) would be bettered in the future by other rookies. Harrison, who missed the last four games with a shoulder injury, and Small each had seven receiving touchdowns. Mora, who deemed his quarterback's performance "pretty incredible," was smugger than a 3–13 coach had a right to be. But he had seen the future.

Senior Class

The family patriarch, Elisha "Buddy" Manning, shown here in the 1928 Drew High School yearbook (far right), departed from his ancestors by avoiding the Mississippi Delta cotton fields to sell farming equipment.

E.A. MANNING WITTIEST BOY

Buddy's wry sense of humor won him "Wittiest Boy" honors in his class. But as he aged, beset by health and financial distress, he grew despondent as his son, Archie, moved upward in big-time college football. In the summer of 1969, Archie would find Buddy's corpse after he had committed suicide in their home.

A 15-time letterman at Drew High, Archie poses proudly in the uniform of his favorite sport—baseball. But while he would be drafted by three big-league teams, his natural talent as a quarterback made King Football his path to fame and fortune. (Getty / Collegiate Images)

The Archie Manning that America would become familiar with: a baby-faced man-child in an Ole Miss uniform. (AP Photo)

Craggy-faced John Vaught was not only Archie's coach at Ole Miss but his surrogate father. Vaught allowed him remarkable latitude to carry the ball as well as pass it, and Archie would set nearly every quarterbacking record at the school—some of which would be broken by his son Eli. (Getty / Collegiate Images)

Despite the records and glory, Archie paid for his notoriety in pain. Often injured, sometimes getting out of a hospital bed to play, this shot of him grimacing as he flexed his damaged wrist was an all-too-common sight. (AP Photo / Jack Thornell)

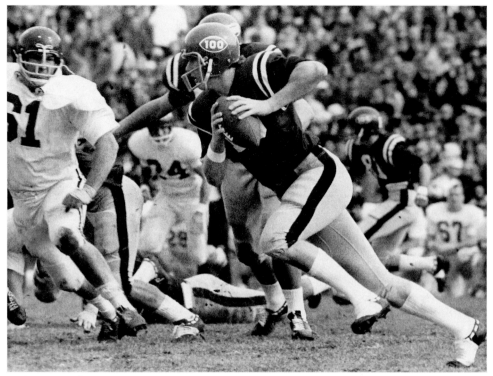

Archie was at his best at the 1970 Sugar Bowl, leading Ole Miss to an upset victory over No. 3–ranked Arkansas in what was to be the last bowl game between two all-white teams. (AP Photo)

Drafted by the New Orleans Saints with the second pick of the '71 draft, Archie would see the world this way—upside down on the way to the hard turf—for most of his decade-long tenure there. Here, during his rookie season, he is upended by the Atlanta Falcons. (AP Photo)

Having married former Ole Miss homecoming queen Olivia Williams, Archie set down roots in New Orleans's Garden District. Their antebellum-style home, surrounded by an iron gate, was where they would raise their three sons, Cooper, Peyton and Eli, and where Archie would throw them passes from the second floor. (Nikreates / Alamy Stock Photo)

All three sons would star at Newman High School, where their Green Wave uniforms are enshrined in a glass case in the athletic department. (AP Photo / Pat Semansky)

When the players' union went out on strike in the summer of 1974, Archie walked the picket line, earning the enmity of Saints owner John Mecom and further souring his relationship with the team. (AP Photo / Jim Bourdier)

Sacked 49 times in 1975, Archie had to constantly take off and get yardage on his own. Here, in a 1976 game, he eludes Rams tackle Mike Fanning and breaks into the open field. (AP Photo / NFL Photos)

Persistence paid off for Archie in 1978. After years of agony and defeat, he won the NFC Player of the Year award, earning him a trip to the Pro Bowl and a chance to bask among the quarterbacking elite before the game with Terry Bradshaw and Bob Griese. (AP Photo / Wally Fong)

Having been loyal to the Saints through losing and tumultuous changes, Archie was crushed when he was traded to the Houston Oilers at the start of the 1982 season. "It's kind of tough," he said at a press conference, biting his lip to keep from crying. (AP Photo)

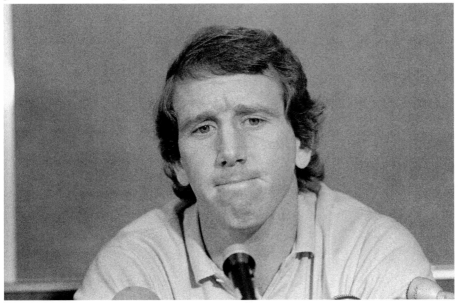

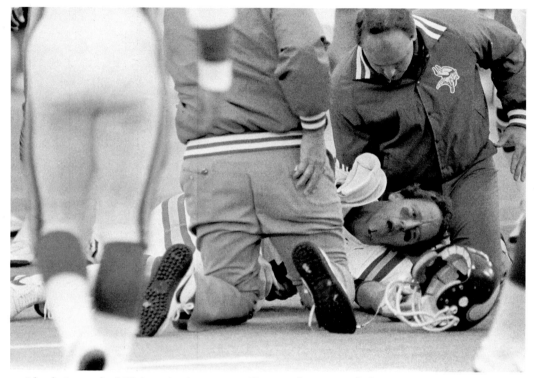

After being sacked 27 times in six games in Houston, he was traded again in 1983 to the once-haughty Minnesota Vikings—but with no relief. This shot of him writhing in pain after one of the 11 times he was sacked by the Chicago Bears captures the agony of his entire pro career. (AP Photo / Steve Green)

In this 1978 photo with his first two sons, Cooper (top) grabs Archie around the neck while Peyton glares into the camera as if thinking, "Who you lookin' at?"—a reticence he would soon learn to live with. (Getty/Bettman)

Though Archie tried to be a good father to his sons, and is seen here playing with a young Eli, it was Olivia who Eli identified with. He grew up insulated from his older brothers, but when he began playing football, he found himself. (Getty / Bill Frakes)

While it had to sting that Peyton chose to go to Tennessee rather than Ole Miss, a smiling Archie proudly leads his son through the corridor of Neyland Stadium after a Vols game in 1997. Like Archie, Peyton's college career would be filled with glory as well as big-game defeats. (AP Photo / Wade Payne)

Fame and success have rewards. Getting very used to both, in this shot following the Vols' victory over Ohio State in the 1996 Citrus Bowl, Peyton is congratulated by an affectionate Tennessee cheerleader. (AP Photo / Chris O'Meara, File)

In the shadows of Peyton's hype-filled college career, Eli was just beginning his own career at Newman High, coached by Frank Gendusa, who had been an assistant coach on the Green Wave when Peyton was throwing passes to Cooper. The youngest Manning's phlegmatic look and manner led Gendusa to call him "Easy Eli." (AP Photo / David Rae Morris)

Inevitably, the Indianapolis Colts made Peyton the first pick in the 1998 NFL draft. He is seen here coolly and confidently answering questions from the media as Archie, who had gone second in his draft, stands behind him with a beaming Olivia and Cooper. (AP Photo / Michael Conroy)

Making an immediate impact, Peyton set NFL records for first-year quarterbacks. (Reuters / Alamy Stock Photo)

Easy Eli turned his draft day upside down in 2004. He had declared that he would not play for the San Diego Chargers, who had the first pick. When they chose him, he reluctantly held up the team jersey, but waited hopefully as the Chargers negotiated a trade with the New York Giants. (Reuters / Alamy Stock Photo)

An hour later, when the trade was made, Eli and the family's mood brightened considerably as he draped himself in Giants gear, surrounded by his parents, his girlfriend, and Peyton and his wife. But as Archie knew, Eli was walking into "a hornet's nest." (Getty / Chris Trotman)

The first "Manning Bowl," when the brothers faced each other in a game, was the 2006 season opener at Giants Stadium. Though both played down the hype, for Peyton it was a matter of honor to beat his little brother, as he did all three times they met. Afterwards, he commiserated with a grim Eli on the field, ringed by cameras. (Getty / Travis Lindquist)

Always the good son, Peyton dutifully stands and waits as Archie makes a call from inside their cart during their stint at a celebrity golf tournament. For Archie, being the good father made fans discover him all over again. (AP Photo / Gerald Herbert)

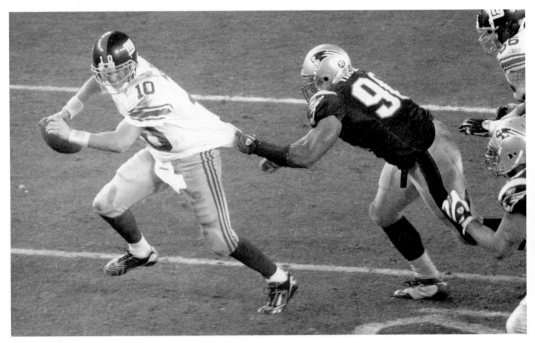

In perhaps the most celebrated and unlikely play ever made, Eli, trailing the undefeated Patriots late in Super Bowl XLII, somehow breaks the grip of Rashad Moore before squaring up and heaving a long pass down the field . . . (Francis Specker / Alamy Stock Photo)

. . . . where unheralded receiver David Tyree snares it by pressing the ball against his helmet as he grapples with Patriots defensive back Rodney Harrison. The "Helmet Catch" preceded Eli's game-winning pass to Plaxico Burress, earning Eli his first ring and a reputation as the top clutch quarterback in the league. (Reuters / Alamy Stock Photo)

Despite his two Super Bowl appearances and one championship, multiple surgeries forced Peyton to miss the 2011 season, leading Colts owner Jim Irsay to release him. At the announcement, an emotional Manning grimaced as Irsay praised him; then the quarterback eloquently thanked Colt fans for their years of support. (Reuters / Alamy Stock Photo)

Peyton's second NFL career began when he signed with the Denver Broncos. A key factor in his decision was his admiration for the jut-jawed John Elway, whose Hall of Fame career with the team preceded his role as general manager. Elway vowed that a Manning comeback would deliver a championship to Denver. (Reuters / Alamy Stock Photo)

Every pass an exercise in pain, Peyton still threw for a record 5,477 yards and 55 touchdowns with just 10 interceptions in 2013, winning his fifth MVP award and getting the Broncos to the Super Bowl. (Reuters / Alamy Stock Photo)

In 2015, breaking down to the point where he could barely feel the ball or move without buckling, Peyton missed the last six games, but returned for the playoffs. While the Broncos won mainly on defense, he made the plays he had to and beat his nemesis, Tom Brady, in the AFC title game, before winning his final game, Super Bowl 50. (Getty / Donald Miralle)

CHAPTER 15

"AN AMBIVALENT RELATIONSHIP WITH HIS IMAGE"

When Peyton was beaten out for the NFL Rookie of the Year award by Vikings receiver Randy Moss, it seemed to revive all the hedges about him that the Heisman voters had had: he was undeniably a star, but there was something about him that prevented him from being fully accepted. Peyton himself eschewed bravado, considering that, numbers aside, he had found himself for the first time unable to do anything about losing. Feeling like he needed some family comfort, he rode with Archie back to New Orleans in his Chevy Suburban, an 11-hour trek, talking the way they almost never did about coping with losing and the downside of stardom. They also went to see Tennessee win the national title in the Fiesta Bowl, and then took a two-week hunting trip. Peyton used his guest pass to take Cooper to the Super Bowl in Miami; at a league party, he looked around and there was Coop, apparently sloshed, dancing on a table.[1]

He was also getting tighter with the kid brother he used to brush by on his way out the door. Eli was preparing for his senior season at Newman High, and whenever Peyton got home, he would tutor him. As Eli recalled, "He'd tell me, 'This is what we're learning at Tennessee: On your three-step, make that second step real short and quick to get the ball out."[2] Back then, he listened to such tips only because he had to. Later, he knew he'd been given a million-dollar education.

Eli would decide where to go to college with far less fanfare and self-absorption than Peyton had, by doing what Peyton was *supposed* to do. But first came his senior season, in which he would be swathed in the building story of the second son of the local legend. One national wire story placed him among the top 10 schoolboy quarterbacks in the country, along with another family legatee, Chris Simms, son of Phil, the former Giants QB.[3] His yardage slipped to 2,381 but his touchdowns rose to 30, with just eight picks, during Newman's best-ever season, 11–1—which was marred, as usual, by a playoff loss, to Riverside. Said Frank Gendusa: "Eli got us to the quarters twice, and I take the blame for those games. It seemed we were always one play or one drive away, we just couldn't push it over the edge. Eli took it very hard."[4]

In truth, he didn't need to run up his stats or win a state crown that year. It was all just the run-up to his choice of college, although that decision was predetermined. Eli always believed he belonged at Ole Miss. He did go through the charade of narrowing it down to a handful of schools, but unlike Peyton, he often had no earthly idea who the coaches were or what their records were. Where Peyton strung recruiters along, when they called Eli he would simply tell them he wasn't interested—if he returned their calls at all. Archie and Peyton would warn him he had to call back, for appearances' sake. Eli would nod, then promptly ignore the advice. It was Archie who called back. Once, Eli referred to a "Coach Woodenhoffer," mispronouncing the name of Vanderbilt's Woody Widenhofer. Furious, Archie barked at him, "Eli, he's the head coach!" Eli merely shrugged. "I didn't see myself playing for Vanderbilt," he explained.[5] Maybe Eli did know a few things; Widenhofer, coming off 3–8 and 2–9 seasons, was a disaster both at Missouri and then at Vanderbilt.

For some reason, Eli agreed to visit the Austin campus of the University of Texas, where school officials fell all over him, Archie, and Olivia. During a tour of the stadium, the sound of Three Dog Night's "Eli's Coming" was pumped through loudspeakers. Longhorns coach Mack Brown had them over to his house for dinner. Ole Miss didn't need to suck up to him beyond sending a private jet to pick him up and take him to Oxford. By a not-so-curious coincidence, the Rebels' new head coach—after Archie turned down an offer—was David Cutcliffe, the man Peyton called his surrogate father. Yet Eli had already made up his mind months before that. He had not even bothered to discuss it with Archie and Olivia, assuming they had to know.

The day before he made it official, he told them his choice. Olivia asked him where he was going. "Oh. Ole Miss, of course," he said. Archie said of that moment, "He didn't have much to say. He felt good about what he did, but wasn't real excited. He was just Eli."[6] He was prohibited by rule to reveal this to the public until after the final game of the Greenies' season. Then, word went out to the papers and wire services. The *New York Times*' headline read, "Eli Manning Inherits the Reins at Ole Miss." Later that morning, at a hastily convened press conference at the athletic center, looking like he'd rather be anywhere else, he said, "I wanted to make my decision early, finish out my senior year and have fun." He felt he needed to add, "This really didn't have anything to do with my father playing at Ole Miss. That was over thirty years ago. The students on campus don't know what he did, either." That reality was quite remarkable, considering the Archie Who mythology and the streets named after him there. But to Gen X, all that was *meh*. Just to make sure all the bases were covered, he added, "I'm not comparing myself to Peyton, either. I can't really look at myself that way."

His words were Manning-like, clipped, though more ingenuous than Peyton's weighting of every syllable with care. Reporters left the room that day not knowing if he had it in him to lead a high-visibility team. And truth be told, neither did Archie. Still, Archie was satisfied that history had self-corrected. "It probably would have been tougher on Peyton at Ole Miss, because he is such a hard charger and attacks everything," he said. "Eli's got his mother's disposition. I don't know what his agenda is. I know he doesn't worry about a whole lot."

Peyton had spoken with his kid brother about the pitfalls ahead, warning that "there would be some attention to come his way and for him not to get involved with it."[7] Cutcliffe would help in that regard. With his wire-rimmed glasses and low-key manner, he was more professor and psychologist than fire-breathing coach. He also had every intention of redshirting Eli. Cutcliffe would not even venture a guess about when and whether he would even get in, as the incumbent Rebel quarterback,

Romaro Miller, was a junior. Whatever his fate, Eli seemed to know he had crossed a Rubicon of some kind. In his senior yearbook, under his blithe, Nietzschean deep thought, he wrote, as if he was going off to a gulag, "To Arch and Mom—Even though I never said much or showed any emotions, I love you and I'll miss you."[8]

In that same yearbook, Peyton had scribbled, "Watch out, world, Eli is the best one." And that spring, as Peyton was going through his drills at the Colts' minicamp, this writer jocularly asked him if, rather than Ryan Leaf, his real future competition would be his kid brother. Instead of chuckling, he pondered for a few seconds.

"That's a good question," he said.[9]

───

When Peyton got to the Colts' summer training camp in '99, the team had made big moves. One was a stunner—moving Marshall Faulk, their sole Pro Bowler. Mora figured he really needed a big back, a truck, who could pound it out but also block for Manning on passing plays. And Faulk, his contract up, was demanding more money—a lot more. When the word started circulating about the Colts coveting the University of Miami's all-purpose halfback Edgerrin James, Faulk wanted out. Polian accommodated him, trading him—cheaply—to the Rams for second- and fifth-round picks. The April draft then gave Polian the opening to land James, who set school records with fourteen 100-yard games and two straight 1,000-yard seasons, with the fourth pick. Most scouts preferred Ricky Williams of Texas, who had led the nation in rushing and set or tied 20 NCAA records, but Polian wondered about Williams's occasional lapses of judgment on and off the field.

Draft day came with Polian holding a high enough card to land James. This was going to be the mother of all quarterback drafts, the first three picks used to get QBs. Polian *really* could have cleaned up had he accepted a desperate offer pushed by Mike Ditka, now the coach of the Saints, to swap his No. 12 pick so he could draft Williams. Ditka dangled *six* Saints picks, plus the first two in the next draft. Had Polian agreed, he likely still would have been able to get James *and* have all those extra picks. Instead, not sure Ditka really was after Williams, he declined, and the Saints made a deal with the Washington Redskins for their No. 5 pick. Still, the Colts got their man, and so did the Rams. Faulk would help turn the Rams into the "Greatest Show on Turf," winning a ring that year along with the first of two MVP awards. For a time, Polian took heat even from his own staff for passing on Williams, more so when James held out, missing spring camp. When he eventually inked a seven-year, $49 million deal, he was slow to round into shape, leading one wag in the press to write: "They've got Peyton Manning and Ricky Williams. Oops, they passed on Ricky, didn't they?"[10]

Peyton entered his second season a little testy, perhaps haunted by losing as a rookie. He blamed all those interceptions on "a lot of tipped passes ... some bad decisions, and I guess the defensive backs made some good plays." When this writer asked a benign question about whether the blitzes and defensive fronts fooled him, he bridled.

"Are you looking for me to agree with you?" he said, glaring.

"About what? All I asked was if—"

"I don't know how much you know about the actual Xs and Os of the game. People who don't are always looking for you to say the right things, to give the NFL credit, to say how hard it is to play in this league. Sure, it's hard. But, really, once you play, you kind of get a feel for it."

Or at least he hoped so.

There was no question the team was his, for better or worse. But Polian did guess right. Ricky Williams would end up a mixed bag, traded after three years and several failed drug tests, and in and out of football for the next decade. Meanwhile, James was a gem. Polian also bolstered the defense, signing veteran linebacker Cornelius Bennett and safety Chad Cota. Manning tried to establish an egalitarian mind-set. He demanded no special favors. Even in the weight room, he said, "I don't believe in having a separate workout for quarterbacks. Other players hate that." During practices, he volunteered to play on the kickoff-coverage squad, because the "defensive tackle who has been going hard on every rep sure does appreciate the breather."[11]

In the Colts' season opener against Buffalo, he was comfy enough to crack up the huddle, calling a play by doing a dead-on imitation of Jeff Spicoli, Sean Penn's stoner character from *Fast Times at Ridgemont High.*

He threw for 284 yards that day with two touchdowns to Harrison—who, with E. G. Green, had more than 100 yards, just the third time in team history that two receivers gained that many. James ran for 112 yards and a touchdown, catching four passes. The next game, in Foxborough, Manning hit Harrison with two touchdowns in the first quarter, another to James in the second. The Colts led 28–7 at the half, and then bent when Drew Bledsoe heaved three of his four touchdowns, followed by a field goal with 35 seconds left that won it for the Pats, 31–28. As maddening as the loss was, it proved what the Colts could be. Then they beat the Chargers, *sans* the injured Leaf, with Peyton throwing for 404 yards.

They folded again late against the Dolphins, but then Manning went off on one of his Vol-like streaks. He beat the Cowboys, Jets, Bengals, Giants, and Eagles, the Colts racking up 455 yards in the last. Most games were well balanced between pass and run; only once during the season would he go over 300 passing yards. The defense would allow more than 20 points only four times, over 30 just once.

Week by week, Peyton became more rarefied. *Sports Illustrated* did its first piece on him as a pro in late November. Titled "Thoroughbred," its writer, Ivan Maisel, judged him to be "as comfortable on the field as any passer with his limited experience has been in at least a decade, perhaps since Dan Marino blew into Miami in 1983. He is a burgeoning superstar who's at ease speaking in front of 10,000 people or singing before five times that many country-music fans." Maisel presented him as a man playing not only against opponents but also his own legacy, with "an ambivalent relationship with his image: It both comforts and annoys him, clearly beating the alternative—would he rather be Leaf?—while sometimes making his actions appear contrived." Peyton, as always pitch-perfect, said, "I see myself as very normal. Growing up in New Orleans as Archie Manning's son, I felt like a target, and I've always known that whatever I'd do, people would hear about it. So I've had my guard up, and maybe that's molded my personality. But if there's something I want to do, I'm going to do it."

Ashley Thompson, still working in Knoxville, now in land development, added, "He's a very genuine and real person, but not everyone sees that. Even if he wasn't a big star with a famous father, he'd still hold back in public because that's his personality. He knows what he wants, and he has a passion for it. Football makes him happy." And if he couldn't bring himself to use the word *love* about her, he tried for some poetry: "She can flow through all the madness, and she's bright and funny. I probably like her so much because she's like my mom, thoughtful and caring." Still, he admitted, "At times I do get lonely. A lot of my buddies are married, and I get tired of being the third wheel. One reason I put in so much work at the facility is that I have nothing to go home to. That's by design."[12]

———

But then, what about him wasn't? He had already filmed his first TV commercial for Gatorade, with Michael Jordan and Mia Hamm, his status as a winner abetted by the fact that Ryan Leaf wasn't. Leaf had only played in 10 games the year before, with two touchdowns and 15 interceptions, before being benched. Heckled by fans, he nearly attacked a reporter in the locker room.[13] He missed this season with a shoulder injury, and then he'd be released, fail with two other teams, and in retirement be jailed on drug and burglary charges,[14] dubbed "the biggest bust in the history of professional sports."[15] Trying not to gloat, Peyton's take on Leaf was: "There's a lot of pressure in a situation like ours. You'll lose it without the right frame of mind and preparation."[16]

By contrast, the "Perfect Peyton" script was in full bloom, complete with the little quirks the public loves to read about pampered superstars. This one, wrote Maisel, had "charming clumsiness. . . . There's something disarming about a multimillionaire innocently hanging up jeans in his locker with PEYTON printed in indelible ink on the inside of the waistband." An old friend described Peyton as "too easy to make fun of. He's mature beyond his years as a public figure, and he has an amazing grasp of what to do on the field, but he can't do anything else on his own. He's always going to be the guy who steps in dog poop, and every time he eats a sandwich or a hamburger, he'll end up with ketchup down his leg, mustard on his ear. He's a terrible driver, and he can't sing, though he thinks he can." For good measure, Cooper told of the time Olivia visited Peyton's apartment and saw him "turning his underwear inside out so he wouldn't have to use the washing machine. A couple of weeks ago he called my wife and asked her how to heat up soup." Ashley also reported that when he didn't know how to order Chinese food, she did it for him—from Knoxville.[17]

An article years later by Robert O'Connell in the *Atlantic* recalled him in his early pro years as a "gangly" guy seemingly playing "in borrowed, ill-fitting pads" with "a massive forehead that featured a real pressure-induced spot whenever he removed his helmet and revealed his Tintin-like haircut," who "moved about the pocket as if stepping barefoot on summertime blacktop," whose "throwing motion looked overstudied, even a touch robotic." Other descriptive phrases were "inelegant bodily style" and "stiff and awkward shambling."[18] And yet, even in this context, he was a rising paradigm of a new age of cerebral quarterbacking—the same article noting that his "mental diligence replac[ed] physical toughness as the defining characteristic" of the football culture. Of course, that was an oversimplification; no one took a hit better, got up to face more punishment quicker, or hated coming out any more than Peyton Manning.

In midseason, on consecutive weeks, the Colts swept the season series with the Jets, then subdued the Dolphins on a winning field goal at the gun after Miami tied it with 36 seconds left. They reeled off 11 straight wins and clinched a playoff berth, a loss to the Bills on the last Sunday bringing their record to 13–3—a perfect reversal of the year before, the largest turnaround in NFL history and the first season of double-digit wins for the Colts since '77. Winning the AFC East by two games over Buffalo, one win off Jacksonville's league-best record, they sent Peyton, Harrison, and James to the Pro Bowl. James had a league-best 1,553 rushing yards, Harrison the most receiving yards, with 1,663. Peyton threw for 4,135 yards with a 90.7 rating—behind only Steve Beuerlein and Kurt Warner in both categories—had 26 touchdowns, 15 interceptions, and a mere 14 sacks. The Colts offense was ranked third, the defense fourth. The reward was a first-round playoff date two weeks after the turn of the new millennium, at the RCA Dome against the Tennessee Titans, who also went 13–3 but made the playoffs as a wild card.

This was a pungent irony for Peyton, as a good many fans coming in from Tennessee were Vol alumni and fans. The Titans were a conservative unit. Coach Jeff Fisher and his offensive coordinator—none other than Les Steckel, Archie's old foil in Minnesota—didn't ask much from quarterback Steve McNair. Fullback Eddie George carried the load. The defense had rough customers, like ferocious rookie All-Pro end Jevon Kearse. The Colts were favored by 5½ points, and some of the talking heads on the pregame shows talked them up—one, former quarterback Boomer Esiason, saying he liked the Colts' chances to go to the Super Bowl.[19] Few figured the Titans could rope Indianapolis into a defensive battle, but that's what happened. The first touchdown came in the third quarter, when George—who rushed for 162 yards—broke through for a 68-yard touchdown jaunt, putting the Titans up 13–9. Harrison was double-teamed, and Peyton, under duress, cracked. He went only 19 of 42, for 227 yards, and James did little, with 56 yards on 20 carries. The Titans took a 19–9 lead with four minutes to go. Then Peyton dropped back from the Titan 15, saw a gap, and ran it in with just under two minutes left. But it ended there, at 19–16. "Colts Dream Season Falls Incomplete" was the headline in the *Star*.

The Titans moved on to the Super Bowl, where they lost to Faulk's Rams. For the Colts, there were bigger problems than the ones exploited by the Titans. Before the game, it was reported that four players had been convicted of assaulting women, prompting vows by the team to "address off-field abuse,"[20] which they never really did. And the Manning training room escapade was soon to break open again. Yet overall, the season was an enormous success, propelling Peyton to a close second-place finish behind Warner as the league's MVP. The implications were clear: the Colts, led by their shiny young quarterback, were a new power. And if the Manning brand wasn't bullish enough, there was another one just like him down in Dixie, biding his time.

CHAPTER 16

ELI'S COMING

Upon Eli's arrival at Ole Miss in the spring of 1999, retracing steps Archie had taken three decades before, the sacred rites of Saturday afternoons in Colonel Reb country were less racially tinged but still pungent. The pregame walk through the Grove, down paths named for Archie Manning, was still lined with tailgaters and magnolias, and the marching bands inside Vaught-Hemingway Stadium played the same old songs. But the fact that, a year later, a Republican governor from Texas would run for the presidency as a "compassionate conservative" was a telltale sign that it was no longer quaint to cherish Jim Crow. At Ole Miss, the rebel flag and Colonel Reb himself were banned from the pregame pageantry after a student body vote in 1997. The same year, the school—by now attended by students from 73 countries and all 50 states, 12½ percent of them black[1]—was granted a Phi Beta Kappa chapter. No one had to defend that the biggest football and basketball recruits were black men from points far beyond the state.

Young Southern white men like Eli had no investment in representing that heritage, more into white rap than white nationalism. To them, the South was about family, not historical grievances with the North. Archie himself had engendered a subtle change in that culture; Ole Miss, a history professor at the school said, was "a mean and ugly place and then Archie came along. He was Mississippi's own Tom Sawyer and he gave us all something to cheer."[2] Now Eli would lengthen the delayed family chain at Ole Miss, on his back the same number, 10, that Cooper had worn for those precious weeks before fate did him dirt. Eli launched himself into his marketing studies, making the Chancellor's Honor Roll and the Dean's Honor Roll twice each, and the SEC Academic Honor Roll every year. As for football, for now it receded as, to Archie's relief, he wore the red shirt. David Cutcliffe's quarterback, Romaro Miller, was important to the school, a black man leading onto the field a team called the Rebels. In '99, he would throw for 2,201 yards and 16 touchdowns, taking Ole Miss to an 8–4 record, finishing with a win over Oklahoma in the Independence Bowl. Not much was heard by or about the Manning boy, though just being who he was might land him in a headline somewhere, even if not the kind he was supposed to make.

On January 31, 2000, tanked up on beer, he stumbled out of his dorm and began puking on the street and causing a disturbance. Cops were called, took him in, and charged him with public intoxication. No real punishment was deemed necessary beyond the embarrassment he caused himself and his family when headlines like "QB Manning Arrested" began hitting the papers that week. Worse, someone took a picture of him in the dorm before the puking, cuddled with a blonde coed, bottle in his hand, eyes rolling, mouth in a salivating half grin. It made its way onto the internet, where it has proliferated since.[3] Humiliated, he called Archie with a tearful apology. Cutcliffe summoned him to his office. "I asked him if he really wanted to be a big-time quarterback, or was he just here to play a little football, have a good time and get through," Cutcliffe said. "And I told him to think about it before he answered."[4]

He did buckle down, studied film, hit the weight room, and waited his turn without further incident as the Rebels began their '99 camp, Eli's first as an active player. Cutcliffe watched him look more and more like Peyton, making all the right throws, the right decisions in practice. In one intrasquad scrimmage, he beat Miller and the first team, driving his side 70 yards to a late victory. And that first team was loaded. Senior fullback Deuce McAllister rumbled for over 700 yards rushing and 14 touchdowns that season, breaking every Ole Miss rushing record. But the

Rebels were in and out. Ranked in the top 20 in the preseason polls, they finished at 7–4. Eli got into six games, mostly mopping up, completing 16 of 33 passes for 170 yards. In the finale, the Music City Bowl, they lost to West Virginia 49–16. Late in the game, he grabbed his mop again. But this time he turned heads, throwing three touchdowns, making a 49–38 loss into a minor headline for him and providing a taste of what would begin in earnest the next season, as he stood in the shoes of Archie Who.

In the heartland, Peyton faced the millennium hoping his time had come as a title winner. The Colts entered the 2000 season as favorites in the AFC East. However, after 13 games they were no better than 7–6. They did win their last three, over the Bills, Dolphins, and Vikings, to just scrape into the playoffs as a wild card. It was Peyton who got them there. He passed for a league-high 4,413 yards and 357 completions, sharing the lead with 33 touchdowns, and had just 15 interceptions, his passer rating 94.7. James, an invaluable asset, led the league with 1,709 yards rushing, with 13 touchdowns, and would rack up more yards in his first two seasons than anyone ever had except Eric Dickerson. But Marshall Faulk won the Offensive MVP award, leading *Sports Illustrated* to say James was "getting hustled," as some sort of residual effect of his holdout, something that had never affected Manning.[5] The Big Three—Manning, James, Harrison—were All-Pro selections.

In the playoff game, the Dolphins relied on the run, amassing 258 yards on the ground. That let them control the clock and keep Manning off the field, limiting him to 194 yards, though he did hit Jerome Pathon with a 17-yard touchdown pass to go up 14–0 in the third quarter, and the Colts led 17–10 with under five minutes left. But the defense failed to stop Jay Fiedler, and Miami came back to send the game to overtime. Then Lamar Smith, who gained 209 yards that day—second most in playoff history—took a handoff on the Colts 17, broke free, and carried defensive back Jeff Burris on his back like a mule as he crossed the goal line. With cause, Peyton said afterward, "Everybody is just frustrated," blaming "missed opportunities."

Hours later, word came that Jane Nelson "Sis" Manning had died quietly at 81 in the same house where she had raised Archie and where she kept his room tidy and lined with his old trophies. Days before, as if knowing the end was near, she had written a letter to a friend in which the lifelong resident of the town said, "Drew has been good to me," and that she had spent "the happiest part of my life here."[6] Archie and his boys and the rest of her surviving family came home to lay her to rest in Drew Cemetery, next to Buddy, where a grave had been saved for her. Both their names were engraved on the same shale blue headstone marking the plot. Pam Manning, who had gotten a degree from Mississippi State, soon moved with her husband to Oxford, where she could watch Eli channel her father. The family would assemble again a few months later when Peyton finally asked Ashley Thompson to marry him. They did, on March 27, 2001, in New Orleans, after which he bought an abandoned home to renovate on a large plot of land in Indianapolis, and another in the Garden District, though she still did business in Knoxville. They were a neomodern professional couple, the woman not giving up her career for a husband. A sure sign that the South, as Buddy, Sis, and Archie knew it, would not rise again. And good riddance.

———

Another sign was that, at Ole Miss, a black quarterback had broken almost all of Archie's records, throwing for 6,311 yards and 43 touchdowns. Now, with Romaro Miller gone to the pros, Eli Manning moved to the fore, amid headlines like "Another Manning Era Begins at Ole Miss."[7] Little used as he was as a freshman, he nonetheless was already a BMOC. He was given new digs off campus in the social and cultural hub of Oxford, the South Lamar Avenue town square, marked by the magnificent pillars and snow-white walls of the Lafayette County Courthouse, which was razed by the Union army, then resurrected and declared a historic monument in 1977, its clock tower looming over a statue of an unknown rebel soldier. Faulkner wrote *The Sound and the Fury* in an office in the square, a title that might be an epitaph of the Manning family.

Not that Eli had produced much of either yet, or believed he was about to. Coming out of high school, he recalled, "I was unsure of myself. . . . I had doubts because of all the things that Peyton had accomplished. I didn't think I was as good as him."[8] Being blindly named to the 2001 preseason All-SEC team meant little. It did help that his first game as the new Rebel rouser was, fortuitously, against a cream puff, Murray State, at home, all the pregame trappings surrounding him. Cutcliffe had made it easier for him, with a swarming defense and returning tailback Joe Gunn. He also put on the team Chris Collins, a champion sprinter who would now be catching Eli's passes—including his first touchdown, of 17 yards, with 5:57 to go in the first quarter. His second also went to Collins, for 21 yards. Eli went on to set a school record, completing 18 passes in a row. After three quarters, *his* mop-up man came in for a final score of 49–14.

Eli's numbers made one gulp: 20 of 23 passes complete, 271 yards, five touchdowns. Archie could relate, but to see this in his boy's first start must have been something almost psychedelic. People came away from Vaught-Hemingway humming Eli's name. And Cutcliffe, who had been cautiously saying that Eli and Peyton's paths would be "very different," had instead seen their paths merge. Of course, Eli had lots more to prove. The next game was his SEC debut as a starter, against Auburn on the road. He was harassed and hurried; 11 times he threw a pass out of bounds or in the dirt, another to the other team. By halftime he had hit on just 6 of 10 for 39 yards, never moving beyond his own 42-yard line. "The crowd noise made it hard to communicate with my receivers at first," he said later, "and the Auburn defense was sitting on all of our curls." After that, he got on track, but it ended 27–21, Auburn. Archie, who was there, was philosophical. "Eli got a little banged up today," he said. "Last week was rosy, this week wasn't. You learn from both."

All of which became speck-of-dust insignificant three days later— September 11, 2001—when the Twin Towers came down and lay in smoking ruin. In the aftermath of those terrible hours, no one would feel like playing games that week, and the NCAA, like the NFL and Major League Baseball, postponed its next round of games, one of which would have pitted Ole Miss against Vanderbilt. During that week of grief and mourning, and the next, with the Rebels on a bye, the Mannings spoke for hours on the phone to each other, dealing with the common feeling of helplessness by retrenching to the comfort of family. When Eli was back on the field, he tamed the Kentucky Wildcats 42–31, then pulled off another two-TD performance in a 35–17 blowout of Arkansas State. These were walkovers, but not the next, against Alabama, whom the Rebels hadn't beaten since 1988. Stymied most of the game, down 24–14 in the fourth quarter, Eli directed a long drive capped when Charles Stackhouse ran it in. Then, from the Tide 38, with under two minutes left, he moved to the three with 46 seconds left. He rolled out, drew defenders toward him, spotted Gunn open in the end zone, and tossed the winning score.

His spectacular game, 325 yards and eight completions to Collins for 110 yards, moved the *New York Times*'s Joe Drape to breathless prose: "From the juke joints of the Delta to the feed stores of northern Mississippi, he is called Archie's boy, a son of one of sports' most famous Sons of the South. In Tuscaloosa, Ala., in Knoxville, Tenn., and in every other castle in the Southeastern Conference football kingdom, he is Peyton's brother. . . . Last Saturday, Eli Manning followed his father into Ole Miss lore [and] looked a lot like his older brother Peyton . . . coolly slinging passes over and between Crimson Tide defenders on that final drive. [He then] hugged his parents, did not want to talk much about the game and attended to his friends and the guests of his parents. Later, he put on a pair of boots and a cowboy hat to attend a country western concert."[9]

After two more blowouts, against Middle Tennessee State and LSU, the Rebels were a Cinderella at 6–1. Next came 4–3 Arkansas, at home. A tight contest, it was tied at 17 in the fourth quarter. The Razorbacks went up by a touchdown, then Eli took the Rebels 72 yards, hitting Jason Armstead from the three with 4:50 left to tie it. The game went into overtime . . . and then some. It was still tied after one OT, then another, and still another. After the third OT, NCAA rules prohibited any single-point touchdown conversions, and neither team could score the required two points after six straight touchdowns, whereupon the game went to a sixth OT. No one dared leave what had become a national curiosity, with people all across the country tuning in to the game on ESPN.

Wearily, the players trudged out again, and Eli threw touchdown number five, 12 yards to Doug Zeigler. This time, the Rebels made the two-pointer to go up 50–42. But the 'Backs scored from the two and they too made the two-pointer—sending it to OT No. 7, which was unprecedented. Now Arkansas scored first. Down to another last shot to tie and move on to perhaps an *eighth* overtime, Eli guided the Rebels on a nine-play drive and tossed a three-yard pass to Armstead. Needing to make the two-pointer, he floated one out to Ziegler, but the 'Backs pulled him down on the two to end the wild, near five-hour marathon at 10:20 p.m. The stats of the 58–56 spectacle were appropriately outrageous. With a 106–92 edge in plays, Arkansas ran 80 times for 271 yards, two players going over 100. Eli went 27 of 42 for 312 yards, six touchdowns, and zero interceptions. Amazingly, there were only eight penalties, and the teams made all five fourth-down conversion plays.

Eli won more praise in defeat, something Archie—who watched the agonizing game, seeing his son beat his old Ole Miss single-game touch-down record—could surely relate to. Normally, he had no such agita at Eli's games. "Archie told me that he doesn't get nervous when Eli is quarterback because Eli is so relaxed," said a family friend, Pat Browne Jr., a champion blind golfer. "Peyton is very intense and Archie feels that."[10] But he and Eli knew the defeat was costly. The next match was against No. 23 Georgia, and the Rebels were trampled, 35–15. Then came Mississippi State and a 36–28 loss. The finale, a 38–27 win over Vanderbilt, only made the 7–4 season a touch more respectable. For Eli, however, there was no real downside. In his first year as a starter, he had completed 63.5 percent, racked up 2,948 yards, and thrown for 31 touchdowns with only nine picks, good for a 144.8 rating. Not enough to push him past guys like David Carr, Rex Grossman, Luke McCown, and Heisman winner Eric Crouch, but well into the big boy quarterback club.

─────────

Up in Indianapolis, meanwhile, the 2001 season was again frustrating for the older Manning sibling, and signs of strain were beginning to show. Jim Mora, now 66 with a postseason record of 0–6, had lost his rosy glow. He'd gotten snappish about Manning ever since he was late for a team meeting the year before, when a TV interview ran long. Once again, Peyton found himself "having words," as he recalled it, with a coach, whom he blamed for scheduling the practice at the last minute.

"Dammit, Coach," he yelled, "if we're gonna play in big games around here, I think we should go about it without changing everything."[11]

But if there was an increasing tension between them, it was overshadowed by Edgerrin James's more overt problems with the team. When spring camp began, James, feeling underappreciated, was a no-show; then, in the summer, he feuded with Mora about the need to even come to practices. Six games into the season, leading the league in rushing, he tore up his knee and was done for the year. By then, the season was pretty much done as well. Arians had left to become offensive coordinator of the Cleveland Browns, and Peyton, who on Arians's advice took to wearing a knee brace for protection, clearly missed him. The Colts started unevenly—one of their early games, against the Patriots on September 30, marked the first start of Tom Brady's career, after Drew Bledsoe had gone down the previous week. Before this game, Peyton encountered the gawky-looking Brady during warm-ups. "Hi, Tom," he said pleasantly. "I'm Peyton."[12]

Manning outpassed him that day, 196–168, but threw three interceptions, two taken back for touchdowns. The Pats romped to a 44–13 win. Three weeks later, in the return match, Peyton rang up more yards again, 335–202, but Brady threw three touchdowns and the Pats swept the series with a 38–17 rout, two games that helped send the Pats to their first championship season under Bill Belichick. In midseason, the Colts stood at 4–3, then went on to lose the next five and seven of eight, thrice giving up 40 points or more. After one of those, a 40–21 clinker against the 49ers in which Peyton threw four ugly interceptions, one returned for a touchdown, Mora had another of his memorable postgame snits. Asked whether the team could make the playoffs, he contorted his face and hissed, "*Playoffs?! Don't talk about—playoffs? You kidding me? Playoffs?!* I just hope we can win a game!" He got his wish: they won the last game to finish 6–10, buried in fourth place in the division.

Not culpable for any of this, Peyton had passed for over 4,000 yards—second to Warner, who won his second MVP—but with just three fewer interceptions, 23, than touchdowns, a good reason why he received no MVP votes. He did make Harrison an All-Pro by feeding him 109 passes and 15 touchdowns. But with the Colts wobbly, Jim Irsay let Mora go. The new man was slender, erudite Tony Dungy, who as coach of the Tampa Bay Buccaneers had lifted that doormat team into the playoffs four times in six years, mainly on the backs of his defenses. This was why Irsay wanted him, but the risk was that Dungy, a former defensive back and longtime defensive assistant, had little expertise about offense. That was why the Bucs fired him after the 2001 season and hired Jon Gruden, who juiced it up and took the team to a championship the next year.

Dungy, an almost inanimate evangelical Christian, as muted as Mora was manic, believed that as a black man he was not only a victim of racism on the street (he had once been hauled to jail in Kansas for not signaling a lane change), but in NFL front offices as well. He expressed uncompromising anger at the prejudice that he believed had kept teams from hiring him for so long. Sometimes, he said, he'd be asked in job interviews if he planned to hire black assistants.[13] The Colts gig was a no-brainer for him. After eight seasons squeezing all he could from Mark Brunell, he now had a chance to coach the best quarterback in football. Dungy retained Tom Moore as offensive coordinator and would leave the Colts attack to him. He also brought his quarterbacks coach in Tampa, Jim Caldwell, who had been the first African-American head coach in the Atlantic Coast Conference, with Wake Forest. But it would be up to the serene, Zen-like Dungy to calm and motivate a team full of fraying nerves.

─────

In the spring of 2002, with Ole Miss having sunk millions into expanding Vaught-Hemingway Stadium, Eli had certainly cleaned up his act. There were no further drunken episodes, and he had found a girl. She was a sophomore, Abby McGrew, a native of Nashville who, like the other Manning women, was beautiful in an elegant, manicured way. Whatever it was about these smart and centered women, the Manning men were instantly hooked. Eli was ready to tell his family he had met his future wife, and that when the time came for a wedding, he would let them—and Abby—know. Until then, as Peyton had done with Ashley, he would string her along as he made the same climb upward on the football stairway to heaven.

The '02 Rebels started 5–1, reaching a milestone in a tight win against Vanderbilt in which Eli rang up a personal-best 368 yards passing—and his record fourth 300-yard game, putting him one ahead of Archie. He also did what Peyton never could, beating Florida, now coached by Steve Spurrier's former assistant Ron Zook. The Gators were ranked No. 6 at the time, and it was the first time since '97 the Rebels had beaten a top-10 team, putting Ole Miss in the top 25. They then moved up to No. 21 by razing Arkansas State 52–17.

But the fun ended there. They lost their next three, to Alabama, Arkansas, and Auburn at home. There would be two more defeats—to a pair of ranked teams, SEC champion Georgia and LSU—with two more Manning interceptions in each, before the bleeding stopped. The season was partially salvaged by wins over Mississippi State and Nebraska—the latter by a 27–23 score in the Independence Bowl, Eli copping the game's MVP award by going 32 of 52 for 313 yards. At 7–6, the Rebels had fallen from contenders to also-rans, and Cutcliffe's job security was suddenly in question. Eli's stock dipped too after he threw 10 fewer TDs and six more picks. Cooper didn't pull his punches, saying of his brother, "I don't think Eli has tapped his full potential. . . . The last couple of years on offense Eli has panicked because he felt if he didn't put up a lot of points, he was letting the team down. . . . [W]hen people say, 'I think Eli's going to be the best [of the Mannings],' they're full of it. He might end up being great, but I don't see how you can be better than Peyton."[14]

But that presumed Peyton would reach *his* ultimate potential in Indianapolis. It still seemed a good bet. The Colts' first-round draft choice in 2002, All-American defensive end Dwight Freeney, a 270-pound monster out of Syracuse, would set a rookie record, forcing nine fumbles. On the other hand, Edgerrin James was back, but not at peak level; he would gain 989 yards rushing, but with only two touchdowns. As for Manning, he was already deep into a streak of starting every game as a pro, one despite a broken jaw. The Colts won four of their first five games, then lost three straight. But he pulled them up again, beating the favored Eagles 35–13 with a 319-yard, three-touchdown game—two to Harrison, one to Reggie Wayne. They would win six of their last eight, Manning's apogee a 417-yard passing show, including two touchdowns to Harrison, in a 28–23 victory over the Browns.

At 10–6, a game behind the Titans in the newly realigned AFC South, they clinched a wild-card playoff spot and were six-point favorites against the Jets in the first playoff round—and were promptly run off their own field. The Jets led 24–0 at the half and cruised to a 41–0 stunner. The Jets quarterback, Chad Pennington, threw three touchdowns. The Colts, managing just 10 first downs, were outgained 396 yards to 176 by a team blown away the next week by the Raiders. James gained 14 yards on nine carries. And Manning lost his cool. He forced 31 passes, completing 14, putting two in the hands of Jets defenders. He had wasted one more fine season, having thrown for 4,200 yards, 27 touchdowns—one behind the leader, Tom Brady—a manageable 19 interceptions, and completing 66.3 percent. He had five game-winning drives and his rating was 88.8. He was 27 now, moving to the top of his craft, keeping pace with Brady, who had already won a ring. Brady, a natural cover boy, seemed just a bit cooler and more than a bit better in the big games. But both were awesome enough that it seemed as if the next decade and a half already had its two main protagonists, and a theme: Brady versus Manning.

CHAPTER 17

MR. INHUMAN

The awkwardly structured dual memoir of Archie and Peyton, published in 2001, was a mostly harmless ego exercise. But it did have a sprinkling of candid personal takes, one of which was Peyton betraying a lingering grudge against Jamie Whited. Just addressing the little-noticed "mooning" episode meant that he was flouting the gag order attached to the 1997 settlement agreement between Whited and the University of Tennessee. Apparently, he, and the lawyers who vetted the manuscript for HarperCollins, believed he was on safe ground by admitting he had acted in an "inappropriate" manner, and that Whited should have nonetheless "shrugged it off as harmless." Bizarrely, he added that had Cooper done the same thing, his gift for joking would have made it all benign, never mind the crudeness of the act. (Ironically, Eli, a sometime prankster, *did* moon someone in college—his backup quarterback, David Morris, whom he then spanked while singing, "How you like me now?!")[1] More bizarrely, Peyton could not stop fulminating about women in men's locker rooms and about Whited, whom he tarred for having a "vulgar mouth" and for not appreciating how much he "went out of my way" to "be nice to her."[2]

If the lawyers didn't know of the gag order in force, Jamie Whited knew. Now divorced and using her maiden name of Naughright, she was working as an assistant professor at Florida Southern College and suffered more indignity when the school fired her after the book was published, for bad publicity—the second time, as she saw it, that Manning had cost her a job. She then filed a defamation suit in Polk County Circuit Court in Florida, naming as co-defendants Archie, Peydirt Inc., ghost-writer John Underwood, and HarperCollins, for portraying her as "an overly sensitive, predatory woman looking for incidents to bolster a lawsuit against her employer." The Manning camp, trying to gain sympathy for him, released a letter written in December 2002 from Malcolm Saxon, the track man he claimed he was mooning when Whited got in the way, apparently hoping that Saxon confirming that scenario would obscure that the missive was full of damnation.

"Peyton, you messed up," it read. "I still don't know why you dropped your drawers. Maybe it was a mistake, maybe not. . . . Please take some personal responsibility here and own up to what you did. . . . Bro, you have tons of class, but you have shown no mercy or grace to this lady who was on her knees seeing if you had a stress fracture. It's not too late. She has had a tough go of it since leaving UT. . . . Do the right thing here!!"[3]

Rather than take the advice, the Mannings decided to fight. After hiring big-time New York lawyer Slade Metcalf, they filed a motion to dismiss the suit, characterizing it as an attempt to extort money from a famous athlete, though Naughright originally asked for only $15,000. When pretrial sessions commenced in March 2003, Naughright claimed that since the settlement, Manning had taunted her, re-enacting the incident on two occasions and calling her a "bitch." She also claimed that, two years before the incident, she had been helping teach a class that Peyton was taking, and when he allegedly cheated on an exam and she reported him, he sought revenge.[4]

Worse for Manning, in pretrial depositions some ex-Tennessee teammates, whom he assumed would back his opinion of Naughright, did not. And when he himself was deposed, the timing could not have been worse. Only months before, during the 2003 Pro Bowl, he gave a most un-Manning-like sideline interview—or, perhaps, one that was *more* Manning-like than he wanted the public to see. He was asked about Colts kicker Mike Vanderjagt, who had casually critiqued him and Dungy for having restrained emotions on the field. In a lather, Manning called Vanderjagt "an idiot kicker" who "got liquored up and ran his mouth off," and that "if he still is a teammate, we'll deal with it."[5] Naughright's lawyers presented the tape of the remarks as evidence of his nasty, vindictive side. Still another hit came when a document was produced in which John Underwood said that not only Peyton but Archie had defamed Naughright—although the words came out of Peyton's mouth in the book, it was Archie who had said she was "kinda trashy" and had a "vulgar mouth," and in an unprinted allegation, she had spent time "with a lot of black guys and up in the dorm." Under oath, Archie admitted he made the derogatory remarks, which hardly did *his* image any good.[6]

As all this was happening, Peyton began the 2003 season, and the case wasn't making much news. In one rare exception, Christine Brennan wrote on CNN's website on November 6, "So you're a sports fan, and you want to believe, and for quite a few years, you've had many wonderful thoughts about Peyton Manning. They're still there, but now, something else is there, too. You thought you knew the guy. Turns out you're still learning." Shrugging off any damage to his reputation, Peyton was prepared to go on fighting to quash the suit. But late in November, Judge Harvey Kornstein ruled that Naughright's case could proceed to trial, because there was enough evidence to suggest both "that the defendants knew that the passages [from the book *Manning*] in question were false, or acted in reckless disregard of their falsity" and "that there were obvious reasons to doubt the veracity of Peyton Manning's account of the incident in question."[7]

These words shot like poison-tipped arrows into the Manning brand and presaged a humiliating defeat in court. Around Christmastime, he and Archie capitulated, personally settling with Naughright for an undisclosed six-figure sum. The Mannings said nothing to the press, and details of the case were sealed. Even now, the story was hardly mentioned in the media, and for one columnist, the *Roanoke Times*'s Dr. Reginald Shareef, that in itself was an outrage. Shareef fumed on January 8, 2004, that "the media promotes certain white athletes [and] Peyton Manning is one of the NFL's most sparkling images. Most football fans were not aware of the defamation suit he recently settled against a woman he has harassed for years. . . . The settlement of the suit makes it 'go away' and allows the media to maintain the 'Perfect' Peyton image, especially among the NFL's female fans."

That image would take more hits in the gossip churn of the internet. In 2005, a former Colts cheerleader who had been fired for canoodling with players on a team trip to Tokyo told *Playboy* that when she entered her hotel room, "a high-profile player" was "hiding in my shower,"[8] which many assumed was Manning, since no other Colt at the time matched that description. Another rumor was that when the actress Renée Zell-weger divorced Kenny Chesney, she filed papers enigmatically claiming that the singer's close friendship with Manning had been a factor in the breakup. *Deadspin* reported on the rumor under the snickering banner headline "Peyton Manning Going All Brokeback Mountain on Us?"[9]

The mooning episode would of course be recycled, with fresh allega-tions that, as a scion of white privilege, Manning had avoided the scru-tiny and opprobrium directed toward black athletes for, say, marijuana use. Headlines ran, such as one in the *New York Daily News* just after his Super Bowl requiem, reading, "Peyton Manning's Squeaky-Clean Image Was Built on Lies."[10] But his ability to insulate himself from this sort of sludge was perfected early. Even back in 2003, he was immune to things mortal men might have to atone for. As if to prove it, even if he had to pay more than he ever made in royalties from the book, he *still* wouldn't let the obsession with shaming Jamie Naughright go, and he would have to pay up again.

———

To most fans, the matter seemed trivial when compared with what he was doing on the field. The Colts blasted out of the gate, winning their first five games. Playing two straight overtime games, they beat the Bucs, then lost to the Panthers. They were 11–3 in mid-December. Most of these games were close, none more than their match against the newly set-tled AFC power, the Patriots, who had won seven straight behind the maddeningly effective and annoyingly hunky Brady, who came into the Dome and staked his team to a 31–10 lead, aided by a 92-yard kickoff return for a touchdown. Then Peyton went off, throwing three of his four touchdowns in a six-minute span over the third and fourth quarters, to Wayne, Harrison, and Troy Walters, tying it. Brady, who was even slower than Manning but had a preternatural ability to stay upright and complete a pass even in a dense forest, fired a 13-yard touchdown to Deion Branch for the lead.

The game was a killing field, players limping off all day. Peyton kept the offense moving, but when it stalled with 3:27 left, Dungy took a field goal, hoping his defense would get the ball back. They did, and Manning took them all the way to the two-yard line. Three plays gained nothing. Then, on fourth down, 14 seconds left, James tried powering it in. but linebacker Mike Vrabel wrapped his arms around his shoulders and wrestled him down on the one. Game over. Manning won the stats battle—29 of 48 for 278 yards, with one pick, to Brady's 26 of 35 for 236, with two touchdowns versus two picks—but one suspected that in the many clashes to come between them, beating Brady and Bill Belichick would require more—the big play, over and over like thrusts of a sword, until the beast was slain. The Colts, at 12–4, won the AFC South, and Manning was given his first MVP award. He shared it with the ill-fated Steve McNair, whose numbers paled next to Manning's but whose 24–7 touchdown-to-interception ratio and 100.4 passer rating were superb. Manning had a league-leading 4,267 yards—making him the first ever to clear 4,000 yards in five straight seasons—29 touchdowns, only 10 interceptions, and a Colt-record 67 percent completion rate. He rang up three 5-TD games, all without one rusher in the top 10. On his arm alone, the Colts had the third-best offense, and the defense was fifth best.

The first playoff round brought in the wild-card Denver Broncos, who had beaten the Colts 31–17 in December. But by this point, Manning almost literally could not have been better. This was his apogee, beginning on the first drive, when he hit Brandon Stokley with a 31-yard touchdown pass. At the end of the quarter, he found Harrison with a 46-yard strike for a 14–3 lead. In the second quarter, he hit paydirt with Harrison and Stokley again, the latter galloping 87 yards for a 28–3 lead. He tacked on a fifth TD, seven yards to Wayne, in the third quarter before retiring to the bench. The final score was 41–10. Of his 26 passes, only four touched the ground. He threw for 377 yards. He wasn't sacked once. He won his first playoff game, and according to the NFL's passer rating system, he scored a perfect 158.3. Before that game, 48 men had achieved that grade, either in real time or applied retroactively. Peyton himself had done it twice in regular-season games, against the Eagles in 2002 and the Saints in 2003, but only Terry Bradshaw and Dave Krieg had done it in the playoffs.

The second round was tougher, against the Chiefs in Kansas City. But he was still on fire. A 29-yard touchdown to Stokley and a two-yard touchdown to Tom Lopienski, sandwiched around a short touchdown run by James, had the Colts up 21–10 at the half. A 19-yard touchdown to Wayne in the third quarter made it 31–17. It ended at 38–31, with Manning putting up 304 yards. That sent the Colts to the AFC title game against, who else, Brady and the Patriots—in Foxborough, on a raw, snowy afternoon. Up to now, Manning had engaged Brady three times (post-'01, they were in different divisions), and had come away losing them all. Moreover, the Pats had motivated themselves by pouting that the media were biased against them. During the week, citing one of the many exemplars in the press about Peyton's last two games, Patriot players took to sardonically calling Manning "Mr. Inhuman."[11]

When the game began, Brady struck first. With Belichick going for it on a fourth down, Brady floated one to David Givens for a seven-yard touchdown. The Pats' blitzing, hidden by unfamiliar defensive sets, kept Peyton out of sync; he would throw four picks, three to cornerback Ty Law, who covered Harrison like a blanket. The other pick, by safety Rodney Harrison, was in the end zone, after which Peyton stomped to the sideline, cursing, arms flailing, head shaking. Indeed, as it shaped up, the Pats' strategy, as one writer put it, was to "torture Manning and the Colts instead of just soundly beating them,"[12] citing the fact the Pats had gotten inside the Colts 16-yard line seven times but settled for five field goals as evidence that they wanted to keep the game close enough to keep beating him up.

That was preposterous, but the Patriots certainly did beat him up. The Pats' defensive coordinator, Romeo Crennel, often inserted backup defensive end Jarvis Green as a second tackle beside veteran Ted Washington. As a result, paths opened for Green to sack him three out of the four times he went down. As *Sports Illustrated* saw it, the defense "contained more wrinkles than a Rolling Stones tour jet."[13] Even so, Peyton hung tough and made it a game, his seven-yard TD to Pollard cutting it to 21–14 with 2:27 left. After regaining possession with 46 seconds left, Peyton tossed short passes aimed on third and fourth downs for Pollard in the flat. Both times, Pollard was jostled and probably held by linebackers Willie McGinest and Roman Phifer and couldn't get to the ball. Pollard and Manning screamed for a penalty each time, Peyton ostentatiously miming a holding gesture. "It ain't a call unless they call it, right?" a sheepish Rodney Harrison chuckled afterward.

When it ended, Brady and Manning—each of whom had, eerily, passed for 237 yards—engaged in the ritual man-hug at midfield that Peyton hated so much. But the agony of his own failure, of being jerked around by the officials, and the personal nature of the beatdown ate at him like battery acid. The snarking of the normally protective media was widespread; one story, about the Panthers' Ricky Manning intercepting three passes that day in another playoff game, led with "This Manning was busy grabbing interceptions instead of throwing them."[14] Michael Wilbon in the *Washington Post*, referring to Peyton, wrote, "Sometimes it's painfully obvious when one player is overwhelmingly at fault for losing a football game. . . . He didn't have to be perfect yesterday, nowhere near it. All he had to be was good and he wasn't anywhere close to that either."

As always, Peyton was courtly and platitudinous in defeat. While saying the Pats "did nothing super special" on defense, he conceded, "I didn't play the way I wanted to play. I made some bad plays and bad decisions." It was, he said, "frustrating, disappointing, all of the above." But that was a front. Suddenly, it wasn't business but indeed personal; winning it all now was predicated on leaving the prone body of Tom Brady in the dust along the way. Knowing it would be unbearable to watch Brady win his second ring in the Super Bowl, he passed up attending or even watching it on TV. Neither was he pleased when, during George W. Bush's State of the Union address days after the AFC championship game, Brady was seated for all to see beside the First Lady in the gallery, apparently to tweak John Kerry, the Democratic senator from Massachusetts who had surprisingly won the Iowa caucuses. It would not be the last time Brady allowed himself to be used as a political prop. Not that Peyton, a Bush booster, wouldn't have been there had he been invited. But Brady had more upside, more pizzazz. He was the sexy one. The *winner*.

======

Eli had one season left at Ole Miss in which to do something big himself, and his draft position would depend on it. As one headline in the spring of 2003 read, "Manning Has Last Chance."[15] David Cutcliffe, entering his fifth season at the Rebel helm, the last on his contract, knew on whose arm his future rode. He gave Easy more incentive by naming him senior captain of the offense, a position of added responsibility for a guy who would prefer to listen to metal music than get all rah-rah with teammates. As Peyton had done, Eli had already earned his degree, his last college season no more than an NFL tune-up. He was being projected as the first quarterback to be picked in the next draft and already held 24 school records, many of which had been Archie's. Yet his phlegmatic manner kept him on a low flame, nowhere near Archie in terms of emotional attachment among Rebel fans. He had all the tools, but it seemed doubtful he could inspire a team—as it was, he had only beaten two high-ranked SEC teams: LSU in '01 and Florida in '02.

Cutcliffe had 17 returning seniors, but in the opener against doormat Vanderbilt the lowly Commodores, led by quarterback Jay Cutler, took a 21–14 lead in the fourth quarter. Eli then directed a 75-yard drive climaxed by a 23-yard touchdown pass to Mike Espy to tie it. A subsequent drive and 54-yard field goal by Jonathan Nichols saved the game, and a lot of shame. At least for a week. Against Memphis, who hadn't beaten Ole Miss in a decade, the Rebels took a 34–21 lead on Eli's fourth TD pass, but then Memphis scorched them for 23 points. Eli, who wound up throwing 48 times, served up two picks in that span, an old bugaboo he just couldn't shake.

The Rebels split the next two games, but now came an impressive run. First, Eli led Ole Miss past No. 24 Florida at the Swamp, 20–17, conducting the game-winning drive as the clock was dying. Then they blasted Arkansas State 55–0 and Alabama 43–28, with three more TD passes from Eli in each game. Next, they clocked No. 20 Arkansas 19–7 to grab the SEC West lead and make the Top 20. In high gear, Eli fired passes for 398 yards and three touchdowns in a 43–40 win over South Carolina. And against Auburn, down 20–17 late, he took the team 80 yards, three times converting on third downs before the Rebels ran in the winning score.

During this streak, Ernie Accorsi, the New York Giants GM who had broken into the game watching Johnny Unitas as the Baltimore Colts' PR director, filed a glowing scouting report on Eli. In it, he wrote that Manning was carrying "an overmatched team entirely on his shoulders . . . so much so that he doesn't trust his protection. Can't. No way he can take any form of a deep drop and look downfield. With no running game [and] no real top receivers, he's stuck with the three-step drops and waiting til the last second to see if a receiver can get free. No tight end either. No flaring back. So he's taking some big hits. Taking them well."

Accorsi drew some heavy conclusions. Eli, he concluded, was "a little like Joe Montana" and had "courage and poise. . . . [M]ost of all, he has that quality you can't define. Call it magic . . . Peyton had much better talent around him at Tennessee. But I honestly give this guy a chance to be better than his brother. . . . If he comes out early, we should move up to take him. These guys are rare, you know."[16]

———

Ranked 15th at 8–2, the Rebels hosted the biggest match of the season, against No. 3 LSU, who were 9–1 and had taken the SEC West lead. A record crowd of 62,552 crammed Vaught-Hemingway for the nationally televised game, and Eli was given a deafening ovation in the introductions. But the Tigers made their mark on defense and zeroed in on him, sacking him three times and disrupting his timing. He would just get to 200 yards, but go only 16 of 36 and throw a pick. LSU took a 17–7 lead in the fourth quarter, and then Eli found Brandon Jacobs with a 10-yard touchdown. He got the ball back late and drove to the Tiger 18, but Nichols missed the tying field goal.

It was yet another soul crusher, but Eli did throw three touchdowns the next week to beat Mississippi State 31–0 and finish with Ole Miss 9–3 and ranked No. 16. It also earned him a high-visibility finale to his Rebel career, in the Cotton Bowl against No. 21 Oklahoma State. He killed it there, throwing three touchdowns and running one in himself to go up 31–14 in the last quarter. The Rebels held on, 31–28, Eli winning the game MVP on 259 passing yards. It had taken 32 years for Ole Miss to have a 10-win season—the last time was the year after Archie left—and with the Cotton Bowl win they had a final ranking of No. 13, saving Cutcliffe, if only for one more season.

For Eli, the numbers from his senior year were dizzying: 3,600 yards, 29 touchdowns, 10 interceptions, 62.4 completion percentage, 148.1 passer rating. In his four active years, he compiled over 10,000 yards, 81 touchdowns, and a 137.7 rating and left with 45 school records. Cooper, who had worried that his baby brother just didn't have what it took, had no doubts now, saying he was now "a little more in awe of what" he turned into.[17] Archie, who had burned thousands of miles on a crazy quilt of travel getting to 31 of his sons' games that fall, said he'd never had as much fun. One writer called those overlapping months the Mannings' "near-perfect season." But not quite near enough. Eli came in third in the Heisman voting to Oklahoma's junior QB Jason White and Pitt receiver Larry Fitzgerald. While he was first-team SEC, the conference MVP, and won the Maxwell Award, he didn't make All-American—not that he cared much. He was, by all indications, going to be the No. 1 draft pick. And, confirming that it's the quiet ones you have to watch, he was going to make a loud commotion.

———

Draft day was April 24, again at Madison Square Garden. But the plot had thickened two weeks earlier when word broke that the Chargers, who had the first pick, were talking to the Giants about swapping picks, the latter holding the fourth slot. Both teams were awful, though in retrospect their quarterbacks were quite adequate; the Giants' 31-year-old incumbent, Kerry Collins, was a future Pro Bowler, and the Chargers' 24-year-old starter, Drew Brees, was a diamond in the rough. Indeed, the Chargers could get more value from Eli as barter. Eli was not eager to play in Southern California, where the living was *too* easy for a guy who needed to feel the heat of battle to keep his eyes focused. This, of course, was a crazily ironic twist, the exact reverse of what Ryan Leaf had wanted the last time a Manning headlined the draft. During the spring, Eli kept mum about his preference but had a simple calculus: he may have wanted to play in the bright lights of New York simply because Peyton *hadn't*. It has also been speculated that Eli—and Archie—saw a lot of the old Saints in the Chargers; and, like John Elway decades before wanting to avoid the Colts, Eli didn't want to end up like Archie. Then, too, the Giants had glamor and glory. But not even Eli seems to have known the reason why he was turned off to the Chargers. In 2013, asked what it was, his answer was hidden behind pure Eli-speak.

"I forgot, I think," he said. "I just can't remember. . . . Been 10 years. It slipped my mind."[18]

The first hint of intrigue arose two weeks before the draft when Accorsi—likely prodded by Tom Condon, whom Eli had also hired as his agent—held a private meeting with Chargers GM A. J. Smith. Given Accorsi's high regard for Eli, he was prepared to make a deal to obtain him. This was doable because in Smith's mind the key get wasn't Manning but Philip Rivers, North Carolina State's four-year starter who had thrown 95 touchdowns and set a record with 51 consecutive starts. In a bit of subterfuge, Accorsi pledged to take Rivers fourth and then swap him for Manning, along with a third-round pick in the current draft and a first and a fifth in the next year's—a heavy price to pay, but worth it, as Accorsi swore to owner Wellington Mara and the Giants' new coach, the ruddy-faced Tom Coughlin.

These terms were leaked to the press, but it would not be a done deal until draft day, when the Chargers drafted Eli and the Giants Rivers. It was an awkward scheme, even more so for Eli, who would remain in limbo and need to feign being happy to be going to San Diego, and then wait out the next three picks before he was traded. Meanwhile, Collins, a crowd and team favorite, felt like he had been kneecapped. He had bled for the Giants after being traded there in '99, twice leading them to double-digit-win seasons and to the Super Bowl in 2000, where they were mashed by the Ravens 34–7. Now, feeling betrayed, Collins was disconsolate. "I feel accountable to the tradition, to the history, to all the seasons and all the players who've been involved with the Giants," he said.[19] He said he would even play behind Eli if need be. But since that would require a large cut to his $8 million salary, he wouldn't be *that* accountable.

Clearly, Eli was no naïf. Two weeks before the draft, after Condon made an endorsement deal with Reebok, Eli had filmed his first TV commercial. Spoofing himself, and exploiting the hubbub he had created, he made the spot holding a Chargers cap in one hand, a Giants cap in the other. When he arrived in New York for the draft with Archie, Olivia, and Peyton, all of them were wary that something might happen to scuttle the deal and leave Eli to somehow get along in the warm sun, near sandy beaches and French bikinis—"Woe is he," commiserated a sportswriter.[20] Seeing to it that it would not go down that way, at a press luncheon the Thursday before the draft, Eli revealed he had notified the Chargers that he did not want them to pick him. He had also, Elway-style, begun to drop threats about sitting out the season if they did—or even quitting football altogether and going to law school. Smith, whatever his team's intentions, took these threats as proof that it was the Mannings who were queering the deal, and he blamed Archie for controlling his son's thoughts. Years later, Archie would still deny the allegation. The threat, he said, "was a decision that Eli and Tom Condon kind of made. . . . I can't say it was pleasant from our end. Most people thought I orchestrated it, but I didn't. I don't tell my kids what to do or make their decisions."[21]

Whoever called the shots, Archie felt he needed to step in, insisting Eli wasn't trying to manipulate the draft. In fact, the Mannings felt the deal was falling apart. Smith was hemming and hawing, saying that he would do what was best for his team. Just as with Peyton, things were still in limbo come Saturday morning. The plan was still on the table, but neither team was sure it would be carried out. The first move was the Chargers taking Eli, who was seated in front of the stage, carefree as usual. When Paul Tagliabue called out the first pick, Eli did his best to grin while biting his lip. As the second Manning brother to be so anointed rose to the stage, hoots from Giant fans unconvinced the trade scenario would play out filled the theater. As Eli stood on the stage with Archie and Olivia, all of them looked like hostages posing with a smiling Tagliabue. Someone gave Eli a Chargers cap and jersey, which he held in his hand rather than putting them on. Other fans, anticipating the swap, showered him with boos for his gall in trying to force a trade before throwing an NFL pass. As the family left the stage, with Eli repeating his law school threat, they walked through the crowd toward an interview room. One guy shouted, "Peyton is great, but Eli is bush!" Surreal as it was, Eli shrugged off the "venomous" reaction, as *Sports Illustrated* described it. "When you play in the SEC," he said, "you get booed."[22]

In the side room, Eli handed Olivia the Charger gear and refused to stand with anyone from the team. Reporters peppered him with questions about sitting out, which he deflected, saying, "It's an honor to be selected with the first pick, but it's not what we wanted." Everyone's attention then turned to the next step, watching on a TV as the second and third picks went by. When the Giants' turn came, they kept to the plan, taking Rivers, who exhibited the same ambivalent reaction. Now, the conditions met, the Chargers tried to squeeze even more compensation out of the Giants. As the tense minutes ticked on, Archie, feeling stressed, was clearly upset that people were so turned off to his son.

"I heard one person say Eli was a punk," he said. "Well, he's not a punk. We're nice people, and we tried to do the best we could in a tough situation."

Finally, after a very long hour, as one reporter wrote, "The Chargers blinked . . . unwilling to call Manning's bluff."[23] Closing the deal, the teams broke the news to the media people. Accorsi handed Eli a Giants cap and he quickly slid it on. "Obviously," he said coyly, "we wanted something of this nature to happen. I'm excited about the whole situation." Olivia asked if she should give away the Chargers stuff. Eli told her to keep it, acknowledging with a smug laugh, "It might become a collector's item one day."

Among the reporters waiting to interview Eli was Peyton, who had been hired for a day by DirecTV to cover the draft. When he pulled his brother over, he conducted a semi-serious colloquy, putting Eli's ability to deadpan to an early test. He grinned awkwardly, but was game.

Q: It's been rumored that you have said you are better-looking than Peyton. That's a bold statement.

A: It is a bold statement. That is my opinion, and I feel very strongly about that opinion. And people I've talked to feel strongly about it, too. Peyton may not agree, but I don't think he's a high [ranking] person who can answer that question.

Q: It's also been reported, and I can't believe it, that you feel you also have more natural talent than Peyton.

A: I don't know if I said it in those exact words. Yes, in basketball, tennis, and Ping-Pong. He beat me at football when I was six and he was 11. But that wasn't really fair.

Q: What will happen when you play against each other?

A: It's not like he's gonna be playing cornerback. If he was, I'd throw there every single time, and he would try to give me some cheap shots. Peyton thinks he knows me. But I've got a few tricks up my sleeve.

The interviews done, the brood then headed across the river to Giants Stadium for a draft-day party of 3,000 Giants fans who chanted Eli's name as he stood atop a platform clad in blue Giants gear. Archie, who looked particularly relieved, said afterward, "It felt good to see Eli and our whole family happy. This situation took a toll on everybody."[24] That Eli had taken heat for what he deemed a principled stand was proof that, as one writer put it, "Manning may look as fresh-faced as your paperboy [but] he had a toughness that he'll need to play quarterback in the Big Apple." Archie could only hope so. Having suffered slings and sacks after he vaulted into the pros, he predicted that his enigmatic youngest son was walking into a "hornet's nest."

———

Condon won another sweet contract for the Mannings. When Eli came to training camp, the Mara family had signed off on five years and $46 million, including a $3 million signing bonus, his rookie salary set at $1.74

million. In the second year, a $9 million bonus would kick in on a salary of a mere $305,000; the third, $7.3 million on a $1.6 million salary; the fourth, $6 million on a $6.5 million salary; the fifth, $2.5 million on an $8.5 million salary. (Much of this structuring, as with any other team's contracts, was done to allow the Giants payroll to fit under the salary cap.) Although it is now submerged in history, a number of Giant players believed that Accorsi had gone in the wrong direction, paying a fortune for a new quarterback instead of filling other needs. Doing so, said All-Pro defensive end Michael Strahan, had "changed the game" and "throws a little bit of a wrench there," meaning the team's stability.[25]

Neither was Coughlin sold on Eli. A former receiver eons before at Syracuse, he had put in years as a college assistant and then as Bill Parcells's receivers coach on the Giants' second Super Bowl championship team in 1991. He took his able quarterbacks coach in Jacksonville, John Hufnagel, with him to New York as offensive coordinator and rehired Kevin Gilbride, who had once been his offensive coordinator in Jacksonville and would now be his quarterbacks coach, and coordinator again three years later. He was no softie, apt to blow his top over very little, his face turning beet-like as he sputtered at players and officials. Fifty-eight now, he was called "Colonel Coughlin" for imperious ways that included mandating that players be at meetings five minutes before the scheduled time or be fined. On the sideline, he sometimes seemed too wound up to think straight, losing awareness of the down or the clock. Players never knew if they measured up in his eyes, since he rarely praised them directly. Eli certainly appealed to him, physically and intellectually, having scored a record 39 correct answers on the Wonderlic IQ test at the combine, where, despite his seemingly slow feet, he ran the 40 in 4.7 seconds.

After Collins was traded, a cautious Coughlin convinced the Giants to sign Kurt Warner, who had broken his hand in '03 and had been let go by St. Louis. Given a two-year deal, Warner was told he would be expected to help tutor Eli, but as a past league and Super Bowl MVP, he regarded the job as more than a placeholder and did little tutoring. Eli's progress in practice would be slow. At the team's May minicamp, he fumbled a couple of times and threw a pick, prompting a typically New York tabloid headline: "All Eyes on Eli in a Dud of a Debut."[26] Warner started in the season opener against the Eagles and was awful, the game ending with Eli mopping up in a 31–17 loss, his first two pro passes incomplete before he got one right, a 34-yard strike to running back Tiki Barber. He threw five, completing three, then was sacked and fumbled.

But Warner then won five of six, with the overhyped rookie, his No. 10 jersey unsullied, riding the pine. After losses to the Bears and Cardinals, Coughlin, feeling the pressure to make a move, handed Eli the ball for the next game, November 21 against the 7–2 Falcons in Atlanta. "You Da Manning" was the headline in the *New York Post*. In another story, the paper's sometimes delirious football writer Steve Serby dubbed him "Heir to the Throwin'," "New York's new diaper dandy," and "Eli Messiah," a man "born for this moment" who "wasn't afraid of New York. He won't be afraid of any grits blitz today. Because Mannings just aren't."[27] The Falcons, led by quarterback Mike Vick, were coached by, of all people, Jim Mora, who during the week sounded loath to fawn over another Manning, sneering that his team had more to worry about than "Eli Manning and his personal tendencies."[28] Eli seemed imperturbable—less so than a nervous Peyton, who had clobbered the Bears in Chicago 41–10 in an early game and called to wish him luck from Mike Ditka's restaurant, where he and Cooper would catch the Giants game on TV. But Eli played jittery, his throws erratic, suffering a pick to defensive end Brady Smith, who dropped into coverage as Eli was confused by a zone blitz. "I thought I had the slant open," he said later, "but I threw it right to [Smith]. I guess you'd call it a rookie mistake."[29]

But then, down 14–0 early in the third quarter, Eli began at his own 28 and led a remarkable, 16-play, nearly eight-minute drive. Converting four third-down plays with pinpoint passes, he found tight end Jeremy Shockey from the six for a touchdown. He did much the same in the fourth, with a 12-play march, though he overthrew Ike Hilliard on third-and-goal from the eight, settling for a field goal to cut the lead to 14–10. He got the Giants close on their final drive, but he was suckered by linebacker Keith Brooking, who feigned leaving Shockey open, but then quickly closed in on him and batted the ball away to preserve the win.

His numbers—17 of 37 for 162 yards, two picks—weren't the story as much as those two drives, with high praise liberally dished out by teammates and opponents, especially for his quick reads and reactions. Shockey said the receivers had "betrayed" Eli with dropped passes. Magnanimously, Mora chimed in: "I'm glad we got Eli in his first start and not his fourth or fifth. I think he's going to be just like his brother in a few years." Paul Zimmerman judged his game as "a triumph if you look at the big picture [and] the players seemed to get a lift from the kid."[30] The rabid tabloids went easy on him, the *Post* calling his debut "shaky" but allowing that he "shows promise." It was pointed out that of the last 13 No. 1–drafted quarterbacks, nine lost their debuts—including Peyton Manning.

However, the positive spin went bad fast, as Big Blue became Big Black and Blue. Over the next five weeks, they lost, mostly big, and the initial rush about Manning dissipated into a dull ennui. Paying his dues, in the Eagles game he was sacked five times, hurried, and shoved by Jeremiah Trotter into the Giants bench, causing a sideline skirmish. He wasn't booed often at home the way Archie had been, but the media love affair turned colder, with words like "overmatched" and "mistake-filled" freely appearing in game stories.

Eli accepted that he was indeed in a hornet's nest. He eased into the cultural clash of being a city slicker, moving into an apartment in blue-collar Hoboken, New Jersey, and mourning that he could not find a single good Southern-style restaurant. He thought it might be a good idea to mingle with tailgating fans before games at the Meadowlands. That didn't last long. Back at the Grove, he said, "I could go there after games and not get harassed or bothered that much." What did he think of Giants fans? "I've heard," he deadpanned, "they can turn on you really quick."[31] A 28–24 win in the finale against the Cowboys, Barber running one in with 11 seconds left, closed out a 6–10 season. Eli could not brag about his stats—1,043 yards, six touchdowns, nine interceptions, a 55.4 rating, all inferior to Warner's numbers. But Warner knew the score. As hard a lesson as the season was, Manning was, wrote Peter King in *SI*, "a force to be reckoned with."[32] Warner, caught in the revolving door, would soon void the second year of his contract and sign with the Cardinals, where his renaissance would run uninterrupted.

Another victim of Eli, the Chargers, had a happier ending. They made the playoffs at 12–4, not with Rivers but Brees, who went to the Pro Bowl. Rivers, who held out in camp before signing, sat that season and the next before Brees inked a huge free-agent deal with the Saints. Meanwhile, the big rookie story that year was Ben Roethlisberger, who won the Rookie of the Year award with the Steelers. But when the post-season rolled around, rookie quarterbacks were forgotten. It was time for the elder Manning to get his next shot at Tom Brady.

CHAPTER 18

PEYTON, FINALLY

That year of 2004, with Peyton's contract running out, Condon struck again. He had already renegotiated the original deal, and by '03, Manning's salary had escalated to $9.8 million. When the Colts re-signed him for seven years, he took a minimum salary of $535,000 in exchange for a series of outrageous bonuses—$3.4 million up front, then two more totaling $19 million in '07 and '08, the total deal worth $98 million. A year later, Marvin Harrison would be extended for seven years as well, for $67 million. This was corporate capitalism run amok, and Peyton was the poster boy for it.[1] By contrast, Tom Brady seemed relatively indigent. Having come in as a low draft pick, even after two championships he was pulling down a puny $535,000 in salary, though restructuring bonuses pushed his yearly take to $6 million, which would double in '05. Perhaps that was a motivating factor, one that spurred him to keep his advantage over Peyton.

They had opened the season playing a marquee match on a Thursday night at Gillette Stadium. Peyton had the upper hand early, directing a nine-run drive ending in a Dominic Rhodes touchdown, then after hitting tight end Dallas Clark on a play-fake for 64 yards, flipping a three-yard TD pass to Harrison for a 17–13 halftime lead. But Brady, who out-passed him 335–256, threw two scores in the third quarter. Peyton got one back with a touchdown to Stokley, making it 27–24, but with the clock running out, he screwed up, a blitzing Willie McGinest sacking him, moving a game-tying field-goal attempt back 13 yards. When Vanderjagt missed, the Pats escaped. Manning didn't pick on Vanderjagt; rather, he blamed himself for playing "like a dog."

Both teams would rampage through the season, the Colts' with terrifying ease. They put up at least 30 points 11 times, and five times over 40 points—once 50. Peyton passed early and often, and in the end no one since Dan Marino's record 5,084 yards in '84 had come as close as he did with 4,557; and he beat by one Marino's single-season touchdown record, notching 49—bettered since only twice—by himself and Brady.

The Manning-Brady tango was, in fact, a strange, distorted reality. Brady, the bland matinee idol soon to win the supermodel wife, was impossible to root for, at least outside of New England, mainly because of his linkage with an assumedly sinister coach who would soon be caught spying on an opponent's practices, leaving a permanent bathtub ring on both; meanwhile, the guy who dropped his scrotum on a woman's head, then tried to sully her, the guy whose calculated image was second to none, was the *real* deal, and if one didn't look too hard, he fit the bill of the anti-Brady.

As Peyton's stats grew, so did his status as an icon. Early in his Colt career he had, with Tom Moore, devised a no-huddle system, wreaking mass confusion by hurrying to the line for a series of plays before defenses could even set themselves, with Peyton making the call at the line. Moore called it "Lightning," but unlike the usual hurry-up schemes, it was actually hurry up and wait, designed to give Peyton extra time to decipher the defensive shifts. Thus did the world come to spend long minutes watching him pointing, moving people around, making weird gestures such as putting an index finger on each side of his helmet, like a *toro* in a bull ring.

The guy who had to wait out the routine before snapping, Jeff Saturday, explained it this way: "As you are walking to the line, a play is being delivered and you knew from the week of practice before kind of what was coupled with that play. So if it was going to be a check, you knew there were two or three different things that we possibly liked to check to."[2] Even after the snap, Peyton would continue scanning the field, waving a hand or giving a quick nod to a secondary receiver to break from the pattern. Manning then executed pump fakes that could momentarily freeze even the most seasoned defender.

This was PhD-level quarterbacking, both an art and a science—because it had to be. Unlike Tom Brady or Aaron Rodgers, Manning was never a pure passer; less true and firm than Eli's, his spirals didn't spin tightly, but wiggled and wobbled. Without knowing exactly where to throw it and when, and with perfect timing, they would have no chance. But the scheme also depended on one man's judgment, an imperfect element that made it all too human. After an early-season Colts win over the Titans, Peter King waxed that "it is performances like [that] that make Manning watchers believe they are seeing the Unitas of his generation." But then he added, "As great as he can be, Manning still makes bad decisions at bad times."[3]

Indeed, drama seemed to attach to him, on and off the field, much of it built into the family subplot. When the Ravens decimated the Giants before playing the Colts, Paul Zimmerman wrote, "In the movie version of *Peyton Manning: Gunslinger*, the part of the hero would be played by Jimmy Cagney, looking for the guy who killed my brother."[4] He took care of the Ravens, 20–10, throwing for 249 yards and ending their playoff hopes. On the cover of the December 20 *SI*, Peyton's eyes burned behind his face mask, "Top Gun" emblazoned across the image. His wingmen enjoyed their own headlines. Harrison caught 15 touchdowns, Wayne 12, Stokley 10. And Manning did all this with a scant 10 interceptions, completing 67.6 percent. His 121.1 rating beat Steve Young's record by eight points and is still the second-highest in history, to Aaron Rodgers's 122.5 in 2011. The Colts had the No. 1 offense. Manning, James, and Harrison went to the Pro Bowl, as did Dwight Freeney. Peyton won his second MVP award, one vote short of unanimous. The Colts, at 12–4, winning eight of their last nine, clinched the division going away, *SI* calling it a "Season to Remember." They then obliterated the Broncos in the first playoff round, 49–24, with Manning amassing 458 yards, going 27 of 33 with four touchdowns; when Harrison was double-teamed, he simply threw to other receivers, Wayne reeling in two touchdowns.

The next Sunday delivered the goods—Manning and Brady, mano a mano, in Foxborough, a Super Bowl ticket on the line for the winner. Peyton had come up a loser five straight times to Brady, and the Pats had also toyed with the league, going 14–2, with Brady throwing for 3,692 yards and 28 touchdowns against just 14 picks. They were just as high-powered, and balanced. And that was the rub: the Colt defense was, in a sense, a victim of the offense. As one writer noted, the offense "takes up more than 70 percent on the salary cap, the most lopsided proportion in the NFL," leaving the defense to be "built mostly from spare parts."[5] This left some wondering, as *Sports Illustrated* asked, "In three or four years will Indianapolis collapse under the weight of fat contracts?"[6] But Manning was talking big before the game, citing his biggest asset. "My dad used to call it, 'Refuse to lose,'" he said. Vanderjagt declared that the Pats were "ripe for the picking," whereupon Rodney Harrison called him "Vanderjerk."[7]

However, what might have been big pregame news came and went, as similar news had in the past. This was the latest repercussion of Manning's seeming vendetta against Jamie Naughright. Interviewed for a recent ESPN *Sports Century* biography of him, he couldn't keep his lip zipped about the matter, claiming that *she* had "taken advantage" of *him*. And, with splendid timing, on the Friday before the Pats game, Naughright filed a motion charging him with breaching the confidentiality agreement. Again. Months later, she would prevail. Again. And he would have to pay an undisclosed sum. Again.

One of the few sportswriters who even heard of the new lawsuit, Mike Freeman, wrote on the eve of the Colts–Pats game, "The idea of saying 'I'm sorry' seems like a phrase that Manning does not like to utter. . . . Manning is worth millions, has the massive NFL PR machine at his disposal, and ESPN, the most powerful sports media entity in the world, promotes him as the prince of pigskin, as do other media outlets. Yet a petite personal trainer from Lakeland took advantage of the powerful NFL thrower? If Manning simply ignored the court agreement, then his reaction smacks of entitlement."[8]

But Peyton could take comfort that the more pressing business on the field that day submerged the story that refused to die. Not long into the game, however, the Pats had gotten the jump. The day was bone-cold, the windchill 16 degrees, and Belichick's defense, even missing two starters out with injuries, played unrelenting smashmouth ball. They applied sharp elbows to Colt receivers' backs out of sight of the officials, causing the receivers to flinch, drop passes, and fumble twice. Though the game stayed close and the Colts sacked Brady three times and held him to 144 yards passing, the intense pressure got to Peyton, who also fumbled one and could not complete a pass for more than 18 yards. It was only 6–3 Pats at the half, but Brady took his team 87 yards in the third for a 13–3 lead. The Pats had the ball for 38 minutes in the game, Corey Dillon running for 144 yards, and when Brady led them on a 94-yard march and took it in himself from the one midway through the fourth quarter, it was 20–3, and a wrap. Peyton did get to the Pats 20 before being picked off by Rodney Harrison in the end zone, his 238 passing yards meaningless in a game where he could put only three points on the board. In *Sports Illustrated*, Michael Silver's postmortem was that the Pats had "neutered" the Colts offense so profoundly that all of Manning's records "seem like a mere footnote."

After grimly glad-handing Brady in the ritual he had come to detest, Peyton put a positive spin on the disaster. "It was an excellent run, a fine year," he muttered. "Eventually, it will be our time."[9]

The Pats, whose time it always seems to be, went on to beat Roethlisberger's Steelers for the AFC title, and then so unnerve the Eagles in the Super Bowl that Donovan McNabb threw up his lunch on the field in the fourth quarter. Peyton knew how he felt, all too well.

———

During the last days of August 2005, New Orleans braced for the first impact of what meteorological models forecast as one of the most potentially catastrophic hurricanes ever to hit the United States. Hurricane Katrina had battered Florida and was heading across the Gulf of Mexico, bearing right for the home grounds of the Manning clan. On Sunday, August 28, Katrina—now a Category 5 storm—hit its peak strength with

175-mile-an-hour winds and 28-foot surges. On the 29th it made land-fall, drenching the city with eight inches of driving rain, the storm surge overwhelming the levees, flooding hundreds of square miles. That was when the images hit the national media of people pleading for help from the roofs of their submerged homes and of lifeless bodies in the rivers that snaked through the streets of mostly poorer, and blacker, neighbor-hoods. Reports later told of prisoners left to die in their cells as prison guards and officials took refuge.[10] Some of the most gruesome images came from inside the Superdome, which was being used as a shelter and where six people would die.

At the time, Tony Reginelli, who had suffered various ailments since retiring as Newman High's football coach, was laid up in Memorial Medical Center for treatment of a liver infection. Despite his weakened condition, he crawled from his bed, got down the stairs, and climbed into a National Guard truck with other survivors. "I was the last one to get out," he recalls.[11] He rode the truck to Baton Rouge, where his daughter-in-law, a nephrologist in the hospital, remained there with bedridden patients. Like other hospitals, victims were taken to Memorial, where 45 dead bod-ies, the most of any hospital, filled the morgue and the hospital's chapel.

Fortunately for the Mannings, the Garden District was spared from the teeth of the storm. Archie, Olivia, and Cooper all got out, to the relief of Peyton and Eli as they watched their hometown sink under water on TV, the death toll rising to over 1,500. As rescue efforts began to slowly bail out the drowned city, some neighborhoods still not resurrected to this day, the economic toll was placed at $150 billion, devastating the state; over a million people were displaced. Up north, the Manning brothers tried to pitch in as they prepared for the opening week of the season. Peyton, who said, "The whole town is like family, so it's very much a personal issue," arranged with Eli, who had also given heavily to charities following 9/11 and the Japanese tsunami—and whose own home in New Jersey would be flooded in the later Hurricane Sandy—to pay for an Air Tran cargo plane in Atlanta to fly up to New York, pick up Eli, then to Indianapolis, filled with relief supplies. With the brothers aboard, it headed for Baton Rouge, where they helped unload the sup-plies and then checked out their neighborhood.

As a result of the disaster, Eli's team would catch a break. With the now-mortuarial Superdome out of commission, not to be made available for a full year, Saints games were shifted to the Alamodome and LSU's Tiger Stadium. But their first home game, against the Giants on the second Monday night, was too soon to secure grounds, and so the league decreed that it would be played at the Meadowlands, an extra home game that had Giant-haters howling. It turned out to be Eli's second straight win to start the season—one in which, as Kurt Warner had foreseen, Eli would take every snap.

Even though the Giants had traded two high draft picks to get him, Accorsi made the most of his picks. His third-round selection, Notre Dame's defensive end Justin Tuck, would be a vital third-down pass-rush specialist. Accorsi also lured free agent Plaxico Burress away from the Steelers with a six-year, $25 million deal. A first-round pick out of Michigan State in 2000, at six foot five and 230 pounds, Burress was long and lithe, a perfect jump-ball target who had once gained 253 yards in an overtime game. But he was also a gamble, having been involved in a variety of misdemeanors, bounced checks, and traffic incidents for which he would be sued at least nine times.[12] In 2004, he had been suspended for going AWOL the week before a game. The Giants bet on him to keep out of trouble.

Eli's work was also made easier by Tiki Barber, a first-team All-Pro that year with a career-best 1,860 yards rushing and 54 receptions. As it happened, the opener was against the Cardinals, meaning Warner was looking for retribution. And he did outgun Eli, passing for 264 yards and a touchdown, while Manning went 10 for 23 with 172 yards and two interceptions. But Eli put the game away in the fourth quarter, finding Burress for a 13-yard score to send the Giants to an eventual 42–19 win. That led them to the "bonus" home game, in which the Saints wore their home colors even as Giant fans cheered their team's 27–10 win. Now, though, Eli had to go where he had mortally offended an entire region—San Diego—sure to take more verbal abuse. While Charger fans were satisfied to see LaDainian Tomlinson trample the Giants with 192 yards on the ground and Brees throw two touchdowns in a 45–23 rout, Eli didn't bow down. He threw for 352 yards and two touchdowns. The next week, he threw for 296 yards and four touchdowns, two to Burress, beating the

Rams 44–24. The Giants then lost in Dallas in overtime—one of three OT contests they would play that season, losing two.

But what seemed a blow became a rallying point. On October 25, Giants owner Wellington Mara died at 89. His life had paralleled that of the team; he started as a ball boy in 1925, when his father, Tim, founded it, then was given the roles of treasurer, secretary, and vice-president. When Tim died in 1958, Wellington became co-owner with his brother Jack, who died in 1965. It was then that the team went into a long dry spell while Wellington and his nephew Tim, who with his mother and sister owned 50 percent of the team, feuded. But Mara guided a renaissance in the 1970s, ceding authority to powerful general managers, and championships in the '80s and early '90s restored the Giants to their status as the bedrock franchise of the league.

The grief over his death, however, ignited the Giants' season. Charged up, wanting to "win one for Well," they won the next three, beating the Redskins and 49ers on consecutive Sundays, 36–0 and 24–6. With a 6–2 record, Burress was paying off big, and Shockey had become *the* third-down receiver in the league. They would run off another three-game winning streak in December, including dumping Parcells's Cowboys. Looking up after finishing 11–5, they had won the NFC East with a quarterback no longer wet behind the ears, who had meshed beyond expectation with his receivers—Burress, Shockey, and Amani Toomer each had at least 60 catches and six touchdowns. Eli did have his foibles, his 17 picks and completion rate barely above 50 percent keeping him from the Pro Bowl. And in the first playoff round, against the wild-card Panthers, he never had a chance. Exposing the Giants' weakness against the run, fullback DeShaun Foster ran wild, gaining 151 yards as the Panthers kept the ball for almost 43 minutes. Rarely getting the ball, Eli could only manage 18 passes, completing 11 and, behind all game, heaving three interceptions in a 23–0 slap in the face.

As Peyton could have told him, progress was measured in pain. Indeed, both Manning brothers could vouch now that ending a great season in the shame of defeat was about the lowest a man could sink and still be able to get up and think straight again. But he had to, no matter how often.

After the physical beating the Colts took from the Pats, Polian drafted some rough-tough Big Ten defensive backs, Marlin Jackson and Kelvin Hayden, to complement his already hard-hitting safeties, Mike Doss and Bob Sanders. Dungy would use a four-tackle rotation that would blunt the rush, and linebacker Cato June had more leeway to roam around and lay people out. But nothing changed on the other side of the ball. The passing attack was the Colts' signature, with schemes built on precise Manning play-action fakes, a quick squaring up, and a perfectly thrown lead to a receiver running patterns without deviation.

This was what had made Manning unstoppable—except, it seemed, to the Patriots. As it happened, though, when Indianapolis faced them midway through the 2005 season, in Foxborough, the tide had shifted. The Colts had ripped through their first seven games, giving up fewer than 10 points in four of them, running up 437 yards against the Houston Texans. The Pats, again racked by injuries, were only 4–3. For a change, the weather was good. Dungy, making a subtle but important distinction, called the game "probably a must-win for the Patriots, and more of a must-win for us from a mental standpoint."[13]

And so it was that the world turned upside down. Manning had the Colts ahead on the first drive, which ended with a one-yard touchdown toss to Harrison. With nine seconds left in the half, he found Wayne with a 10-yard scoring pass to go in leading 21–7. The icing was a fourth-quarter, 30-yard strike to Harrison, making the final tally 40–21. The Colts outgained the Brady bunch 453–288. Peyton, with time to set up and throw and the Pats' elbows a safe distance from the receivers, went 28 of 37 for 321 yards and three touchdowns, making Brady's three seem trivial. The title of the *Sports Illustrated* game story was trenchant: "Peyton, Finally."

The rub was that the regular season was such a breeze that, other than routing the AFC's other big power, the Steelers, 26–7 on a Monday night late in November, there was no other game that was crucial. This was a problem for Dungy, who could sense a decreasing intensity. They would finish a league-best 14–2, scoring the second-most points and giving up the second fewest. Peyton, first-team All-Pro for the third straight year, had the lowest passing yardage of his career, 3,747, due to frequently playing with the lead, but with 28 touchdowns and 10 picks, had a 104.1 rating. James ran for 1,506 yards, Harrison caught 12 touchdowns. But there were ominous signs, and one kick to the gut administered by another cold, hard, irrational dose of reality.

On December 22, Dungy's 18-year-old son James was found dead by his girlfriend in the bedroom of his Tampa college dorm, a belt tied to his neck, hanging from a ceiling fan. As with Buddy Manning, there was no explanation that would suffice; two months before, depressed, he had overdosed on hydrocodone, but after recovering seemed to be okay. Coming as it did just before Christmas and the new year, his death seemed particularly tragic. Dungy's soft-spoken words could have made the hardest man weep. "I would want America to know our kids need us," he said. "Spend as much time with your kids as you can. Enjoy them. Be with them."[14] Something Buddy probably would have wanted to do more than anything.

The Colts vowed to win for the coach. But unlike the Giants' response to Mara's death, the tragedy may have taken the brine out of them. Two days later, they lost their second straight, 28–13 to the Seahawks. And they still were not right entering the playoffs. The first round would bring in the Steelers, itching for revenge and having won five in a row, including their first playoff game, against the Bengals. Pittsburgh's fist-faced coach, Bill Cowher, had a team suited to its home city—tough, rusty nails and trench players—and in Roethlisberger a jumbo-sized quarterback as skilled as Manning (and similarly flawed; after a more serious transgression than Peyton's, he would be suspended for six games in 2010 after being accused of, but never charged with, rape).[15]

When the game began, the Steelers got the jump. Big Ben threw two first-quarter touchdowns and controlled the ball. Peyton, sacked five times—twice by linebacker James Farrior—and his running game stuffed, could not get untracked until it was 21–3 entering the fourth quarter. Mounting a furious comeback, he sent a pass soaring to Dallas Clark, who snagged it for a 50-yard touchdown. Another touchdown and it was 21–18 with 4:29 left, the crowd up and screaming. The Colts held, but Peyton, from his own 18 with 2:31 left, faltered and was sacked twice—the last on fourth down at the Colts two. All the Steelers needed to do was take it in from there—but the ridiculously reliable future Hall of Famer Jerome Bettis *fumbled*, and Nick Harper—who the night before had been stabbed, fortunately not seriously, by his wife in a domestic dispute—ran it the other way, stopped only by *Roethlisberger*, who lumbered down the field after him and just did trip him up at the Colts 42.

With stunning capriciousness, this had become one more insane game involving the Manning family. Given another chance to tie or win, Peyton hit Wayne for 22, Harrison for eight more, to the Steelers 28. Two passes to Wayne were incomplete. Now, with 21 seconds left, on fourth down, in came Vanderjagt, the guy savaged by his own quarterback. From the 46, he sent the kick on its way . . . and it sailed wide right. As Colts cursed and crumbled to the ground in agony, Vanderjagt went mental. In a rage, he yanked his helmet off and slammed it on the turf, incurring an unsportsmanlike conduct penalty, lamenting later, perhaps tweaking Dungy, "I guess the Lord forgot about our football team."

Peyton, who threw for 290 yards in vain, barely knew which cliché to dust off about his latest failure, though he did know he wasn't going to condemn Vanderjagt. He, and all the Colts, echoed Dungy in saying they couldn't have been any better positioned. "I couldn't tell you," he said, eyes glazed, in the morgue-like locker room, "how much I studied these guys over the last two weeks. It's disappointing. . . . At this point, it is hard to swallow. But I'm going to keep trying, that's all I can say."[16] The reporters wouldn't let it go at that. One asked about the lack of protection he had received from the Colts' offensive line. His jaw tightening, he seemed for a second to think of how to respond, then just gave up and ducked it.

"I'm trying to be a good teammate here," he uttered with a faint grin, saying more than he likely intended. Then, needing to go a step further, "Let's just say we had some problems in protection. I'll give Pittsburgh credit for the blitzes and their rush. Those guys rushed. But we did have some protection problems."

That didn't sit well with some crowded into that locker room. One, the *Los Angeles Times*'s J. A. Adande, wrote that the response, guarded as it was, "sold out his offensive line" and "whether you're a good loser or a bad loser, the problem is you still go down as a loser. There has never been a more sympathetic figure in defeat than Indianapolis Colt Coach Tony Dungy. . . . But his quarterback, Peyton Manning, lost points by his willingness to point fingers everywhere but at himself. Different vibes, same unavoidable conclusion. They didn't get it done in the play-offs. Again."[17]

One barometer of where each Manning stood when the 2006 season commenced would be the very first game of the season, when the Colts invaded Giants Stadium. Not only would this be the first time brothers had faced each other in an NFL game at quarterback, but never before had the two of them competed against each other in a real game, let alone an NFL marquee game on Sunday night. They did now because the league knew how high the TV ratings would be, and it would be in the Meadowlands, in the eye of the New York media circus, guarantee-ing what *Sports Illustrated* touted as "pro football's most hyped season opener, ever." The magazine's story, titled "May the Best Manning Win," cleverly paired photos of the brothers to make it seem like they were pointing at each other.[18]

Publicly, they professed no particular emotional investment in the game. "For the other 52 guys on each team," said the poker-faced Eli, "it's a football game, not a [story]." Peyton also had other matters to worry about. Edgerrin James had taken a $30 million deal from the Cardinals—although this was good timing for the Colts, since James was never again the same and they mined a gem in the draft, LSU fullback Joseph Addai. Peyton, a year older, had one fantasy football columnist pronouncing, "His stock has dropped slightly from last year," though he was still rated the top QB.[19] And Eli was being given little chance. A former Giant player was anonymously quoted before the game as saying that Coughlin and Hufnagel—in words that echoed Accorsi's criticism of the Ole Miss coaches—"have him thinking so much at the line, I don't even know how he gets through his reads. How can you not play stiff?" Eli admitted that, upon reaching the pros, Peyton was no longer a tutor. "Before, I would study him on film and ask him questions about what he saw and compare notes about other defenses," he said. "That's all stopped."[20]

The New York hype-makers were typically loopy. Steve Serby predicted that Eli would best Peyton in the Super Bowl that year and that, given the pressures of the New York market vis à vis Indianapolis, the heat was more on Eli to win.[21] Diplomatic as ever, Archie, who would watch with Olivia from a VIP box, said he'd be happy with a tie.

As the game rolled out, Peyton went up 13–0, but Eli battled back, finding Burress from 34 yards out, then Shockey from 15 to make it 16–14 after three quarters. But Peyton was always a step ahead. A 20-yard completion to Harrison and a face mask penalty set up a Rhodes touchdown. Eli then led a long drive capped by a touchdown run by Brandon Jacobs, who was drafted that year out of Auburn to replace the retiring Tiki Barber and at six foot four and 265 pounds was a human SUV. That cut it to 23–21, and Adam Vinatieri—who had bolted the Patriots and signed as a free agent with the Colts, who were quite willing to let Vanderjagt go as a free agent—booted a 32-yard field goal with a minute left, but it wasn't over until Eli's bomb to Burress fell incomplete on the last play. Peyton, who passed for 276 yards to Eli's 247, had cause to say he was proud to be Eli's brother that night. He could see up close how Eli could make a team, any team, sweat bullets.

The two of them went their own ways. The next week, Eli had another thriller, against the Eagles. Down 24–7 at the half, he again proved how good he was at coming back, going 31 of 42 for 371 yards and three touchdowns—his 31-yard dart to Burress winning it in overtime, 30–24. By midseason the Giants were 6–2. But then it all crumbled. Eli was awful in a 38–20 mauling by the Bears, then lost the next three, the last a soul crusher to the Cowboys. Down 20–13 in the fourth quarter, Eli took them a 17-play, seven-minute drive, tying it on a five-yard pass to Burress with a minute left. However, the Giants failed to cover a 47-yard heave by Tony Romo to Jason Witten, and a field goal won it with one second on the clock.

Further hobbled by Burress's groin injury, they ended at 8–8, a step back that a cheap wild-card playoff berth couldn't salvage, though the Eagles had to endure what the Colts had gone through in the opener. After they pulled ahead 20–10, Eli once more clawed back, his 11-yard pass to Burress tying it with five minutes to go. Now, though, veteran journeyman Jeff Garcia, who took over when McNabb was injured during the season, handed off to Brian Westbrook six times and completed one pass to move close enough for another field goal with three seconds left—to nail it down, 23–20. The closeness of these matches was in itself a marker of how close Eli—who passed for over 3,200 yards and 24 touchdowns, but with 18 interceptions—was to crossing over into Peyton territory. But if few were ready to recognize that, it was only because the season would play out as Peyton's own deliverance, at long last.

═══

The '06 season was a reckoning for Peyton and Harrison, who in December would become the fourth player to catch 1,000 passes and was behind only Jerry Rice, Cris Carter, and Tim Brown on the all-time list, all while possibly not speaking 100 words. "I'm not going to be loud, but I do talk," he insisted, amusing teammates with superstitions like sitting in the same left-row seat on planes and placing a white towel on the sideline bench, marking his—and *only* his—spot. His work habits in practice were even more maniacal than Manning's; his favorite line was "I get paid to practice. I play the games for free."[22] He, Manning, and Jeff Saturday were the gravitational center of the team, the latter a real rags-to-riches story. Cut by the Ravens in '98, Saturday was a 325-pound undrafted free agent who was working in a hardware store when Polian rescued him; he would play with the team for 12 years, an All-Pro six times, Offensive Lineman of the Year in '07.

But the big buzz of the year was Addai. Not starting any game that season, he swiveled and slithered for over 1,000 yards, leading all rookies and tying a rookie record with four touchdowns in one game. Of Ghanaian descent, his braided hair streaming down his back, he was a picaresque sight blasting through or around the line. He was of much help to Peyton, who wasn't quite as sharp as the year before but, like all the Colts, used the too-early peaking the year before as a lesson to hold something back in the tank for when it really counted. They still won their first nine, but many were close, including the most satisfying—

27–20 over Brady, again in Foxborough. Not only did he outpass Brady 326–201, but the latter was intercepted four times. A new trope emerged, that the Colts had Brady and Belichick's number. But this didn't seem of great significance when, in their next game, they just squeaked by the lowly Bills 17–16. They were 9–0 at that point, making a joke of the league—and then, going into safe mode, they lost their way, falling in four of the next six games, blown out in one, 44–17, by the Jaguars, who rushed for an amazing 375 yards, forcing Manning to throw 50 times. Bill Polian was so despondent afterward that he told Jim Irsay, "It's over."

"What are you talking about?" Irsay shot back. "We're in the playoffs. It can't be over."

Polian persisted. "Too many injuries. It's over."[23]

Winning their division was a given—since 2002, they had led the AFC South all but seven weeks. Despite losing three of the last five games, Peyton finished the regular season with the usual Pro Bowl numbers— 4,397 yards, 31 touchdowns, nine interceptions, and a league-best 101.1 rating, feeding Harrison 12 touchdowns—though he only garnered two MVP votes, putting him well behind LaDainian Tomlinson. But while the Colts had the third-ranked offense, the soft spot was their defense against the run, which was dead last. Clearly, people in Indianapolis were nervous when the wild-card Chiefs rolled in for the first playoff game. The game was no blowout, Peyton allowing the Chiefs to stay close with three picks, but the Colts did put the pieces together. Peyton went 30 of 38 for 268 yards, his late touchdown to Wayne clinching a 23–8 victory. The suspect defense, meanwhile, yielded just 126 yards, a mere 44 rushing, and had four sacks.

They now had to go to Baltimore to play the 13–3 Ravens, whose defense could make grown men tremble and its offense make them giggle. Giving up just 12.6 points a game, at their core was their linebackers' shifting, disguised sets. All were Pro Bowlers, anchored by the scabrous man in the middle, Ray Lewis, who could psych you out just doing his pregame war dance, which looked more like a full-body seizure. If receivers could get to the secondary unmolested, they would encounter two more All-Pros, Ed Reed and Chris McAlister. They were a mouthy bunch, Lewis and fellow linebacker Bart Scott taunting

Addai, whose gentle demeanor and ancestry apparently translated into being not tough, smart, or even *American* enough to beat them. Scott blathered, "It's going to be a painful day for Joseph Addai."[24] Defensive coordinator and circus clown Rex Ryan added, "If you don't disrupt Peyton's timing and his rhythm, you have no chance. But as big a challenge as we face in Peyton, he faces a bigger challenge in us."[25] Doing their part, Ravens fans showered the Colts with verbal abuse when they arrived for the game.[26]

Peyton busied himself watching film—but not just of the Ravens. Because they used a plethora of finely tuned defensive formations, he ordered up the film of the Patriots' first-round playoff win over the Jets, who also used a lot of sets only to be flummoxed by Brady with a hurry-up offense. "I came in and told [Jim Caldwell], 'Let's look at the film to see how Brady did that,'" he recalled. "I knew that against the Ravens if you don't throw changeups, you can't win."[27] Of course, the Colts used their own no-huddle scheme; now, though, Manning would forgo all the crazy signal calling. That week, it went into the playbook under the name "The Quick."

Played in balmy 63-degree weather, the defenses swarmed. Both Manning and Steve McNair were intercepted twice. But the Colts, four-point underdogs, kept the edge, with Peyton indeed quick, keeping the Ravens from having time to alter defenses or bring in substitute players. He didn't throw much, and his stats were mundane against that brutal defense. His biggest passes were, at times, completed even with Ravens hanging off receivers. But the Colts never trailed, aided immensely by a running game that gained 100 yards, while the defense read and reacted almost perfectly. With the only scoring coming from field goals, Vinatieri's five kicks—the fourth giving him a record 33 in playoff games—certified the 15–6 victory. That, however, seemed a lark compared with the next test looming for Manning: the AFC title game, January 21, which fate decreed could only have been played against his blood enemy.

———

This time, the Colts would meet Brady and the Patriots in the controlled climate of the RCA Dome, and it provoked hysteria around town. For

Peyton, the game required a balancing act, ego against history. There was no way he could be overconfident—not when history reminded him of the heartaches he had suffered in two playoff games against Brady and Belichick, and certainly not with his middling numbers against the Chiefs and Ravens: one touchdown, five picks. Meanwhile, the Pats beat the Chargers in the divisional playoff round 24–21, a San Diego fumble and missed field goal letting New England survive Brady's three interceptions.

Dungy said he never saw Peyton put more effort into practices than those preceding that game. Manning and Harrison had a pact in practice: the ball never could hit the ground; if it did, they would do the same pass over and over. None did, but they reran every pattern numerous times anyway. This, of course, was his meat: preparation, execution, an almost extrasensory feel for where to throw and when. "Whoever they play," Ravens cornerback Corey Ivy had said, "Peyton will be ready. He's the best out there. He knew what we were going to do before we did. How do you prepare for that?"

Few knew, however, that he wasn't too proud to borrow from Brady's methods. Or that in the off-season they had sent emails back and forth and played golf together. Amusingly now—though not so much to Brady—they had persuaded the league to change how game balls were prepared. "We're both kind of football junkies," Peyton said. When they met up on those occasions, "we're usually discussing football, trying to improve our games."[28]

The Colts wouldn't play hurry-up in the game, since the Pats were prepared for it. In fact, it seemed that the Pats had the fates. Early on, Brady tried to run it in and fumbled, but teammate Logan Mankins fell on it in the end zone. Down 14–3 in the second quarter, Peyton threw short for Harrison—but it was intercepted by cornerback Asante Samuel, who ran it back for a 39-yard touchdown. Behind 21–6 at halftime, Manning began the first possession of the second half with a 14-play drive that took it to the Pats one. He then ran it over himself. On the next drive, a pass interference penalty again put it at the one, and on a tackle-eligible play, he flipped a touchdown to Dan Klecko; the two-point conversion tied the game, 21–21.

So now it was a new game. The kickoff was returned 80 yards and Brady threw a six-yard TD pass. That should perhaps have, well, deflated the Colts. But in the fourth quarter, in a remarkable turnabout, Rhodes fumbled into the end zone—only this time, Saturday pounced on it for the tying touchdown. The Pats' new kicker, Stephen Gostkowski, and Vinatieri matched field goals. Then Gostkowski nailed another, and Peyton took the ball at their 20 with 2:17 to go, yet another unbearable defeat awaiting failure. He passed to Wayne for two first downs to get into tying field-goal range, but after Addai ran it to the doorstep, on third-and-two from the three, 1:02 left, he shot up the middle through a massive hole excavated by a Saturday block that drove nose tackle Vince Wilfork out of the play—a wipeout that had a giddy Saturday trying to convince reporters to officially call it "The Block."

The touchdown nearly tore the dome off. Now it was Brady who was reduced to a desperation fling, and his interception ended it, 38–34, Manning having led the biggest comeback in conference title game history, completing 27 of 47 for 349 yards to Brady's 21 of 34 for 232. With the Indianapolis Colts punching their first Super Bowl ticket, Peyton could now console Brady—whose luck ran out, several passes muffed by receivers—on the crowded field, oozing the same clichés Brady had so often dispensed to him. After both teams had left their locker rooms, they met up again to shmooze; Brandon Stiley took a picture of them on his cell phone, smiling in unison. So it was left to the Patriots defensive backs to grouse, Ellis Hobbs insisting, "We let them off the hook."[29]

It had taken Peyton nine years to get to the summit. Only a fool would have wondered if he was ready. As Dungy said, his time was now. The local papers were dutiful courtiers, the *Star* blowing kisses with headlines like "Manning, Colts Break Through with 2:17 of Magic" and "Magic Manning." Wrote the AP, "A comeback, a drive, a legacy. And, yes—finally—Peyton Manning gets his Super Bowl trip." *SI*, a Manning courtier from way back, gave him the cover again, with the line "Yes, He Can." And yet, there was lingering doubt that could only be removed by him, in Super Bowl XLI in Miami's Dolphin Stadium on February 4, with 100 million pairs of eyeballs trained on his every move.

The last remaining obstacle would be the NFC champion Chicago Bears. Not nearly as fierce as the Ditka-led team that had last gotten to the summit, the Bears, embodied by middle linebacker Brian Urlacher, a hot-wired madman, still had the best defense in the conference, but the surprise was quarterback Rex Grossman, who had avoided his usual mistakes and injuries and thrown 23 touchdowns. The big boy in the backfield, fullback Thomas Jones, rushed for 1,210 yards. After going 13–3, they edged the Seahawks in overtime in the first playoff game, then blew away the Saints. Much like Dungy, Chicago coach Lovie Smith was a low-key motivator who had been Dungy's linebackers coach in Tampa Bay. Not only were the two men close, but this would be the first time both Super Bowl coaches were African-American, and, as one scribe noted, "two nice men who have shown the world a head coach doesn't have to be a raving lunatic to reach a Super Bowl."[30] The bettors made the Colts 6½-point favorites. And, in truth, the Colts' biggest problem was overconfidence, combined with a natural letdown after the Pats game. As the team leader, Peyton felt he needed to go full Bolshevik. Before the trip to Miami, after Bill Polian ruled the hotel off-limits to all but players' families, he stood up and objected, "I don't think we should let *anyone* up in the rooms," he intoned. "This is a business trip, and I don't want any distractions. I don't want any crying kids next to me while I'm trying to study."[31]

This was not a popular position. As cornerback Nick Harper recalled, "We were heated. People were saying, 'We're grown-ass men. We've got wives and kids, and we'll make those decisions for ourselves.'" But they knew the deal. On the Colts, the show tune was *Whatever Peyton wants, Peyton gets.* Indeed, when he demanded a film-study room at the hotel, the swank Harbor Club Resort, team brass rented another floor and set one up. Among themselves, some Colts began to grumble about the "Peyton Rules" and that the team should be called the Indianapolis Peytons.[32]

As it was, Manning, while a popular teammate, was never really one of the guys. Players liked to prick him for his cultural retardation—in the iPod era, his idea of high tech was a cheap CD player he took onto bus and plane rides, listening to the same country tunes. Reggie Wayne even took pictures of it, in disbelief. A good sport, Peyton would suck up the jokes, pronouncing himself that his tastes were "retro." But when some Colts took to South Beach, no one asked him along, not only because they knew he wouldn't go, but because they liked it when he wasn't around. As assorted Manning relatives partied at the South Shore Club—Ashley telling him she was "having the best time of my life"—he ate room service, studied the game plan, and nursed a sore thumb he kept quiet about.

The day of the game, it was a very un-Miamian 67 degrees, rainy, and gusty. After waiting around in the rain for the endless pregame pomp and introductions to wrap up, the Colts went out as if in a funk, doing little but watch as the opening kickoff was returned 92 yards by the Bears' Devin Hester. As the heavily pro-Bear crowd hollered, the Colts made a profusion of misplays, with receivers running the wrong routes and Manning underthrowing Harrison and being intercepted. It took half the first quarter for them to awaken. On a third-and-10 from his 47, Dungy allowed Manning to call the play. He chose, in Colt parlance, 66 DX Pump, a fake to freeze the secondary, followed by a deep middle bomb to Wayne. A fraction of a second before he was hit, he let fly. It wobbled a bit but was true. Wayne, running an in-and-go slant, later said the pass "seemed like it hung in the air forever." It came down in his hands and he streaked into the end zone—a 53-yard bolt.

The Colts were still a bit skittish, though. Vinatieri missed the extra point, and after the Bears fumbled away the kickoff, Manning did the same, coughing it up under pressure, and Grossman promptly hit Muhsin Muhammad for a TD and a 14–6 lead. Paul Zimmerman called this mess of a first quarter a "freak show." But thereafter, the Colts' game plan began to grind the Bears down, applying a championship formula: ball control. Both teams used variations of the Cover 2 defense, which drops a linebacker into deep zone coverage. Knowing this, Peyton again kept his throws primarily short to medium-range. Over the game, 13 went short left, 12 short right, and seven short middle—of the 32 attempts, 23 were completed. Of the remaining six, three were thrown into the deep middle, two for completions—one for 17 yards to Clark, and the big strike to

Wayne for 53. Rhodes ripped out 113 yards on 21 carries. Addai had 77 on 19 and 10 catches, the most ever by a running back in a Super Bowl.

The Bears took a different approach. While Jones put up 112 yards rushing, they came on only 15 carries because Grossman believed he could beat the Colts deep. So the Colts blitzed like crazy, at times using defensive backs on blitzes. Grossman sent deep spirals through the wind and rain seven times, completing exactly one. He went 20 of 28, but for a mere 165 yards, only two of his 20 attempts clicking for more than 14 yards. He was intercepted twice. Unable to sustain drives, they were run ragged by the Colts, who controlled the ball for 38 minutes. Meanwhile, gradually racking up numbers, his linemen and backs walling him off from the Bears' pass-rushing stunts, Peyton threw 38 times, completing 25, for 247 yards. Like a slowly invading army, long drives led to three Vinatieri field goals and a short Rhodes TD run. By the fourth quarter, it was still close, 22–17, but the Bears were gassed, and a 56-yard interception return by the Colts' Kelvin Hayden and a subsequent pick by Sanders iced the 29–17 triumph.

———

Up in the VIP boxes, Archie, Olivia, Eli, Cooper, Ashley, and all the family who could fit let loose—even Eli, though typically with less relish. The Colts gathered at midfield—the absurdity of doing these rituals on the field made obvious by everyone's desire to get out of the rain—for the ceremonies presenting Jim Irsay with the Vince Lombardi Trophy and Peyton with the MVP. After the presentations, Peyton bundled both trophies and embraced them as the rain poured. Naturally, the postgame scene revolved around him. His face a mix of relief and redemption, sweat seemed to mingle with tears forming in his red eyes. "Everybody did their part," he said, a statement he had only dreamed about making so many times before. "We worked together. I'm proud to be part of this team."[33]

Ghosts hung heavy in the locker room, tempering the joy with sadness. During the season, prompting memories of James Dungy, Reggie Wayne's brother died in an automobile accident, and defensive tackle Montae Reagor was out for most of the season with injuries sustained in another car crash. The rumbling about the Peyton Rules notwithstanding, Irsay took to the podium and said, "We're so tight-knit. Our bonds have been forged through some real-life tragedies, and those things make you stronger." Then there was Dungy, testifying to the power of prayer and his quarterback, no less than an instrument of God, as he made it. "I don't think there's anything you can say now, other than this guy is a Hall of Fame player and one of the greatest players to ever play the game." No one would have argued the point. Bill Polian went further. "There is no Super Bowl held here without Peyton," he said. "There is no Lucas Oil Stadium without Peyton. Without Peyton, the Colts would probably be [relocated] in L.A. right now."

———

Long after everyone else had cleared out for a victory party at the hotel and the streets back in Hoosierland had been jammed in celebration, Peyton put on his dark suit and tie and shuffled out, a winner. Outside of the stadium, the Colt bus waited for him, his teammates beyond impatient. But he lingered a last minute when he saw in the dim light Archie and Cooper, who had also waited for him in the rain. Cooper began trotting toward his brother. "Dad! Come on!" he yelled to Archie, whose knees made him lag behind. Together, they all hugged in silence, a puddle at their feet. They said a few words and parted. Now, his suit ruined, Peyton was finally ready to climb aboard the bus.

The best part may have been reading the now-unanimous verdict in the media that, as the AP game story read, "Peyton Manning answered the final question. Yes, he can win the big one—and yes, he can do it in a big way, too." *Sports Illustrated* hailed the "Colt Heroes" on its cover, under yet another vibrant shot of Peyton, who was on that cover so often, the magazine might as well have been called *Peyton Illustrated*. There was, however, a mild clucking of irritation among the Colts that he was hogging the spotlight. "Everyone thinks this is about Peyton's legacy," said Dwight Freeney, "but listen—this is a 53-man team. Peyton doesn't do everything by himself, and at the end of the day defense wins championships."

He was kidding himself. For a quarterback with self-promotional skills, to win one of these things is a windfall. Even before, Manning had established his entrepreneurial pipes. Now, noted one business writer, his "endorsement price could jump 10 to 20% [and] marketers say . . . he still can increase his appeal with the non-sports audience."[34] To the NFL writ large, he was the main attraction. Not Brady. Not the crumbling Favre. At 30, he had gone where no Manning had, and as the one with the most to gain—but also the most to lose. Like any other addiction, winning had diminishing returns; it was more fleeting than losing, and set up the deepest falls from grace, far deeper than any mooning scandal could have ever precipitated. Even as he left Miami with that shiny trophy and all those headlines, about to spend the next months on a treadmill of appearances and supplemental award banquets, he felt under the gun to keep winning.

At the apex of his career, he went to the Pro Bowl a week later in Honolulu, perhaps a bit too full of himself. Joining in on some locker room byplay, he began ribbing Michael Strahan about his recent divorce. Hearing this, the bull-necked Fox football analyst Jay Glazer, a New York guy friendly with Strahan, wasn't amused and cursed out Manning, who, with a friend, started coming at him until a buddy of Glazer's, a mixed martial arts fighter, came over and Peyton quickly backed down. Glazer would later smirk that if the fight had happened, Peyton would have lasted "about six or seven seconds." He added that he and Manning put it behind them.[35]

Indeed, it seemed that no one—at least in the game or the media—could stay mad at Peyton Manning for long. Not teammates, not opponents. Even Ryan Leaf looked back and conceded that, unlike himself, Manning "handled everything just like he was supposed to."[36] For the Manning brand, nothing could have been a better selling point.

CHAPTER 19

ANYTHING YOU CAN DO

In the off-season, Peyton hosted *Saturday Night Live*, unveiling heretofore hidden talents for subtle, self-deprecating, even cruelly cynical Eli-style humor, if it was in step with cultural cool. The show, which aired on March 24, began with a monologue in which he said he had met his goals for the season—including "appearing in half the nation's TV commercials"—and calling out in the audience Archie, Eli, and Olivia, the last "a real disappointment to us . . . she never made it to the NFL." The best sketch found him working with kids at a United Way–style camp, where he barks complex signals, tells a kid who missed a pass, "You suck!," tries to break into a car with a crowbar, and tattoos a kid's leg with the image of his face. Then he sits with the group, beer in his hand.

"I'll kill a snitch," he tells them. "I'm not saying I have, but I'm not saying I haven't. Whatever. You kids don't know [bleep]." The sketch ends with a voice-over saying, "Spend time with your kids, so Peyton Manning doesn't."

Tom Condon, meanwhile, dealing with reality, restructured Eli's contract, garnering him a $5 million option bonus, a $1 million roster bonus, and a $900,000 restructure bonus. His salary increased to $6.5 million, with additional bonuses down the line. This show of confidence in Eli came as the general feeling around the Giants was that they were on the cusp of their awakening as an honest contender, needing just a few tweaks. Tom Coughlin hired a new quarterbacks coach, Chris Palmer, another of his old Jaguar adjutants, who made some changes in the off-season practice routine, having Eli spend long hours working on patterns with Plaxico Burress and Jeremy Shockey. It was something Peyton did in endless reps with Marvin Harrison and Dallas Clark, mind-melding the most dependable guns of the attack.

But the Giants' '07 season opener, in Dallas on Sunday night, was a bummer. Eli burst out of the gate, throwing a 60-yard touchdown to Burress on the first drive. The Cowboys, with Tony Romo, got back some of it with a field goal, then took the lead on a Marion Barber TD run, and by the fourth quarter Romo had thrown three touchdowns for a 38–22 lead. Tenaciously, Manning accounted for two touchdowns in three minutes, cutting it to 38–35 with four minutes left. But the Giants defense went limp and Romo uncorked a 51-yard touchdown to Sam Hurd to put it away, 45–35. While both quarterbacks threw four touchdowns and combined for nearly 700 yards, the Giants defense was suspect.

Worse, a number of Giants came away hurt, including Eli with a bruised shoulder. With the Packers coming in next, Coughlin could not risk resting him, but Manning's blah game, and Brett Favre's three touchdown passes, sent the team down 35–13. Finding themselves playing for their lives after just two games, game three was a tough nut in D.C., and in the third quarter the Redskins led 17–3. The season appeared lost. But a comeback began, and on a key third-and-eight, Eli picked up 21 on a pass to Shockey, preceding a short Reuben Droughns touchdown run. Then, in the fourth quarter, Droughns ran in another for a 17–17 tie. Getting the ball back with 7:33 to go, a 'Skins pass interference penalty set up Eli's laser to Burress from 33 yards for the lead. Now it was up to the maligned defense, and it bent—far, but with the ball on the Giants' one-yard line, three times they held, the last on fourth down when they hit the runner for a two-yard loss.

That thrilling quarter saved the season, one that would have more magic in store. They won six in a row, seven of eight, nine of 11, and two days before Christmas they were 10–5 and in the playoffs. Eli's numbers overall were middling, throwing for 3,336 yards, his quarterback rating only 73.9, but he was Mr. Clutch. He took the team from behind to win with six game-winning drives, most in the league. When Shockey went down for the season with a fibula injury, things kept rolling with Kevin Boss; so much so that Shockey, the frequent All-Pro, was traded to the Saints after the season.

_____

Meanwhile, the Colts defended their title almost with a yawn. They won their division at 13–3, as Peyton threw for over 4,000 yards and 31 touchdowns versus 14 interceptions, his passer rating 98.0. There was a possibility the Mannings might just decide the Super Bowl between themselves if everything broke right. And because the Giants were in as one of the two NFC wild cards, with no chance to catch the division-leading Cowboys, they normally would have taken it easy in the regular-season finale. But this was no meaningless game. Eli was the only thing that stood between the Patriots and history.

Belichick's team came into the Meadowlands in week 17 having won all 15 of their games, gaining headlines not only for winning, but for doing what many NFL people assumed was part of any of their game plans: cheating. This was, of course, the result of "Spygate," Belichick's illegal videotaping of the Jets' coaches from the opposite sideline during the season opener, presumably to steal signals, which got him the biggest fine ever assessed against a coach—$500,000—and cost the team another $250,000 plus the forfeiture of its first-round draft pick. Belichick, at his smarmiest, admitted to "a mistake" only technically, insisting he didn't use the tapes that game. He denied the league the tapes, but NFL officials confiscated, played, and subsequently destroyed them.[1] Seeing his record challenged, Don Shula, the coach of history's only undefeated team, the '72 Dolphins, debited the Patriots, saying Spygate "has diminished what they've accomplished," a common conclusion ever since.[2]

Both teams prepared as if the game were a Super Bowl, the Giants playing all their starters, even with nothing to gain. While many of their fans sold their seats to Patriot fans, Coughlin was convinced the team would reap enormous momentum from an unlikely win. To do that, they would need to stub Brady, whose numbers that year were inhuman.

Given an atom bomb when Belichick traded for the seemingly withered Randy Moss before the season, a great team became greater. At 30, Moss seemed past his All-Pro prime, but with Brady he was reborn. The New England offense, with Brady throwing for over 4,800 yards, was the best in the league, the defense fourth-best. But Manning pumped out four touchdown passes, two to Burress. Brady hit on two, both to Moss, the second of which, a 65-yard bomb that put the Pats ahead in the fourth quarter, was the biggie, and quite historic. It broke two records, Brady notching his 50th touchdown pass, eclipsing Peyton's mark, and Moss catching his 23rd touchdown. The Pats held on, Eli's late touchdown closing it to 38–35.

The mind-set coming out of this game was odd; because the Giants had given the Pats hell, it boosted them and pricked the Pats, who seemed vulnerable. The Giants, emotionally wrought all week long, came off the field preening like winners, and should have sounded deluded when they boldly said they'd win the next time around, like in the Super Bowl. Instead, it became a battle cry, and probably one that rankled the Pats. However, the game also gave a shot of courage to other teams who might get a crack at the Pats, the most obvious being the one in Indianapolis.

———

The Colts' season was a steamroller in itself. Though overlooked amid the Patriots' dramatics, they scored the third-most points in the league and surrendered the least. With Marvin Harrison hurt, aging, and on the way out, Reggie Wayne went over 100 receptions. They were more dependent on the rush, scoring the second-most rushing touchdowns, 19. Joseph Addai scored 12 on his own in another 1,000-yard season. Their first playoff game, in the divisional round, brought the Chargers to the RCA Dome. For Peyton, it was a flashback to a nightmare. In November, when the Colts had played San Diego on the coast, he threw six picks, the most he had ever thrown at any level, three to Antonio Cromartie alone. He also threw two touchdowns and had 328 yards passing, and fought back from down 23–0 to make it close, losing 23–21, but the stench of those picks drove him; the Colts didn't lose again until the finale, when he only played half the game.

The Chargers were generally an awful playoff team, and the Colts were 11-point favorites. Peyton put them ahead with a 25-yard pass to Clark, but it became a touchdown-for-touchdown battle between him and Philip Rivers as they combined for seven touchdowns. Rivers was more economical; he threw only 19 times but completed 14, for 264 yards, while Peyton, his running game static, heaved it 48 times, hitting on 33 for 402 yards. In the third quarter, down 14–10 but on the Charger doorstep, he panicked and aimed a short pass at running back Kenton Keith. Safety Eric Weddle sneaked underneath and snatched it.

Manning did rise up and throw TD passes to Wayne and Anthony Gonzalez, and with 10 minutes left, Indianapolis led 24–21. Rivers was now gone with a knee injury and little-used backup Billy Volek was in. But Volek, helped by a Colt face mask penalty on a third-down pass, took the Chargers to the Colts one, then ran it in for a 28–24 lead with 4:54 left. Peyton would get the ball back twice. The first time, he got it to the Chargers seven. In a strange set of play calls, three straight times he threw a short pass for Addai—and all three fell incomplete. The last series was a four-and-out. Season over.

As ignominious as it was—"Implosion" was the headline in the *Star*—Dungy, his contract up, freely spoke about retiring. Peyton, his ambivalence about the perils of winning driven home in the span of one year, spoke of going back to square one and relearning what it took to win. He included himself in that indictment, with cause. Because if a case could be made that the Colts' defense, save for one year, never seemed to come up big in these playoff games, there was an equally strong case that neither did Peyton Manning. Dungy rightly says that those Colt teams understood the biblical truism that nothing is ever promised, but that Peyton's value was that he gave them the right to feel it was. If so, they also understood that the positive energy ebbed when Peyton's knack for making the big play vanished in the haze. The Chargers would get the Patriots, full of optimism. Antonio Gates, their great tight end, said, "We got something special now."[3] Or so they thought. The Pats pushed them aside, 21–12, moving on to the Super Bowl, looking to close out a perfect season, but they were no doubt just a tad nervous about who was waiting for them.

The Giants, fueled by the glorious defeat in week 17, were still juiced when they blew by the favored Bucs. Next came a higher bar, and one with more history: the Cowboys in the divisional playoff, with Dallas salivating after sweeping their two regular-season games. The bettors made them seven-point favorites, and they would hold the ball 13 minutes longer, gain 106 more yards, and pick up 10 of 16 third downs. Marion Barber ran for 129 yards. But Tony Romo, a Pro Bowler for the second year in a row, went 18 of 36 for 201 yards, his longest a mere 20 yards, as *his* reputation as a big-game schlemiel grew. Eli was a modest 12 of 18 for 163 yards, but two of those were touchdowns to Toomer. Early in the fourth quarter, Jacobs scored for the lead. The rest of the game saw Romo cranking up but never getting it done. With 26 seconds left, he was close, at the Giant 23. Two incompletions and an end-zone interception later, it was over, 21–17. The Mannings could appreciate his postgame admission.

"It hurts," he said.

Each of these upset victories fed the Giants' hunger for more. The NFC championship game would be at Lambeau Field, and the Packers had their own incentive, the 38-year-old Brett Favre having said he'd retire after the season. (He wouldn't, of course, signing with the Jets, and then the Vikings, perpetuating a tiresome annual will-he-or-won't-he retirement fandango.) Favre, the greatest quarterback to be born in Mississippi—though, like the second-greatest, his roots had also been transplanted to Louisiana—had broken John Elway's career records of 148 regular-season wins and 162 overall victories and had broken several passing records, including yards, touchdowns, and pass attempts.

In a throwback year, he passed for over 4,000 yards with 28 touchdowns. Going 13–3 under coach Mike McCarthy, the best the Pack had been in a decade, Favre and his big target, Donald Driver, were bound for the Pro Bowl. Fresh off a 42–20 stomping of the Seahawks in the first round, they were 7½-point favorites.

For the Giants to pull off another upset, they would need to control the ball and keep Favre off the field, and they were aided by treacherous conditions. The temperature at Lambeau was minus-1, the windchill minus-23, reminiscent of the legendary 1967 Ice Bowl game on this same field. The Pack, with a weak running game, could only manage 28 yards on the ground, while Jacobs and Ahmad Bradshaw would eat up 134 yards, freeing Eli to throw for 251 yards. The Giants owned the ball for 40 minutes, but Favre threw for 236 yards. Early in the second quarter, all he did was make the longest touchdown in team history—90 yards, to Driver. In the third quarter, Eli led an eight-minute march, converting three third-down plays, and a Jacobs touchdown made it 13–10. Favre then came back with a 12-yard TD to Donald Lee. It was 20–20 in the last minute. Eli expertly moved into field-goal range, only to have Lawrence Tynes miss from 36 yards. This brought about that wonderful playoff treat: overtime. With nightfall having turned the field into a slab of ice, Favre tried to find Driver, but Corey Webster picked it off. Tynes, making amends, booted the 47-yard game winner.

For many, Eli had arisen during this crazy dream sequence as Peyton's better when the pressure was on. He still had the interception bug, but was so calm and collected when staring at a big play that the joke was he actually could make the play in his sleep, because that's what he seemed to be doing anyway.

———

This ongoing upset spree, the last delivering their fourth NFC title, created a mythic veneer for the Giants, who now had what they wished for: the rematch with the Patriots, winner take all, on February 3. Co-opting any slights from the Belichick gulag, the Giants started right in, with vigor. Burress predicted they'd win 23–17. Brady, yukking it up, answered, "We're only going to score 17 points?"[4] It did seem a preposterous notion; the Pats had scored an average of 36.8 points a game, twice going over 50.

At least the Giants were entertaining. When they landed in Phoenix six days before the game at the University of Phoenix Stadium in Glendale, Arizona, they wore black suits and ties, boasting that they were "dressed to kill." Seeing it on the news, Randy Moss responded he would be wearing black *after* the game—to mourn the Giants.[5]

On a technical level, the Giants were convinced that they had the answers. Coughlin swore the Pats had some weaknesses, that they were slow picking up blitzes by defensive backs and the weak-side linebacker—a specialty of Giants defensive coordinator Steve Spagnuolo. They also saw from the film that the Jets had confused Brady by lining up linemen in different slots than usual. The Giants were a voracious sack team—52 on the year, the aging Michael Strahan and the young Justin Tuck combining for 19 of them. Still, it was a grim task. The Giants came in no less than a 12½-point underdog, one of the biggest spreads in Super Bowl history. The Pats had already paid to register the trademark "Perfect Season 19–0." And Burress, who had been playing on a sprained ankle, slipped in the shower at the hotel, injuring a ligament in his knee, making him cry like a baby when he thought he couldn't play. He did, but couldn't practice all week.

Still, this would be a war of attrition. The first two drives took the entire opening quarter, each team slogging a few yards at a time toward the end zone, the Giant drive, spanning 9:59, the longest in Super Bowl history. The Pats led 7–3 at the half and went on a 16-play drive to start the second half, but the Giants held when Belichick went for it on fourth-and-13 from the Giant 31 and Brady misfired. The Giants front four was shutting down the Patriots offense. Brady found his sawed-off receiver Wes Welker 11 times, Moss five, but his longest completion was just 19 yards. Unable to set and throw because of a well-timed blitz or sack, he went down five times, which had not happened since 2003—twice he was cornered by Tuck, who lined up in various positions, and weak-side linebacker Kawika Mitchell was often in his face. His runners gained all of 45 yards; Laurence Maroney, who had gained 244 yards in the first two playoff games, had 36. Brady, the touchdown machine, went without any. Moss would later say he was surprised that the Giants' intensity "was greater than ours."

But when the Giants went ahead on Eli's five-yard touchdown pass to spare receiver David Tyree, it was the preface to the game's ultimate, and most unlikely, play. A Jersey native, Tyree had been a sixth-round pick out of Syracuse in '03 but was mainly a special-teams guy, partly due to addictions to booze and pot, for which he was busted in 2004.

He managed to salvage a career by affirming a newfound faith in God. But the '07 regular season ended with him having only four catches for 35 yards. At a pregame practice, he had dropped a bunch of passes. Eli reassured him, "Forget it. You're a gamer. I know you are." Not that this seemed to matter when Brady led another long march, passing on 11 of 12 plays, finding Moss with a six-yard touchdown with 2:45 left, leaving the Giants fully spent and, as one reporter wrote, "limping off the field."[6]

So now the Giants had it at their own 17, down 14–10. Eli, who had thrown a pick earlier trying to force things, kept it conservative. On second-and-five from the Giant 44, Manning went to Tyree down the right sideline, but overshot him. Asante Samuel, his eyes widening, leaped for a sure interception, but the ball slid through his hands. Given life, on third-and-five with 1:15 left, Manning took the shotgun snap and looked deep over the middle, but from the right side, defensive end Jarvis Green closed in. Eli eluded him and stepped up into a crowd of blockers and tacklers, Green clutching a fistful of his jersey. The Giants seemed to ease up, expecting that the play had ended, as did most everyone else—but not Tyree, who when he saw Eli in trouble, broke off his post route and headed down the middle. When Eli slipped free of Green and retreated five yards back to the 33—"That looked like Archie running around at Ole Miss," Olivia would say—he caught sight of Tyree.

His arm cocked before he set his feet, he let fly a wobbly spiral. As it fell to Earth inside the Pats 25, Tyree, picked up by Rodney Harrison, jumped before Harrison could. Both elevated as if for a jump ball, arms rising high. Harrison, seeing the ball up near Tyree's head, kept reaching to grab either it or Tyree's arm. The ball had slipped through Tyree's hands, but, remarkably, he pressed the ball against his helmet as he fell, securing it. Coming down on top of Harrison, the soft landing helped him maintain control of the ball. Harrison, the ball in Tyree's hands, violently rolled over him, trying to jar it loose.

On the Fox telecast, Troy Aikman exclaimed, "My God!" Replays from numerous angles showed what looked like an optical illusion. Nobody could remember seeing anything like what would go down in history as Tyree's "helmet catch." On the field, the players and coaches had their eyes glued to the giant screen, the catch seeming crazier with each replay, the Pats in absolute disbelief. The Giants took their second time-out with 59 seconds left. Then Eli was sacked, but on third-and-11 he zipped one to Smith for 12. First down on the 13-yard line, 45 seconds to go. Now, going to Burress on a play the team called a "sluggo"—a slant and go—he took the snap from the shotgun and then took two quick steps back. Burress slanted to the inside, changed course, and cut for the left side of the end zone, freeing himself from cornerback Ellis Hobbs. He turned just as the ball came down right into his hands. The Giants swarmed over Burress and slapped Eli on the helmet as he came off the field. The television camera trained on the Manning brood in their VIP box showed Peyton clapping wildly. Brady had 74 yards to go in 29 seconds. After a sack and three incomplete passes, it was over—17–14.

The Manning clan could now celebrate the apogee of the dynasty: two seasons, two championships, one for each brother, the younger avenging the older against a shared opponent. It was every bit the classic people were already calling it, Tim Layden in *Sports Illustrated* codifying "the second-greatest upset in a Super Bowl" after Joe Namath's victory in Super Bowl III and "the culmination of a season in which a team, a quarterback and a coach found themselves linked by a deep resilience and rode it to the top of their sport."[7] The Pats were left in a funk. Eyes glazed, Hobbs said, "I've never been a witness to anything like that. Every play went their way. Every play."[8] And while Burress's prediction about the 17 points was dead on, the klieg lights shone most brightly not on the defense that had held the Pats to 274 yards (the Giants had 338), but, as almost always, on the winning quarterback. Given the game's MVP award and a gaudy Cadillac Escalade, Eli was lionized the next day the way Peyton had been—he was "Mister Cool," wrote an AP reporter.

For Tyree, it was one shining moment, one immortal catch—which he called "supernatural." The next year, he injured his knee, then was cut in '09, to make news trying to persuade the New York State legislature not to allow gay marriage, calling it "sliding toward anarchy."[9] Eli, like his brother, was part of something larger than any given game. He knew it, too, saying through the ear-splitting din and champagne-spraying mayhem in the locker room, "It's just surreal." He danced into the morning at the team party at their hotel, the Sheraton Wild Horse Pass Resort in Chandler, Arizona, at one point getting up and joining with his brothers to sing endless choruses of "New York, New York." The headlines in the hometown papers bathed him in adulation—"Super Men—Giants Kick Pats In"; "Big Blue Heaven"; "Eli Leads Greatest Victory Ever"; "Giant Upset." And yet, Eli had some cynicism about being the toast of the town. "I've had a lot of downs in New York," he said. "A lot of times I've thought, Why have I gotten this treatment? Do I deserve this?" But it was really the *family* that had won. That was what Manning Inc. meant. As another headline put it, "Winning Now a Family Business for Mannings."[10]

———

After stringing Abby McGrew along for years, Eli now decided the time was finally right for a wedding. She had moved to New York to study fashion, then worked for the Pamella Roland boutique (which offered a crystal-trimmed, shoulder-silk caftan for $6,985). They had been living together in Eli's Hoboken pad. Then, in the spring of '07, he took her to his hometown for Mardi Gras. He stopped into an Adler's jewelry shop and ordered a ring with an emerald-cut stone and emerald-encased diamonds. Then he took her to dinner, got on a knee, and popped the question. They set a date for the spring and, two months after the Super Bowl, made it official at a resort hotel in Los Cabos, Mexico, with sweeping vistas of the Sea of Cortez. A New Orleans high society website noted that Abby wore a Monique Lhuillier gown; Eli, his father, and brothers wore tan suits.

The newest Mr. and Mrs. Manning began making appearances at events like a film society gala tribute to Alice Tully Hall, hosting exclusive charity dinners, and running with her corps d'elite friends on Park and Madison Avenues and out in the Hamptons. For a rebel who once detested such pomposity, he was getting rather comfy with these rituals, even enjoying getting gussied up in a tux and smiling for cameras. While Peyton had consciously avoided wanting to play in New York, for Eli it was a gas. But New Orleans was still in his blood, so he also made plans to build a home in the Garden District, as had Peyton and Cooper. Still, he was comfy in the lap of old-money Yankee aristocracy, and whatever it took to stay with the Giants, he would do. The last step was starting a family, and their first child, Ava Frances, was born in 2010, followed by daughters Lucy in 2013 and Caroline Olivia in 2015—the exact opposite of Archie's three boys.

Eli had seen intimately how Archie had had to navigate issues like favoritism, life-and-death reactions to games, and constant involvement in matters he thought he had left behind, and he wanted none of that. He was glad to have daughters, knowing he would never be turned inside out watching them play big-time football. It was hard enough watching Archie not being able to kick back and enjoy his senior years, still living and dying on every down.

CHAPTER 20

"THE POWER OF PEYTON"

Eli Manning, of all people, was now part of the glitterati. After the Packer win, he and Abby had dinner at Rao's, a chi-chi Italian restaurant in East Harlem. Getting up to go to the bathroom, he was given a standing ovation by the swells. He could, of course, well afford such epicurean dining in the most stupidly expensive city in creation. His salary for '08 would kick in at $8.5 million, plus $2.5 million in bonuses—about $600,000 less than Peyton, though what was a half million or so between brothers? Indeed, in the Mannings' prime the NFL's corporate ceiling not only rose but flew away, and both guaranteed themselves the kind of money that only their accountants could tabulate.

A *New York* magazine profile of Eli, written before the Super Bowl, based his entire net value as a city mahatma on the game's outcome. The author, Adam Sternbergh, lamented that while glamour puss Tom Brady would be "the perfect New York quarterback," Eli was "the anti–New York quarterback," a "poker-faced yokel" who "isn't a fire-in-the-belly kind of guy [but] a well-balanced breakfast in the belly. . . . [O]ff the field, he's just as disappointing. He talks to his mom on the phone nearly every day. He can't even get stalked properly." However, if he somehow beat Brady, "Eli will become a bigger hero than the efficient Phil Simms, bigger even than glamorous, amorous Broadway Joe [Namath]." In which case, he would be, in a town of front-runners, "the perfect New York hero for these times."[1] Apparently, a steady hand was the fixative for times skidding into recession due to capricious spending—something the NFL had no fear about falling victim to. But whether or not Eli actually was a perfect heroic metaphor, he had no qualm about being able to run now with the same parvenus who tut-tutted about his yokel-ness, no doubt appreciating the irony that he could buy and sell them. However, as Peyton found out, in the inbred world of football, success can undo the chemistry of winning. In May, at the Giants' minicamp, Burress sat out, complaining that he was underpaid at his current $3.25 million salary. The team agreed to a $35 million contract extension, but he was miffed that so much was contingent on incentives. In camp, he was dour and hostile, not a good sign.

The season began with a bang. In the opener against the Redskins, Eli ran one in from a yard out and the Giants cruised to a 16–7 win, Burress grabbing 10 passes. They won their first four games, lost to the Browns, then ripped off the next seven, standing 11–1 on November 30. That was when the Burress time bomb exploded.

In September, his wife had obtained a restraining order on him after two calls to police about domestic violence, though the order was dismissed.[2] He also made derogatory remarks about officials—and actually slapped one in the face—incurring $60,000 in fines. Repeating an old bit, he went AWOL during midweek practices and was suspended for a game. On November 2, he caught his 500th career pass. Then, on November 28, partying at a nightclub, he reached for a gun that he felt slipping in his pocket. It accidentally discharged, putting a bullet in his thigh. Though he wasn't seriously hurt, as the news and inevitable jokes spread, he was charged with criminal possession and reckless endangerment.[3]

Indicted by a grand jury in July, he copped a plea and was sentenced to two years, serving 20 months. This lunacy had little impact on the team. The '08 season was very much like the Colts' post-championship one the year before. Without much trouble, they finished 12–4. The offense ranked seventh, the defense fifth. Eli went to the Pro Bowl, throwing for 3,238 yards, 21 touchdowns, a mere 10 interceptions, and amassing an 86.4 rating, the draft bringing him another promising receiver, Mario Manningham. Domenik Hixon stepped in for Burress, joining Toomer,

Smith, and Boss. Jacobs and Derrick Ward ran for over 1,000 yards. Strahan's retirement did nothing to crimp the defense, which piled up 42 sacks, Tuck with 12 of them.

The wild-card Eagles came to the Meadowlands for the first playoff game, a very beatable team that quickly showed why. Donovan McNabb went 22 of 40 for 217 yards with two picks. The Eagles gained all of 59 yards on 28 carries, to the Giants' 138 rushing yards. But Eli was a jittery 15 of 29 for only 169 yards, with two picks of his own, the first deep in his own territory only seven minutes in. In the end, the Eagles won 23–11. For Eli, the sweet smell of success turned to the old putrefaction of failure. Suddenly, no one was seeing him as a hero of the times anymore, just that little-bit-odd fellow who threw all those passes to the other team. As endless stand-up comics have said about New York, it's a tough crowd.

———

As for the "other" Manning, he had a new workplace in '08: the 67,500-seat, retractable-roofed Lucas Oil Stadium, a couple of blocks from the abandoned RCA Dome. He also had to deal with his first serious physical hurdle. During the off-season, Peyton had surgery on his left knee, which had given him periodic problems, but by training camp he had healed well enough. Tony Dungy had decided to return for another go-around, believing the Colts had learned their lesson. Like the Giants, they rolled to a 12–4 record, and Peyton to first-team All-Pro honors, cracking 4,000 yards again. Four of his receivers had at least four touchdowns, including Harrison in his last year; the same kind of balance had Addai and Rhodes gain almost the same yardage, 544–538. The defensive ends, Dwight Freeney and Robert Mathis, combined for 22 sacks. Although they had given up home-field advantage by finishing a game behind Tennessee in the AFC South, even as a wild card they were favored over the Chargers on the road in the first playoff round.

Trailing 14–10 in the third quarter, Peyton went deep down the left sideline to Wayne, who broke for a 72-yard touchdown—helping him run up over 300 yards with no interceptions, towering over Philip Rivers, who had 217 yards and was sacked four times. But even with the Chargers fumbling at the Colts' nine-yard line and Rivers throwing a pick, Peyton could not put it away; a field goal sent it to overtime, and after taking the kickoff Rivers went on a long drive that was kept alive by three Colt penalties. Darren Sproles, on a bad ankle, ran it in from the 22 to end it, 23–17. The Colts were livid about the penalties. "Those were the worst fucking calls I've seen in a long time," raged Freeney in a rant that would cost him $20,000 in fines. "It's just disgusting. It's not like they made one bad fucking call—it's three calls, in overtime. They need to start investigating."[4]

It was also the death of the Manning-a-Manning Super Bowl fantasy, although the Giants extended Eli's contract into a six-year, $97.6 million deal (with the one year of his old deal left, it translated to seven years at $106.9 million). His salary was a league-high $15.3 million, with signing bonuses of $13 million each year—the cherry a $12.5 million option bonus deferred to 2010, when his bonuses would total, gulp, $26 million.[5]

Jerry Reese, who had succeeded Ernie Accorsi as general manager in '07, becoming the third African-American GM in the league and first to reach the Super Bowl, issued a justification: "He is a franchise quarterback. He has done everything we asked him to do. He has come in, taken a lot of flak from you guys [the media] and he just keeps going. He does what we ask him on the field and he does what we ask him to do off the field." And while all this lucre battered the spending cap, limiting the team's ability to make moves, Eli earned his keep well, passing for over 4,000 yards for the first time and amassing his most touchdowns yet, 27, with just 14 interceptions and a 93.1 rating. (He also notched, as had Peyton in '04, a perfect passer rating, in a game against the Raiders.) The offense was there, with the surprise emergence of third-year running back Ahmad Bradshaw, who ran for 778 yards and eight touchdowns. The Giants won their first five games, then went flaccid, dropping four in a row and six of the last 10, giving up at least 40 points five times, allowing the second-most points and rushing touchdowns in the NFL. The team went 8–8, out of the money.

Meanwhile, Peyton was just getting started, the old drama queen just coming out of intermission.

═══

Peyton's salary that '09 season was $14 million, with two years left on his contract, the last of which would bring in $23 million in bonuses. (The Colts had to work within tight salary-cap constraints, having given Freeney a six-year, $72 million contract in 2007 with $30 million in guarantees, and Jeff Saturday a $13 million extension and $7.5 million bonus.) While Eli had been paid so well to reignite the fire in the belly of his team, it was Peyton who did that for his, turning in arguably his best season. With Dungy retired, Jim Caldwell was elevated to head coach, with the same hands-off policy toward his quarterback. Tom Moore stuck around as de facto offensive coordinator; the real boss, his quarterback, decided to all but forgo the running game. The Colts would have the second-fewest carries and fewest rushing yards in the league—and the second-most passing attempts and yardage, to go with the league lead in touchdowns.

Marvin Harrison, who had outlived his considerable usefulness to the team, was gone after getting to third place in all-time receptions. He had refused to take a pay cut and asked for his release just as the "quiet man" was embroiled in a mess back home in Philadelphia, stemming from a 2008 confrontation with a convicted drug dealer who was shot in the hand. Even though a gun traced to Harrison was found, authorities didn't press criminal charges. The dealer and a bystander who claimed he was wounded in the back filed a civil suit against Harrison, whereupon the dealer was shot again and claimed Harrison had done it. Yet again, he was not prosecuted, even after the FBI investigated.[6]

Peyton did his own gunslinging. The opener was nothing to brag about, a 14–12 win over the Jaguars, but Manning's 301-yard game was an appetizer. They won 14 straight, including another satisfying decision over the Patriots in mid-November at Lucas Oil Stadium—a classic guns-blazing match with Brady, the two of them with almost identical stats that day: Brady 29 of 42 for 375 yards and three touchdowns, with one pick; Manning 28 of 44 for 327, with four TDs and two INTs. But Peyton survived the picks and came up big late. Trailing 31–14, he hurled a touchdown to Pierre Garçon; then, after a Gostkowski field goal, a short run by Addai got the Colts to within six. With 2:08 left, on a fourth-and-two on his own 28, Belichick riskily eschewed a punt and went for it. Brady, who feasted on these situations, fired a safe pass to Kevin Faulk, who was wrapped up by defensive back Melvin Bullitt. It looked like Faulk had the first down, but the ref spotted the ball short as Belichick screamed in frustration the way the Colts had in past meetings. Taking over, Peyton guided a perfect two-minute offense, getting it to the one-yard line. And with 16 seconds to go, he took a quick snap and sent a slant pass to Wayne that won it with the extra point, 35–34.

Caldwell now had a decision to make. The team had clinched home-field advantage throughout the playoffs. Like the Patriots the year before, he could have gone for the undefeated season, but the Pats' Super Bowl letdown seemed to him like the result of too much needless pressure. Others argued that it would take a Lourdes-level miracle to beat them and that pride, as well as keeping the killer instinct, would be an advantage. The coach decided to rest the regulars in those last two games, which the Colts lost. This did not cheapen Manning's stats in another MVP season—4,500 passing yards, a conference-leading 68.8 completion percentage, 33 touchdowns (one behind Drew Brees), 16 picks, only 10 sacks, and a 99.9 rating. But more than a few in the Colts locker room would have preferred the plum of perfection.

As it was, the first-round playoff opponents were the Ravens, who in addition to their thorny defense and manic jive by Ray Lewis, now had a real quarterback, Joe Flacco, and in Ray Rice one of the top breakaway running backs. They had beaten the Patriots in the wild-card round, 33–14, in Foxborough, and the defense was naturally stingy, stopping the Colts' ground game cold. In a freak turn, the perennial All-Pro free safety Ed Reed, a master of the interception, picked Manning off twice on the same drive, fumbling away the first and a penalty wiping out the second. But Caldwell's own defense was sizzling. "These guys moved the entire game," Rice said later. "We don't see this on a regular basis. Everything we see is a 3-4 front. They play a spread offense, and they have a speed defense."[7] Defensive backs Antoine Bethea and Jerraud Powers picked off Flacco passes, and he fumbled twice. Behind Manning's 30-for-44, two-touchdown effort, it ended 20–3.

Tough as the win was, it gave hope to the surprise challengers in the AFC championship game, the Jets. Coached into relevance again by the bloated Rex Ryan, whose clownish bluster masked his expertise as a defensive strategist, and his defensive coordinator, Mike Pettine, the Jets' defense was a stone wall that allowed the fewest yards and points in the league. They sent two defenders to the Pro Bowl: end Shaun Ellis and first-team All-Pro Darrelle Revis, the consensus lockdown cornerback. Fullback Thomas Jones, who ran for over 1,400 yards, was essentially the offense; quarterback Mark Sanchez was almost never permitted to throw long. But Ryan changed things up in the playoffs. Sanchez cranked up 30 passes, throwing for 257 yards and two touchdowns—the first, to Braylon Edwards, breaking for 80 yards—to lead 17–6.

The Colts, 8½-point favorites, had little going right. The Jets overloaded the deep zone with up to seven defensive backs. Early on, Peyton struggled, nailed by some of Ryan's hidden blitzes. Cooper later said the mood in the family's VIP box was "tense." But seven times during the season, they had won when they were trailing as late as the fourth quarter. Several of them reminded each other of being down to the Pats by 18 three years before in this same game. Peyton, who had watched film of Ryan defenses going back to his days as the Ravens' assistant coach, kept attacking and hit on three unanswered touchdowns, the game changer a 46-yard strike to Austin Collie between two defenders just before halftime, then Garçon and Clark, pulling away to a 30–17 final score. In the end, Peyton ripped Ryan's schemes for 377 yards. Eli, coming into the locker room, hugged him. "I'm really proud of you," he said.

On the pedestal after the game, Peyton was handed the Lamar Hunt Trophy for winning the AFC championship. As Lee Jenkins wrote in *Sports Illustrated*, he "looked at it as though he were being handed a pair of used socks," nothing like the giddy dancing they did around the same trophy three years before, when he finally exorcised the demon of Tom Brady. Freeney had said back then that it "felt better than the Super Bowl." Now, wrote Jenkins, "the Colts acted as if they'd just beaten the Jaguars in September." The headline of the *SI* story credited their drive to get back to the only game that mattered to one primal force: "The Power of Peyton."[8]

Or perhaps it was the power of the *Mannings*. After all, the coming Super Bowl would mark the third time in four years that Manning Inc. was the real winner, as the centerpiece of the highest-rated TV show of the year.

═════

That climactic game would be on February 7 against the Saints, on the same field where the Colts had last won it all, Miami's newly renamed Sun Life Stadium. Archie's old team had at long last become an elite bunch, the ghost of the bag-wearing, margarita-slinging days slain by Drew Brees's arm and an offensive line Archie would have killed to work behind. Even though a lot of time had elapsed since those days, for the Manning family, playing against the Saints still carried a bit of the dread Peyton had felt when he first played against Ole Miss. Archie naturally felt it the most, having also worked for years as the team's radio analyst. Seeing the mild-mannered Brees—whom Eli would have had to beat out had he signed with the Chargers back in 2004—rise as New Orleans's superhero on and off the field, Archie must have seen as much of himself in Brees as he did in his own sons. Indeed, Archie and Olivia had helped Brees find a house in New Orleans. On their recommendation, Tom Condon was his agent. A voluble Christian, Brees gave much time and money to Katrina relief and other charities, churches, and schools, such as funding the city's after-school ballet program.

As saintly as Brees was, Peyton Manning was just as charitable. On the strength of a significant donation, Indianapolis renamed its children's hospital after him in 2007. In 2010, a local high school basketball player named Kevin Massey, who had a brain tumor and was given 24 hours to live, was sent to the hospital for treatment; he is still alive today.[9] But Brees was the new flavor. Working on a six-year, $69 million contract, Brees was a penthouse quarterback, throwing for more yards over the previous four seasons than anyone and tied with Peyton for most touchdowns. A tremendously accurate passer—his 70.6 percent completion rate in '09 was then a record—under coach Sean Payton he bucked the shorter-pass trend, heaving bombs anytime, on any down and distance.

By 2012 he would become the first quarterback with three consecutive 400-yard postseason games.

In the Saints' 13–3 season, this fusillade had wrought the most points and yards in the league, and while Brees's 4,388 passing yards were down in the pack, his 34 touchdowns and 109.6 rating were the best. He only threw 11 interceptions. Brees was so dominant it didn't matter that Reggie Bush, the former Heisman Trophy winner and the Saints' top pick in '06, whose jersey was the league's second-best seller next to Peyton Manning's, was oft-injured and soon to be traded. Manning's jersey sales aside, the Colts were nowhere near the fan favorites that the Saints were. What's more, the Saints had the underdog mentality, with the Colts installed as 4½-point favorites and on the rim of historic elitism. "Another win," wrote Lee Jenkins in *SI*, "and they'll go down as one of the best teams ever. They realize, though, that few outside of Indiana will be pulling for them. They don't have a civic cause like the Saints, and they aren't as entertaining at press conferences as the Jets."[10]

The proximity to New Orleans made it virtually a home game for the Saints, and the French Quarter vibe rang all week. Grown men took their seats for the game in drag, an homage to the late Buddy Diliberto, who had vowed that if the Saints got to the Super Bowl, he would pad down Bourbon Street in a dress. This was reason enough for the Colts to think like underdogs. Mighty as they were, the running game had about died. Addai and Donald Brown, their first-round pick that year, had barely cracked 1,000 yards, the team dead last in rushing. Even so, Peyton's return to the Super Bowl made it tough to bet against him.

When the game was a quarter old, and he had thrown a 19-yard touchdown to Garçon for a 10–0 lead, it had the feel of a coronation. He still had a lead, 10–6 at the half, but Garçon had dropped a sure touchdown pass, and on the second-half kickoff, Payton caught Caldwell completely unaware, calling for an onside kick. The Colts' Hank Baskett had it in his hands but bungled it, allowing the Saints to fall on it. Brees threw a touchdown to Pierre Thomas to take the lead on that possession, and even after the Colts answered with a short scoring run by Addai to retake it, Brees put the Saints back up with a two-yard pass to Jeremy Shockey.

Now it was 24–17 with 5:42 remaining, ball on the Colts 30. Peyton, passing each down, hit on four short ones to move to the Saints 31. Two more were incomplete, and it was third-and-five, 3:24 left. At the line, sorting out the defense, Peyton thought he saw a blitz coming from the right side and directed Wayne to line up left and Collie to go in motion. Down the field, cornerback Tracy Porter, who had seen in the films that Manning often threw the short slant to Wayne in these situations ("It was a good play for us all year long," Peyton agreed later),[11] inched up on the receiver, playing him to the inside. "I had it in my mind I was going to jump the route," Porter said in footballese.[12] And he got an enormous break when, in a rare foul-up, Wayne stopped and buttonhooked. When the pass sailed too far inside for him, it hit Porter right in the numbers—one of the most stunningly inopportune interceptions in Super Bowl history. Worse, Porter took it back 74 yards for an absolute beast of a touchdown, one that Colts linebacker Clint Session called "a dagger in the heart." After it ended at 31–17, Session could only shake his head. "Peyton is always 100 percent in those situations," he would say, more fanciful than factual. "I guess it shows that no one is perfect. Even him."

———

Of course, Manning had almost never been close to perfect. But the reappearance of his mortality came as a shock. He had outpassed Brees and posted winner's numbers: 31 of 45 for 333 yards. But Brees's 32 of 39 for 288 yards and a staggering 114.5 rating let him take home the MVP award and the Saints the Lombardi Trophy, causing a highly emotional scene on the field, one that Peyton could not bear to witness. As the platform for the winners was being erected at midfield and the TV cameras moved into place in front of it, Peyton took a few steps onto the field, then veered off to the sideline and jogged for the locker room. Breaching protocol, he didn't greet the winning quarterback, and he kept his head down, avoiding eye contact with several Saints players and coaches who tried to catch up to him.

He did seek out and congratulate Brees and others—in private—before he left, but even seeing the Saints' celebration later on the news made him turn away. The Saints players had fused into the bayou culture, living there all year round. In the celebration, they took turns shouting names of towns in the Gulf. While Archie and Olivia mourned Peyton's latest big-game demise, the sting must have been eased by the Mardi Gras–level celebrations all around town that week,[13] which Archie no doubt had imagined four decades ago, before all such thoughts were knocked cold by the next grim sack. When Brees was named *Sports Illustrated*'s Sportsman of the Year, credited with no less than ushering in a "rebirth of a great American city,"[14] it was a what-might-have-been moment for the old Saint martyr. For his son, an actual native who today was the outsider, the Saints fans' shouts of "Who Dat?"—the old Cajun/ minstrel idiom adopted as the team's chant—sounded like it was aimed at him.

The *Indianapolis Star* ran a story with a headline stating the obvious— "Family Rallies around Manning"—noting that Eli and Cooper were waiting for Peyton when he made it inside and stood behind him, Eli rubbing his neck, as Peyton ran through his well-practiced post-defeat mantra of disappointment, repeating for each new wave of press that Porter "made a great play. That's all I can say about it. . . . It was great film study. The coaching staff did a great job of preparing for that route." But this time, something was different. Losing makes a man look old. Or older. He was nearly 34 now, lines creasing his face, his big forehead starting to crowd out his hairline, his voice hoarse. Ominously, he had played the season with a pinched nerve in his neck, for which he would undergo surgery in February. It was as if all the years of seamless football seasons, practices, bumps, bruises, sacks, and hours of watching grainy tapes, learning tendencies and keys, were reaching a critical mass.

A win would have masked these effects; the loss magnified them. Caldwell had said of the coaching profession, "You're hired to win Super Bowls."[15] The same could be said for quarterbacks, and Manning had lost another.

He was now 9–9 in playoff games, whereas Brady was 14–4 (though their overall ratings were almost identical: Brady 88.5, Manning 87.4). Some sportswriters pounced, one writing of him, "The greatest of all time? Nope. Not even close now. The [greatest] doesn't throw that kind of awful interception. Joe Montana didn't throw those in the Super Bowl. Has Tom Brady? Manning has one ring and a bushel of stats and records.

He deserves accolades and praise, but the [greatest] talk must stop now."[16] Others, with 20/20 hindsight, traced the defeat to the two games the Colts had conceded rather than going for the undefeated season, losing intensity they couldn't get back. He may have felt that way, too. If so, he probably felt robbed of what should have been his—but which now was a reminder that he might simply be a great quarterback on his way down.

Being pitied, of course, would be the worst way for Peyton Manning to go through life. He could only imagine how it had eaten into Archie's pride. The old man's hunted look always reappeared when one of his boys lost, and defeats like these were hell on the whole brood. Naturally, Peyton wanted back in, fully aware that he would need to cheat nature and biology, and with the suspicion that the peak he had reached on that field in Miami had ebbed on that same field. He believed he could do it, just like he could do anything, control any situation. After the Super Bowl, he was shocked when a Colt official handed him a phone and told him Barack Obama, a year into his first term, was on the other end. The president, calling to offer words of comfort, told him, "I hope you get back here while I'm still in office." As it turned out, he would need every year of those two terms.

CHAPTER 21

ONE DOWN, ONE UP

Peyton Manning now faced a crossroads. While the surgery on his neck, done at Northwestern Memorial Hospital in Chicago, did not affect his timetable of preparation, he was a year from the end of his contract—which, even with a salary of $15.8 million due in 2010, was a bargain. Now, his client having had two surgeries in service to the Colts without missing a single game, Tom Condon let it be known that the next deal would need to be big: nine figures, a budget buster by all measures. In 2009, Jim Irsay was affably saying, "With Peyton, it's about the last thing you worry about. You know that he's going to be with the top guys at the position. It comes down to just getting things worked out and moving things forward." However, he added, "I expect it to quietly get done, but there are no conversations going on with the season going on."[1]

That was a clue that all the sonnets meant nothing when a quarterback ages another year, even a quarterback who had missed exactly one regular-season play because of injury and taken 11,623 of 12,047 snaps entering the new season. As the roster turned over, young players would need to be kept happy. At the same time, the clock was now ticking on a highly significant factor, the end of the players' collective bargaining agreement with the league. The union was demanding a higher salary cap, naturally, but the league was starting to stand firm, or firmer. Talk was getting around that there might be another lockout before the '11 season, which would freeze all expiring contracts, leaving Manning in limbo. To be sure, he wanted to stay a Colt, something Irsay wanted, too. In the sports culture, Manning was inviolate; the *Wall Street Journal* earnestly reported that there were 106 pets in the US named after Peyton Manning, compared with 32 after Drew Brees.[2] (It didn't say how many were named for Tom Brady.) When he came to summer camp for the 2010 season, he was the old Bolshevik, pissed off at every botched play in practice, keeping the workouts going for as long as he deemed necessary.

Already having made the Colts totally pass-reliant, he had a newer agenda for himself, which would not coincidentally help to keep his value high: passing for geyser-like numbers. This was in line with the newest stage of football evolution, the game having become nearly a pass-off between the best quarterbacks trying to keep pace with each other—at first a product of the West Coast offense gone amok, starting with a flurry of short passes, followed by Brees bypassing the shorter stuff to chuck long. Back in Archie's day, when fewer plays were run, a 4,000-yard season was the unreachable star; Joe Namath got there in '67 during a 14-game season in the pass-crazy AFL. In the '80s and '90s, when it became child's play—in 2009 alone, 10 QBs did it—5,000 became the new goal, reached only by Dan Marino in '84. Then came Brees, swinging the 5K door open in '08, daring everyone else in the brethren to step through. Not one to be left behind, and with his pride and future riding on going higher, Peyton—who had already gone over 4,000 a record 10 times—was prepared to go for it. In truth, he didn't have much choice, given that, as the *Star*'s beat man, Mike Chappell, wrote, "the Colts' running game has hit rock bottom."[3]

The season began ominously with a 34–24 loss to the Houston Texans. Next came Manning Bowl II, on another Sunday night, after another round of pregame hype and pain-in-the-neck questions for Peyton and Eli about how consumed they were supposed to be by these matches. This one, Eli said, was "going to be fun," unlike the first, when he was a bit overwhelmed.

The game was on Peyton's turf this time, and the Colts had the good timing to show that the "rock bottom" running game had some life in it. Addai and Brown tore up the Giants defense, gaining 160 yards on 43 carries, giving Peyton openings to rack up another 255 yards passing and three more touchdowns, one a 50-yard bomb to Clark. Eli had his own bomb, 54 yards to Mario Manningham, but it was 24–0 Colts at the half, ending not a second too soon at 38–14, cameras encircling the brothers as they embraced at midfield. Both would go on to routinely excellent seasons, though Peyton rose to a level surreal even for him.

Still, this was no romp for the Colts. Despite his fireworks every week, the running game and the run defense often collapsed, making for some long afternoons. In November they lost three straight, the first to the Pats, 31–28 in Foxborough—Manning nailing four touchdowns to Brady's two, but also throwing three picks in a comeback that fell just short. Another late comeback, against the Cowboys, was lost in overtime with Manning having thrown four interceptions. At that point, they were 6–6. They saved their season by winning the last four to take the division, but three were close calls. The first playoff round, the wild-card game against another of Rex Ryan's overachieving Jets teams, looked like a mismatch. Manning, even after losing Dallas Clark during the season with a broken wrist, had ravaged the league, having thrown for 4,700 yards, averaged 42.3 passes per game, and completed 66.3 percent, with 33 touchdowns against 17 interceptions.

But the Jets posed a danger because their running game was fourth-best in the league, while the Colts' run defense was in the bottom 10. New York's defense gave up the sixth-fewest yards. And so it was that, after Peyton put the Colts ahead with a 57-yard touchdown pass to Garçon, the Jets controlled the clock, running for 169 yards. Trailing 14–10 late in the fourth quarter, the Colts inched back and took the lead by two on a 50-yard field goal with 53 seconds left. Yet it was the maligned Sanchez who made the big plays, the last an 18-yard pass to Braylon Edwards with 29 seconds left to put the Jets in field-goal range, Peyton visibly angered on the sideline. As Bob Kravitz wrote in the *Star*, before the play, an "exasperated" Manning—not knowing why Caldwell called time, thereby giving the Jets a chance to discuss the play—"lifted both arms into the air, a clear gesture that said, 'What are we doing?'"[4] The field goal won it with three seconds left, 17–16.

Even by the standard of crushing Manning losses, this one was excruciating. Here was Peyton Manning, on his own field, having to congratulate Mark Sanchez for beating him in a big one. However, things happen for a reason, and for numerous reasons this inglorious nadir would turn out to be more significant than anyone thought that day. Because no one thought it was the last time they would see Peyton Manning in a Colts uniform.

═══

Neither Manning brother made it past the first week of January. Like Eli, the Giants of 2010 were an enigma wrapped in an interception. They had a high-voltage offense and a stingy defense. Eli had his second straight 4,000-yard season, with 31 touchdowns. Ahmad Bradshaw rushed for 1,235 yards, and he and Brandon Jacobs combined for 17 touchdowns. Hakeem Nicks caught 11 touchdown passes. They began 1–2, but at midseason they seemed to be cruising, their record 6–2, their fifth straight win a 41–7 blowout of the Seahawks—on the road, no less. But then they drooped, losing four of the next seven games and finishing at 10–6—good, but not good enough for a playoff berth. If one had to pinpoint the most revealing stat, it was Eli's 25 interceptions.

For Peyton, this winter would be eventful. Ashley, who had become pregnant before the last season, found out she was going to have twins, and on March 31 she gave birth in an Indianapolis hospital to a son, Marshall Williams, and a daughter, Mosley Thompson. Suddenly, Peyton had a brood of his own, and he took them home to the Garden District, beseeching Eli to give him advice on fatherhood. But he had scant time to learn before he would find himself in a hospital again. When the brothers were throwing a ball around in the backyard one day, Eli told Peyton he was short-arming his tosses, not completing the motion. Peyton said it was because he was feeling pain that started from his neck and ran down his back. He had been putting off seeing a doctor, but now he did, fearing that, as doctors warned him long ago after Cooper's diagnosis, his own latent spinal deformity had risen up. An MRI of his spine did not show stenosis but confirmed that he had a herniated disk and would need surgery on his neck.

He tried to believe it was not a big deal. The doctors said the surgery would be minimally invasive, and he only told the Colts about it in late

May, days before he went into Northwestern Hospital again, to be oper-
ated on by the same surgeons who had relieved the pinched nerve in
his neck. It all went fine. He woke up in his room without the neck pain
he had lived with so long, and although his right arm was still numb,
doctors explained that the disk had been pressing on a nerve, and it
would take time for residual numbness to go away. Impatient that it was
still there weeks later, he went back in for follow-up surgery amid such
secrecy that there were no press reports of it. Doctors reassured him he'd
be good to go when the season began.

With the owners having locked the players out in February as negotiations on a new CBA limped along, he would have the luxury of privacy as
he worked his way back into shape. "There is plenty of time for recovery,"
he said, downplaying the surgery by saying that, had it not been for the
lockout, he wouldn't have gone under the knife at all.[5] Privately, though,
the doctors—who were not affiliated with the league or the Colts and, in
the interest of medical confidentiality, could not exchange information
with the team—changed their rosy tune and told him he had maybe a
50-50 chance of playing again, and that the surgery might not work at all.

At the time, he was prohibited from contact with the team, anyway.
In fact, no one knew when or if football would be played again. With
spring minicamps padlocked, the players had to find other ways and
places to practice on their own. Eli and the Giants receivers did it on a
high school field in Hoboken, New Jersey. Peyton found refuge all the
way out in Colorado. As it happened, Todd Helton, whose brief, thorny
bisection with him at Tennessee truly was a lot of water under the bridge,
was in a similar situation, dealing with a degenerative back condition
just as he signed his last contract with baseball's Colorado Rockies. Reading of Peyton's surgery, Helton invited him to Denver to work out with
him at Coors Field during pregame and off-day hours and get treatment
from trainers who knew how to rehabilitate throwing arms. He did, with
a zipper scar on his neck. To keep from prying eyes, he and Helton began
working out in an underground batting cage. The first time Peyton tossed
a football to Helton, just 10 yards away, it bounced halfway there. Helton,
believing Peyton was joking around, laughed.

"C'mon, man, quit kidding," he said.

"Man, I wish I was," Manning replied.[6]

He quickly grew despondent when the numbness in his arm refused to subside. Rather than the cocky character Helton had known, Peyton seemed a sad, even pathetic figure—"He walked different. He carried himself different"—who was so embarrassed about his throwing that "he had a hard time turning around to look at you."

=====

Back in Indianapolis, Irsay stalled on offering Manning a new contract. He had not kept his promise to make his quarterback the highest-paid player in history before the end of the previous season, and now that reports were drifting in about Peyton's condition, he seemed to waver, saying, "No surgery is minor if it's on you or your franchise quarter-back."[7] Still, back in February, Polian had attached the franchise-player tag to Peyton, with the "exclusive" designation that prevented any other team from negotiating with him, and locked him in at $23.1 million for one year if a long-term deal wasn't reached. But even before the surgery, the *Star*'s Mike Chappell, going off the reservation, had pondered, "Is it too early to start looking down the road?"—meaning drafting a quar-terback, since the team had no viable alternative for a future without Manning.[8]

Irsay didn't want to look down that road. He wanted to re-up Man-ning. He had to, lest he become the enemy in his own town, having invested $146 million in him so far. There was also Polian's encomium about Manning after the championship Super Bowl, how he had saved the team from relocating. They did owe him, big. As a sop to Manning, Polian, now vice-chairman and grooming his son Chris to take over as GM, used his two top picks in the April draft on offensive linemen, leaving the likes of Andy Dalton and Colin Kaepernick on the board. Irsay put an offer of $100 million for five years on the table, saying hopefully, "He's had things tougher than this before." But then things started getting complicated.

First, there was the pertinent fact that Peyton was *not* recovering nicely. In fact, he wasn't recovering at all, not that he and Tom Condon had any qualms about keeping that quiet. After quitting the humiliating workouts with Helton, Peyton had gone to Thibodeaux for the Manning

Academy, mainly because those young quarterbacks had paid good money to mingle with him. But he never picked up a ball. One high school kid asked him to toss just one pass to him. "I just can't," he told him. "Eli will throw you one."[9] His depression was obvious to Archie and his brothers. "He's not very good at disguising how he feels," Cooper said. "You can hear it in the first hello and the last goodbye. I saw him vulnerable for the first time. And then I saw him get emotionally around the idea that, Hey, this may be too much to battle back from."

Archie recalled Peyton asking him, "Am I gonna throw like a 40-year-old man?" According to Archie, "He didn't want to be out there if he didn't belong." Archie was preparing to comfort his son if he chose to retire right then. Olivia, however, was more of a fighter. She told Peyton he owed it to himself to do all he could to get back, knowing how miserable he would be if he gave up without trying. There was no denying the task before him, which perhaps was the most burdensome any quarterback ever had to contend with, given his age and the perilous nature of spinal injuries. "The frustrating part," Peyton would say, "was there was no one to call who had this, no other thrower. There was no protocol."[10]

———

But the good son did as his mother told him. Virtually alone, he would be making it up as he went along, needing to relearn the mechanics of throwing, not to mention getting back that old confident swagger. When he decided he'd give it a shot, some around the league thought he was nuts. At first, however, the decision was made for the easiest of reasons: money—specifically, the money in the contract negotiations with the Colts. Talks had continued during the winter and spring, with the $100 million offer on the table. But then came the second complication. In July, the players and owners agreed to a new CBA, ending the lockout. The big change was that the salary cap would be limited to $120 million. That meant the $100 million was off the table, since it would leave little room for other signings. So Peyton did Irsay a favor. Brimming with altruism, he said he would take less—the proverbial "hometown discount," for the good of the team. Brady, he said nobly, could have the league's top salary, which, per his four-year, $72 million deal the year before, averaged out to $18 million, though he too had taken less on occasion for the same reason.

The deal was signed at the start of training camp, for $90 million over five years, with a $28 million signing bonus and $3 million roster bonus. It was $10 million off the nine-figure plateau Condon had once set as a floor, but not gruel, either; contrary to Peyton's comments about ceding the top salary to Brady, he would own it, at least for a year. Irsay took to Twitter to proudly announce that Manning would make $69 million over the first three years of the contract, for a yearly average of $23 million—$26 million in '11—highest in the game, as promised, leaving out that the last two years would each carry a salary of $10 million, dipping the average over the full life of the contract to $18 million, the same as Brady.[11] (These figures included bonuses; his actual base salary was kept low for cap purposes, at $3.4 million the first year. Brady would have a 2011 base of $5.7 million, bonuses bringing it up to $19.7 million. By this metric, Eli's salary of $8.5 million would be the highest, but he was due to receive almost no bonuses.)[12]

The numbers were also temporary. When the league signed a new TV deal in 2014, it would raise each team's income—and the salary cap—and permit contract renegotiation. All in all, then, it was a very good day for a quarterback who still couldn't throw, and a very risky move for the Colts, who didn't know that the man signing that contract could hardly feel the pen in his hand. The nerve connected to the disk that ran to his right arm still left his arm so numb that he could neither grip a ball nor a three-pound dumbbell in the gym. During the lockout, so desperate for relief, he had flown to Europe to consult doctors he had learned of online, boasting of miracle cures for spinal injuries; trying some with no luck, he would call the methods "voodoo."

Now, in camp, feeling useless, he stayed in bed in his room in the dorm some days rather than doing anything else. Bob Kravitz had already written that Manning wouldn't be ready to start the season. And now, with him kept out of practice and out of pads, working on throwing in private but with no good news ever coming out of it, the big issue in the media was the Colts' failure to draft or trade for a reliable quarterback rather than having to go with the middling Curtis Painter.

Although Peyton still went along with the con job about maybe, perhaps being ready at some point in the season, he knew better. Looking back, he recalled, "It's hard to explain but I kind of lost awareness of my arm in space. When you had the same throwing motion for so long—golfers talk about repeating their swing—well, quarterbacks repeat too. But I couldn't repeat. That was scary. Just discouraging."[13]

========

All during the preseason, Peyton held a clipboard beside Caldwell on the sideline. Though Irsay coyly spoke of perhaps signing the retired Brett Favre, he wound up bringing in none other than 38-year-old Kerry Collins on a two-year deal. The Manning watch was still on, however; in late August, the *Star* reported that Peyton "hopes to be ready in week 1." But then ESPN's Chris Mortensen learned that Manning, "concerned over the slow healing . . . is being re-evaluated by several doctors."[14] And the bad news shook the Colts down to their cleats. The problematic disk in his neck was now reherniated, necessitating another operation, the fourth procedure to deal with the same nagging problem. The previous ones had taken a conventional approach, decompressing the disk by widening the nerve passageway in the spinal canal. Now, major surgery awaited him, the kind never performed on an athlete, especially one in a brutal contact sport seeking to *continue* playing in a brutal contact sport: a single-level anterior fusion to stabilize the neck by removing the troubled disk and replacing it with a tiny bone graft, welding two vertebrae into one solid bone, a metal plate screwed into it for reinforcement. This would finally relieve the nerve in his arm and allow free movement. It was a common but delicate procedure that can take hours and requires around four months of inactivity afterward.

The surgery was scheduled for September 9, to be performed by a top spinal neurosurgeon, Dr. Robert Watkins, co-director of the posh Marina Spine Clinic in Marina Del Rey, California. Before he flew to the coast, Peyton detoured to New Orleans to be with Ashley, the kids, and his parents, perhaps giving himself one last chance to be talked out of the operation and simply retire. For his part, he was as close to doing that as he could have been. "I'll listen to the doctors," he said. "If they say after this that I still can't play, then it's been a good ride."[15] Even so, there really was no escape from the operation; like Cooper, he would need to have it done simply to get through life without pain and numbness. And when Ashley told him, "You've got to try," he packed for the trip to L.A.

The operation came two days before the Colts began their season against the Texans with Collins at quarterback, unable to ring up a point until the fourth quarter, when Houston had run up a 34–0 lead, ultimately winning 34–7. In his Marina hotel room, Peyton put the game on the TV and winced. "It was hard to watch," he said, not just because he knew his team was moribund, but because of the uncertainties he faced. "I was disappointed, I was down, because I wasn't able to do what I love and I didn't know where I was headed. I didn't know if I'd ever be able to perform again. I had those thoughts. They were real."[16]

Back home in New Orleans, he would not be cleared to pick up a football for three months but would try to throw anyway. David Cutcliffe, now the coach at Duke, dropped in on him. Seeing him struggle, he barked, "Stop throwing!" lest he damage his elbow or shoulder—or get further depressed. He had good days and days when he wallowed in self-pity. While his movements were free of neck pain and his arm regained its elasticity and strength, the fingers of his right hand were still numb, and doctors said they always would be. The only thing he could do was condition himself to "feel" with those fingers through familiarity with routine sequences; he would grip the laces of the ball with his fingers just by knowing where they *should* be. He also had to adapt to throwing at a different angle, at a slightly different release point, the range of motion in his arm and shoulder limited by the lesser stretch of the nerve running down his right side. To help do this, he would simulate his throwing motion in front of a full-length mirror—looking at someone he now had trouble recognizing.

The upside was that he was a full-time father, which offered him a greater perspective about life without the game. "I had a real peace," he would say, sounding like a Hallmark card. "I don't know if many people believe that, but I had a peace if this was not to be. . . . The one year the Lord took my greatest physical gift, he gave me the greatest gift you could have in children."[17] Sentimental, even weepy at times, he went over to the first house he lived in and knocked on the door.

"Hi, I'm Peyton Manning," he told the owner, "and I'd like to see my room."[18]

═══════

Manning mojo moved in mysterious ways. Eli and Peyton's respective fates in 2011 suggested John Coltrane's "One Down, One Up," though it would take some doing for Eli to keep going up. When the season began, the Giants sprinted out of the gate, winning five of their first seven games before meeting the Patriots at Gillette Stadium. The Pats, who hadn't been back to the Super Bowl since that maddening defeat by the Giants, came in 5–2 and were nine-point favorites. The Giants' top rusher and receiver, Ahmad Bradshaw and Hakeem Nicks, were both out injured, and Eli's receiving corps was mostly new, including Brandon Stokley. But the Giants stymied Brady early, intercepting him twice.

It was a back-and-forth game that came down to the last minute. With 1:36 left, trailing 20–17, Eli launched a drive, picking up an enormous third-and-long play with a 28-yard completion to tight end Jake Ballard. Now the Pats cracked, interfering on a pass to the end zone, and from the one, Manning found Ballard for the touchdown that won it, 24–20. It was a real statement game, the victory achieved even without key players and with the satisfaction of hearing spoiled Pats fans, perhaps for the first time ever, booing Brady despite his passing for 342 yards.

However, the Giants would falter, sliding to 7–7. Their shot at a playoff spot rode on the outcome of the last two games. In the first, a crosstown tilt with the Jets, Eli was subpar, hitting only 9 of 27 passes, while Mark Sanchez threw 59 times, completing 30. But it was Eli who pulled off the play of the game, maybe the year. Trailing 7–3 in the second quarter, on a third-and-10 from his own one, he took the shotgun snap five yards deep in the end zone and fired one to Victor Cruz, who caught it at the 11 between two Jets, hip-shifted through both of them, and beat the only defender left down the sideline for a 99-yard touchdown. The Giants won 29–14. Now, needing to beat the Cowboys, who were also 8–7 and with a win would reach the postseason, all the forces of the universe came together. With Eli going 24 of 33 for 346 yards and three touchdowns, they won in a walk, 31–14, gaining 437 total yards.

Finishing atop the NFC East at just 9–7, the Giants seemed one-dimensional, a pass-heavy team with the worst running game in the league and the sixth-worst defense. In this framework, they really did live and die with Eli. Yet, as in 2007, they gelled when they needed to. Indeed, the postseason was a virtual replay of the cosmic climax of that season, with the team sent into the fray having yielded just 14 points in each of their last two games—the surprise of the season being defensive end Jason Pierre-Paul, the first-round pick in 2010. The son of Haitian immigrants, he was a remarkably quick 270-pound man whose sack total exploded from 4½ as a rookie to 16½ this season, earning him first-team All-Pro honors. One lingering memory of the season came in the first tilt with the Cowboys, when he stretched up and blocked a game-tying field goal in the last seconds of a 37–34 win. And Eli was money, nearly hitting 5,000 yards with 29 touchdowns, a 92.9 rating.

In the wild-card playoff, the Giants brushed aside the Falcons, 24–2. Then they would need to win on the road, their next stop—just like the last time—in Green Bay against the defending NFL champs, who went 15–1 in Aaron Rodgers's first MVP season. The Pack were eight-point favorites, but their weakness was a defense that was last in yards allowed and against the pass. And on a sultry 31-degree afternoon at Lambeau Field, Eli tore them apart. Racking up 330 yards, he threw three touchdowns, one spookily similar to the helmet catch, when, from the Packer 37, six seconds left in the half, he flung a Hail Mary that Nicks grabbed and held against his face mask as he fell to the turf.

Rodgers, the reigning Super Bowl MVP, threw for 264 yards, but, playing from behind, he never had a chance, harried and sacked four times. The score was 37–20, a victory *Sports Illustrated*'s Damon Hack called "a postseason splash fit for a Leviathan." As Archie, who was hopscotching the map to be at each game, said afterward, "He was tired of people talking about how many interceptions he threw last year. What he was saying was, I've been around for seven years. I know I can play this game."[19] The title of the *SI* story confirmed that opinion with sweet nectar:

"Eli, as in Elite."

CHAPTER 22

MIRACLE, REDUX

All the Giants had to do next was fly to San Francisco for the NFC championship game and upset another power, the 49ers. Coached by the volatile Jim Harbaugh, the Niners had gone 13–3 on the backs of their punishing defense; ranked first against the rush, they had five All-Pros, three on the first team: linebackers Patrick Willis and NaVorro Bowman and tackle Justin Smith. They got to the title game by subduing the Saints, by far the best offensive team in the league, and winning on a touchdown pass by Alex Smith with nine seconds left. Smith was unspectacular but reliable, having thrown a modest 17 touchdowns during the season but only five interceptions, mainly handing off to Frank Gore, who ran for over 1,200 yards.

The 49ers were motivated to bring Manning down to earth. All that week, he was being drenched with slavish praise as a miracle worker and a refreshingly understated hero. Damon Hack, for example, with the sort of heavy cream *Sports Illustrated* usually reserved for Peyton, wrote, "Overshadowed by voluble teammates like Michael Strahan and Tiki Barber early on, Manning has now imbued the Giants with a stoic vibe that seems ideal for the pressure-filled postseason."[1] Through all this, Archie was looking far more beaten down than his boy. With Peyton sidelined, he had told Olivia that each week was "just three hours of nervousness instead of six." But after the Green Bay game, looking like he had gone 10 rounds, he confessed that the contest "felt like six hours." Yet there he was, with Olivia and Cooper, chewing at his fingernails in Candlestick Park.

During a midweek practice, Eli had said to his teammates of the 49ers, "Their lifeline is turnovers, so you've got to protect the football. . . . Just don't give them any points, and we'll have a chance to win it at the end."[2] For inspiration, Coughlin brought to the coast three Giants from previous glory days: Mike Strahan, Mark Bavaro, and Rich Seubert, who addressed the team at their hotel on the eve of the game. Coughlin had also pointed out that the way Brees, in defeat, had carved up the vaunted 49ers defense for 462 yards was their road map. In the muddy, cake-batter turf of Candlestick, saturated by rain and lying under gloomy fog, no one dared lose the ball. Each team stopped the other's running game, the Giants doing so even though Harbaugh inserted a massive defensive lineman as a blocker. Eli was able to control the ball with short and medium throws. Smith had a strong game, too, throwing a 73-yard touchdown to Vernon Davis early, and after Eli hit little-used tight end Bear Pascoe on a six-yard TD and took a 10–7 lead at the half, Smith found Davis from 28 yards out to take a 14–10 lead.

In the fourth quarter, Eli moved the Giants to the Niners 17. To that point, Manningham hadn't caught a ball. But the cornerback who had locked him down, Tarell Brown, went out injured, and on third down Eli zeroed in on the scrub, sending Manningham on a post over the middle for the touchdown and the lead. When the 49ers tied it on a field goal, an already exhausting game went to overtime. Although Harbaugh's defense savaged Manning, sacking him six times and leaving him with an angry red welt on his shoulder, they never could pick him off, even as he was passing more than any other Giant quarterback ever had in a postseason game—58 times, completing 32 for 316 yards. It was the 49ers who made the big blunder. With five minutes gone in the OT, a Giant punt was fielded by Kyle Williams, who ran five yards, then was stripped by Jacquian Williams. The Giants had the ball at the Niners 24, and on third down Lawrence Tynes kicked the game-winning field goal—repeating history, his overtime three-pointer following a Packer turnover in the playoffs four years before.

Archie did not know how many more of these he could stand, his nerves always far more on edge than Eli's in these pressure-cooker games. And he had another ordeal still to endure: his boy in the cross hairs of Brady and Belichick, still smarting from four years ago.

———

Naturally billed as "The Sequel," Super Bowl XLVI was in, of all places, Lucas Oil Stadium—which, when it was chosen, had a decent chance of providing a hometown advantage for the Manning brother whose image was splashed all over its exterior walls. As Peter King pre-codified it, "Peyton Manning's brother versus Peyton's archrival in the House That Peyton Built."[3] The Pats, who had gotten here with a too-close 23–20 win over the Ravens, were favored by three. But the Giants were confident— the day before the game, their website began hawking apparel reading "The Giants Are Super Bowl Champions!"[4] Sixteen players from the '07 team were on the roster, conditioned to the task of beating the Patriots; one, Victor Cruz, spoke of the team's "destiny."[5] Coughlin had ingrained that mind-set; the night before the contest, he ran a film of highlights from their last six games, choosing as the soundtrack Phil Collins's grimly foreboding "In the Air Tonight."[6]

Besides revenge, the Pats had their own leitmotif. Bob Kraft, the leprechaun-like owner, had dedicated the season to his late wife. They also had the second-best offense in the league and the second-best passing game. Meaning, of course, that they had Brady. Eli spent much of the week—when not engaged in practice or entombed by Coughlin's chalk-talks—hanging with Peyton at his and Ashley's house with Archie and Olivia, inhaling fast food and then picking Peyton's brain for insights he might not have already known about the Pats. On Friday night, he treated his linemen to dinner—on Peyton's recommendation— at St. Elmo Steak House.

The Pats, as they often did, began slowly. Brady, on his very first play, from his own six-yard line, came under a heavy rush and grounded the ball in the end zone for a two-point safety. Eli then led a 10-play drive, throwing a two-yard touchdown to Cruz. After the Pats woke up, Brady hit on two touchdowns in the third quarter to go ahead 17–9. Again Eli was successful with short and medium passes, going 30 of 40 for 296 yards, while Brady, harassed by the Giant front four, was mortal: 27 of 41 for 276 yards, with one pick. But the Giants could only get two field goals closer until given a monumental break when, in the fourth quarter, Wes Welker muffed a long pass that should have been a killer touchdown. Eli now stood on familiar ground, not only from four years ago but from seven times during the season when the Giants had orchestrated fourth-quarter comeback wins. There was 3:46 left, the ball on his own 12, down 17–15, a strangulating defense waiting for them. Upstairs, Wellington Mara's widow, Ann, pulled out her rosary beads and prayed. "I asked the Blessed Mother to tell him where to throw the ball," she said. Olivia, on the other hand, was typically calm, saying later, "I have to tell you, I am always happy when the ball is in Eli's hands."

According to the play sent in by Kevin Gilbride, Eli was to check the deep safety, Patrick Chung; if he covered Manningham, the sole receiver on the left side, the latter would hug the sideline deep down the field. But Eli never even looked at Chung. Seeing Manningham breaking free, he cranked up and put the ball right into his hands just as Chung and cornerback Sterling Moore both closed in on him. Manningham managed to plant both feet before tumbling out of bounds and came up holding the ball—a dizzying 38-yard gain, longest of the game, this year's Biggest Catch Ever. "That's a huge play right there," Eli would say, without objection. And apparently, one he hadn't gotten the hang of before now. As Eli's backup, David Carr, said, "That's not a throw he's made in practice or a game on that play all season."

The Pats seemed to sag—and how familiar was that? Four more completions took it to the Patriots seven with 1:04 left. Then Eli got a little wavy. Knowing what Brady can do on a short clock, he actually didn't want the Giants to score, but rather to keep the clock running and make the Pats call their last time-out. Only he forgot to tell Bradshaw, who blasted through a crater-sized hole left open intentionally by the Pats, who wanted the ball back. The end zone in his sights, he heard Eli yelling, "Don't score!" Said Manning later, "I should have said something in the huddle, but I didn't think of it. I thought about yelling back to him before we snapped the ball but I didn't want to confuse things." But shouting to Bradshaw confused the running back so much that he tried to stop short and plop down on the one-yard line, but couldn't impede his momentum and, twisted like a pretzel, he fell backwards into the end zone. A magnificently strange and wondrous touchdown. The two-point conversion failed, but the Giants led 21–17, and Brady had 57 seconds to make it go away. He got as far as the Giants 49, but with only seconds left sailed a Hail Mary into the end zone, a rainbow that Tuck said was up there long enough for him to write a novel. The Giants slapped it down and it was over.

———

The Manning family box exploded in celebration at a victory that proved Eli really *was* elite. He was the one consoling Brady, the one covered in confetti on the platform at the 50-yard line, the Super Bowl MVP once more. Archie, finally relieved, looked down from the box, later saying, "We're just kinda pinching ourselves." He went on, "It's amazing, really, because Eli wallowed around so much that we didn't even know if he would like sports."[7] Olivia, meanwhile, waited outside the locker room as champagne corks popped inside, next to Abby, the three girls, and Cooper's seven-year-old son, who had two uncles sharing three Super Bowl MVP trophies. "And we have another one on the way," she said. "This is my grandson, Arch Manning. Watch out, world."

Above the din, Eli was saying, "This isn't about me. It's about the organization and Coach Coughlin and all our coaches." But it *was* about him. And Peyton. Eli had bridled a bit when reporters leaned on the story line that he was trying to transcend Peyton on his home turf. But now, as the waves of media swarmed around him, Peyton was seated next to him, as if giving his blessing to the kid brother who had finally become an equal. Indeed, in the throes of his own uncertain future, he seemed to gush over Eli, explaining their unique, sometimes odd bond.

"I don't think people understand our relationship," he said. "I always used to look after him. I used to drive him to school. He used to come to all my games. Our relationship is so much one of support and help. I've given him every piece of knowledge I've had about playing quarterback, and he gives it to me. Love is what that is. I want to do the best I can for my team, but when that's done I hope Eli surpasses every record. I hope he wins five more Super Bowls." Then, "I hope I win five more too."[8]

It was hard now to think about one without thinking of the other. The *Sports Illustrated* game story was titled "One Giant Leap for Manningkind," a pun meant to be inclusive of Manningham but epitaphic of the broad reach of the Manning family. Well into the morning, when the Giants carried on at a nightclub just down the block from the stadium, the Manning clan mostly hung out in one corner, as if it was the throne of ultimate power, of which Eli was now ruling liege. The day after, in the *New York Daily News*, Mike Lupica swooned hard. Eli, he averred, was "as great a clutch athlete as we have ever had in New York, in anything. Nobody takes his team down the field and does it like this twice with an NFL championship on the line, not Johnny Unitas or Joe Montana or anybody. Only now Eli has."[9] There was another parade down Broadway, and he was the toast of the town that winter, of course, burnishing his good-guy cred with charity gigs—though he was not averse to spoofing even that image.

Getting his own appearance on *Saturday Night Live*, he was in a spot remarkably similar to the "United Way" spoof Peyton had performed on that stage. Surrounded by kids in a "Little Brothers" program, he was asked by a wide-eyed kid, "Are you Eli Manning?" "No, I'm your worst enemy," he sneered with his best maniacal look, proceeding to hold the kid by his heels over a flushing toilet and aiming a crossbow at another. There was also a sketch with him as "Richard," a nerd said to have once been part of Cheech and Chong's act (something not as far-fetched as it seemed) and later "turned into Mitt Romney."

There was now a new round of Eli puff pieces. *Sports Illustrated*'s entry, titled "The Big Easy," floated the theory that Eli had refashioned the hero-quarterback role. To writer S. L. Price, Eli, unlike his brother, "forces us to rethink what we expect in a star." Wrote Price, "Bart Starr and Bob Griese carried themselves like NASA engineers. Eli Manning, peering out from under a 10-year-old's haircut, is the NFL embodiment of cognitive dissonance. . . . At certain harried moments Manning resembles no one so much as [Michael] Dukakis in the tank. No wonder his favorite Seinfeld episode is 'Bizarro Jerry,' where everything is reversed.

In Eli's world last is first, omega man trumps the alpha males and the lesser quarterback always wins." Price also revealed the nugget that Eli cheats at Ping-Pong.[10]

The article quoted Boomer Esiason, a physically imposing quarterback in his day who only tasted bitter fruit in New York, saying with great envy, "To have two Super Bowl parades and be on the lead float, looking like a bobble-head doll? What is going on here? But that's the beauty of Eli. I can't tell you just how amazing his story is. If I had a vote, even if his career ended today, he'd be in the Hall of Fame." That was surely a stretch, the issue still pending today. Phil Simms, whose Giants passing records he was dismantling, demurred, "No, he is not one of the elites. Because when I hear the word elite, I'm thinking about guys that can make unbelievable plays on the field by themselves."

Although Eli had a comeback, questioning whether Simms himself qualified for that rank, he let it slide. Winning, he now knew, was the only retort a Manning needed.

CHAPTER 23

GOODBYE, HELLO

Without Peyton, the Colts bounced from one quarterback to another and ended the 2011 season a woeful 2–14. For Jim Irsay, it became harder to accept that he had given all that loot to a guy who hadn't been straight with him. By early 2012, he seemed less interested in Peyton's recovery, which was progressing well. Peyton had gone back to Durham, North Carolina, in February to live with Dave Cutcliffe and have the coach oversee his reorientation, Peyton in his Colts helmet as he did drills with the Blue Devils squad. Cutcliffe had him start with basic exercises and drills he hadn't done since he was a kid. Again, this took place under cover, the Duke people keeping it from the media, and even the Colts.

But by now, Irsay had committed to rebuilding his team. He had fired Jim Caldwell and his staff and the two Polians, not even allowing Bill Polian the dignity of retiring. Peyton, seeing himself on an island being deserted, came to the Colts' offices during Super Bowl week. After a perfunctory meeting with the new GM, Ryan Grigson, and sensing a growing depression in the office, he was moved to tell Bob Kravitz of his findings: people were "walking around on eggshells," and he himself had no idea whether the team intended to keep him.

That might have ripped it for Irsay. A few days later, when he introduced Chuck Pagano as the new coach, he was asked about Manning's remarks. Clearly "irked," as a reporter wrote, he bit his lip as he said, "I have so much affection and appreciation for Peyton. I mean, we're family. We always will be and we are." Then, biting harder, "He's a politician. I mean, look at . . . when it comes to being competitive, let's just say on a scale of 1 to 10, 10 being the highest, we're both 11s, OK? So there's been plenty of eggshells scattered around this building by him with his competitive desire to win."[1]

Though *politician* was the exact word for Peyton Manning, the implicit criticism stung him. He rang up Kravitz and sought to clarify his own words. "I wasn't trying to paint the Colts in a bad light," he began, "but it's tough when so many people you've known for so long are suddenly leaving. I feel very close to a lot of these guys and we've done great things together. It's hard to watch an old friend clean out his office. That's all I was trying to say." He went on, "Mr. Irsay and I owe it to each other and to the fans of the organization to handle this appropriately and professionally, and I think we will. I've already reached out to Mr. Irsay, . . . and when the time is right for Mr. Irsay and I to sit down, I look forward to a healthy conversation about my future."[2]

Irsay also toned it down. Taking to Twitter again, he cooed, "Peyton and I love each other, that goes without saying." The next day, he was asked by a reporter if it was possible Manning had played his last game as a Colt. Trying to sound noble, he said, "This isn't an ankle, it isn't a shoulder. Often times the NFL is criticized for putting someone out there at risk, and I'm not going to doing that. I think he and I just need to see where his health is because this isn't about money or anything else. It's about his life and his long-term health."

But in truth, it was about something else. March 8, the day when Irsay would have to pay Manning's next bonus, a weighty $28 million, was fast approaching. Having been hoodwinked about Manning's condition the year before, or so he believed, the last thing Irsay needed was to be fleeced again. Anticipating this as an undercurrent, Manning announced a week later that Dr. Robert Watkins had checked him out in Marina del Rey, found his neck sufficiently healed, and cleared him to play again, though there would be residual blips such as finger numbness and weak triceps muscles. Even so, as a *Star* headline tellingly pointed out, "Doctor, Not Team, Clears Manning."

In early March he was back at Duke, having invited Jeff Saturday, Dallas Clark, Austin Collie, and Brandon Stokley to work with him—all of whom had been either summarily released by the Colts or, in Saturday's case, was a free agent and not wanted back. Whether that sat well with Irsay, only the owner knew for sure, though if he sincerely wanted Manning back, it should have cheered him that these workouts proved he was making real progress. Running the same drills with the receivers that they did in Colts practices, he put them through exhausting paces. At one point he had them simulate the 2010 AFC championship game against the Jets, minute by minute. "It was a little over the top," Stokley recalled of how they ran the same plays and even took time-outs at the exact intervals that they had been called in real time. For his part, Cutcliffe was amazed at his old pupil's reanimation. "You hear and read about people who overcome things they shouldn't," he said. "I saw it with my own eyes."[3]

———

Manning had not heard from Irsay since they uneasily tried to smooth things over. It was a good sign that Pagano brought Bruce Arians back to Indianapolis as his quarterbacks coach. But the other omens weren't so good. Given Peyton's age and uncertain future, the owner was now looking past him to a new, young savior, one he could acquire, ironically enough, only because of Manning—or, more accurately, his absence: the Colts had the first pick in the draft. Irsay had already determined that his team would use it to draft Stanford quarterback Andrew Luck, considered the best, surest quarterback prospect to enter the draft in a generation. Some believed the Colts had tanked the season just for that reason. The town was buzzing about it, though most assumed Luck would back up Manning for the foreseeable future. Then, on March 6—a month before the draft, and two days before he would have to write Manning a check for $28 million—Irsay dropped the hammer, announcing he had given Peyton Manning his outright release.

It was a shock, one that tore Manning up and hurt his pride. Said Archie, "I think it broke his heart. I think he understood the reality [was], 'It's time for me to go.' And then I think he reconsidered and said, 'No, I'm supposed to play my whole career here.' So he went back and told them, 'I'll help Andrew, and we'll make it work. I want to stay.'"[4] Irsay was deaf to the pleas, though in fairness he probably did Peyton a favor by not creating a situation where the fans would be calling for Luck if and when Peyton faltered. As Kravitz wrote, "The moves were made, ultimately, because they had to be made. Because as the late, great 49ers coach Bill Walsh once said, you're best to move a player one year too early than one year too late."[5] Indeed, drafting Luck was the easiest way to justify ending the Manning era, even if, when the team called a farewell press conference a day later, these hard, cold realities had no place in the mawkish rite of counterfeit sorrow.

Irsay was right about one thing, saying, "It's been very hard on everyone around here, and it's been very hard on Peyton, too." But he had been eager to turn Manning from icon to castoff in one year. Already, the huge image of him affixed to the exterior of Lucas Oil Stadium was being torn down when, looking regal in a gray suit, he entered the room and stood towering over the stubby, goateed Irsay, neither exchanging a glance, both looking like they should be at a funeral. Manning and Polian, who had himself swallowed his pride to help Irsay's spilling of tears and tributes, were sincerely emotional, and Irsay, his own distraught emotions no doubt eased a bit by the money he had saved himself, began by saying, "The number 18 jersey will never be worn again by a Colt on the field."

Peyton then stepped to the microphone and was extraordinarily gracious toward Irsay, which was perhaps the best acting he's ever done. "I've been a Colt for almost all of my adult life," he said, fighting back tears, voice quavering, "but I guess in life and in sports, we all know that nothing lasts forever. Times change, circumstances change, and that's the reality of playing in the NFL. Jim and I have spoken extensively about where we are today. And our conversations have led both of us to recognize that our circumstances make it best for us to take this next step."

He went on: "This town and this team mean so much to me. It truly has been a[n] honor to play in Indianapolis. I do love it here. I love the fans and I will always enjoy having played for such a great team. I will leave the Colts with nothing but good thoughts and gratitude to Jim, the organization, my teammates, the media, and especially the fans. . . . And as I go, I go with just a few words left to say, a few words I want to address to Colts fans everywhere: Thank you very much from the bottom of my heart. I truly have enjoyed being your quarterback."[6]

And that was it, a "classy farewell," wrote Kravitz, by the man who had set a cornucopia of records in that uniform and now was exiting stage right, taking the team's identity out the door with him. Before Elvis left the building, he lingered with around two dozen employees of the team. "Maintenance, secretaries, equipment guys, everybody who'd been there a long time," he recalled. "Some guys leave a place after a long time, and they're bitter. Not me. But it was important for me to get closure."[7] He was driven to the airport by an equipment manager who recalled, "There were a lot of tears."

The fans would have a new toy to make the sense of loss, even anger about seeing him go, easier to get over—though the Luck era would roll out fast, and then seem to run dry after a few seasons. And Peyton Manning's new priority would be selling himself to other teams as a 36-year-old rewired quarterback with numb fingers, coming off unprecedented surgery, who hadn't played for a year. Any new team would need to pay him the stratospheric money Irsay had backed out of—a big risk. But after a year of hell, he would go into the hunt without compromising. He'd made the commitment to keep Manning Inc. a valuable stock, and now it was someone else's turn to buy into it.

=====

At first, he had no idea what a free agent is supposed to do. But this was just another subject for him to study from top to bottom. He began to draw up a pros-and-cons list of teams that needed a quarterback, weighting each one based on front office stability, tenure of the coaches, style of offense, and possibility of winning. The money, he trusted, would fall into place according to how badly a team wanted him, another factor. Besides Condon and Crosthwait, he placed a good deal of trust in Cutcliffe's opinions. Indeed, that link no doubt led the Tennessee Titans to put in a bid, the nostalgia of coming "home"—his real home had a guy named Brees—to the scene of his pro apprenticeship and his old rabid fans, as well as giving him a chance to beat Irsay twice a season. Another early contender was San Francisco, with whom he could walk in the footprints of Joe Montana (who had also been forced out late in his career, which he finished in Kansas City).

Following his release, he spent time at his vacation home in Miami, where local reporters pestered him for interviews. He walled himself off to even old friends—his family, Condon, and Crosthwait forming a protective shield that his old favorite Vols receiver, Marcus Nash, found "a little sad," given that the Peyton he knew, the one he saw every day, had hated the notion of needing to be shielded. After his maniacal research, one team met all the criteria: the one whose personnel decisions were being made by the quarterback he revered most, after his own father. That, of course, was John Elway in Denver, who really, really needed a quarterback. The one he had, the former Heisman Trophy winner Tim Tebow, had taken the Broncos on a weird, wild ride. Taking over early in 2011 when they were 1–4, he somehow got them into the playoffs at 8–8, even beating the Steelers in the first round of the playoffs with a long touchdown pass on the first play of overtime. But he never proved he could be better than his anemic completion rate of 46 percent. As popular as Tebow was, he simply was not the future. Elway pushed the Broncos' owner, Pat Bowlen, to pursue Manning, which, while obviously desirable and the best conceivable way to disappear Tebow, seemed impossible given the team's usually conservative spending habits.

Indeed, Tebow would be making just $1.5 million the next season. The *Denver Post*'s football writer, Mike Klis, ventured, "Once all the bids come in and the recruiting pitches are made, the Broncos probably will have as much chance at signing free-agent Peyton Manning as Tim Tebow does of starting an interview without thanking the Lord."[8] Added the antediluvian columnist Woody Paige, "Despite all the shrieking and screeching, Peyton Manning is not coming to Denver to play—unless he's on the visiting team."[9] But only three days after Peyton was released, Bowlen, Elway, head coach John Fox, and offensive coordinator Mike McCoy flew to Miami, picked him up, and brought him to the

team's office facility in Englewood, Colorado. He had a great time with
Elway, the pair arguably the best quarterbacks of their respective generations, but Manning's head was still spinning and he felt rushed. As in
Miami, TV reporters got wind of him being there and followed him right
from the moment the plane landed. The Broncos had seven vans go to
and from their Dove Valley training complex to the Cherry Hills Country
Club, where Manning was staying, so the media wouldn't know which
one Peyton was in. The Broncos fawned all over him. As another *Post*
scribe, Mark Kiszla, wrote, Tebow "took the most vicious hit of his NFL
career Friday, when he got run over by the red carpet that Denver rolled
out for Peyton Manning."[10]

Elway, as an inducement, was about to sign Brandon Stokley, and
during his stay Peyton threw a ball around with his old Colts receiver.
At the time, Elway described Manning as being "in shock" about being
released. "Everybody kept telling him he was going to get released, and
he didn't believe them until it happened." Peyton had also set up a meeting with Redskins coach Mike Shanahan, who lived in Denver. Indeed,
Fox, a rah-rah type who had coached the Panthers for nine years before
taking the job in Denver in '11, recalled that Manning "sounded bothered" on the visit and "wasn't in his comfort zone."[11] Elway was wise
enough to know the hard sell would turn him off. Having made the team's
pitch, he told Peyton to take his time. But with spring camps only weeks
away, there was little time left. Back home, he and Cutcliffe went over all
the possibilities, a process Peyton says was "a full-court press situation."

One of six other teams wanting a shot at him was the Redskins,
though it would have meant facing Eli twice each season, with all the
hysteria that entailed; when news broke that the Redskins had traded
up in the draft to be able to get Robert Griffin III, they came off the list
anyway. While Peyton was in Colorado, Seahawks coach Pete Carroll
impulsively flew in to make a pitch, surprising Peyton. Carroll said he'd
fly him to Seattle and show him around. However, Peter King wrote in
Sports Illustrated, "Peyton Manning does not like surprises. He said no
thanks. Carroll flew home."[12] Driven to the airport by Stokley, Manning
went to Phoenix, where he met with the Cardinals, and then had a Dolphins front-office party meet him at the airport in Indianapolis, where

he would spend one day before heading off to Nashville and the Titans. Then he was back with Cutcliffe again in Durham, where he swore he thought he saw Jim Harbaugh watching him throw—from a distance, through binoculars, a hoodie over his head. Speaking on the phone with Olivia, Peyton said she'd never guess who he saw watching him under a hoodie.

"Bill Belichick?" she said, cracking him up.

═══════

Elway and Fox also watched him throw at Duke, though not through binoculars. Other teams were pending, too, the Jets and Chiefs among them. Peyton made some calls to people he trusted for their advice, including Tony Dungy and Bill Parcells. As Dungy says, rather than anything football, Peyton wanted to find the closest thing he could to the "family" womb he'd had in Indianapolis, at least until Irsay blew that up. That was what he felt with Elway and Fox. Frank Tripucka, the first Broncos quarterback in the AFL days, whose No. 18 jersey had been retired by the team, graciously said Peyton could wear it.[13] Even President Obama offered his opinion that Manning seemed right for the Rocky Mountain scenery, "if natural beauty has anything to do with it."[14] Other quarterbacks had felt that way, until losing set in. Post-Elway, Jake Plummer, Jay Cutler, Kyle Orton, and Brady Quinn had all fled the team. And three Broncos were to be suspended for four games each for using performance-enhancing drugs.

But the other pieces were in place. The team seemed a quarterback away from becoming a serious contender in the AFC, and now the best quarterback in the game may have wanted in.

Not that this appealed to everyone in Denver. Kiszla thought merely courting Manning had damaged a good thing. "Without taking a snap for the Broncos," he wrote, "Peyton Manning has engineered one of the biggest upsets in the history of a storied NFL franchise. He killed Tebowmania. After the anticipation of a Hall of Fame quarterback wearing orange and blue, how can Denver possibly go back to Tim Tebow? With all due respect to Manning and his recent medical issues, however, the quarterback who has his neck on the line is Broncos executive John Elway."

Kiszla also wondered about "the consequences should Manning get hurt, while Tebow is doing his thing for the Dolphins in Miami? There are not too many things that would tempt me to bury [Elway's] old No. 7 jersey in the closet, but that would rank at the top."[15]

Ol' No. 7 was willing to risk it. It was implicit that anyone wanting Peyton knew he wouldn't come cheap; in fact, the inability of some teams to fit him under the $130 million salary cap was one of the factors he considered. For example, the Cardinals had to know what his decision would be before their deadline to pay a $7 million bonus to quarterback Kevin Kolb; when Manning refused to rush his decision, they dropped out. The Broncos, though, thanks to their history of chintzy spending, had all the room they would need. Speculation mounted that they might even pony up a $100 million deal.

Manning made his decision on Sunday, March 18. That morning, he called Elway, who was with Fox at the time. When Elway got the good word, he shot the coach a thumbs-up. Jumping up out of his chair with glee, Fox recalled, "I almost pulled both hamstrings." Condon and Elway talked turkey later in the day. The next morning, Peyton flew out to Dove Valley for the announcement, even as the contract was still being written. When he arrived at the Broncos office and shook hands with a "thrilled" Bowlen, some issues were still being ironed out. In the end, the contract was for five years, projected to perhaps $96 million—but with a lot of ifs. He would make $18 million in '12—paid out in 17 game checks of over $1 million each—but the Broncos wisely protected themselves with an "injury waiver"; if he passed a physical after the first season, he would be guaranteed $40 million over the 2013 and 2014 seasons, with a salary cut eased by a $10 million restructuring bonus in '13. If at any time he reinjured his neck or flunked a physical, the contract could be voided. No one in the Manning camp objected. Grateful as Peyton was, he even kicked in a $4.3 million gift to child-services charities around Denver.

Manning, who knew the color well, held up his new orange No. 18 jersey for the cameras, smiled with Bowlen and Elway and oozed, "I'm very excited to begin the next chapter of my playing career for the Denver Broncos." He said he "hated" having to reject the other teams, but in the end, "I felt the Broncos were just a great fit." He also said he wasn't "where I want to be" physically.[16] But if pride had to do with it, Elway, in his welcoming remarks, put it best.

"We signed a Hall of Famer with a chip on his shoulder," he said.

Making time for each reporter or microphone carrier, when Peyton was done he walked downstairs to the locker room, put on shorts and a T-shirt, and began working out in the gym. He followed that routine for the next three days, during which Tebow was traded to the Jets, to be dumped after a year and then be out of the game after two brief, failed attempts to catch on. Notice was taken of the two Frankenstein's monster–like scars on Manning's neck, but as iffy as he was, it was already being reported that the team was banking on an economic boom, his arrival sure to spike local TV and radio ad rates, stadium revenues, licensing fees, and merchandise sales (though Tebow's was the second-highest-selling jersey in the league). He was already doing TV promos for the team. The league would schedule his debut, at home at Sports Authority Field at Mile High against the Steelers, as the first Sunday night game of the season. Elway immediately went about spending what was left in the coffers to give Manning pieces, signing several receivers, among them free agent Andre Caldwell.

The offense in '11 had been entirely built around the run, leading the league in rushing yards, Willis McGahee gaining nearly 1,200 and Tebow over 600. They were next-to-last in passing, even with receivers like Eric Decker and Demaryius Thomas. The defense was unsettled but on the rise, blitzing outside linebacker Von Miller winning the Defensive Rookie of the Year award. Expectations were clearly high; Mike Klis wrote in the *Post*, "Merely by closing the deal with Peyton Manning . . . Elway has become a leading candidate for NFL executive of the year."[17]

———

When Peyton began working out informally with the receivers, gradually building intensity through spring and summer camp, he was still getting his sea legs. But Fox put the offense in his hands, his ear-numbing word salad and gesticulations prior to the snap to remain intact, and of course the endlessly mimicked "Omaha!" added to the glossary. His first official practices in early August drew such attention that the Broncos moved an intrasquad scrimmage to Mile High, where it was played before 20,000 fans. Each of Manning's passes was charted in the paper.

His regimen was under the eye of a Denver trainer, a masseur, and a private chef. Peter King noted that "Broncos nutritionist Bryan Snyder directs Manning's cook on what to prepare for him on which days (Thursday is pasta night), and accompanies Manning on walks through the team cafeteria. 'It's, "You can have one piece of that, two pieces of this,"' Manning says, 'like you would with a child.' "[18] As for his mechanics, his whole neurological system had to be reprogrammed. As Luke Richesson, the Broncos' strength and conditioning coach put it, "We broke him down like a car—take the motor out, get the alignment straight, then focus on the horsepower."[19] Finding Manning weak and "really detrained," hardly able to even pick up a medicine ball, Richesson started him with light weights most men would scoff at.

He looked like a retread, limping onto the field with his knee brace visible and a thick therapeutic glove swaddling his right hand, but his timing was all but perfect again, and of course his mind was never an issue. Right away, his presence galvanized the team—"You want to be better because it's Peyton Manning," testified Demaryius Thomas. "I know I'm a better player because he's here." The fans embraced him instantly. From day one, he was getting over 300 letters a day, leading him to hire two staffers to screen them for him, and he personally answered the ones that moved him, saving a copy of each in a big computer file. Many were from people who had or would have neck surgery. In Dove Valley, food shops near the team's training field sold out their supplies to the mobs of fans who came to catch a glimpse of him in practice. Televisions all around the state tuned in the Broncos' preseason games, in which he played little and wowed no one, throwing three picks in the first two games.

As he had on the Colts, he had his own routines. He would sit with the team's equipment managers, draining cans of beer, watching game film on his iPad, sometimes running a single play back for half an hour. One guy had to carry his baseball cap, which he'd put on when on the sideline; another was in charge of his chin strap.[20] Others would help wrap his legs and torso, even his feet, in tape to help cushion his body, a painstaking task that took an hour. The rituals, of course, would mean nothing if he didn't recover his form in a whole new way. Though his arm wasn't quite as strong as before, he adjusted by getting more power from his legs, producing arm velocity as would a pitcher driving hard off the rubber. His footwork was more intricate, with less wasted movement. Knowing he was hitting it again, the old cockiness was back, his recent softer side discarded. When people had told him they were praying for him, he had been taking it to heart. Now, he would look at them with annoyance.

"I'm fine," he'd say. "You don't have to do that."

Despite the progress, he was still a shadow of himself, bewildering fans who had no idea how far he had fallen. He had his timing, but the little bit of zip he lost on throws turned those old wobbly completions into aimless passes or even interceptions. Fox was a conservative coach who wanted to pound on the ground, but he gave Manning the reins, aware that when the Colts won the title, they had the league's worst running game. The Colts' hurry-up Lightning offense was adapted as the Broncos' Bolt offense, as a collaborative effort with McCoy and quarterbacks coach Adam Gase. In many ways, the swirl of passing patterns was indistinguishable from the Colts'.

When the opener arrived on September 9, Peyton was well aware of the pressure he was under. "End of the day," he said, "my contract really is only a one-year contract," given that only the first year was guaranteed.[21] He set out to become the first quarterback to win championships with different teams. The bettors were on board. With Manning having won at least 10 games 11 times and thrown for 4,000 yards 11 times, the Vegas oddsmakers gave the Broncos the third-best shot to win it all, behind the Patriots and Packers. But was he *that* Manning?

On the first drive of the game, played on an 85-degree night in the Rockies, with an electric current in the air and people making a ruckus all around Mile High, Manning's first pass as a Bronco was a 13-yard completion to Decker. In the second quarter, he led a drive on which he ran seven yards for a first down and halfback Knowshon Moreno ran it in from seven yards. But the Steelers led 10–7 at the half, and a nine-minute drive directed by Ben Roethlisberger then made it 13–7. Two plays later, the ball on the Broncos 29, the Steelers tried to disguise a blitz by lining up a linebacker on the tight end. But Peyton read it and called a quick screen to Thomas. Center J. D. Walton and guard Zane Beadles got out ahead of him, and their blocks sprang Thomas for a 71-yard touchdown romp. That pass made history—it was Manning's 400th touchdown pass, a mark previously reached only by Favre and Marino. Thomas, whose end zone shtick is to drop the ball like a hot mic, didn't realize it. Naturally, Manning did. "Peyton asked me why I didn't have the ball," Thomas recalled, "so I went back and got it."[22]

Manning was on a roll. In the fourth quarter, he hit on six of seven passes, the last a one-yard touchdown to tight end Jacob Tamme, followed by another to McGahee for the two-point conversion and the lead, 22–19. After a Broncos field goal, a 43-yard pick-six by cornerback Tracy Porter—the same guy who had sealed the Saints' Super Bowl win over Manning with the 74-yard interception—made the final 31–19. It was a heck of a debut, with Peyton going 19 of 26 for 253 yards, with two touchdowns and a passer rating of 129.2. And it set in motion a season in which Manning was able to override his physical limits, although it took the defense belatedly congealing for the Broncos to get in gear.

The Broncos finished 13–3. They had the fourth-ranked offense and second-ranked defense, giving up a mere 13 rushing touchdowns. They closed out the regular season by blasting the Chiefs 38–3, Manning going 23 of 29 for 304 yards and three touchdowns, a 144.8 rating. That gave him 37 touchdowns against 11 interceptions, 4,659 yards (41 shy of his career high, two years before), a 68.6 completion percentage, and a 105.8 passer rating, second to Aaron Rodgers. These numbers seemed like science fiction, considering he was still working his way back. His performance won him his sixth selection as first-team All-Pro. Thomas—his new Marvin Harrison or Reggie Wayne—was on the second team, catching 94 balls, 10 for touchdowns. Five receivers had over 40 catches. Three runners combined for over 1,500 yards. Von Miller was a first-team All-Pro, Elvis Dumervil and cornerback Champ Bailey making the second team. Elway *should* have won Executive of the Year, but he placed second to, ironically, Ryan Grigson—for drafting Andrew

Luck, who led the Colts to an 11–5 record and a playoff berth. Both Jim Irsay and Pat Bowlen had profited quite handsomely from the fall and rise of Peyton Manning.

═══

A stunning success in every way—he was beaten out for MVP only by Vikings halfback Adrian Peterson, who broke the 2,000-yard barrier, and Brady—his comeback put him back in the lead of the Manning brothers' one-on-one rivalry. Eli had another fine season of his own—3,948 yards, 26 touchdowns, 15 interceptions. In a game against the Bucs, a 41–34 Giants win, he went 31 of 51 for 510 yards, the fourth 400-yard game of his career and just the 13th time a quarterback had gone over 500, a threshold not crossed by Peyton. But with the team sitting at 6–2, the defense collapsed, keeping Eli off the field a lot, even though, as they lost five of the last eight games, the question around the city was: What's wrong with Eli? Finishing 9–7 and out of the playoffs, it was the first of four straight seasons of the same.

And so Peyton had the playoffs to himself, and a pathway to delivering another championship. The first playoff encounter was against the Ravens, who had disposed of the Colts but had only gone 10–6 during the season. The danger for the Broncos was that the Ravens had the second-best pass defense. And Joe Flacco had matured into a near-elite quarterback. They also had motivation; Ray Lewis had recently announced that he would be retiring at season's end. The Broncos had mauled the Ravens 34–17 during the season. But they were a rabid bunch, talking trash and unnerving people. And they had a familiar face at offensive coordinator: Jim Caldwell.

It was also the Ravens' type of weather: 13 degrees with a wind-chill of 2. But Manning's passes cut through the Colorado wind—as did Trindon Holliday, the Broncos' five-foot, five-inch return specialist and former college sprint champion who took back an early punt a playoff-record 90 yards for one touchdown and the second-half kickoff 104 yards for another, making him the first to score two TDs on kick returns in a postseason game. In a game of wild swings, Flacco torched Bailey for two long touchdown passes and Peyton threw first-half touchdown passes to Stokley and Moreno, but also had a pick returned for a 39-yard touchdown by Corey Graham. His third TD, 17 yards to Thomas, had Denver ahead 35–28 with 7:11 to go. They looked to be in the clear when, with just a half minute left, Flacco faced third-and-three on his own 30 with no time-outs left. Denver dropped eight men back into coverage. Flacco stepped up in the pocket and heaved one, long and high enough to almost cross into the haze of the lights, all the way to the Broncos 20, where Jacoby Jones had slipped past free safety Rahim Moore and cornerback Tony Carter. Moore leaped too early to bat the ball down. Jones grabbed it and jogged into the end zone.

The sudden game-tying, 70-yard touchdown seemed to stun John Fox. He had 31 seconds, the ball on his own 20 and two time-outs. But he had Manning take a knee and send it into overtime. He then had him play conservatively instead of making risky long throws. No one could score, and with a minute left, Peyton, looking to get into field-goal range, rolled right, then threw left, a difficult task for any quarterback, much less one with reduced throwing strength. Aimed at Stokley, the ball died in flight and was picked off, again by Graham—a turnover only slightly less awful than the killer interception by Porter, and one that Mike Klis called an "egregious sin."[23] So now it went to a second OT, in which Ray Rice ran it close enough for the Ravens to kick the winning field goal. After four hours and 11 minutes of heaven and hell, Peyton was once more explaining the pain of a loss he *couldn't* explain, his 290 yards and three touchdown passes wasted.

No one could have quibbled with him calling his interception a "bad throw" and remarking, "Probably the decision wasn't great either." But many fans blamed Fox for playing it so cautiously. Leaving the recriminations to others, Manning recycled the good-loser sap he kept stored in his bark for these moments, saying, "Certainly we did a lot of good things this season, but as of right now, it's hard to think about anything besides the loss tonight."[24] Showing class, he dressed and then trudged into the Ravens locker room, holding his son Marshall's hand, to congratulate Lewis, who was about to win his second Super Bowl, perhaps by turns envying Lewis for not needing the game anymore—and pitying himself that he *did*.

CHAPTER 24

"HE THROWS DUCKS"

As it turned out, Peyton was prescient to wonder, when he was considering signing with Denver, if John Fox and Mike McCoy would stick it out with the team. Fox stuck, but McCoy split, taking the head-coaching job with the Chargers. Adam Gase took over as offensive coordinator, and the Broncos picked up right where they left off, as did Manning. He cranked up 659 passes in 2013, getting in line with the massive numbers being compiled by Brees, who had gone over 5,000 yards and 40 touchdowns two years in a row, and Rodgers, who just missed 40 for a second straight season. In the past, crazy air numbers like that generally accompanied losing teams, and teams in general threw much more often with much less efficiency. Now, it was expected that fewer passes would gain big. In '12, four quarterbacks, old and young, had just missed 5,000 yards—Brady, Romo, Matt Ryan, and Matthew Stafford—and the rookie Luck had 4,374. Now, the man who had already thrown 49 touchdowns, way back in 2004 (that record, alas, bettered by Brady in '07), was about to do something really crazy.

The opener, on the first Thursday night, brought in the world champion Ravens, not on ice but an 83-degree evening, a lovely Rocky Mountain high—but only for the home team. Peyton, numb fingers, mummified anatomy, and all, was never better, a tribute to spinal fusion and Scotch tape. The Ravens took a 17–14 halftime lead, then were steamrollered.

Manning, who had thrown two touchdowns to Julius Thomas, the new starting tight end, went on a ridiculous spree. Within 27½ minutes, on three straight possessions and five of the last eight, he finished off drives with a touchdown pass, only once needing more than five plays. Leaving the deep backs watching aerials fly over their heads, he threw one for 28 yards to Andre Caldwell, with the playoff hero Graham clutching at him and called for holding. To give him another major weapon, Elway had signed Wes Welker as a free agent, and Brady's former target got the next serving. After a blocked punt, Peyton flipped a five-yard touchdown to him; then on the next drive, a two-yard touchdown. It was 35–17 then, and, padding the lead, he hit Thomas with two more, from 28 and then a short one that broke for 78 yards. Final: 49–27. Seven touchdowns, 462 yards, 141.1 rating. Zero picks. Statement made.

In the carnage, he became the sixth man to throw for seven scores (though, attesting to how the game had changed, just that year it would happen *again*, the Eagles' mediocre Nick Foles doing it against the Raiders; and Brees would get there in 2015). It was also his 11th 400-yard game, at the time putting him one behind Brees—three days before Eli rang up his fifth, against the Cowboys. As it happened, the brothers then met for the third Manning Bowl, at MetLife Stadium, meaning more distractions for each—and another sympathetic postgame pat on the head by Peyton, whose second touchdown pass, to Julius Thomas, early in the fourth quarter broke open a close game and sent the Broncos to a 41–23 rout. For Eli, it was a four-interception nightmare and an early augury that the yin would again be the yang, and Eli again the "other" Manning.

Never getting traction, the Giants offense was a shambles. The defense was crippled before the season even began; on July 4, Jason Pierre-Paul was setting off fireworks, got too close, and damn near lost his right hand. His thumb and forefinger fractured, the latter was so badly damaged it had to be amputated five days later. He resolved to return, and did, on a one-year deal worth $4 million less than the year before. He played surprisingly well, recording six sacks and returning a fumble 43 yards for a touchdown in a game against the Browns, but in December he went down for the season with a sports hernia. During the season, the Giants were thumped by the Panthers 38–0 and the Chiefs

31–7. The Cowboys pretty much ended their season in late November, when, after Eli led another of his comebacks, tossing two touchdowns to tie the game 21–21 with 4:45 left, Romo led his own 13-play drive and Dallas kicked the winning 35-yard field goal with four seconds left. The Giants finished out of the money at 7–9, not even reaching 300 points for the season.

Eli, in another sharp fall from grace, passed for 3,818 yards but only 18 touchdowns—and, the killer stat, 27 interceptions, a product of the complete failure of the running game. Of the receivers, only Victor Cruz was a game-breaker, and Eli only found him for four touchdowns. He was the Giants' all-time passing leader, but some wondered if he had peaked too soon. Or if David Tyree and Mario Manningham had saved him from being Jay Cutler, a fate to which he would now revert.

———

At the other end of the scale, the Broncos won their first six games, scoring over 50 points in back-to-back games. Peyton already had thrown for 20 touchdowns, compared with six Bronco rushing scores. (He also vaulted past Marino for second on the all-time passing yardage list, behind Favre.) The team set a record for points scored in five games. Manning set another for most touchdowns (20) without a pick. As Mike Klis wrote, "This is not so much about the Broncos. This is about Peyton Manning."[1] If it was about his pride, two games later came the one he *really* wanted, his return to Indianapolis, the buzz making the Manning Bowl seem mild. The week-long run-up to the October 20 contest was, predictably, a re-airing of old grievances, sparked by Irsay saying there was "no way" the Colts' reemergence, led by Luck, could have happened "if [Manning] is in Indy."[2] This was merely logical, of course, but it came out as a dig, which was why John Fox called it "inappropriate" and a "cheap shot" at Manning.

Peyton seemed relieved that the Denver media focused more on the Broncos' self-inflicted screw-ups. Just within the past two weeks, both kicker Matt Prater and Wes Welker were suspended for four games each by the league for violating its substance abuse policy. That story dominated the week, and Peyton curiously said, "I guess I wasn't shocked" about Welker, and that "I guess I had an idea that it might be happening," though he went no further.[3] On Wednesday, on a video hookup with the Indianapolis media, he kept it positive, refusing to bad-mouth Irsay. The *Indianapolis Star*'s Bob Kravitz had come to Denver to interview him, and, cornering him in a hallway, asked if he harbored any resentment toward the Colts. "It's just easier not to answer anything along those lines," he said. Kravitz wrote that "there was something very telling in his body language. . . . [H]e clearly has some issues now with . . . Irsay, and he'd be perfectly happy to drop about 60 points on the Colts Sunday night. Maybe 70."[4]

His return to Indy pulled the highest local TV ratings in a decade, yielding a 71 percent share of the city's televisions in both Indianapolis and Denver. Lucas Oil Stadium was a zoo, the fans beginning with intense ovations for Manning during a big-screen tribute, while Irsay, playing the nice guy, stood and cheered when Peyton took the field. Warming up on the sideline, Peyton removed his helmet, smiled, and waved. Luck called the vibe of the moment "rocking. The energy, you could taste it."

The 6–0 Broncos were six-point favorites over the 4–2 Colts, and Peyton hit Decker from 17 yards out for the first score. But the Broncos were mistake-prone this day. After Manning's second touchdown pass, to Julius Thomas, the Colts' Robert Mathis smashed in and forced Manning to fumble out of the end zone for a safety. The crowd, even those wearing No. 18 jerseys, had quickly shifted their enthusiasm to Luck, who threw two touchdowns in succession to go ahead 26–14 and keep ahead, running one in as well. Manning's TD pass to Demaryius Thomas and Moreno's rushing touchdown cut the lead to 36–30. But late in the game, throwing under duress, he was intercepted. On the next possession, backup running back Ronnie Hillman fumbled at the Colts three. Manning outpassed Luck 386–228, and the Broncos outgained the Colts 365–213, but the rookie was the victor, 39–33.

Peyton trudged off his old home field, head down, and of course he played it humble, praising Luck, who would go 11–5, losing in the second playoff round to the Patriots, and be named second-team All-Pro behind Manning. Of the reception the fans gave him, Peyton said, "It's something I'll always remember, and I'm very grateful for that." But this was a week he could have done without. The Colts' punter, Pat McAfee, said, "I think he got emotional . . . and I think it got to him a little bit."[5] There was no doubt this one really hurt. The rest of the league would pay for that.

———

The Broncos rebounded by wrecking the Redskins 45–21, Manning completing 30 of 44 for 354 yards and four more touchdowns (albeit with three interceptions), while the other quarterback he'd been shoved aside for, Robert Griffin III, was yanked for Kirk Cousins. Denver would go 5–2 the rest of the season, with the beleaguered defense regrouping, giving up more than 30 just once—a brutal 34–30 overtime loss to the Patriots, in which they collapsed after leading 24–0 at the half, then mostly watched as Tom Brady threw three touchdowns and the Pats stormed back to win in overtime.

Otherwise, the beat went on, accentuated by a 51–28 mugging of the Titans. Not even the loss of their coach slowed them. Before the season, Fox had been diagnosed with aortic valve damage but put off surgery. During the bye week, he felt dizzy, and doctors told him to go under the knife right away. He was replaced by defensive coordinator Jack Del Rio, who had once coached the Jaguars, for the last eight regular-season games. On autopilot, the Broncos again closed at 13–3, with numbers prompting double-takes.

Mostly Manning's. Two years after his career seemed moribund, all he did was break Brady's single-season record with his 51st touchdown pass in the penultimate game. "I'm sure it's just a temporary record," he said, "but I will enjoy it." Then, the next week, before which he already had 430 more yards and 16 more touchdowns than any other quarterback, he scorched the Raiders with four more, stretching the record to an unfathomable 55, which just might last as long as DiMaggio's 56-game hitting streak. He had racked up 5,477 yards—exactly one more than Brees's record—and done it on 659 pass attempts, 20 fewer than his previous high, with only 10 interceptions. He completed 68.3 percent. He averaged 342 yards a game. His quarterback rating was 115.1. Yet, hardly forgotten, the running game, opened by defenses spooked by the pass, gained 100 yards in all but four games—and as many as 280 in the New England game. The Broncos notched a league-high 606 points, though they did give up a hefty 399.

Manning's numbers more than earned him his fifth MVP and another first-team All-Pro designation. These honors began before the playoffs; another came when he finally made *Sports Illustrated*'s Sportsman of the Year, his grizzled face and wide forehead taking up most of the cover, the main picture inside of him in a jacket and tie, standing in the end zone, grimly gazing into the distance. He had a right to be introspective. The previous season's promise had ended ingloriously, and some mavens were jaded about him. On one website, the former *New York Times* writer Mike Freeman noted that Manning had a 9–11 playoff record, and was 1–4 in divisional games at home. Not only was the blown game against the Pats "extremely Heimlich-y," wrote Freeman, but "[i]f he's eliminated early [again] his NFL epitaph will [be] 'Here lies Manning's NFL career. One of the best at generating statistics. One of the worst at winning big.'"[6]

He would have home-field advantage through the AFC rounds, and first up were the Chargers. The heavily favored Broncos' running game did most of the damage, Moreno and Montee Ball gaining 134 yards between them, while Peyton only needed to throw for a modest 230 yards and two short touchdowns to Demaryius Thomas and Welker. The Broncos led 24–7 in the fourth quarter, sacked Philip Rivers four times, and won 24–17. Next came the AFC title game, one anticipated all season: the next big-game war with the hated Patriots, who, with yawning regularity, went 12–4. But Brady's numbers had been ebbing over the past three seasons. His touchdowns fell to 25, his fewest since 2006, and his 87.3 passer rating was his lowest since '08.

No one expected a defensive battle. And for one quarterback, the pickings were never easier. That quarterback was Peyton Manning, who came in having lost 10 of 14 games to Brady, and two of three in the playoffs, not that the numbers, or creeping age, mattered much. As one scribe wrote before the game in no less than *Forbes*—on whose annual Celebrity 100 list each quarterback had appeared four times—Manning versus Brady "is the greatest current individual rivalry in sports, and arguably up there with the ranks of Bird/Magic, Chrissie/Martina, Wilt/Russell and Ali/Frazier."[7]

But this time, Manning was better, a lot better. Denver was favored by five points, and acted like it. Peyton toyed with the Pats' cheesecloth defense, made even more vulnerable when Aqib Talib went down in the second quarter with a knee injury. Peyton used the short-to-medium passing game to control the ball—"We just couldn't get off the field," moaned Pats defensive end Andre Carter later—his goal-line scoring tosses to Jacob Tamme and Demaryius Thomas putting Denver up 20–3 at halftime. Despite two late New England touchdowns, they waltzed to a 26–16 victory—having laid 507 yards of offense on Belichick, 400 of them via Manning's arm. In line with his surreal regular season, he completed 32 of 43 passes, his rating a shiny 118.4. Brady, of course, wasn't bad, going 24 of 38 for 277 yards, but he needn't have shown up on this day.

It was so one-sided that, for some, the game was a *letdown*, though clearly not in the Mannings' VIP box, where, *Sports Illustrated* noted, "Archie, and brothers, Cooper and Eli [were] pogoing with joy." *SI* hailed a "Manning at the peak of his powers. He was dictatorial in his approach . . . democratic in his rule . . . and efficient in his execution. And there wasn't a damn thing the Pats could do about any of it." Seeing it as a kind of exorcism for Manning, writer Andrew Lawrence posited that Peyton "has one more ghost to K.O."[8] That being *himself*—specifically, his self-doubts after his Super Bowl failures. If so, he seemed to have let skeptics like Freeman affect his swagger.

Archie may well have been speaking for his son when he found he had to stick up for a four-time MVP and past champion. "As a parent, I get tired of it," he said with restrained anger afterward. "[W]hat's he played in? Twenty-two postseason games? And he's kind of being ridiculed. I mean, I played in zero postseason games. I can tell you a bunch of guys in my era, quarterbacks, buddies of mine—they'd love to say they played in 22 postseason games. My text count just hit 108 since the game's ended. The last one I got is [from] Fran Tarkenton."

While Fox and the other Broncos basked in the confetti streams and the fireworks detonating above the stadium, wearing AFC title caps and T-shirts, Lawrence said Peyton went through the ritual with "the frowning, furrow-browed expression that is as much a part of his persona as his nimble wit," which the writer interpreted as "the face of frustration." In the locker room, no more joyous, he was telling reporters, over and over, "There is still one more game to play."

═══

Playing in that game would make him the third starting quarterback to get to the big enchilada with two different teams, after Craig Morton and Kurt Warner. But the unknown known was that the NFC entry in Super Bowl XLVIII, played in Eli's backyard, MetLife Stadium, on February 2, was the Seattle Seahawks, a team for years lost in near obscurity. Even a five-year playoff run in the early-to-mid-2000s and a losing trip to the Super Bowl in '05 didn't generate much fire. That is, until boyish-looking football lifer Pete Carroll—a human windup toy who had coached the Patriots in the '90s, left his sinecure at USC to try again in the pros—took over the team in 2010. Two years later, they drafted a new-age quarterback, the smallish, eel-like Russell Wilson—who only a few years before had attended the Manning Academy—giving Carroll a leader who could run and throw, and throw *while* running, to go with brick-house fullback Marshawn Lynch.

In '13, Wilson, at only 25, threw 26 touchdowns and ran for 539 yards. Lynch rumbled for 1,257 yards and 12 scores; both went to the Pro Bowl, aided to no end by the defense, coordinated by Dan Quinn. Ranked the best in the league, dubbed the Legion of Boom and the Angry Birds, they were No. 1 against the pass, No. 7 against the run, and No. 1 with 39 takeaways. The sine qua non was first-team All-Pro cornerback Richard Sherman, a bug-eyed Stanford grad whose skills were often overshadowed by his loud mouth and brash behavior. The Seahawks figured they could disrupt all those Bronco crisscrossing patterns with their hybrid zone-man coverage, with Sherman and the other corner either inside or outside, interchanging with free safety Earl Thomas, another first-team All-Pro, and the strong safety, second-team All-Pro Kam Chancellor. One of their fleet linebackers would play midzone, and everyone was fast and smart enough to create double coverage at the point of most any pass.

The Vegas boys made the Broncos a two-point favorite, dragged down by the Manning big-game "choke" effect and the suspicion that his numbers had an inflated feel about them; and that, as Sherman said, "His passes will be accurate and on time, but he throws ducks." Hearing that, Peyton grinned tightly and said, "I believe it to be true as well," he said. "I've thrown a lot of yards and touchdowns with ducks. I'm actually quite proud of it."[9] Sherman also made the valid technical point that when Manning took the snap, "he doesn't necessarily catch the laces all the time," due to the numbness in his fingers. However, just as important was that two valuable Broncos, Von Miller and left tackle Ryan Clady, were out injured.

Though heavy snow was forecast for the New York area after the game, the day itself was an almost tropical 49 degrees, the wind calm. Yet, only 12 seconds into the game, the Broncos snapped the ball too soon, sending it over Manning's right shoulder and rolling into the end zone where Moreno fell on it, a safety. "There's no explanation for it," center Manny Ramirez would say, and that went for the rest of a very long evening for the Broncos, during which, S. L. Price wrote in *Sports Illustrated*, "Manning never lost the harried, confused look of those first moments; the game once expected to be a career topper soon became a potential legacy mangler."[10]

Rushed hard late in the first quarter, he overshot Julius Thomas and was intercepted by Chancellor; a few plays later, Lynch ran it in to make it 15–0. Late in the half, at the 'Hawks 35 and on a 16-play, eight-minute drive, he dropped back to pass. As he threw, his arm was clipped by defensive end Cliff Avril, the ball fluttered, and linebacker Malcolm Smith, the eventual game MVP, plucked it and ran 60 yards for a touchdown—yet one more crushing pick. That made the second half moot—especially when, again, just 12 seconds in, the 'Hawks returned the kickoff for a touchdown. Working under the deep zone, Peyton would end up completing 34 passes—a Super Bowl record—out of 49 attempts and a touchdown to Demaryius Thomas, who set a Super Bowl record with 13 catches. Manning's 280 yards lifted him past Brady for all-time playoff passing yardage. But when the game ended at 43–8, he had taken the worst Super Bowl loss since 1990, when the Elway-led Broncos were pummeled by the 49ers 55–10. The Wilson kid, the second black quarterback to win the Super Bowl, the one with the $526,000 salary, threw one more touchdown than the aging, millionaire record holder.

The punishment over, Peyton sought out the winning quarterback and other players—on the field this time—and then repaired to the locker room. He said nothing as he peeled off his uniform and tape. He donned a suit, packed his bag, and slowly fulfilled his duty to answer questions at the press conference. "You can what-if all you want," he said. "I don't know if you ever get over it. It's a difficult pill to swallow. You have to find a way to deal with it and process it, and if you can, you try and fuel it to make yourself a better team next year. Guys are disappointed. It takes some time." Later, encountering the *Denver Post*'s Mark Kiszla, he had a simple missive. "I'm sorry," he said. As Kiszla recalled it, "he spoke straight from the heart, as if [he] felt obligated to send a message to every, last Broncos fan."[11]

Sherman, who hurt his leg and ended the game on crutches on the sideline, said the 'Hawks defense had deciphered Manning's hand signals. But he rhapsodized about the man he'd denigrated. Peyton, he said, had specifically sought him out after the game. "He was really concerned about my well-being. After a game like that, a guy who's still classy enough to say 'How are you doing?' To show that kind of concern for an opponent shows a lot of humility and class." Later, he tweeted, "He's a Hall of Fame player, he's a living legend, he's a record-holding quarterback, he's a Super Bowl champion."[12] Yet most everyone else might have seconded Price's rumination in *SI*: "Everyone knows that it's never a one-man game, but you've got to wonder: Why doesn't Peyton win more?" And even Archie seemed to have had his fill of these psychodramas ending in such pain. So tied in knots was he from watching Peyton being abused that he made his weary admission about how he hated this ulcermaker called football.

The headlines in Denver were brutal—"Shame Won't Disappear in Just 12 Seconds" sat atop Kiszla's story in the *Post*, his game story leading with: "It took Peyton Manning 37 years to build a reputation as the best quarterback in NFL history, and only 12 seconds in the Super Bowl to fumble it away. Duck, Peyton." Mike Klis added that "the Broncos suffered from a horrific case of stage fright. Jitters turned to panic. Panic leaked to disaster. Disaster became humiliation." And Benjamin Hochman: "Sunday stunk. It was embarrassing, and I don't care if Peyton Manning doesn't like that word." Now the question was whether Manning would be back again next year, or go out with his record-breaking season. Even the fans were split, one letter to the editor of the *Post* reading, "Dude, you're kidding, right? What will it be like next season, when Manning is a year older and a year slower?"

Peyton kept repeating that he had no plans to retire, not exactly an emphatic answer. When last seen on that latest dreadful Sunday, after being consoled by the family, he was pushing his way past autograph hunters on the way to the team bus. At one point, he stopped and signed a few. Some in the small group threw some more questions at him, but he engaged none and quietly slipped onto the bus. The door closed behind him.

⸻

Most things Peyton Manning did now were framed by history. For instance, the season before, when he played in the Pro Bowl, the rules were bent so that Jeff Saturday, who was retiring after playing out his career in Green Bay, could cross sides and snap the ball one last time to Peyton, the sideline shouting match they'd had years before long forgotten. While retirement for Manning was entirely logical, his greatness and his ability to beat the odds and the laws of biology proven, at 38 *he* needed closure. He hadn't worked his way back only to pack it in after a blowout soiled his legacy. Naturally, money was also in the equation. He had earned the second year of his tentative contract, and so he was prepared to reach down and take whatever he had left. But this was a Peyton Manning steadily, even precipitously, in decline from week to week, and easy to frustrate. During a preseason game with the Texans the next year, a scrub safety, D. J. Swearinger, knocked Welker out of the game with a concussion. On the next play, Manning threw a touchdown and violated his own protocol by taunting Swearinger, drawing the only fine of his career. His body, meanwhile, was breaking down, and he could be painful just to watch. However, what he had was enough most games.

The 2014 season would run much like the one before it, though the rarefied numbers were dialed back to merely great. To his good fortune, he wasn't required to carry the team; the Broncos defense, with lockdown players at most positions—now including two high-profile free-agent acquisitions: Aqib Talib, who jumped the Patriots to sign for $57 million over six years, and 32-year-old outside linebacker DeMarcus Ware, the all-time Cowboys sack leader who signed for $30 million over three years—would set him up within smelling distance of the enemy goal line. Eleven Broncos would make All-Pro, five on defense and, across the line, Manning, both Thomases, Clady, second-year halfback C. J. Anderson, and the newest receiving gem, Emmanuel Sanders, who left the Steelers and signed as a free agent, replacing Decker, who signed with the Jets.

There was payback the very first week, when the Colts came in on Sunday night and, unlike the traumatic game in Indianapolis the previous year, Peyton made mincemeat of his old team's defense. He fired three touchdowns in the second quarter—all to Julius Thomas—and had a 24–7 lead at the half. This time, Luck didn't have any. Abused all day, sacked three times, he had to throw 57 times, gaining 370 yards (to Manning's 269) with two touchdowns and two interceptions, closing the gap before losing 31–24. In the third game, the Broncos went to Seattle for a rematch with the Seahawks, and now it was Manning who had to claw his way back. The 'Hawks led 17–5 in the fourth quarter, but an interception set up a short touchdown pass to Julius Thomas. Then, after a field goal, Manning got the ball back on his own 20 with 59 seconds left, down 20–12. Slicing up the secondary, he got to the Seattle 26 with 24 seconds to go, then zipped one to Tamme for the touchdown. The two-point conversion sent it into overtime. However, the 'Hawks won the coin toss and moved right down the field, winning the game on a six-yard run by Lynch.

Still, Manning's 303 passing yards against the team that would make it back to the Super Bowl that year showed he was in the groove. Winning five of the next six games, he and the Manning brand were purring, his jersey selling briskly, his cluttered "Omaha" cadences alone a major public curiosity. That season, ESPN thought it necessary to dispatch a crew to Omaha, Nebraska, to glean the reaction of the locals to the town's new notoriety, and Omaha Steaks was doing peak business. As it was, the only real drama of the regular season was the latest match with the Patriots, in week nine.

Belichick's team had started off slowly, some mavens wondering wistfully whether Brady was finished, but they evened out and were now 6–2, again seemingly beatable only with a stake in Brady's heart under a full moon at midnight. Even on a blustery day in Foxborough, both quarterbacks went right to the pass and never stopped, Manning going 34 of 57 for 438 yards and two touchdowns, Brady 33 of 53 for 333 yards. The difference was that Brady hurled four touchdowns to Manning's two, and one pick to Manning's two. The second was off a muff by his receiver, but the first was a killer—into the teeth of a mid-depth zone right to linebacker Rob Ninkovich. The final score was 43–21, prompting Peter King to write that, in light of history, Belichick was "so far inside Peyton Manning's head that he's built a condo in there."[13]

They were upset by the Rams in week 11, despite 389 yards from Peyton, who threw four more touchdowns in a win over the Dolphins. But now, dehydrated and hurting, he felt so poorly before a December game against the Chargers that he lay on a trainer's table, hooked up to an IV drip, going through four bags of fluid. In that game, a 22–10 win, he threw for 233 yards but strained his right quad, partly because of dehydration, and came out late for his backup, Brock Osweiler. The next week, he passed for 311 yards and two touchdowns in a 47–28 loss to the Bengals. In the finale, he destroyed the Raiders with five touchdown passes in 14 minutes and 340 yards in a 41–17 rout, ending the regular season at 12–4. All this even as Archie grimaced, believing, he would say, "I'm not sure he should even have been playing."[14]

His numbers were routinely glittering: 4,727 yards, 66.2 completion percentage, 39 touchdowns, a reasonable 15 interceptions, a 101.5 rating. The offense ranked fourth in the NFL. With the Bronco run defense a stone wall, teams passed like crazy, netting 29 touchdowns, but overall the defense was No. 3 in the league, those five All-Pros—Miller, Ware, Talib, strong safety T. J. Ward, and right cornerback Chris Harris—knotty and opportunistic. And when their first-round playoff game was played—with added drama, against the Colts—the oddsmakers made the Broncos seven-point favorites. However, Chuck Pagano knew that Manning's painful thigh was still limiting him.

Hell, *everything* was. Manning was even telling people he would need a hip replacement one day, like many other old-timers. The films showed he had been getting less on the ball and was reluctant to throw his usually devastating slant passes—which, if he was even a centimeter off or a mile an hour slow, would be ripe for a pick. He took to throwing higher-percentage sideline passes, which were also risky, tempting a pick-six. Colts players tauntingly spoke of wanting to "put the game in Peyton Manning's hands," and even some in the Denver media were chary about him, having watched him labor through games even as he won them. Wrote Woody Paige, "Which Peyton will perform in the postseason? The Powerfully Persuasive Peyton or the painfully pitiful Peyton?"[15] In Indianapolis, the misty tributes over, they were already looking past Manning to an even better future than he had given them in the past.[16] Irsay, for his part, spoke smugly of "transition[ing] to the next level" and "the destiny of this franchise." The halcyon era having begun with the replacement of Manning with Luck, he added blithely, with all of three years' perspective, "the rest is history."[17]

═══

It seemed easy enough to put that history in its proper place when, on their first possession of the postseason, Peyton took the Broncos 68 yards, hitting Julius Thomas with a 32-yard laser, then finding Demaryius Thomas from the one-yard line for the early lead. But the Colts carried out their game plan well, holding the ground game in check and indeed taking their chances with Manning. They overplayed to the middle, predictably detouring his throws to the sidelines for manageable yardage. The Colts held the ball for nine more minutes, and even though Luck threw two interceptions and Manning none, the breaks went their way. In the second quarter, linebacker Jonathan Newsome sacked Peyton, causing him to fumble. Luck's short scoring pass gave his team the lead, 14–7, and Manning was indeed pitiful. He went 26 of 46, but for a measly 211 yards, converting only 4 of 16 third downs. Luck, marginally better, had 265 yards and two touchdowns. Final score: 24–13.

As darkness fell over the Rockies, the writers had the long knives out. Mark Kiszla, who had lobbied the Broncos to stick with Tim Tebow instead of throwing Manning a life buoy, had seen enough of the old dog. "He's done. Deep in his heart, Peyton Manning must know it. He's done. NFL legends never die, but they often are cruelly required to slowly fade away.... Broncos fans [are] praying for a football miracle Manning can no longer deliver with any reliability. He's done. Oh, Manning can return to the Broncos for the 2015 NFL season and gallantly give winning a championship another shot at age 39. But would it be a fool's errand?"[18] Patrick Saunders's take was: "'Orange Crush?! Really? How about Orange mush?' Those angry, painful words sprang from the lips of [a] longtime Broncos season-ticket holder. [Luck] outplayed the Broncos' Peyton Manning, who looked every bit like a 38-year-old quarterback."[19]

Elway now had a decision to make about 2015, but before that, so did Peyton. Asked repeatedly if he would be back, he didn't bother with a false front. "I guess I can't just give that simple answer," he said. "I'm processing it. So I can't say that. I could not say that."[20]

John Fox would not have a choice. He was fired the next day and replaced by 46-year-old Gary Kubiak, the Ravens' offensive coordinator and former coach of the Texans, who had been Elway's backup quarterback for his entire nine-year playing career. Kubiak was committed to at least one more season of Manning, but the future, he believed, was Osweiler, the team's second-round pick in 2012. A devotee of the West Coast offense, he saw Osweiler, a six-foot-seven, 235-pound telephone pole, as a good fit. Right after the season, Elway told Peyton to take his time deciding whether he would return, but applied the franchise tag to Demaryius Thomas, not Manning, and not Julius Thomas—who, with the Broncos in a budget-cutting mode, skipped out and signed as a free agent with the Jaguars. As a *Denver Post* headline saw it, the team was "Already Moving Past Peyton."

What's more, Peyton himself was again in what-to-do mode. Back in New Orleans, he had deep discussions with his family and his personal trainer, Mackie Shilstone. One factor he had to consider was learning a new offense yet again, since Kubiak was much more of a run-oriented guy. "It was pretty obvious they were going to change systems," Archie said, "and that was going to be a big transition for him."[21] And yet, if anything, seeing Brady take home another title and Super Bowl MVP—thanks to Pete Carroll's ill-fated, goal-line pass call—seemed to presage what was possible for him. Indeed, Brady restored some semblance of sanity to the notion that a new order was here by roughing up the Colts in the conference final, 45–7.

Once Manning indicated he was returning, Elway moved to accommodate him, but with a condition—the same one Peyton had had to accede to in Indianapolis: a pay cut. Condon could have played hardball, since on March 9 the Broncos would be contractually obligated to pay Peyton his full $19 million salary if he passed his physical. But again, Peyton was the good soldier. He agreed to take $15 million, with incentives that, if he won the AFC crown and the Super Bowl, would make back the $19 million.[22] He would still be among the highest-paid quarterbacks, albeit behind the likes of well-paid lemons like Jay Cutler ($15.5 million)—but, astonishingly, still ahead of Brady, who would pull in just $13 million with incentives (but in 2016 would profit from a $28 million signing bonus).

Yet, even as he signed, and passed the physical, Peyton knew the score. He would turn 39 on March 24, and a fifth year at age 40 would be highly problematic. Just how obvious an issue this was for him was exhibited in August when, during court hearings in Tom Brady's Deflategate saga, some of Brady's emails came to light, one of which said, "I've got another 7 or 8 years. [Manning] has 2." Brady immediately apologized to Peyton for it,[23] though in truth, he was a year too generous.

CHAPTER 25

"GONNA DRINK A WHOLE LOTTA BEER"

li, again the forgotten Manning, had suffered through one more arduous season in 2014—though he did find a nuclear weapon, Odell Beckham Jr. The kid from Isidore Newman School had been drafted as a junior out of LSU in the first round, and after battling early hamstring injuries, finished with 91 catches, 13 touchdowns, and a league-high average of 108 yards per game. He made All-Pro and was named Offensive Rookie of the Year. In May 2015, he would beat out Rob Gronkowski for the cover of the *Madden NFL 16* video game. And he actually seemed relatively humble and well adjusted. The rest of the season was a bust, the Giants sinking to 6–10, but Eli had no obligation to cut *his* salary, and at 34 was about to sign his fattest deal.

Negotiations between Tom Condon and Jerry Reese lingered until September 12, one day before the opening game, on Sunday night against the Cowboys in Dallas. It was a four-year, $84 million contract extension, with a no-trade clause and a $31 million signing bonus. The $65 million in guaranteed money equaled that given Philip Rivers as the most ever. Almost all of this was in salary, with only minimal bonuses. In total, he would pocket $68.5 million over the next three seasons, $101.5 million over the next five. At $17.5 million in salary the first year, he could finally leap ahead of Peyton, behind only Rodgers ($22 million), Wilson ($21.9 million), Roethlisberger ($21.8 million), and Brees ($18.8 million). If he made it through five years, he would earn $235 million over his career, to Peyton's $248.7 million. And he would still only be 38.

He began earning this kingly meed with what had become a normal Giants tease, leading to a fall. Tony Romo, himself making $15 million for an ongoing career of big-game failure, completed 36 of 45 for 356 yards and three touchdowns in week one, but his two interceptions and a 57-yard fumble return for a touchdown allowed Eli, despite a humdrum 20 of 36 for 193 yards and no touchdowns, to hold a late 23–20 lead. That was when Eli began to overthink. After killing four minutes with a long drive, he had a first-and-goal at the four. He then revived the strategy from the Super Bowl; trying to take more time off the clock, he called runs for Rashad Jennings on the next two plays, telling him, "Don't score!" Then, on third-and-goal from the one, Dallas having burned their time-outs, he rolled out and, when no one was open, tossed the ball out of bounds—stopping the clock with 1:43 to go rather than, by taking a sack, keeping it running. Losing the chance to put the game on ice, the Giants made the field goal but left Romo too much time, and he moved crisply from his own 28 down the field, finding Jason Witten from 11 yards away for the winning score with 13 seconds left.

Eli took the hit for the snafus, saying it was "100% on me and that can't happen.... It hurts, but it's supposed to hurt."[1] Coughlin tried to mitigate the fallout. "I completely trust Eli, always have," he said. "He's extremely into the game. He's aware of all the circumstances, and as he comes over to the sideline, he relates what he sees and so on and so forth from his position. To be honest with you, nothing like that has ever happened. His mind was in the right place here, he just didn't have the facts right, and unfortunately we didn't get it corrected."[2] The papers wouldn't let him off the hook. One headline was "Comedy of Errors," with Manning called "boneheaded," "clueless," and "absentminded." Wrote Steve Serby in the *New York Post*, "Shockingly, it was the team's rock, Manning, who let it down the most."

<hr />

The Giants sputtered thereafter, their chance to break through ruined by two more almost identical soul-crushers. At 5–4, they met the unbeaten Patriots at MetLife Stadium. Though heavy underdogs, the Manning–Beckham connection was already lethal. Moments after Brady threw a first-quarter touchdown, from his own 13 Eli went bombs away down the right sideline and came away with an 87-yard touchdown. A one-yard TD pass to receiver Dwayne Harris gave New York a 17–10 halftime lead, and after Brady hit Gronkowski with a 76-yard touchdown to go up 24–23 in the fourth quarter, Eli led a 15-play drive that ended in a field goal and produced a 26–24 lead—but again, leaving too much clock, in this case 1:47. Brady squeezed in 12 plays and got his field goal to win 27–26.

Beckham had become more flamboyant in this second year. His hair half-dyed blonde, his post-touchdown gyrations bad Tootsie Rolling, he'd drawn a few fines for taunting. He was still humble enough to take the blame, saying, "I lost the game for us" by not getting himself open enough.[3] But the only memorable things about the season were his increasingly bizarre impulses. His ego fed by tons of puff pieces, he had begun to see confrontations with defensive backs as personal wars, sending him careening out of control. This came to a head when the undefeated Panthers, led by the second-biggest showoff in the game, Cam Newton, came to MetLife on December 20. Both Newton and the Panthers' All-Pro cornerback, Josh Gordon, were prone to preening. For the Giants, who still had a long-shot hope of making the playoffs, the game was not unlike the end-of-season Patriots game in '07, for pride and manhood.

For Beckham, it was almost literally so. The Panthers were said to have latched onto rumors that made their way around the league that he was gay, as if that would matter in any way. Beckham had heard homophobic slurs during games and didn't have the maturity to ignore them. During pregame warm-ups, Michael Irvin would later say on ESPN, several Panther defensive backs, including Josh Norman, assembled close to where Beckham was putting on his usual pregame show—grabbing long passes one-handed, emulating several catches he had made during games that way, video clips of which were all over the internet. Irvin said a Panthers scrub, defensive back Marcus Ball, carried over a baseball bat and pointed it at Beckham, which was construed as some kind of phallic gesture.

When asked about this, Panthers coach Ron Rivera denied his players engaged in any slurs and said the bat was a common pregame prop—one the league prohibited upon hearing about it. Giants punter Brad Wing agreed that he heard no such slurs before or during the game. But he did say that when Beckham tried to shake Ball's hand, the latter refused and issued a "legitimate threat," to wit, "He said he would be the reason Odell would not play, today and other days," an odd thing for a scrub to say.[4]

Whatever set Beckham off, his sights were on Norman, not his pass routes. Early in the game, he was provoked when Norman body-slammed him to the turf, and no flag was thrown. For nearly the first 42 minutes, he went without a catch. Instead, he and Norman yapped at and grappled with each other. Three times Beckham was flagged for personal fouls, Norman twice. Late in the third quarter, the Giants down big, Beckham stalked Norman, then came at him with a helmet-to-helmet collision. Flags flew and whistles blew, each man penalized, Beckham later fined. Players grabbed and held each other.

Yet the aging Coughlin, who seemed not in control of his own team anymore, never did rebuke Beckham or remove him for even a single play. Attesting to his talent, Beckham wound up with six catches in 15 minutes as Eli, being Eli, mounted a furious comeback. As the two-minute mark approached, down by seven, he hit Beckham with a slant that broke for 40 yards, then hit him from 14 yards out to tie it, 35–35. But Newton quickly got the Panthers into Giant territory, and a last-second field goal ended the game. Afterward, a remorseless Beckham admitted no wrongdoing, but all around him, the questions were about his grand display of monomania. Eli, weaseling out, said of Beckham and Norman, "I don't think either one was in the right, but I didn't think one was worse than the other."[5]

Coughlin even insisted he hadn't seen the flagrant foul, and that "I will defend the young man, and the quality of the person."[6]

After the Giants closed out the season again at a listless 6–10, Coughlin was spared further bootlicking. He was canned, his two championships just fading memories. Eli, of course, was as safe as a man could be. He had performed admirably once more, throwing for a career high 4,432 yards, his 35 touchdowns one behind Brady. He had only 14 interceptions, completing 62.6 percent, his 93.6 rating also a career best. He went back to the Pro Bowl for the first time since '12. But he was stuck on a treadmill, sandbagged by the worst defense in the game, and sacked 27 times due to a leaky line. And after finding Beckham 96 times, 13 for touchdowns, he would face the future knowing the rest of his career would be interlocked with a man who was destined either for the Hall of Fame or a straitjacket. Or both.

———

Almost 2,000 miles away, Peyton could feel fortunate that he had a defense that prevented that sort of season. But just as obvious was that Peyton was a shadow of the old Manning—the one from the year before. The opening game, against the Ravens, was a gruesome affair, with both teams combining for fewer than 400 total yards, the two quarterbacks throwing three picks and no touchdowns. Manning passed for 175 yards, Joe Flacco 117. But the Broncos won 19–13, using a simple template: swarming defense and a few key passes.

The Broncos continued not scoring much, and after he threw three touchdowns against the Chiefs and two against the Lions, he tailed off, his yardage down and his interceptions way up—11 in the first seven games, all of which were wins. By then, he had sustained rib and foot injuries. Clearly shying from contact, his timing and footwork were out of sync. In an article in the *Atlantic*, Robert O'Connell believed many of his passes were "torturously slow or misaimed," and that "he curls and tumbles at the approach of a defensive lineman as if to protect a skeleton made of chalk. . . . Each of his drop-backs triggers a hint of fear, from the viewer if not from the player himself. The words spine and neck linger, and nightmare scenes of paralysis flash. His slow and lanky limbs seem ready to fall apart at the slightest knock."[7]

ESPN the Magazine piled on with a piece describing a virtual cadaver: "his pale arms and torso are covered in fresh scrapes and old bruises, some the color of strawberries, others a shade of eggplant . . . the crooked pink scar on the back of his neck is still visible. . . . As he slices away at the thick layers of athletic tape supporting his ankles, he looks like a surgeon operating on his own leg without anesthesia. . . . It's hard not to wonder: How much longer can he possibly keep this up?"[8] This was a question being asked freely in the media before the 10th game, against the Chiefs. In the first quarter, his first pass was intercepted. Next possession, he was sacked and threw two incomplete passes. Next time, he managed one completion—for one yard. Then he completed another, for 17 yards to Demaryius Thomas, breaking Brett Favre's record for career passing yardage, before ending the drive with an interception. He would throw two more picks, the last with 9:41 to go in the third quarter. By then he had managed to complete exactly five of 20 passes, for 35 yards; his passer rating was 0.0. The score was 22–0 Chiefs, and the Mile High crowd was booing. That was enough for Kubiak. He benched Manning and went with Osweiler, who heaved 24 passes, completing 14, with a touchdown that brought the final score to 29–14.

Afterward, Peyton was diagnosed with a tear in his plantar fascia near the left heel. "Those last couple games," Archie confirmed, "he admitted to me that he shouldn't have been playing."[9] Kubiak had to point out that "Peyton is our quarterback." However, people began to wonder if this was the dawning of the new era of Brock Osweiler. One analyst opined, "Whatever Brock Osweiler is, it's got to be better than what we've seen from Manning."[10] Osweiler responded well, leading the Broncos to an overtime victory over the Patriots in his second game and throwing three touchdowns against the Steelers in a close 34–27 defeat. He was executing the West Coast offense well, and could be clutch, winning another overtime game against the Bengals. Whether Kubiak ever considered staying with the hot hand, and in effect, letting Manning rot, it looked like the leading passer in NFL history just might exit on that 0.0 game.

======

Before that question would be resolved, Peyton ran into an added complication. On Saturday, December 26, two days before the Broncos played the Bengals on Monday night, the cable news network Al Jazeera America, a little-watched but highly credible branch of the worldwide Al Jazeera news operation, ran an investigative documentary called *The Dark Side: The Secret World of Sports Doping*. The indeed-noirish "undercover" report traced the secret doings of a source with the too-perfect name Charlie Sly, a shadowy pharmacist whom the network's reporter quoted as having been a party to providing an "HGH derivative" to pro athletes that included Manning, Steelers linebacker James Harrison, Packers defensive lineman Julius Peppers, and baseball players Ryan Howard of the Philadelphia Phillies and Ryan Zimmerman of the Washington Nationals. Manning, Sly said, had been supplied during his time as a Colt through the Guyer Institute of Molecular Medicine, a chic, new-age "anti-aging" clinic in Indianapolis.[11]

Especially coming from a respected news organization that had won numerous awards for its journalism, the accusation was damaging enough; worse was Sly saying the stuff had been mailed to Ashley Manning, and that the couple had visited his clinic after hours for "intravenous treatments."[12] Waking up to this bombshell, all of the players denied being involved with any such thing, with Peyton the most irate. Going into attack mode, he released a statement reading: "For the record, I have never used HGH. It never happened. The whole thing is totally wrong. It's such a fabrication," adding—debatably—"I'm not losing any sleep over it, that's for sure."[13] On Sunday, he told ESPN he was "angry, furious . . . disgusted is really how I feel, sickened by it. . . . [C]omplete trash, garbage. . . . [A] joke, a freaking joke. . . . [T]ime ended up being probably my best medicine, along with a lot of hard work, and that really stings me that whoever this guy is insinuated I cut corners, I broke NFL rules, in order to get healthy."[14]

There were a few things wrong with these heavy-breathing allegations, though they were too complex for many sportswriters to understand. For one thing, the drug in question had little to do with HGH. Rather, it was something called Delta-2, a synthetic steroid precursor, or prohormone, originated for use in breeding elephants, goats, and pigs. As such, it was reminiscent of androstenedione, the prohormone that Mark McGwire had gotten into trouble using during his home run onslaughts of the late 1990s and which was soon banned by sports leagues, as was Delta-2 in 2004. Yet the latter apparently grew so popular in the sports underground that some called it "the new normal" in performance-enhancing drugs, especially since it leaves the bloodstream quickly and makes it harder to detect. But all this was a con, a marketing scheme. In reality, the substance is sold under the counter and on the internet, for as little as $30 a bottle—*The Dark Side* asserted that one former player had bought out all the online supplies by himself.[15] Yet, because it showed no proven effects other than perhaps making men sprout breasts, the former trainer who had admitted supplying baseball players with PEDs during that scandal investigation said Delta-2 was "like offering tea to a man who needs a stiff drink."[16]

In light of Sly misidentifying the drug, Peyton's denial of using HGH was perfectly truthful; as was Guyer's denial he supplied him with it. Manning never would address whether he used prohormones, nor did anyone ask him. Instead, he did admit he had attended the Guyer clinic around 35 times, but only in 2011. He said it was only for its hyperbaric chamber, nutrient therapy, oxygen therapy, "and other treatments that are holistic in nature," which likely caused a few snickers. In response to the stinging assumption that he was using his wife as his beard for those deliveries, he turned it back onto the reporter, British hurdler Liam Collins, as the lowest possible insult. His jaw tight, his mouth sneering, he went on, "My wife has never provided any medication for me to take,"[17] adding that he was "sick" and "nauseous" that she was "being brought into this."[18]

═══

However, what he didn't let on was that this news was not a surprise to him. In fact, he had been working his own "undercover" operation for five days, ever since Al Jazeera fact-checkers had sent word to him and the other athletes, informing them of the allegations. After his lawyers hired private investigators, someone at the Guyer clinic ratted out Sly as the source of the allegations, and two undercover dicks went looking for Sly—wearing black suits and overcoats, their aim apparently to intimidate him into recanting his story. They appeared with no warning at the suburban Indianapolis home of Sly's parents, who later said one of the men told them he was a law enforcement officer, but had no badge. They so unnerved the Slys that they called 911.[19]

The "officers" never did find Sly, but knowing they were after him may have led him to do what Manning wanted, because when the program ran, he already had a statement ready, and a YouTube video recanting. Admitting he wasn't a pharmacist, he nervously said he had "made it up," never saying why, though his lawyer said, "It was pure puffery. He was manufacturing a story to bolster his own appearance." Sly went on to say he had never met the Mannings, never saw any of their files, and then confessed that he "was in no state of mind to be making any coherent statements as I was grieving the death of my fiancée." For what he had wrought, he added, "I feel badly."[20]

Both the Colts and Broncos issued their own statements supporting Manning, as did Tom Condon. But the frontal assault on the story and the network—which, predictably, was the target of virulent Islamophobic invective—put Al Jazeera immediately on its heels. Needing to defend its own honor, it also had to defend a scoop that fell apart from the first day, walking the fine line that the report had never actually said Manning had *used* the drug. And within a few days, Peyton's freshly hired "crisis management" spokesman, former George W. Bush press secretary Ari Fleischer, quietly acknowledged that Ashley had indeed received "shipments" from the clinic in the mail, citing her right to privacy in not specifying exactly what was shipped, legal or otherwise.

Peyton's word, of course, was good enough for Archie, who called the story "pretty shabby journalism." He said his son told him, "I didn't do that." He went on, "I always had a saying when he was going through everything and he had to talk to a lot of different doctors and trainers, and I always said, 'No voodoo.' That was kind of our theme. And he didn't. He said he didn't. He didn't." Because Ashley had been dragged into it, Peyton believed that she had been "violated,"[21] something he or Archie had shown little concern about doing to Jamie Naughright.

Unlike the mooning story, this one took hold, at least for a few days, though the most telling part of it was that, despite some other big names accused, it seemed to only descend upon the one who did all the commercials. The documentary aired to a fair amount of gawking, but there were diminishing returns. Manning spoke of possibly filing a lawsuit against the network and Sly. (Howard and Zimmerman did file one.) He had no reason to worry about a fan or media backlash. Not everyone bought his denial, but even those who didn't seemed to subscribe to the "everybody does it" school of thought. This was a rather amazing contrast to the Brady Deflategate story, with one internet scribe concluding that the differing response "exposes the Brady haters" as blatant hypocrites, and that it was proof the public was "bored by [the subject of PEDs] and rightly so. I can think of no mystery less interesting than whether an aging athlete with a broken neck used a substance that might not even work to return to a playing field where cortisone injections are given out like chewable Vitamin C tabs. The PEDs debate is over,"[22] never mind that players in all sports are routinely suspended for such infractions.

The NFL and Major League Baseball, at least acting as if it were a grave matter, launched investigations; seven months later, the former concluded that there was "no credible evidence" Manning had used HGH or any other PED,[23] the other players shoved aside for later clearances. Since he was retired by then, this too set off a few cackles; after all, what would Roger Goodell have done if the allegations were true—suspend him for four commercials?

Al Jazeera America, meanwhile, didn't retract the story but stopped defending it. And, perhaps anticipating more lawsuits and with growing internal trouble, it closed up shop in April 2016 after three years on the air. As with the Jamie Naughright scandal, the "HGH" allegation would not completely go away, and the *Manning* haters would have fun with it. But within the media, and the parochial relationships of the NFL, it was just another minor distraction that legendary men like Peyton Manning ought never to have to endure.

―――――

Asked on that first day of the scandal that wasn't what the effect of the story would be, Peyton had said, "I plan to go throw today a little bit harder. My ball has a little extra heat on it today. I've got some built up anger, as you might understand, and I'll try to do what I can to help the Broncos get a win tomorrow night." But while he didn't get into the win over the Bengals, he was more prophetic than he knew.

A week later, going into the regular-season finale against the woeful Chargers, the Broncos were 11–4 and needed a win for the top seed in the AFC playoffs.

In that game, Osweiler started hot, throwing a 72-yard touchdown to Demaryius Thomas. But then the Broncos began bumbling, with three fumbles and two interceptions on their next seven drives. An appreciative Chargers squad led 13–7 with eight minutes left in the third quarter. Kubiak now made a providential move. He sat Osweiler and put his dinosaur in. Peyton's foot and thigh had healed, and he had worked hard in practice to stay ready. And as he said, his arm was angry. On his first drive, he hit on three straight passes to move into Charger territory, and Anderson ran it in from the one to get the lead. Philip Rivers took it back with an 80-yard touchdown pass, Manning maneuvered into position for the tying field goal, then the Chargers fumbled one away and Hillman ran in the game winner. It wasn't that Manning looked so great; rather, he looked in charge, his acumen uncontested. At this point, that was enough. The defense would do the rest.

For better or worse, he would be under center for the postseason, on a team not geared around him. Chris Harris, for example, had no problem describing the Hall of Fame quarterback's role as no more than a "game manager." As Greg Bishop wrote in *Sports Illustrated*, "He didn't need to win games so much as he needed not to lose them."[24] That seemed to suit Manning fine. The Broncos placed not a single offensive player on the first- or second-team All-Pro team, for Manning the first time that had happened, other than the season he missed, since 2001. His numbers were painful: 2,249 yards, nine touchdowns, 17 interceptions, 67.9 rating. Osweiler in two fewer games had 10 touchdowns and six interceptions. Yet Manning's record was 7–2, such was the defense. And the offense did ring up decent running yardage (burnished by 210 yards on the ground in that Charger game), Hillman with 863 yards, Anderson 720. Demaryius Thomas pulled in 105 passes and six touchdowns.

But the defense was bred like hounds from hell to strike first and worry later, coordinated by 68-year-old Wade Phillips, who had twice coached the Broncos. He not only bridged the years between Archie and his son, having been an assistant on Archie's last Saints team, but had been the defensive coordinator of the teams against whom Peyton had twice set the single-season touchdown record. Under him, the Bronco defense would reach its peak. Von Miller was first-team All-Pro, Talib, Ware, and Harris were on the second team. Still, no one knew quite what to make of the Broncos. They had won seven games with fourth-quarter drives, and were 11–3 in games decided by a touchdown or less, and no other championship team had walked the line of defeat so often. Manning was a sentimental favorite, and so the Broncos were seven-point favorites in their first game against the Steelers, who had beaten the Bengals in a street fight of a wild-card game the week before.

The game in Denver was brass-knuckled from the start. The Steelers lost All-Pro receiver Antonio Brown with a concussion and halfback DeAngelo Williams with a foot injury, but they still led 13–12 entering the fourth quarter. The home crowd had been booing when Manning, with just under 10 minutes left, started on his own 35. On third-and-12, he drilled one deep down the middle to rookie receiver Bennie Fowler for 31 yards. Burning up the clock with runs, with 3:04 left Anderson punched it in and Manning tossed the two-point conversion to Demaryius Thomas. After Ware sacked Ben Roethlisberger on fourth down, a field goal made it 23–13, enough for Denver to withstand a late scare and win 23–16.

It wasn't pretty, but it was gritty. On one memorable play, Peyton fell to his knees, then got up and fired a 34-yard pass to Sanders. Knowing that the Patriots would be next—the ultimate battle royal for the AFC crown—didn't help. Already, Peyton was feeling pressure. As Greg Bishop wrote in *Sports Illustrated*, "When Manning strode into the interview room that narrative had already been established. He felt no need to contribute to it. He answered two questions about Brady and the Patriots without saying the words Brady or Patriots. He wanted to enjoy this win first."[25] When he was given the game ball, having completed 21 of 37 for 222 yards and sacked only once, he in turn gave it to Thomas, whose mother had just been released from prison as a result of a pardon by President Obama.

Said Archie of the victory, "Peyton hasn't enjoyed the year he's had in other seasons. But if he had one contribution to getting [Denver] to the Super Bowl, it was what he did that day."[26]

―――――

The AFC title match was being called "The Last Tango" on the assumption that this, their 17th meeting, would be the last time Manning and Brady squared off. That week, reporters quoted players who had played with both. Adam Vinatieri equated Brady to "a kid on the playground, just does his thing," as opposed to Manning, "who's meticulous, almost OCD; I've never seen a guy prepare, study that hard. S——, he might as well be the coordinator, the GM and the coach. He may be the smartest player I've ever seen." However, *Sports Illustrated*'s Jack Dickey ventured that "few seemed to consider his Broncos anything other than the worst team remaining in the playoffs."[27]

If so, then all he had to do to was slay the best one. Belichick's bunch was the usual steamroller, third in scoring, while allowing the 10th-fewest points. Not so hot in rushing, but Brady's passing was unstoppable. At 38, with no signs of aging save for perennially tortoise-slow feet, he had thrown for 4,770 yards, the second most of his career, with a league-best 36 touchdowns, and a microscopic seven interceptions. His rating was 102.2, and he was coming off a two-touchdown, 302-yard playoff win over the Chiefs. His über-weapon, the semi-insane Rob Gronkowski, was the first-team All-Pro tight end for a third time, and managed to stay healthy.

The Broncos needed no motivation. Like practically everyone else outside of New England, defensive end Derek Wolfe said, "I hate everything about them."

The game, played on a cool, 46-degree afternoon at Mile High, was a brutal back-alley street fight, players bitching and moaning to the officials about non-calls. The Pats, favored by three points, didn't fool around trying to establish the run; Brady went right to the pass and stayed with it, throwing 56 times. However, while gaining 307 yards, he would complete only 27 of them and was picked off twice. The Broncos had him under thunderous assault. They would sack him four times—two and a half by Von Miller, who seemed shot out of a canon and also intercepted a pass intended for Gronkowski—and make contact with him 23 times, the most by any team in a game all season. Wolfe, playing his best game of the year, had a game-high six tackles.

Even so, this was not enough to slay Brady. Manning threw two touchdowns in the first half to spare receiver Owen Daniels, one up the middle, the other in the corner of the end zone. But he also fumbled deep in his own territory, and the ensuing Pats touchdown kept them close, down 17–9 at the half. Archie, who said he'd made a new year's resolution to stop biting his nails, wore thick gloves, and he'd need them. The Broncos led 17–12 going to the fourth quarter, and Manning, taking no chances, took what he was given. His stats were mediocre—he completed 17 of 32 for 176 yards, and was sacked three times. He overthrew an open receiver in the end zone. He threw an unwise lateral that fell short and was recovered by the Pats. But he also scrambled once for 12 yards and a first down, looking, wrote *Sports Illustrated*, like "a giraffe on ice skates."[28] The Pats helped him, too; Gostkowski missed an extra point, something he had not done in a decade, and in the fourth quarter Belichick opted to pass up a field goal to go for it on fourth down. A screen pass to Julian Edelman was snuffed by Chris Harris, despite playing with a bad shoulder.

But with the sputtering Bronco offense unable to kill the clock, with 1:52 left, trailing 20–12, Brady had a last gasp. He drove down the field, hitting Gronkowski for 40 yards on a fourth-and-10. After taking it to the doorstep, on another fourth-and-goal, he found him again in the back of the end zone with a four-yard touchdown, 12 seconds on the clock. Now, needing the two-point conversion to tie and go to overtime, Brady rolled right and lofted it for Edelman at the goal line, where it was tipped by the ex-Pat Talib and grabbed by extra cornerback Bradley Roby. The onside kick failed, and Manning had a storybook ending to his rivalry with Brady.

The huzzahs, however, were rightly for the defense—"La-D-Friggin'-Da," *Sports Illustrated* titled its game story. Miller, regaled for having played one of the greatest games ever by a defensive player, said he wasn't surprised by how the game went, and indeed it was a microcosm of the season. As for Manning, watching him over these last miles, Brett Favre said he looked "sort of un-Peyton like." In the locker room, the fizzy celebrations seemed built not around the old boy but the younger, louder players, especially the defensive guys, who were the first to claim their preeminent roles. Nearing his end of the line, deep circles under his eyes, he made his way to the interview room, Marshall peeking his head out from behind him. Almost embarrassed at what he couldn't do, he said, believably, that this one was "special," "a sweet day," and "a sweet victory" that would usher him out with a Super Bowl. That he wasn't the critical factor in the win, he said, was "a great example of what this entire season has been like."

The last one to leave the locker room, before heading out, he slowly walked back onto the chewed-up field in the basin of the now-deserted, garbage-strewn stadium. The big screen still read, "NEXT GAME: SUPER BOWL 50." For a few minutes, he stood there, looking around. Then he headed off, a pale shadow of himself, but one with perhaps an ounce of almost palpable magic still left in him.

═══

The climactic encounter of the season was the exact opposite of the Last Tango. Super Bowl 50, as the league billed it—sans Roman numerals—played on February 7 in Santa Clara's Levi's Stadium, would match the quarterback on the way out with the one on the way up. Cam Newton had run and passed the Panthers to its near-perfect record and the MVP trophy, and so the themes of the match wrote themselves: New versus old, brash versus stoic, black versus white, mustang versus army mule, dab versus drab. Peyton Manning, the oldest quarterback to start a Super Bowl, found himself not a Bolshevik but a Borgia, though one clad in an outdated preppy suit costing a fraction of Newton's $900 zebra-print Versace jeans. The backstory was that Newton, the Heisman winner and the first pick of the '11 draft, had in his first NFL game thrown for 422 yards, smashing Peyton's first-game record by 120 yards. He had by now already been named All-Pro thrice, this year as the first-team choice, passing for 3,837 yards and 35 touchdowns and running for 636 yards and 10 touchdowns. No other quarterback came near his buffet of talent, and the bettors made his team a quick six-point favorite.

On closer inspection, however, the Panthers were right in the wheel-house of the Broncos' mobile, wily defense. The Panthers had amassed the most points in the league, but the Broncos zeroed in on what made it all work: Newton's arm and legs, but just as much his head. He had fine pieces around him, like All-Pro halfback Jonathan Stewart, tight end Greg Olsen, as well as Josh Norman at corner, linebackers Luke Kuechly and Thomas Davis, and defensive tackle Kawann Short. Another, full-back Mike Tolbert, defined the team's creed. "If you don't want us to have fun," he said during the week, "stop us."[29] Taking that dare, the Broncos' plan was to swarm Newton, angling him off outside so he couldn't get wide, while pouring through the middle; when the Panthers had to dou-ble up on blocks, alleys would open up for the blitzers, mainly Miller. That, in turn, would require a receiver or back to stay in and block, leav-ing a path for a safety corner to blitz—Wade Phillips's "green dog" blitz package. Newton ran a flowing offense, with complex zone-reading option plays. Disrupt it, the thinking went, and chaos would ensue. New-ton had little playoff experience and, high-strung as he was, he might even melt down.

Manning's job would be to take good field position, get a lead, and play ball control. But, true to form, he was pulling rank during the team's preparations. After they arrived in Santa Clara, he tried to have Kubiak set a curfew. Said Peyton, "I threw out 9 (p.m.) and that didn't get a lot of (positive) reviews."[30] But while the curfew was set at 10, most things ran on Peyton Time. Save for Newton, he was the most interviewed player during the media crush, sitting down with everyone from the network guys to Snoop Dogg, who asked him if he got a discount at Papa John's pizzerias. "Absolutely," he said. And he was the same old ornery Manning when he swatted down Mark Kiszla for bringing up Super Bowl XLVIII.

"I was having such a good day," he hissed. "Thanks for bringing up a bad memory."[31]

The night before the game, he and DeMarcus Ware got up to address the team, both with such fire that Miller said later he wanted to "run onto the field and hit someone right there."[32] During warm-ups, when a wheeled stage to be used by Lady Gaga in a pregame concert was rolled across the field, it nearly struck Manning. A roadie yelled through a bullhorn to get out of the way; Peyton shouted back, nearly getting into a fight with the guy. As for whether it would be his last game, he said he wouldn't talk about it until it was over, but the die was cast. Linebacker Brandon Marshall predicted as much, adding, "I want to win for Peyton."

The whole Manning clan rolled into town, the last big-game reunion they might ever have, and Olivia made no bones about hoping her little "Peytie Pie" would walk away from the game thereafter. In fact, the night before the Patriot game, *SI* reported, "Archie and Olivia took a moment. Their eyes welled with tears as they acknowledged what Peyton refused to say publicly, even on Sunday night: that the game could be his last. Archie hugged his wife and said, 'Hey, this really has been fun with this guy. Let's see what happens.' "[33]

What happened was that, when the whistle blew in Santa Clara, Manning played as if already retired. The first drive of the game, the Broncos kicked a field goal. Then, over seven drives, the offense had four first downs and gained 38 yards; three drives actually lost yardage. Manning, aided by Hillman's 34-yard run, had the ball on the Panther 24, looked for Sanders short, but defensive tackle Kony Ealy dropped back into coverage and picked it off—Manning's fourth career Super Bowl pick, tying Elway's dubious record. And still, at the half they *led* 13–7, the defense saving his fairy tale. Miller had sacked and stripped Newton, sending the ball squirting into the end zone, where tackle Malik Jackson covered it for a 10–0 lead. Tackle Darian Stewart then separated Tolbert from the ball, and linebacker Danny Trevathan fell on it. In the third quarter, with the ball on the Denver 28, Newton rushed a throw for Ted Ginn that was picked off by T. J. Ward.

Manning, meanwhile, was working on a string of misery, converting exactly one of 14 third-down situations and being sacked five times. The fact was, the best ex-Vol on the field this day was the kicker, Britton Colquitt. Yet Newton was just as inept, and the Broncos had padded the lead to 16–7 by the fourth quarter. Peyton gave the Panthers an opening when, sacked by Ealy, he fumbled. The Panthers got a field goal out of it, but, minutes later, Miller again swooped into the backfield, reached in, and hit Newton's arm as he threw. The ball came loose and rolled around near Newton's shoes. He seemed to be deciding whether or not to fall on it when a pile swarmed, with Ward finally grabbing it at the four. A minute later, after a defensive holding call on Norman in the end zone, Anderson ran it over to ice the game.

Then came the last pass Peyton Manning ever completed: for two yards, to Bennie Fowler, making the two-point conversion that made the final score 24–10. In the end, he was 13 of 23 for 141 yards, with no touchdowns. His passer rating for the game was a sickly 56.6—but even that was better than Newton, who went 18 of 41 for 265 yards, had two fumbles, was sacked a Super Bowl record seven times, and had a rating of 55.4, third-worst of all time in the big game. Messing with Newton's head had all but demobilized the Panther offense. In the Broncos' historically dominant defensive performance, Miller had two and a half sacks, propelling him to the game's MVP and appearances in postseason TV commercials, but Ealy tied a Super Bowl record with three. Even two dumb penalties by a near-out-of-control Talib, for taunting and grabbing an opponent's face mask, didn't hurt.

As it had been all along, the fairy tale was the story. Elway had gotten a lot of mileage out of what he said he had told Manning when he signed with the Broncos, that he would do "everything in my power to make sure you finish your career the way I finished mine," and though Peyton limped across the finish line, Elway had delivered. Manning was one of a dozen quarterbacks to win two rings, the same number Eli has. And of course, he was now the only quarterback to win with two teams. All in all, not a bad day's work. In the afterglow, the cameras zoomed in on Peyton as he met with Newton, who wept on the bench and whose anger and shame would come spurting out minutes later in the interview room, ruining his manufactured sunny image. As the bedlam of the celebration proceeded on the field, Peyton held both Marshall and Mosley, who clung to him around his neck. He lifted the Lombardi Trophy above his head and waved around a cap reading "Super Bowl Champions." There was some sheepishness in his postgame comments, but the overwhelming emotion was simple relief, rivaling that of the anxiety-ridden Archie, who had been as reluctant as the pickle-pussed Eli to celebrate upstairs until the last second ticked away, as if something truly terrible could still take it away.

Peyton wasn't so emotional that he forgot a few duties he had agreed to perform for corporate benefactors. When CBS's Tracy Wolfson corralled him and asked, "Is this your final game for your career?" he gushed, without shame, "I'm going to drink a lot of Budweiser tonight, Tracy, I promise you that," mentioning the brand of suds again for good measure. When he saw John Schnatter, the equally shameless owner of Papa John's, in the mob on the field—Peyton having arranged for his VIP field pass—he went over and planted a highly visible kiss on his cheek. *Now* his day was complete.

In the interview room, trying to ignore the stinging irony that his biggest win came with one of the worst games he had ever played, he acknowledged, "This has been an emotional week, an emotional night, and I've got a couple of priorities. I want to go kiss my wife, kiss my kids, and I want to go drink a lot of beer. Von Miller's buying." Like an Oscar winner, he went through a litany of acknowledgments, thanking "coaches, family members, and friends" for standing by him, making him believe he could get here again. "I do not take this for granted," he allowed. "I know how difficult it is. I'm very grateful and I'm very appreciative."[34]

After putting his preppy blue blazer and orange tie back on, he met up with Archie in the hall outside. He and the old man embraced, grabbing each other tight for a moment—a moment 40 years in the making—before they broke and the son gave the father a quick pat on the back. It was all that was needed to express from deep within thoughts rarely spoken by either man, both of them bred in the old South, where real men weren't permitted to get mushy or reveal weakness. The kind of gesture Archie had never shared with Buddy Manning. But for father and son, no matter the twisting, jarring culture collisions of the past four decades, the glue that had kept them bonded was the unstated truth that they were still what they were born as: kinsmen.

<hr>

The CEO of Manning Inc. went into the night a winner, with a joyous requiem shared by everyone except the Peyton-haters across the social media. One Patriots website cheeked, "Congrats to P.M. on his 2nd Super

Bowl victory, and officially becoming half as good as Tom Brady."[35] Another: "I don't have to pretend that it's heartwarming to see Manning and his size-12-head limp his way to the title, after a long career of wiping his ass on trainers' faces and [having] HGH delivered to his doorstep. And I won't have to watch him ruin what ought to be a touching and genuine sports moment with subliminal mentions of shitty beer and even shittier pizza."[36]

Indeed, the mooning incident still had legs. A women's group called for Manning's corporate sponsors to ax him from the commercials.[37] At the same time, six more former Tennessee coeds sued the school for mishandling recent complaints of sexual assaults—and dropped in his name for historical context, which university lawyers moved to strike in order to "protect his name."[38]

Down in New Orleans, however, none of this mattered. Tony Reginelli, who had watched the game from his hospital bed after back surgery, couldn't believe it when he got home a few days later and there was a box on the doorstep. "My son brought it in, we opened it up, and there was a gorgeous hanger that looked like it must've cost around forty dollars itself. Then he pulled out an NFL carrying case, unzipped it and there was this beautiful Broncos jacket with 'world champions' on it. I said, 'C'mon, man,' couldn't believe it. With all that was goin' on out there, he found time to send this beautiful jacket to me. Well, that's Peyton. He remembers. He remembers people who were there along the way. It made me feel so great that he would think of me. And I haven't put it on. It hangs in a special place."[39]

═══

The only thing left now was his retirement announcement. Keeping mum about the subject during the victory parade through downtown Denver on Tuesday, he left it dangling. His natural penchant for teasing the media reflected the feelings he had always had when the bumps and bruises from the season began to heal and he got that old itch in his arm. Elway once again told him to take his time. But unlike the last time he dispensed that advice, Elway had no intention of signing him. His hope was now pinned on Osweiler, whose contract had run out but was assumed to be eager to re-sign so he could take the reins of the offense. But the delay led some to think Manning just might come back again for a farewell lap. And he did give it some thought, though he knew Elway and Bowlen wanted him to quit—and do it before March 9, when, if he passed a physical, the Broncos would owe him another $19 million. He could have made things sticky for them, and himself, since Elway would have pulled an Irsay and coldly cut him a day before the deadline. And finding yet another team to rent him for a year would be . . . a challenge.

He made it easy on everyone. On Saturday, March 6, after Peyton had spoken with Elway and Kubiak, Broncos president Joe Ellis released a statement making it official, saying how proud the team was "to have called Peyton Manning our quarterback." Only hours later, they made Osweiler a big-time offer of $13 million a year for three seasons. When Manning called Irsay, the owner who had jilted him felt him out about signing a one-day contract so he could retire as a Colt. But the next morning, he was in Denver, standing in his blue suit and tie, giving his final valedictory address. He took a few questions from the press—one about the new court motions in the Tennessee sexual abuse scandals. Then, with executives and a collection of former teammates that included Jeff Saturday in the front rows, he began a prepared, 15-minute speech.

His words were sprinkled with humor—he tweaked Von Miller for taking time from *Dancing with the Stars* to be there—and he choked up as he went along. He recalled shaking Johnny Unitas's hand once. "He told me, 'Peyton, you stay at it. I'm pulling for you.' Well, I have stayed at it. I've stayed at it for 18 years. . . . I have fought the good fight and I have finished the race. I have kept the faith." Among the things he said he would miss were the handshakes with Brady, "steak dinner at St. Elmo's after a win . . . Demaryius Thomas telling me that he loved me and thanking me for coming to Denver after every touchdown I threw to him . . . recapping the game with my dad. And checking to see if the Giants won and calling Eli as we're both on our team buses." He spoke of facing "a whole new world of possibilities," but "you don't have to wonder if I'll miss it. Absolutely. Absolutely I will."[40] Just before he stepped off the stage, he uttered, "Omaha." Then he left. All he would say about his future was that he would "consider all possibilities."

Cooper could sense his brother's unease. "You know, it's such a weird thing," he said. "Think about being 40 and saying, 'Now I need to go find out what I'm going to be when I grow up.' It's a great position to be in, but it's also kind of peculiar because you don't really know what to do." One of his old teammates, Marshall Faulk, ventured, "I think there is a small chance he'll coach, there is a great chance he'll run a team, and there is a very high chance him and his family will own a team."[41]

The most logical route was to the broadcast booth. Offers started coming in right after the Super Bowl, but he demurred; it was just too easy. If the past quarter century had proved anything, it was that he needed not a cushion but a chance to rewrite some history.

A few weeks later, he went to Indianapolis for a second retirement speech. In early June, the Broncos were feted at the White House by the lame-duck President Obama, the old Bush ally as gracious as any Southern white boy could be to a Democrat commander-in-chief. A week later, the players got their rings. By then, the Broncos were already feeling the pinch of Manning's retirement. Osweiler stunned them by walking, signing a ridiculous four-year, $72 million contract with the Texans, who would deeply regret it almost immediately. That forced Elway to draft a quarterback in the first round: Memphis's Paxton Lynch. With the offense in the hands of former seventh-round draft pick Trevor Siemian in the meantime, the defense couldn't get the team to the playoffs in 2016. This sent Elway on a new mission of salvation: trying in vain to sweet-talk another old warhorse, Tony Romo, who had been released by the Cowboys. Such desperation was the toll Elway was paying for banking everything on winning right away at the expense of the long term, the quotidian decisions of which rubbed the glow off the Lombardi Trophy for almost everyone except Peyton Manning. His race was done, and won.

CHAPTER 26

LAST MANNING STANDING

Eli Manning, of course, spent the 2016 season gathering up his skills and sanity for the Giants' rise from the dead. Most expected them to be a mess, and in many ways they were. The hirsute Ben McAdoo, promoted from his old job as Tom Coughlin's offensive coordinator, had exactly two good things going for him on that side of the ball: Eli and his chancy receiver branded as "OBJ," and the latter could go very bad very quickly. The surprise was that there was an astounding turnabout from the year before. This year, the offense was often stodgy, finishing 25th, the rushing game a total joke—compiling a total of six ground touchdowns, by far the worst in the NFL. Yet defensive coordinator Steve Spagnuolo suddenly had a monster defense, giving up the second-fewest points in the league, distressing quarterbacks with 35 sacks and 17 interceptions.

However, it still seemed up to Eli to close the deal. That he had to do it living off Odell Beckham Jr. ensured a long road of peaks and nadirs, not to mention psychotic scenes. Worse, in midseason, kicker Josh Brown—who had been re-signed even after his wife filed domestic abuse charges against him eight times—was cut in late October after journal entries and emails came to light in which he admitted to the crimes, for which he was never prosecuted.[1] Along the way, Beckham, who had not moderated his behavior at all, was alternately the hero and the clown. He became the fastest to ever get to 200 career catches and 4,000 yards, but he seemed to carve out new ground in lunacy during an early game against the Redskins when, despite seven catches and 121 yards, he stomped up and down the sideline, making bizarre gestures and facial expressions. And then, in the ultimate *schlimazel* moment, after Eli threw a fourth-quarter interception, Beckham, helmet in his hand, crashed it into the kicking net, which collapsed on top of his chia-topped head. As if he were toe-to-toe with a human enemy, he furiously pushed it away and glared at the wrecked net. He then began to weep uncontrollably.

Eli, seeing this man come unwrapped, came over and stood with him, trying somehow to ease his demons, but said nothing critical afterward. Two weeks later, the Giants, at 2–3 and with the season perhaps on the line, played the Ravens. After Beckham caught a 75-yard touchdown, he ran over to the kicking net and seemed to kiss it, then did a hip-grinding pantomime of a man having sex with an inanimate object, before dropping to his knees and miming a man proposing to the net. Some thought it funny, others disturbing, but most were simply tired of his antics. Then, with the Giants trailing 23–20, 1:43 left, on a fourth-and-one, he ran a short slant, caught the ball, and blew by everyone for a 66-yard touchdown. Stripping off his helmet, he strutted around like a bantam cock for a good minute, incurring a penalty.

Winning because of Beckham—who had eight catches for 222 yards—yet *despite* Beckham seemed to be too much for Eli, though typically, his rebuke was weak tea. The next night, he went on a local radio show and, rolling out each word warily, said, semi-coherently, "It's one of those deals where you can get real sick of it if you're not going out there and making plays." While it was nothing close to what one headline labeled a "blast" leveled at Beckham, for Eli, it was. However, Beckham took it as a practical endorsement, as long as he made those catches.[2]

That win probably saved the season. It got them to .500, and Eli's 397 passing yards righted him after a rocky start. He moved past Elway for seventh on the all-time touchdown list, becoming only the eighth quarterback over 300, not that he was so impressed with himself. "After I'm done playing, I'll look back and see where I stand, maybe or maybe not, I don't know," he said in Eli-ese.[3] It also began a six-game winning streak of mainly close games pulled out by Eli, though only four times in that span did he go over 200 yards. While the Cowboys ended up 13–3, the Giants swept their two meetings. Always finding a way, a severely limited team went 11–5 and earned a wild-card spot. The slickest trick was that Eli rang up over 4,000 yards passing, with 26 touchdowns and a modest 16 interceptions, his rating a quite competent 86. But he could not escape blame for imperfection. Read one press dispatch, "Manning has three years left on his current contract with the New York Giants, it's time to start thinking about life without him."[4]

Of course, he was nowhere near ready to think about that, even if his team was aging him beyond his 36 years. When, six days before the Giants' playoff game in Green Bay, Beckham and most of the other receivers jetted off to Miami for a day of partying on a yacht, sparking a kerfuffle in the media, Eli was asked to comment and attempted to calm the storm.

"I think as a team we always pride ourselves on being well prepared," he began, "so when I saw some of the pictures, I was a little disappointed."

Reporters in the room gathered, hushed, already scribbling their "Manning Bashes Beckham" headlines. And then he delivered a quick scoring pass: "Obviously, they didn't pack accordingly. They didn't have any shirts, all long pants, no shorts, no flip-flops. Disappointed on their packing and not being prepared for that situation." He also said he was glad he wasn't in the group because he would have had to "take off my shirt," which is nobody's idea of pretty.

That soothing syrup quieted the situation. In Lambeau Field, scene of two of his greatest games, he did his part, getting the jump on Aaron Rodgers by moving the team to two early field goals while the Pack were seemingly frozen on their famous tundra. But then passes began bouncing off receivers' hands, most grievously Beckham and rookie Sterling Shepard, robbing Eli of two touchdowns.

Neither could the defense stem Rodgers, who threw a Hail Mary touchdown just before halftime—something Eli had done the last time they met in the playoffs. In the end, the Giants were humbled 38–13, sending Beckham banging his head against a locker room door, then punching the wall. Beckham had only one explanation for his dropped balls.

"It was freezing," he said.

Eli, meanwhile, sat at his locker, engaged in another exercise in sportsmanlike defeat. He had gone 23 of 44 for 299 yards and a touchdown. "You got to keep working," he said, "and hopefully, you get more opportunities." Then, unprompted, came a somewhat odd vow, as if he had been debating with himself whether he should consider retiring—"I plan on being back next year."[5]

The shadow of his big brother still seemed to loom over him. Days before, Peyton had been elected to the College Football Hall of Fame, the prelude to his sure induction into the Pro Football Hall of Fame in 2020. For Eli, a third title would likely be *his* ticket to the Hall. But if he gets it, it will probably not be because of personal hubris. Indeed, a piece in *Psychology Today* a few years ago, titled "The Psychology of Archie Manning and Sons," posited that Eli's "nonchalance at times permits him to perform beyond expectations under the greatest pressure."[6] True enough. However, when you're the last of a dynasty, self-sworn to upholding family tradition, it can feel like a cross to bear. As he strode off the field, ice frozen on his helmet, head hung, staring at his dirty cleats, one could almost read his mind. There were many factors involved in the team losing. But only he had let his family down.

<hr />

He had only more reason to bear such private shame in 2017. This edition of the Giants would place a greater burden on him than most expected. Forecast by many to win the NFL East, their unresolved problems—the offensive line and the running game—put them in a hole from the start. Nothing Eli could do kept them from losing their first five, extending to eight their streak of games lost when scoring under 20 points. And Ben McAdoo was playing the blame game with his quarterback. Beckham was lost for the season with a fractured ankle. When Eli's brain freeze on a goal-line play resulted in a costly delay-of-game penalty in a loss to the Lions in week two, the coach didn't hesitate to blame "sloppy quarterback play" for the team's doldrums, rather than, say, sloppy coaching or sloppy general managing by Jerry Reese. A *New York Post* headline had it that Eli had been "thrown under the bus,"[7] while at the same time regurgitating old what-ifs about whether he was through. Eli readily admitted that he "deserved the criticism," though he laughed off a question again being asked on a heavy-breathing ESPN program, "Is Eli done?"

"Everybody had gotten very sensitive," he noticed, not needing to add "*again*." From his perspective, "You play 14 years in New York, you've been criticized. You can take pretty much whatever they throw at you."[8]

All he could do was to keep marching in step with the guiding principle of Manning Inc., which is that work, faith, and family will ultimately be rewarded, at least until time starts marching ahead of you and your team is dead last in offense and defense. Indeed, the only Giant win after nine weeks, 23-10 over Peyton's old Broncos, came despite him not doing all that much, going 11 of 19 for 128 yards and one touchdown—though the most impressive number that day was zero picks. Perhaps sensing he could win a power struggle with his own quarterback and survive the season with the éclat to trade Eli, a seemingly deranged McAdoo ignored his biggest problems—the execrable offensive line and running game— to say Manning was "underperforming" and that no one was untouchable on the Giants—"not even the quarterback."

All this static was before the beyond-bizarre move by McAdoo to yank Eli from the starting lineup for the December 3 game against the Raiders in Oakland. That idea apparently had not been McAdoo's originally but rather, according to reports, brought to him by Jerry Reese, with the implicit approval of co-owner John Mara, though he said he assumed Manning would start the game and be removed for the second half. With the Giants 2–9, it wasn't necessarily illogical. As Mara said, the team's performance "speaks for itself." What's more, some observers pointed out that Eli's quarterback rating was the lowest in the NFL over the past four seasons, and was clearly on the way down. However, McAdoo didn't name as the starter the team's rookie third-round pick, Davis Webb, but a quarterback some did not even realize was still in the league: Geno Smith, who had failed spectacularly with the Jets and was primarily remembered for having his jaw broken by one of his own teammates in an argument about money.

The optics of the change sent New York into a frenzy. The longtime WFAN host Mike Francesa branded McAdoo and Reese as "gutless," and said that the coach should look at Manning's championship rings because "that's as close as you're ever gonna get to one." Eli, maintaining his even-tempered air of nobility, said, "I don't like it, but you handle it." But Archie wouldn't play along. Eli, he said, "isn't bitter, but he is hurt." Smith did little to make his case, losing to the Raiders 20–10, whereupon, with a number of former Giants threatening to show up and stand on the sideline showing solidarity with Eli by wearing his jersey, the experiment ended with Eli being reinstated as the starter, preceding by a few days the merciful firing of McAdoo and Reese and the promotion of Steve Spagnuolo as interim head coach.

Showing he still had it, Eli threw for over 400 yards and three touchdowns against the Eagles, though the close 34–29 loss cemented a fourth-place finish in the division, their worst since 2003. Only an 18–10 win in the finale in Washington, despite Eli relapsing with a 10-of-28, 132-yard wreck of a game, spared them their worst record in team history. In the end, it was best to simply try to forget the season and its frightfully bad numbers—19th in passing yards, 26th in rushing, 23rd in touchdowns. Worse, on defense they were 31st against the pass, 27th against the run. Eli still managed to throw for 3,468 yards, 19 touchdowns, with a modest 13 picks, his 80.4 rating a far cry better than the 69.4 disaster of 2013. And, coming into 2018, he had the commitment of the new coach, Pat Shurmer, who, although his credentials are a tad underwhelming, seemed to fully understand that Eli Manning—whom he called "outstanding" and vowed to keep as the starter—meant something visceral to the franchise. Something Jim Irsay didn't when he drafted a hyped college quarterback who was supposed to make everyone forget Peyton Manning.

Remarkably, being as inscrutable a character as he was, even now, grizzled as he was, he seemed still an evolving, unfinished work whose highest authority was embodied in the demands of his surname. As such, he still was laboring in the shadow of the brother who made that surname into a mark of royalty, and who still bears it. In early 2017, when Peyton was sighted—and there is always a Peyton sighting somewhere—at the Pebble Beach Pro-Am golf tournament, he was surrounded on the fairway by a mob sticking No. 18 orange jerseys and other Manning bric-a-brac in his face, demanding his autograph. It was such a frenetic scene that one sportswriter called it "pretty terrifying."⁹ And yet, not a soul who knew him would have expected to ever find him on a ranch in Montana, hiding behind a big white beard.

He was hopelessly addicted to attention, the great narcotic of fame and the lifeblood of the business that surrounds it. The next step was to film his newest Nationwide commercial with country crooner Brad Paisley, in the guise of a vain, overbearing record producer continually badgering the mellow singer—a perfect metaphor for his on-field persona, which he willingly sent up. He then hosted the ESPY Awards show, nimbly delivering put-downs of the elite sports crowd. His gag about the US Olympic women's gymnastics team being so good that Kevin Durant, the Golden State Warriors' newly signed mercenary superstar, wanted to play for them, played to perfection by a glowering Durant, was the enduring highlight of the show and immediately went viral.

Eli, still keeping pace with him, would leave his mark after all on the 2018 Super Bowl, the first one Brady had lost to any quarterback but him. Still in tune with Beckham, the pair filmed an in-house ad for the NFL that smartly parodied those already-parody end-zone twerkings with a spoof of *Dirty Dancing*, Eli doing something like dancing before crooking an inviting finger toward Odell and then lifting him high above his head. But Peyton's family-oriented "Quarterback Vacation" spot for the Universal theme park was a winner, too, that day, with him batting one-liners back and forth with kids and at one point barking "Omaha" while preparing for a selfie; the best line went to a little girl, trying in vain to tutor him on gaming lingo, then sighing, "You're uncoachable."

Such frivolous but necessary-to-the-brand matters were not in the purview of the patriarch, who begat and handed down all the glory, glitter, and agita of fame. Nearing 70, Archie, the rosy-cheeked, freckle-faced, one-time quarterback of the future who once seemed to be that kind of broader cultural hero, had spanned more historical tides than even a wise man like him could hope to process. But in *his* world, football had insulated him through many roiling waters. He's not regal, wears no championship rings, but of prime importance to him, he chairs the National Football Foundation, winner of that organization's Gold Medal in 2016, and is in the College Football Hall of Fame. Still a New

Orleans staple, he went into the Saints Hall of Fame in 1988, wanting or expecting little more.

He lives equally with pride and agony, still amazed at the wonder of it all. As he waited in the tunnel outside the Broncos locker room in Santa Clara, waiting for Peyton to come out and take his leave from the sport, he was humming his favorite song. Naturally, it's a country song, the kind that reaches deep into the soul: Kris Kristofferson's "Why Me," recorded by, among others, Elvis, Johnny Cash, and Merle Haggard. The first line goes:

> *Why me Lord, what have I ever done*
> *To deserve even one of the pleasures I've known?*

He will never know the answer. But on that day, when the Manning brand ruled the football world, possibly for the last time, his shoes half immersed in a puddle flooding the corridor, smelling the same fetid fragrance from a locker room that he had 50 years ago, Elisha Archibald Manning III would not have wanted to be anywhere else.

NOTES

INTRODUCTION: FAMILY MATTERS

1. Mike Klis, "Peyton Manning Has No Regrets About Retirement, Reveals His New Fall Schedule," KUSA-TV website, June 7, 2016, http://www.9news.com/sports/nfl/denver-broncos/peyton-manning-has-no-regrets-about-retirement-reveals-his-new-fall-schedule/234589181.
2. Ryan Van Bibber, "NFL Debrief: Peyton Manning, Tony Romo & a Trip through the Record Book" *SB Nation*, October 7, 2013, http://www.sbnation.com/2013/10/7/4809926/nfl-week-5-2013-scores-results-peyton-manning-tony-romo-records.
3. Ben Doody, "Peyton Manning Contract & Salary: No. 1 in Career Earnings," *Heavy*, November 2, 2014, http://heavy.com/sports/2014/11/how-much-money-does-peyton-manning-make-salary/.
4. Ivan Maisel, "Archie Manning Faces Family History," ESPN website, September 24, 2013, http://espn.go.com/blog/sec/post/_/id/70758/archie-manning-faces-family-history.
5. Michael Silver, "Thoroughbred," *Sports Illustrated*, November 22, 1999.
6. S. L. Price, "The Big Easy," *Sports Illustrated*, December 17, 2012.
7. Nate Scott, "Eli Manning Looked Miserable When His Brother Locked Up Second Super Bowl," *USA Today*, February 7, 2016.

PROLOGUE: MANNING INC.

1. Mark Ribowsky, "No. 1 with a Bullet," *Sport*, May 1999.
2. Lee Jenkins, "Peyton Manning: 2013 Sportsman of the Year," *Sports Illustrated*, December 23, 2013.

3. Marc Malkin, "Is Ann Coulter the Most Hated Woman in the World? She Was at Last Night's Rob Lowe Roast," *E! News*, August 28, 2016, http://www .eonline.com/news/790558/is-ann-coulter-the-most-hated-woman-in-the -world-she-was-at-last-night-s-rob-lowe-roast.

4. Paul Zimmerman, "Archie Manning Is Too Good for This Place," *Sports Illustrated*, June 8, 1981.

5. Archie and Peyton Manning with John Underwood, *Manning* (New York: HarperCollins, 2000), 356.

6. Dan Ozzi, "Don't Let the Manning Brothers Trick You Into Liking Their Rap Video," *Noisey*, https://noisey.vice.com/en_ca/article/rj7a76/dont-let-the -manning-brothers-trick-you-into-liking-their-rap-video-57a20690078424 ded0752463.

7. Mike Wise, "Peyton Manning vs. Eli Manning, and the Best Brothers in Sports History," *Washington Post*, September 14, 2013.

8. Jaime Uribarri, "Peyton Manning Credits Legal Colorado Pot with Booming Papa John's Pizza Business," *New York Daily News*, September 19, 2014.

9. Jeb 2016 Inc., *Federal Election Commission Form 3P: Report of Receipts and Disbursements*, July 15, 2015, http://docquery.fec.gov/cgi-bin/fecimg /?201507159000160826.

10. Robert O'Connell, "The Inevitable Decline of Peyton Manning," *Atlantic*, October 22, 2014.

11. Damon Hack, "Eli as in Elite," *Sports Illustrated*, January 23, 2012.

12. Tim Rohan, "Eli Manning Is Tougher than You," *Sports Illustrated*, January 4, 2017, http://mmqb.si.com/mmqb/2017/01/03/eli-manning-giants-playoffs -nfl-ironman-streak.

13. "Growing Up a Manning," *Athlon Sports & Life*, April 5, 2011, http://athlon sports.com/monthly/growing-manning.

CHAPTER 1: "THEY AIN'T STOPPIN' IN DREW"

1. Dora Mekouar, "These Are America's Richest & Poorest States," Voice of America website, September 21, 2015, https://blogs.voanews.com/all-about -america/2015/09/21/these-are-americas-richest-poorest-states/, and Sam Dillon, "Study Compares States' Math and Science Scores with Other Countries," *New York Times*, November 14, 2007.

2. "The Most Southern Place on Earth: Music, History and Culture of the Mississippi Delta," workshop given by the National Endowment for the Humanities, http://www.neh.gov/divisions/education/other-opportunities/2015 /the-most-southern-place-earth-music-history-and-culture.

3. Billy Turner, "The Hometown Archie Once Knew Is No More," *New Orleans Times-Picayune*, January 26, 2008.

4. Zimmerman, "Archie Manning Is Too Good."

5. Mississippi Legislature, Regular Session 2009, House Bill 1480 and Senate Concurrent Resolution No. 593.

6. J. Todd Moye, *Let the People Decide: Black Freedom and White Resistance Movements in Sunflower County, Mississippi, 1945–1986* (Chapel Hill: University of North Carolina Press, 2004), 28 and 128.

7. US Census (1940), retrieved at https://1940census.archives.gov/search /?search.state=MS&search.enumeration_district=67-52#filename=m-t0627 -02067-00842.tif&name=67-52&type=image&state=MS&index=12&pages=3 8&bm_all_text=Bookmark.

8. Archie and Peyton Manning, *Manning*, 18.

9. Ken Murray, "Genetics, Athletics Mesh for Mannings," *Baltimore Sun*, December 12, 2004.

10. Archie and Peyton Manning, *Manning*, 16.

11. Zimmerman, "Archie Manning Is Too Good."

12. Author interview with Frank Crosthwait.

13. Archie and Peyton Manning, *Manning*, 17.

14. Zimmerman, "Archie Manning Is Too Good."

15. Archie and Peyton Manning, *Manning*, 18.

16. Ibid., 25.

17. Zimmerman, "Archie Manning Is Too Good."

18. Author interview with Paul Pounds.

CHAPTER 2: MR. DREW

1. "The Forgotten," Southern Poverty Law Center, https://www.splcenter.org /news/2015/07/27/forgotten.

2. "Church Refuses to Marry Black Couple in Mississippi," CNN, July 30, 2012, http://www.cnn.com/2012/07/30/us/mississippi-black-couple-wedding/.

3. "Two Brandon, Mississippi Men Plead Guilty to Committing Hate Crimes Against African-Americans in Jackson, Mississippi," Federal Bureau of Investigation, January 7, 2015, https://www.fbi.gov/contact-us/field -offices/jackson/news/press-releases/two-brandon-mississippi-men -plead-guilty-to-committing-hate-crimes-against-african-americans-in- jackson-mississippi.

4. Archie and Peyton Manning, *Manning*, p. 177.

5. Zimmerman, "Archie Manning Is Too Good."

6. Ibid.

7. Ibid.

8. Archie and Peyton Manning, *Manning*, 34.

9. Ibid., 37.

10. Zimmerman, "Archie Manning Is Too Good."

CHAPTER 3: "AIN'T YIELDING TO NOBODY"

1. "Ole Miss Takes Its Name from Darky Dialect, Not Abbreviation of State," *Mississippian*, May 13, 1939.
2. Zimmerman, "Archie Manning Is Too Good."
3. Stuart Stevens, *The Last Season: A Father, a Son, and a Lifetime of College Football* (New York: Knopf, 2015; repr., New York: Vintage, 2016), 8.
4. United Press International, "Vaught Tells of Being Rebel," *Greenville (MS) Delta Democrat Times*, September 1, 1971.
5. Nick Valencia and Marlena Baldacci, "Ole Miss Racial Incidents Have Many Feeling Uneasy," CNN website, February 22, 2014, http://www.cnn.com /2014/02/21/us/mississippi-meredith-statue/.
6. C. J. Schexnayder, "The Integration of Football in the Southeastern Conference," *SB Nation*, May 9, 2012, http://www.teamspeedkills.com/2012 /5/9/3008248/the-integration-of-football-in-the-southeastern-conference.
7. Archie and Peyton Manning, *Manning*, 48.
8. Becky Gillette, "Williams Brothers General Store Is Something to Count On," *Mississippi Business Journal*, August 19, 2012, http://msbusiness .com/2012/08/williams-brothers-general-store-is-something-to-count-on/.
9. Archie and Peyton Manning, *Manning*, 51.
10. Ibid., 56.
11. Ibid., 66.

CHAPTER 4: "I THINK BUDDY'S DEAD"

1. Archie and Peyton Manning, *Manning*, 58.
2. Author interview with Frank Croshtwait.
3. William F. Reed, "Red-Letter Year for Quarterbacks," *Sports Illustrated*, September 14, 1970.
4. Zimmerman, "Archie Manning Is Too Good."
5. "Ole Miss Launches 'Project '69,'" *Greenville (MS) Delta Democrat Times*, August 24, 1969.
6. Lars Anderson, "Alabama vs. Ole Miss, 1969: The Night College Football Went Prime Time," *AL.com*, October 3, 2014, http://www.al.com/sports/index.ssf /2014/10/alabama_vs_ole_miss_1969_the_n.html.
7. David Moffit, "Archie Sets Three SEC Records," United Press International wire story, October 6, 1969.
8. Zimmerman, "Archie Manning Is Too Good."
9. Pat Putnam, "Answer to a Foolish Question," *Sports Illustrated*, November 24, 1969.
10. "Hustling the Heisman Hopefuls," *Time*, November 16, 1970.

CHAPTER 5: "HE HAS MADE PEOPLE FORGET JAMES MEREDITH"

1. Reed, "Red-Letter Year."
2. Ibid.
3. MediSav drugstore ad, *Greenville (MS) Delta Democrat Times*, January 30, 1970.
4. Reed, "Red-Letter Year."
5. Ibid.
6. Rick Du Brow, "Archie Who? Not Manning for Sure," United Press International wire story, January 11, 1970.
7. "Driftwood," *Greenville (MS) Delta Democrat Times*, November 15, 1970.
8. William F. Reed, "Archie and the War Between the States," *Sports Illustrated*, October 12, 1970.
9. Ibid.
10. *The Ole Miss* (University of Mississippi yearbook), 1970.
11. Lew Powell, "Newmoney Finds Raise Enriching," *Greenville (MS) Delta Democrat Times*, March 26, 1971.
12. Archie and Peyton Manning, *Manning*, 85.
13. Zimmerman, "Archie Manning Is Too Good."
14. Archie and Peyton Manning, *Manning*, 81.
15. "Archie in Canada?" *Greenville (MS) Delta Democrat Times*, April 19, 1971.
16. Susan Klopfer, comment on Benjamin T. Greenberg, "Why Doesn't Mississippi D.A. Mark Duncan Want Assistance from the DOJ?" *Hungry Blues: Ben Greenberg's Blog*, June 5, 2005, http://hungryblues.net/2005/06/15/why-doesnt-mississippi-da-mark-duncan-want-assistance-from-the-doj/.
17. Archie and Peyton Manning, *Manning*, p. 86.
18. "NFL Salary Survey Shows Colts' Pay Highest," United Press International wire story, July 25, 1971.
19. Don Banks, "Oral History of the 1971 NFL Draft: The Original Year of the Quarterback," *Sports Illustrated*, April 21, 2016.

CHAPTER 6: MUDBUGGERS

1. Archie and Peyton Manning, *Manning*, 95.
2. Zimmerman, "Archie Manning Is Too Good."
3. Ross Newhan, "Rams' Front Four Is the Best—Manning," *Los Angeles Times*, September 23, 1974.
4. Zimmerman, "Archie Manning Is Too Good."
5. Archie and Peyton Manning, *Manning*, 119.
6. Zimmerman, "Archie Manning Is Too Good."
7. Archie and Peyton Manning, *Manning*, 118–19.
8. Jeff Duncan, "Arrival of Saints Heralded 'Sea Change' for City of New

Orleans in 1960s," *New Orleans Times-Picayune*, June 1, 2016, http://www.nola.com/saints/index.ssf/2016/06/arrival_of_saints_heralded_sea.html.

9. George Becnel, *When the Saints Came Marching In: What the New Orleans NFL Franchise Did Wrong (and Sometimes Right) in Its Expansion Years* (Bloomington, IN: AuthorHouse, 2009), 131.

10. Duncan, "Arrival of Saints."

11. Peter Finney, "Archie Will Revolutionize Pro Football," *New Orleans States-Item*, May 7, 1971.

12. "Archie Manning, Drew Mississippi and 'The Ballad of Archie Who,'" *The Whited Sepulchre*, August 4, 2010, http://thewhitedsepulchre.blogspot.com/2010/08/archie-manning-drew-mississippi-and.html.

13. Mike Scott, "New Orleans, We Have a Problem: Remembering the Saints' Astronaut Executive," *New Orleans Times-Picayune*, August 11, 2016.

14. Zimmerman, "Archie Manning Is Too Good."

CHAPTER 7: "STRANGLED BY THE TRAUMA"

1. "Archie Is Happy, WFL Interests Him," *Baton Rouge Morning Advocate*, May 24, 1974.

2. *New Orleans Times-Picayune*, June 23, 1974.

3. "WFL Teams Seek Archie Manning," *Baton Rouge Morning Advocate*, June 27, 1974.

4. "Mecom Scores Manning for Leading Picket Line," *Baton Rouge Morning Advocate*, July 16, 1974.

5. "Manning Decision Due Soon," Associated Press wire story, July 23, 1974.

6. "Manning Gets Rich Contract," Associated Press wire story, July 10, 1975.

7. Sam Borden, "A Saint in His City: Archie Manning in New Orleans," *New York Times*, January 26, 2013.

8. Zimmerman, "Archie Manning Is Too Good."

9. Lee Jenkins, "Peyton Manning: 2013 Sportsman of the Year," *Sports Illustrated*, December 23, 2013.

10. *New Orleans Times-Picayune*, October 15, 1971.

11. *New Orleans Times-Picayune*, February 21, 1971.

12. Rick Rosen, "Olivia Manning, Peyton's Mom: 5 Fast Facts You Need to Know," *Heavy*, February 7, 2016, http://heavy.com/sports/2016/02/peyton-eli-archie-manning-mom-wife-family-age-new-orleans-ole-miss/.

13. "Archie Inks 5-Year Pact," *Baton Rouge Morning Advocate*, July 9, 1975.

14. Zimmerman, "Archie Manning Is Too Good."

15. Author interview with Derland Moore.

16. Zimmerman, "Archie Manning Is Too Good."

17. Bob Roesler, "Mecom-Stram Honeymoon Over," *New Orleans Times-Picayune*, December 12, 1977.

18. Gil LeBreton and Marty Mule, "It's Over—Saints Express Shock and Surprise," *New Orleans Times-Picayune*, January 29, 1978.

19. Zimmerman, "Archie Manning Is Too Good."

CHAPTER 8: GOOD LORD, I FEEL LIKE I'M DYING

1. Peter Finney, "Mike Ornstein Case Shows How History Can Be Repeated," *New Orleans Times-Picayune*, October 11, 2010.

2. William Nack, "Football's Little Bighorn?" *Sports Illustrated*, January 26, 1981.

3. "Chuck Muncie," Cal Alumni, http://www.berkeley.edu/news/magazine /summer_99/feature_alumni_muncie.html.

4. Jeff Duncan, "Remembering Chuck Muncie's Star-Crossed Career with the New Orleans Saints," *New Orleans Times-Picayune*, May 14, 2013.

5. "Muncie Not a Saint Anymore after Being Sent to Chargers," *New York Times*, September 30, 1980.

6. Greg Bishop, "Beneath Brown Bags, Saints Had Loyal Fans," *New York Times*, February 4, 2010.

7. "Humor Soon Turned to Ratings Worries," *New Orleans Times-Picayune*, November 25, 1980.

8. Author interview with Derland Moore.

9. Zimmerman, "Archie Manning Is Too Good."

10. Sam Borden, "A Saint in His City: Archie Manning in New Orleans," *New York Times*, January 26, 2013.

11. Zimmerman, "Archie Manning Is Too Good."

12. Archie and Peyton Manning, *Manning*, 125.

13. Zimmerman, "Archie Manning Is Too Good."

14. Ibid.

15. Borden, "A Saint in His City."

16. Associated Press, "Cooper Manning Happy for Brothers' Success," February 1, 2008.

17. Archie and Peyton Manning, *Manning*, 187.

18. Ibid., 135.

19. Ibid., 133.

20. Ibid., 139.

21. Peter Finney, "Requiem for Saints No. 8," *New Orleans Times-Picayune*, September 18, 1982.

22. *New Orleans Times-Picayune*, September 26, 1982.
23. Dave Lagarde, "Olivia Manning: The Pressure's Off," *New Orleans Times -Picayune*, September 18, 182.
24. Finney, "Requiem for Saints No. 8."
25. Archie and Peyton Manning, *Manning*, 142.
26. Don Reese, "I'm Not Worth a Damn," *Sports Illustrated*, June 14, 1982.
27. Ronald Sullivan, "Associates Can't Believe Charges against Strachan," *New York Times*, July 4, 1982.
28. Archie and Peyton Manning, *Manning*, 129.

CHAPTER 9: "A DOGGONE GOOD TRIP"

1. Sam Blair, "Manning's Optimism," *Dallas Morning News*, December 13, 1982.
2. Archie and Peyton Manning, *Manning*, 148.
3. Peter Finney, "Archie Readies for Last Season," *New Orleans Times-Picayune*, May 26, 1985.
4. Archie and Peyton Manning, *Manning*, 153.
5. Finney, "Archie Readies for Last Season."
6. Archie and Peyton Manning, *Manning*, 276.
7. Finney, "Archie Readies for Last Season."
8. Archie and Peyton Manning, *Manning*, 164.
9. William Raspberry, "Reagan's Race Legacy," *Washington Post*, June 14, 2004.

CHAPTER 10: "WE'RE NOT AVERAGE. WE'RE COOP AND PEYT."

1. Zimmerman, "Archie Manning Is Too Good."
2. Author interview with Tony Reginelli.
3. Author interview with Frank Gendusa.
4. Archie and Peyton Manning, *Manning*, p. 179.
5. John Ed Bradley, "The Other Brother: Like His Famous Father, Archie, and Younger Siblings, Peyton and Eli, Cooper Manning Had NFL-Caliber Talent. Then His Body Betrayed Him," *Sports Illustrated*, November 10, 2003.
6. Archie and Peyton Manning, *Manning*, 183.
7. Ibid., 186.
8. Ibid., 194.
9. Author interview with Tony Reginelli.
10. Author interview with Frank Gendusa.
11. Ian O'Connor, "Peyton Manning Shares Lasting Bond with High School Coach," ESPN website, http://www.espn.com/nfl/story/_/id/14718714/

peyton-manning-denver-broncos-shares-lasting-bond-high-school-coach
-tony-reginelli-nfl.

12. John Ed Bradley, "The Other Brother."

13. *Gulfport Sun Herald*, September 29, 1992.

14. "Manning Career Is Ended," *Mobile (AL) Register*, September 29, 1992.

15. John Ed Bradley, "The Other Brother."

16. Archie and Peyton Manning, *Manning*, 197.

17. John Ed Bradley. "The Other Brother."

18. Archie and Peyton Manning, *Manning*, 194.

CHAPTER 11: EVERYTHING'S COMING UP ORANGE

1. Archie and Peyton Manning, *Manning*, 198.

2. Author interview with Tony Reginelli.

3. Author interview with Frank Gendusa.

4. Archie and Peyton Manning, *Manning*, 204.

5. Press release, Gatorade Circle of Champions, December 30, 1993.

6. "Archie's Son Spurns Ole Miss for Tennessee," Associated Press wire story, January 26, 1994.

7. Archie and Peyton Manning, *Manning*, 226.

8. Ibid., 247.

9. Tom Sharp, "Manning Happy to Wait for His Turn as Vols' QB," Associated Press wire story, August 21, 1994.

10. Michael Silver, "Thoroughbred," *Sports Illustrated*, November 22, 1999.

11. Archie and Peyton Manning, *Manning*, 235–36.

12. Tim Layden, "Matinee Idol—Now Playing on Saturday Afternoons: Tennessee's Peyton Manning, Who Is Reveling in His Birthright as the Nation's Best Quarterback," *Sports Illustrated*, April 26, 1996.

13. Associated Press, "Bernard King Says He Faced Racism," ESPN website, November 5, 2013, http://www.espn.com/mens-college-basketball/story/_/id/9927621/bernard-king-says-faced-racism-tennessee-volunteers.

14. "University of Tennessee is a 'Cesspool' of Anti-Semitic and Racist Behavior, Anonymous Watchdog Group Claims" *London Daily Mail*, October 25, 2016, http://www.dailymail.co.uk/news/article-3730310/University-Tennessee -cesspool-anti-Semitic-racist-behavior-anonymous-watchdog-group -alleges.html#ixzz4OD4DWZ8c.

15. Layden, "Matinee Idol."

16. Archie and Peyton Manning, *Manning*, 242.

17. Ron Bracken, "Brain Cramps," *State College (PA) Centre Daily Times*, September 10, 1994.

18. Ed Price, "Vols Break In Freshmen Quarterbacks," *Augusta (GA) Chronicle*, September 29, 1994.

19. Mary Foster, "Stewart Has Had Stellar Career," *ESPN College Football*, December 31, 1998, http://a.espncdn.com/ncf/s/1998/1231/25370.html.

20. Archie and Peyton Manning, *Manning*, 252.

21. Layden, "Matinee Idol."

22. Archie and Peyton Manning, *Manning*, 254.

CHAPTER 12: JUST RIGHT

1. Author interview with Marcus Nash.

2. Layden, "Matinee Idol."

3. Mike Berardino, "No Chip Off Old Block," *Augusta (GA) Chronicle*, September 9,1995.

4. Berry Tramel, "Trouble in Tennessee Volunteer Football Program Racked by Scandals," *Oklahoman* (Oklahoma City), September 27, 1995.

5. Archie and Peyton Manning, *Manning*, 257.

6. "Despite Manning's Play, Fulmer Displeased with Team's Performance," Associated Press wire story, August 25, 1995.

7. Tim Layden, "Putting Peyton in His Place," *Sports Illustrated*, September 22, 1997.

8. Berry Tramel, "Trouble in Tennessee."

9. Associated Press wire story, September 15, 1995.

10. "Alabama Preparing for Test by Tennessee QB Peyton Manning," Associated Press wire story, October 10, 1995.

11. Layden, "Putting Peyton in His Place."

12. Ibid.

13. Ibid.

14. "On Any Given Sunday" (excerpt from University of Tennessee investigative report), *Smoking Gun*, January 17, 2000, http://www.thesmokinggun.com/file/any-given-sunday-0?page=0.

15. Employment Discrimination Complaint, Jamie Naughright Whited, Case number 3021596, August 27, 1996.

16. David Keim, "33 Claims Cited by UT Trainer," *Knoxville News-Sentinel*, August 19, 1997.

17. "Manning Mooning Expensive," *Augusta (GA) Chronicle*, August 16, 1997.

18. David Keim, "It Wasn't for the Money," *Knoxville News-Sentinel*, August 24, 1997.

19. Chris Dufresne, "Gators Put Tennessee, Peyton in Their Place," *Los Angeles Times*, September 22, 1996.

20. Layden, "Matinee Idol."

21. "Manning Was Nearly a Rebel," Associated Press wire story, October 3, 1996.

22. Layden, "Matinee Idol."

23. Ibid.

24. Peter Finney, "No Joke: Cooper Manning Really Loves His Brothers," *New Orleans Clarion Herald*, October 1, 2013.

25. Dave Scheiber, "The Other Brother," *Tampa Bay Times*, November 7, 2004.

26. Frank Schwab, "Peyton Manning Recalls Every Detail of Play at Tennessee in 1996, and It Is Simply Amazing," *Yahoo! Sports*, May 2, 2013, https://sports.yahoo.com/blogs/ncaaf-dr-saturday/peyton-manning-recalls-every-detail-play-tennessee-1996-140742956.html.

27. Layden, "Putting Peyton in His Place."

28. Mike Dame, "UF's Wuerffel Nixes Playboy Offer as Top Scholar-Athlete," *Orlando Sentinel*, May 10, 1996.

CHAPTER 13: "I'LL WIN FOR YOU"

1. William F. Reed, "Currying No Favor: Bill Curry Hasn't Had a Winner in Six Years at Kentucky, Where Patience Is Wearing Thin," *Sports Illustrated*, October 7, 1996.

2. Dave Goldberg, "Why Take Jeff George? Because a Lot of Teams Need a QB," Associated Press wire story, September 28, 1996.

3. Jim Sexton, "The Star Who Stayed in School," *Aberdeen (SD) Daily News*, August 17, 1999.

4. Associated Press wire story, August 17, 1997.

5. Archie and Peyton Manning, *Manning*, 260.

6. Ibid., 261.

7. Mike Lupica, "It's Michael on 33d St.: Knicks–Bulls Is Great Theater, but Not Last Act," *New York Daily News*, March 9, 1997.

8. "Peyton's Place Is With the Vols," Associated Press wire story, March 6, 1997.

9. Lee Jenkins, "Peyton Manning: 2013 Sportsman of the Year," *Sports Illustrated*, December 23, 2013.

10. Archie and Peyton Manning, *Manning*, 262.

11. Tony Fabrizio, "Losing May Let Falcons Draft Vols' Manning." *Augusta (GA) Chronicle*, July 15, 1997.

12. Layden, "Putting Peyton in His Place."

13. *Augusta (GA) Chronicle*, September 19, 1997.

14. Archie and Peyton Manning, *Manning*, 270.

15. *Newsday* (Long Island, NY), September 21, 1997.

16. Archie and Peyton Manning, *Manning*, 270.

17. Will Shelton, "Peyton Manning's 10 Best Passing Performances at Tennessee," *SB Nation Rocky Top Talk*, October 20, 2014, http://www.rockytoptalk.com /2014/10/20/7023395/peyton-mannings-10-best-passing-performances-at -tennessee.

18. Ibid.

19. Mike Berardino, "Manning Finally Gets Snapshot for His Memory," *Augusta (GA) Chronicle*, December 7, 1997.

20. Ibid.

21. Archie and Peyton Manning, *Manning*, 267.

22. Ibid., 265–67.

23. John Adams, "Nebraska Had More Credentials to Finish No. 1," Scripps Howard News Service, January 5, 1998.

24. "Colts Lure Mora Back to the NFL," *Augusta (GA) Chronicle*, January 13, 1998.

25. Associated Press, "Hopefuls Flock to Combine," February 6, 1998.

26. Mel Kiper, "Ryan Leaf, QB," *ESPN Sports Zone*, https://web.archive.org/ web/19981207060713/http://nfldraft98-espn.sportszone.com/html/player/ player17.html.

27. Matt Rudnitsky, "An Agent Claims the Colts Wanted Ryan Leaf over Peyton Manning, but Ryan Leaf Told Them to F*** Off," SportsGrid.com, January 21, 2014, http://www.sportsgrid.com/real-sports/nfl/an-agent-claims -the-colts-wanted-ryan-leaf-over-peyton-manning-but-ryan-leaf-told -them-to-f-off/.

28. Silver, "Thoroughbred."

29. Peter King, "The Toughest Job in Sports: As Rookies Peyton Manning and Ryan Leaf Are About to Find Out, an NFL Quarterback Must Withstand Unparalleled Pressure—a Fact Most of Their Young Predecessors in the 1990s Learned the Hard Way," *Sports Illustrated*, August 17, 1998.

30. Leonard Shapiro, "Peyton's Place Is Indianapolis," *Washington Post*, April 19, 1998.

31. Archie and Peyton Manning, *Manning*, 284.

32. Ralph Vacchiano, "In Rare Interview, Tom Condon, Super Agent for Peyton and Eli Manning, Gives Exclusive Look into His World," *New York Daily News*, June 27, 2015.

33. Archie and Peyton Manning, *Manning*, 85 and 267.

34. Mike Freeman, "NFL Draft Day '98: Colts Agonize to the End, Then Pick Manning," *New York Times*, April 19, 1998.

35. Associated Press, "Colts Make Indy Peyton's Place," April 19, 1998.

36. Freeman, "NFL Draft Day '98."

37. Shapiro, "Peyton's Place Is Indianapolis."
38. Freeman, "NFL Draft Day '98."

CHAPTER 14: "A GOLDEN STAIRCASE FROM HEAVEN"

1. Todd Graff, "Replacing Peyton Fit for a Tee," *Augusta (GA) Chronicle*, July 31, 1998.
2. Ben Cornfield, "Peyton Manning Never Beat Florida," *Gator Country*, September 11, 2012, https://www.gatorcountry.com/florida-gators-football/peyton_manning_never_beat_florida/.
3. "American College Football Is Rich with Black History," African American Registry, http://www.aaregistry.org/historic_events/view/american-college-football-rich-black-history.
4. Author interview with Frank Gendusa.
5. Archie and Peyton Manning, *Manning*, 301.
6. Ibid., 303.
7. Ohm Youngmisuk, "Eli Manning Had Super Sense of Future While Still in High School," *New York Daily News*, January 28, 2008.
8. Associated Press, "Manning Watches His Brother Play," October 26, 1997.
9. S. L. Price, "The Big Easy," *Sports Illustrated*, December 17, 2012.
10. Silver, "Thoroughbred."
11. Ibid.
12. Archie and Peyton Manning, *Manning*, 295.
13. Mike Chappell, "A Weighty Matter for Colts' Glenn," *Indianapolis Star*, June 12, 1998.
14. Ribowsky, "No. 1 with a Bullet."
15. "Faulk Excited about Colts' Changes," Associated Press wire story, April 26, 1998.
16. "Colts Rookies Trying to Adjust," Associated Press wire story, April 27, 1998.
17. Author interview with Frank Crosthwait.
18. Robin Miller, "Manning's Absence Becoming Alarming," *Indianapolis Star*, July 24, 1998.
19. "Colts Need Manning in Camp, Former 49ers QB Says," *Indianapolis Star*, July 27, 1998.
20. "Indianapolis, Manning Finally Agree to Rookie-Record, Six-Year, $48 Million Contract," Associated Press wire story, July 29, 1998.
21. Vacchiano, "In Rare Interview."
22. Bill Benner, "Fans Flock for Brush with $48 Million Man," *Indianapolis Star*, July 30, 1998.
22. Silver, "Thoroughbred."

23. King, "Toughest Job in Sports."

24. Silver, "Thoroughbred."

25. Jim Cour, "Rookie Shows in No. 1 Pick," Associated Press wire story, August 10, 1998.

26. Bernie Wilson, "Early QB Edge to Leaf," Associated Press wire story, August 11, 1998.

27. T. J. Simers, "Ryan 'I've Got Personality' Leaf No Prince Charming," *Los Angeles Times*, August 16, 1998.

28. Silver, "Thoroughbred."

29. Associated Press, August 14, 1998.

30. Simers, "No Prince Charming."

31. Associated Press wire story, July 31, 1998.

32. Conrad Brunner, "Manning Impresses in NFL Debut," *Indianapolis Star*, September 7, 1998.

33. Marty Burns, "Growing Pains: Colts quarterback Peyton Manning Showed Flashes of Brilliance in His NFL Debut, but His Inexperience Led to a Dolphins Victory," *Sports Illustrated*, September 14, 1998.

34. Archie and Peyton Manning, *Manning*, 309.

35. Howard Ulman, "Pats Dominate Colts," Associated Press wire story, September 14, 1998.

36. Dave Goldberg, "Quarterbacks Falling Like Flies," *Indianapolis Star*, September 15, 1998.

37. Conrad Brunner, "Polian Furious after Defense Hits Bottom in Shellacking at Hands of AFC East Rival Jets," *Indianapolis Star*, September 21, 1998.

38. Robin Miller, "Manning Growing, But, Oh, the Pain of Learning on Job," *Indianapolis Star*, September 14, 1998.

CHAPTER 15: "AN AMBIVALENT RELATIONSHIP WITH HIS IMAGE"

1. Archie and Peyton Manning, *Manning*, 301.

2. Damon Hack, "Eli as in Elite," *Sports Illustrated*, January 23, 2012.

3. Dwight Foxx, "Sons of NFL Stars among Nation's Top Quarterbacks," *Augusta (GA) Chronicle*, September 4, 1998.

4. Author interview of Frank Gendusa.

5. Archie and Peyton Manning, *Manning*, 332.

6. Joe Drape, "Eli Manning Inherits the Reins at Ole Miss," *New York Times*, October 19, 2001.

7. "Eli Manning Has a Name to Carry On," Associated Press wire story, September 7, 1999.

8. Youngmisuk, "Eli Manning Had Super Sense of Future."

9. Ribowsky, "No. 1 with a Bullet."

10. David Newton, *Columbia (SC) State*, August 29, 1999.

11. Silver, "Thoroughbred."

12. Ibid.

13. "Heckler Gets to Leaf," Associated Press wire story, August 20, 1999.

14. Betsy Blaney, "Ex-NFL QB Leaf Gets Probation in Texas Drug Case," *Seattle Times*, April 14, 2010.

15. Michael Ventre, "In NFL Draft, Watch Out for Next Leaf," NBC Sports website, March 25, 2000.

16. Ribowsky, "No. 1 with a Bullet."

17. Silver, "Thoroughbred."

18. Robert O'Connell, "The Inevitable Decline of Peyton Manning," *Atlantic*, October 22, 2014.

19. John O'Neill, "ABC's Esiason Likes the Chances for Colts to Reach Super Bowl," *Indianapolis Star*, January 15, 2000.

20. Phil Richards, "NFL, Colts Try to Address Off-Field Abuse," *Indianapolis Star*, January 9, 2000.

CHAPTER 16: ELI'S COMING

1. Joe Drape, "Eli Manning Inherits the Reins at Ole Miss," *New York Times*, October 19, 2001.

2. Ibid.

3. Drunk Athletes, Twitter post, February 20, 2015, 9:06 p.m., https://twitter.com/athletesdrunk/status/568954807660228608.

4. Drape, "Eli Manning Inherits the Reins."

5. Michael Silver, "Making Waves: AWOL from Colts Workouts, Edgerrin James is Cruising through the Off-Season at a Pace Worthy of the NFL's Two-Time Rushing Champion," *Sports Illustrated*, June 11, 2001.

6. Turner, "The Hometown Archie Once Knew."

7. "Another Manning Era Begins at Ole Miss," Associated Press wire story, August 16, 2001.

8. Drape, "Eli Manning Inherits the Reins."

9. Ibid.

10. Youngmisuk, "Eli Manning Had Super Sense of Future."

11. Archie and Peyton Manning, *Manning*, 342.

12. Christopher L. Gasper, "17th Time Won't Be Two Too Much," *Denver Post*, January 24, 2016.

13. S. L. Price, "About Time," *Sports Illustrated*, June 10, 1996.

14. John Ed Bradley, "Cooper on Eli: You've Come a Long Way, Baby Brother, and Can Go a Lot Further," *Sports Illustrated*, November 10, 2003.

CHAPTER 17: MR. INHUMAN

1. Price, "About Time."
2. Archie and Peyton Manning, *Manning*, 272.
3. Matt Dolloff, "Malcolm Saxon's Letter to Peyton Manning Speaks Louder than Any Other Evidence," CBS Boston.com, February 18, 2016, http://boston.cbslocal.com/2016/02/18/malcolm-saxon-letter-to-peyton-manning/.
4. Will Hobson, "The Mysterious 1994 Incident between Peyton Manning and a Tennessee Trainer," *Washington Post*, February 19, 2014.
5. Will Brinson, "Peyton Manning Grilled over Article, Colts Kicker in 2003 Deposition," CBS Sports website, http://www.cbssports.com/nfl/news/peyton-manning-grilled-over-article-colts-kicker-in-2003-deposition/.
6. Ollie Gillman, "Peyton Manning and a Dark History His Football Dynasty Family Have Tried to Bury," DailyMail.com, February 13, 2016, http://www.dailymail.co.uk/news/article-3445659/Peyton-Manning-dark-history-football-dynasty-family-tried-bury-Super-Bowl-legend-sexually-abused-college-team-s-trainer-stood-father-smeared-good-name.html, and Shaun King, "Peyton Manning's Squeaky-Clean Image Was Built on Lies, as Detailed in Explosive Court Documents Showing Ugly Smear Campaign Against His Alleged Sex Assault Victim," *New York Daily News*, February 13, 2016, http://www.nydailynews.com/news/national/king-peyton-manning-squeaky-clean-image-built-lies-article-1.2530395.
7. Mel Antonen, "Trainer Has Backers in Suit against Mannings," *USA Today*, November 4, 2003.
8. "Employee of the Month: Lisa Perry," *Playboy*, December 2005.
9. Leitch, "Peyton Manning Going All Brokeback Mountain on Us?" *Deadspin*, September 29, 2005, http://deadspin.com/128185/peyton-manning-going-all-brokeback-mountain-on-us.
10. Shaun King, "Peyton Manning's Squeaky-Clean Image Was Built on Lies," *New York Daily News*, February 13, 2016.
11. Don Pierson, "Pats Lay Down the Law on Peyton, Colts," *Chicago Tribune*, January 19, 2004.
12. Ibid.
13. Michael Silver, "Cold Blooded," *Sports Illustrated*, January 26, 2004.
14. Richard Rosenblatt, "This Manning Going to Houston," Associated Press wire story, January 19, 2004.
15. Josh Kendall, "Manning Has Last Chance," *Augusta (GA) Chronicle*, August 18, 2003.
16. "Ernie Accorsi's Scouting Report: Eli Manning," New York Giants website, June 18, 2003, http://www.giants.com/news-and-blogs/article-1

/Read-Ernie-Accorsis-Scouting-Report-Eli-Manning/02b2f782-cb8c-4eda
-a1c9-531482da5a37.

17. Michael Marot, "Mannings Enjoy Nearly-Perfect Season," Associated Press
wire story, January 10, 2004.

18. Conor Orr, "Eli Manning Still Won't Admit Why He Didn't Want to Play
for Chargers," NJ.com, December 4, 2013, http://www.nj.com/giants/index
.ssf/2013/12/eli_manning_still_wont_admit_why_he_didnt_want_to
_play_for_chargers.html.

19. Adrian Wojnarowski, "Collins, with Departure Likely, Takes High Road,"
Bergen Record, April 16, 2004.

20. Bill Wolverton, "Tillman Worthy of Hero Label," *Rockford (IL) Register Star*,
April 24, 2004.

21. John Breech, "Archie Manning Gives Details on Why Eli Refused to Play
for the Chargers," CBS Sports website, http://www.cbssports.com/nfl
/news/archie-manning-gives-details-on-why-eli-refused-to-play-for-the
-chargers/.

22. Jeffri Chadiha, "What a Manning Wants," *Sports Illustrated*, May 3, 2004.

23. Bob Glauber, "Giants' Trade a Win-Win," *Newsday* (Long Island, NY), April
25, 2004.

24. Chadiha, "What a Manning Wants."

25. *Newsday*, April 30, 2004.

26. "All Eyes on Eli in a Dud of a Debut," *Newsday*, May 8, 2004.

27. Steve Serby, "Heir to the Throwin'," *New York Post*, November 21, 2004.

28. Tom Canavan, "Eli Era Begins in New York," Associated Press wire story,
November 21, 2004.

29. Peter King, "A Rookie Mistake," *Sports Illustrated*, November 29, 2004.

30. Paul Zimmerman, "Dr. Z's NFL Forecast," *Sports Illustrated*, November 29,
2004.

31. Lisa Altobelli, "Eli Manning," *Sports Illustrated*, October 11, 2004.

32. Peter King, "Rating the Young QBs," *Sports Illustrated*, October 10, 2005.

CHAPTER 18: PEYTON, FINALLY

1. "Peyton Manning," *Spotrac*, http://www.spotrac.com/nfl/denver-broncos
/peyton-manning-5028/cash-earnings/.

2. Bob Wolfley, "Jeff Saturday Explains Peyton Manning's Pre-Snap Language
and Histrionics," *Milwaukee Journal Sentinel*, January 18, 2014.

3. Peter King, "Perfect Timing," *Sports Illustrated*, September 27, 2004.

4. Paul Zimmerman, "Dr. Z's Forecast," *Sports Illustrated*, December 20, 2004.

5. Dave Goldberg, "Colts, Pats Have All the Drama This Week," Associated
Press wire story, January 11, 2005.

6. Peter King, "Harrison's Deal: What It Means," *Sports Illustrated*, December 20, 2004.

7. Howard Ulman, "Patriot Blasts 'Vanderjerk,'" Associated Press wire story, January 12, 2005.

8. Mike Freeman, "Manning Still Battling College Foe," *Florida Times-Union*, January 16, 2005, http://jacksonville.com/tu-online/stories/011605/spf_17700659.shtml#.WigqmHNOkwi.

9. Howard Ulman, "Pats 'D' Stops Vaunted Offense of Manning, Colts," Associated Press wire story, January 27, 2005.

10. Amy Goodman, "Left to Die in a New Orleans Prison," *Alternet*, September 27, 2005, http://www.alternet.org/story/26073/left_to_die_in_a_new_orleans_prison.

11. Author interview with Tony Reginelli.

12. "Burress Has String of Debtor Lawsuits," Associated Press wire story, February 9, 2009.

13. Peter King, "Peyton, Finally," *Sports Illustrated*, November 7, 2005.

14. Darren Everson, "The Final Hours of James Dungy," *New York Daily News*, January 1, 2006; "Dungy's Son's Death a Suicide: Medical Examiner"; CBC Sports website, February 17, 2006, http://www.cbc.ca/sports/football/dungy-s-son-s-death-a-suicide-medical-examiner-1.616710.

15. Michael Marot, "Another Poor Playoff Performance Dooms Manning, Colts," Associated Press wire story, January 16, 2006.

16. Ibid.

17. J. A. Adande, "Manning Loses Blame Game Too," *Los Angeles Times*, January 16, 2006.

18. Michael Silver, "May the Best Manning Win," *Sports Illustrated*, September 11, 2006.

19. Mike Arco, "'06 Fantasy Preview," *Rockford (IL) Register Star*, September 3, 2006.

20. Silver, "May the Best Manning Win."

21. Steve Serby, "It's Eli-Mentary—Pressure's on Little Brother, Not Big, to Finally Be Da-Man," *New York Post*, September 6, 2006.

22. Nunyo Demasio, "The Marvelous and Mysterious Marvin Harrison," *Sports Illustrated*, January 8, 2007.

23. Jarrett Bell, "Colts' Jim Irsay: No Regrets Releasing Peyton Manning," *USA Today*, October 15, 2013.

24. Gary Mihoces, "Ravens Target Addai," *USA Today*, January 9, 2007.

25. Peter King, "Freaking 'Em Out," *Sports Illustrated*, January 22, 2007.

26. "Colts Showed Class, Ravens Fans Didn't," *Indianapolis Star*, January 6, 2007.

27. King, "Freaking 'Em Out."

28. Ibid.

29. Curt Calvin, "Patriots' Cornerback Hobbs: 'We Let Them Off the Hook,'" *Indianapolis Star*, January 22, 2007.

30. Bob Kravitz, "Manning, Colts Break Through with 2:17 of Magic," *Indianapolis Star*, January 22, 2007.

31. Michael Silver, "Bringing It Home," *Sports Illustrated*, February 12, 2007.

32. Ibid.

33. Michael Marot, "Manning's Super Bowl Ring Comes with MVP Award," Associated Press wire story, February 5, 2007.

34. "Peyton's Payday," *Indianapolis Star*, February 4, 2007.

35. Nicki Jhabvala, "Jay Glazer Explains His Infamous 2007 Feud with Peyton Manning," *Denver Post*, November 20, 2014.

36. "Ryan Leaf Q&A," *Playboy*, September 2013.

CHAPTER 19: ANYTHING YOU CAN DO

1. "Senator Wants NFL Spying Case Explained," *New York Times*, February 1, 2008.

2. "Patriots Players Dismiss Shula's Comments," *Providence Journal*, January 9, 2008.

3. Jim Trotter, "Chargers," *Sports Illustrated*, January 21, 2008.

4. Tom Canavan, "Giants' D Comes Up Big," Associated Press wire story, February 4, 2008.

5. Tim Layden, "They're History," *Sports Illustrated*, February 11, 2008.

6. Canavan, "Giants' D Comes Up Big."

7. Layden, "They're History."

8. "Fate Runs Out on Brady, Pats," Associated Press wire story, February 4, 2008.

9. Jason Kessler, "Super Bowl Hero Warns of 'Anarchy' if NY Approves Gay Marriage," CNN, June 17, 2011, http://www.cnn.com/2011/US/06/16/new.york.gay.marriage.tyree/.

10. "Winning Now a Family Business for Mannings," Associated Press wire story, February 3, 2008.

CHAPTER 20: "THE POWER OF PEYTON"

1. Adam Sternbergh, "Underdog," *New York*, January 27, 2008.

2. Ed Beeson, "Burress Involved in Domestic Disputes," *Bergen Record*, September 24, 2008.

3. "Guns Seized in Search of NFL Player's Home," CNN, December 24, 2008, http://www.cnn.com/2008/CRIME/12/24/burress.home.search/index.html.

4. "Freeney Fined for Postgame Comments," ESPN, January 10, 2009, http://www.espn.com/nfl/playoffs2008/news/story?id=3823511.

5. "Eli Manning Gets 6-Year, $97M Contract," Associated Press wire story, August 5, 2009.

6. Shaun Assael, "Sources: Police, FBI Team Up in Probe," ESPN, January 15, 2010, http://www.espn.com/nfl/news/story?id=4826851.

7. Judy Battista, "Well-Rested Manning Leads Colts Past Ravens," *New York Times*, January 16, 2010.

8. Lee Jenkins, "The Power of Peyton," *Sports Illustrated*, February 1, 2010.

9. Gregg Doyel, "Brain Tumor Survivor Lives the Big Blue Dream," *Indianapolis Star*, April 3, 2015.

10. Jenkins, "The Power of Peyton."

11. Jim Trotter, "Secondary Matters," *Sports Illustrated*, February 15, 2010, and Gary Myers, "After Disastrous Interception vs. New Orleans Saints, Peyton Manning a Man of Few Words," *New York Daily News*, February 8, 2010.

12. Curt Cavin, "Porter Hairdo a Work of Art," *Indianapolis Star*, February 8, 2010.

13. Lee Jenkins, "For You, New Orleans," *Sports Illustrated*, February 15, 2010.

14. Tim Layden, "Sportsman of the Year: Drew Brees," *Sports Illustrated*, December 6, 2010.

15. "Caldwell: 'You're Hired to Win Super Bowls,'" *Indianapolis Star*, February 7, 2010.

16. Mike Freeman, "Greatest QB Ever? Manning's Case Takes Hit," CBS News, February 8, 2010, https://www.cbsnews.com/news/greatest-qb-ever -mannings-case-takes-hit/.

CHAPTER 21: ONE DOWN, ONE UP

1. Gregg Rosenthal, "New Deal for Peyton Coming Next Year?" NBC Sports, September 18, 2009, http://profootballtalk.nbcsports.com/2009/09/18/new -deal-for-peyton-coming-next-year/.

2. Norman Chad, "'Manning Is Picked . . . I Believe It Must Be an Optical Illusion,'" *Indianapolis Star*, February 9, 2010.

3. Mike Chappell, "Colts Stacked with Top Picks at RB," *Indianapolis Star*, April 16, 2010.

4. Bob Kravitz, "A Day Later, Final Timeout Still Doesn't Make Any Sense," *Indianapolis Star*, February 10, 2011.

5. "Peyton Manning Had Neck Surgery," ESPN, May 25, 2011, http://www.espn.com/nfl/news/story?id=6584790.

6. Lee Jenkins, "Peyton Manning: 2013 Sportsman of the Year," *Sports Illustrated*, December 23, 2013.

7. Mike Chappell, "Manning Has 2nd Neck Surgery," *Indianapolis Star*, May 25, 2011.
8. Mike Chappell, "Is It Too Early to Start Looking Down the Road?" *Indianapolis Star*, April 25, 2011.
9. Lee Jenkins, "2013 Sportsman."
10. Sally Jenkins, "Peyton Manning on His Neck Surgeries Rehab—and How He Almost Didn't Make It Back," *Washington Post*, October 21, 2013.
11. Judy Battista, "Manning's $90 Million Deal Gives the Colts Flexibility," *New York Times*, July 30, 2011.
12. Brad Biggs, "Peyton Manning's Signing Bonus $20 Million," *National Football Post*, August 12, 2011, http://www.nationalfootballpost.com/peyton-mannings-signing-bonus-20-million/.
13. Sally Jenkins, "Neck Surgeries Rehab."
14. Chris Mortensen, "Peyton Manning Being Re-Evaluated?" ESPN, September 5, 2011, http://www.espn.com/nfl/story/_/id/6931858/peyton-manning-indianapolis-colts-neck-being-re-evaluated-doctors-sources-say.
15. Sally Jenkins, "Neck Surgeries Rehab."
16. Lee Jenkins, "2013 Sportsman."
17. Sally Jenkins, "Neck Surgeries Rehab."
18. Lee Jenkins, "2013 Sportsman."
19. Damon Hack, "Eli as in Elite," *Sports Illustrated*, January 23, 2012.

CHAPTER 22: MIRACLE, REDUX

1. Hack, "Eli as in Elite."
2. Peter King, "Déjà Vu All Over Again," *Sports Illustrated*, January 30, 2012.
3. Ibid.
4. "Spoke Too Soon, Guys? Giants Website Claims They've Already Won Super Bowl as Fans Shell Out $16,000 for One Seat at the Big Game," *London Daily Mail*, http://www.dailymail.co.uk/news/article-2096516/Super-Bowl-2012-New-York-Giants-website-claims-theyve-won-seats-sell-16k.html.
5. Victor Cruz, "Cruz Discusses Championship Hopes in Super Bowl Diary," *New York Post*, February 3, 2012.
6. Hack, "Eli as in Elite."
7. Bart Hubbuch, "Archie Proud Father of Eli," *New York Post*, February 6, 2012.
8. Damon Hack, "One Giant Leap for Manningkind," *Sports Illustrated*, February 13, 2012.
9. Mike Lupica, "Once Again, Eli Is Super," *New York Daily News*, February 6, 2012.
10. S. L. Price, "The Big Easy," *Sports Illustrated*, December 17, 2012.

CHAPTER 23: GOODBYE, HELLO

1. "Public Comments Irk Colts' Jim Irsay," ESPN, January 27, 2012, http://www
   .espn.com/nfl/story/_/id/7507255/indianapolis-colts-jim-irsay-upset
   -peyton-manning-went-public-comments.
2. Mike Chappell, "Irsay: Colts Want to Keep Manning—at Right Price," *Indianapolis Star*, February 14, 2012.
3. Lee Jenkins, "2013 Sportsman," *Sports Illustrated*, December 23, 2013.
4. Ibid.
5. Bob Kravitz, "No Easy Way for Irsay to Say Goodbye to Manning," *Indianapolis Star*, February 2, 2012.
6. "Peyton Manning Farewell Press Conference," *American Rhetoric*, March
   7, 2012, http://www.americanrhetoric.com/speeches/peytonmanning
   farewell.htm.
7. Peter King, "Peyton Manning's Long Game," *Sports Illustrated*, April 2, 2012.
8. Mike Klis, "Broncos Ready to Add Veteran QB," *Denver Post*, March 8, 2012.
9. Woody Paige, "Broncos Won't Make Peyton's Final List," *Denver Post*, March
   9, 2012.
10. "Peyton Watch: Look Out, Tebow," *Denver Post*, March 10, 2012.
11. King, "Peyton Manning's Long Game."
12. Ibid.
13. Mike Klis, "Frank Tripucka Would Be Honored If Peyton Manning Wears
    Broncos' No. 18," *Denver Post*, March 14, 2012.
14. "Obama Says Broncos Would Be 'Lucky' to Have Manning," CBS Denver,
    March 12, 2012.
15. Mark Kiszla, "Satisfying Me. B's Request Sends Shivers to Fan," *Denver Post*,
    March 11, 2012, and Mark Kiszla, "Elway's Biggest Gamble," *Denver Post*,
    March 13, 2012.
16. Nate Davis, "Broncos, Elway Introduce Manning after He Signs $96M Deal,"
    USA Today, March 20, 2012, http://content.usatoday.com/communities
    /thehuddle/post/2012/03/report-peyton-manning-signs-five-year-96
    -million-contract-with-broncos/1#.Wjirt_krLIV.
17. Mike Klis, "High Hope Not Just Pie in the Sky," *Denver Post*, March 25, 2012.
18. Peter King, "Stretching the Field," *Sports Illustrated*, November 5, 2012.
19. Lee Jenkins, "2013 Sportsman."
20. Ibid.
21. Woody Paige, "Peyton Not Passing Up Shot at Super Year," *Denver Post*,
    August 26, 2012.
22. Jeffri Chadiha, "Demaryius Thomas Recalls Reboot," ESPN, October 19,
    2014, http://www.espn.com/nfl/story/_/id/11667324/demaryius-thomas
    -recalls-catching-peyton-manning-first-broncos-td.

23. Mike Klis, "Manning's Final Pass of Denver's Season a 'Bad Throw,'" *Denver Post*, January 13, 2013.

24. "Playoff Upset: Ravens Beat Manning and Broncos 38–35 in Double Overtime," Associated Press wire story, January 13, 2013.

CHAPTER 24: "HE THROWS DUCKS"

1. Mike Klis, "Broncos, Peyton Manning Win Texas-Sized Shootout vs. Cowboys at Dallas," *Denver Post*, October 6, 2013.

2. Jarrett Bell, "Colts' Jim Irsay: No Regrets Releasing Peyton Manning," *USA Today*, October 15, 2013.

3. "Peyton Manning, John Elway Dispute Wes Welker's Suggestion that His Suspension Was a Shocker," AP, September 3, 2014.

4. Bob Kravitz, "Peyton Manning's Silence on Jim Irsay Says Enough," *Indianapolis Star*, October 16, 2013.

5. Lindsay H. Jones, "Colts Spoil Peyton Manning's Return to Indianapolis," *USA Today*, October 21, 2013.

6. Mike Freeman, "Peyton Manning's Record* Means Little If He Doesn't Win Super Bowl," *Bleacher Report*, December 22, 2013, http://bleacherreport.com /articles/1898279-peyton-mannings-record-means-little-if-he-doesnt-win -super-bowl.

7. Kurt Badenhousen, "Peyton Manning vs. Tom Brady: By the Numbers," *Forbes*, January 14, 2014.

8. Andrew Lawrence, "Peyton Manning Has One More Ghost to K.O.," *Sports Illustrated*, January 27, 2014.

9. Cindy Boren, "Richard Sherman On Peyton Manning's 'Ducks,'" *Washington Post*, January 30, 2014.

10. S. L. Price, "It's Just the Start," *Sports Illustrated*, February 10, 2014.

11. Mark Kiszla, "Super Apology May Not Need To Be Reissued by Peyton Manning," *Denver Post*, January 28, 2016.

12. Chris Chase, "Richard Sherman Goes Off On Peyton Manning . . . In a Good Way," *USA Today*, February 3, 2014.

13. Peter King, "Where to Begin?" *Sports Illustrated*, November 3, 2014, http://mmqb .si.com/2014/11/03/nfl-week-9-peter-king-monday-morning-quarterback.

14. Greg Bishop, "Von Trapped," *Sports Illustrated*, February 15, 2016.

15. Woody Paige, "Manning Will Trigger a Trip to AFC Title Game," *Denver Post*, January 11, 2015.

16. Gregg Doyel, "Give Luck Time To Surpass Manning," *Indianapolis Star*, January 11, 2015.

17. Stephen Holder, "Jim Irsay Looks Back on Peyton Manning, Ahead on Andrew Luck," *USA Today*, January 6, 2015.

18. Mark Kiszla, "It's All Over for the Legendary Manning," *Denver Post*, January 12, 2015.
19. Patrick Saunders, "Luck Outplays Manning in Shocker," *Denver Post*, January 12, 2015.
20. "Peyton Manning Noncommital for 2015 After Loss to Colts," *Denver Post*, January 11, 2015.
21. Bishop, "Von Trapped."
22. Jeff Legwold and Chris Mortensen, "Peyton Manning Taking a $4M Pay Cut," ESPN, March 5, 2015, http://www.espn.com/nfl/story/_/id/12422106/peyton -manning-denver-broncos-agree-4-million-pay-cut-2015.
23. Arnie Stapleton, "Peyton Manning: Tom Brady Apologized for Email Barb," Associated Press wire story, August 12, 2015.

CHAPTER 25: "GONNA DRINK A WHOLE LOTTA BEER"

1. Eric Prisbell, "Tony Romo, Cowboys Pounce on Giants' Blunder," *USA Today*, September 14, 2015.
2. Steve Serby, "Imposter for a Day: Giants Hoping Never to See Absentminded Eli Again," *New York Post*, September 15, 2015.
3. Howie Kussoy, "I Lost the Game for Us," *New York Post*, November 16, 2015.
4. Ebenezer Samuel, "Giants Players Heard 'Legitimate Threat' Made toward Odell Beckham, No Homophobic Slurs," *New York Daily News*, December 24, 2015.
5. Steve Serby, "Suspend It Like Beckham," *New York Post*, December 22, 2015.
6. Ibid.
7. O'Connell, "The Inevitable Decline."
8. Kevin Van Valkenburg, "The Audacity of Peyton Manning," *ESPN the Magazine*, September 25, 2015.
9. Bishop, "Von Trapped."
10. Drew Loftis, "Remember When Peyton Was the Man?" *New York Post*, November 17, 2015.
11. "The Dark Side: The Secret World of Sports Doping," Al Jazeera America, December 27, 2015, http://america.aljazeera.com/articles/2015/12/27/al -jazeera-investigates-secret-world-of-sports-doping.html.
12. "Documentary Links Peyton Manning, Other Pro Athletes to Use of PEDs," ESPN, December 28, 2015, http://www.espn.com/nfl/story/_/id/14441114 /documentary-links-peyton-manning-other-pro-athletes-use-peds.
13. Ibid.
14. "Transcript: Peyton Manning Interviews with ESPN's Lisa Salters," December 27, 2015, http://www.denverbroncos.com/news-and-blogs/article-1

/Transcript-Peyton-Manning-interviews-with-ESPNs-Lisa-Salters/f07ef954
-bada-42fc-ab64-f9f38dc9fb49.

15. Paula Mooney, "Delta-2 Steroid: D2 Steroid Sold by 'Thomas Mann'—'The Dark Side' Claims Dustin Keller Bought All D2 Stock Online," *Inquisitr*, December 27, 2015, http://www.inquisitr.com/2660292/delta-2-steroid-d2 -steroid-sold-by-thomas-mann-the-dark-side-claims-dustin-keller-bought -all-d2-stock-online-video/.

16. Christian Red, "Sorry Charlie! Experts Say Delta 2 Is a Pretty Weak PED," *New York Daily News*, January 7, 2016.

17. "Documentary Links Peyton Manning."

18. "Transcript: Peyton Manning Interviews."

19. Will Hobson and Justin Wm. Moyer, "Inside Peyton Manning's Secret Investigation into Al Jazeera Documentary," *Washington Post*, February 4, 2016.

20. "Documentary Links Peyton Manning."

21. "Archie Manning Blasts HGH Report Involving Son Peyton," ESPN, February 4, 2016, http://www.espn.com/nfl/story/_/id/14713984/archie-manning -defends-son-peyton-manning-regarding-al-jazeera-america-report.

22. Matthew Rewinski, "Peyton Manning PED Allegation Expose Tom Brady Haters," *Chowder and Champions*, December 30, 2015, https:// chowderandchampions.com/2015/12/30/peyton-manning-ped-allegation -expose-tom-brady-haters/.

23. "NFL Finds Peyton Manning Did Not Use HGH, PEDs," *Sports Illustrated*, July 25, 2016, http://www.si.com/nfl/2016/07/25/peyton-manning-hgh -peds-nfl-investigation.

24. Bishop, "Von Trapped."

25. Greg Bishop, "As Denver Turns," *Sports Illustrated*, January 25, 2016.

26. Bishop, "Von Trapped."

27. Jack Dickey, "Fossil Fueled," *Sports Illustrated*, December 14, 2015.

28. Greg Bishop, "La-D-Friggin'-Da," *Sports Illustrated*, February 1, 2016.

29. David Newton, "Mike Tolbert to Opponents: If You Don't Like Panthers' End -Zone Dances, 'Stop Us,'" ESPN, January 27, 2016, http://www.espn.com/nfl /story/_/id/14661671/panthers-end-zone-dances-stop-us.

30. Troy E. Renck, "Peyton Manning Eager to Help Boost Broncos Offense," *Denver Post*, January 28, 2016, http://www.denverpost.com/2016/01/28/peyton -manning-eager-to-help-boost-broncos-offense/.

31. Mark Kiszla, "Super Apology May Not Need to Be Reissued by Peyton Manning," *Denver Post*, January 28, 2016.

32. Bishop, "Von Trapped."

33. Ibid.

34. "Broncos Defeat Panthers, 24–10, as Von Miller and 'D' Help Peyton Manning in Super Bowl 50," *New York Daily News*, February 8, 2016.

35. "Peyton Manning: Here He Is America . . . The Guy You Sided with Over Tom Brady," *Patskrieg.com: New England Patriots Fan Blog*, January 17, 2014, https://patskrieg.com/2014/01/17/peyton-manning-here-he-is-america-the -guy-you-sided-with-over-tom-brady/.

36. Drew Magary, "Why Your Team Sucks 2016: Denver Broncos," *Deadspin*, September 7, 2016, http://deadspin.com/why-your-team-sucks-2016-denver -broncos-1786098524.

37. "Women's Group Calls for Sponsors to Drop Peyton Manning," *Denver Post*, February 17, 2016.

38. "Vols to Protect Manning's Name," *Denver Post*, February 25, 2016.

39. Author interview with Tony Reginelli.

40. "Peyton Manning Retirement Speech: Full Text," Denver Post.com, March 7, 2016, http://www.denverpost.com/2016/03/07/peyton-manning-retirement -speech-full-text/.

41. Kevin Van Valkenburg, "After the Perfect Ending, What's Peyton Manning's Next Rodeo?" ESPN, February 8, 2016, http://www.espn.com/nfl/story/_/id /14734266/after-perfect-ending-denver-broncos-peyton-manning-next -rodeo.

CHAPTER 26: LAST MANNING STANDING

1. "Giants Release Josh Brown after Domestic Violence Admission," ESPN, October 25, 2016, http://www.espn.com/nfl/story/_/id/17884851/kicker -josh-brown-released-new-york-giants-abuse-admission.

2. Dan Duggan, "Giants' Eli Manning on Odell Beckham: 'We're on the Same Page,'" NJ.com, October 18, 2016, http://www.nj.com/giants/index.ssf/2016 /10/giants_eli_manning_on_odell_beckham_were_on_the_sa.html.

3. Ryan Lazo, "Eli Back on Track with a Giant Effort," *New York Post*, October 17, 2016.

4. Luis Tirado Jr., "New York Giants: Life after Eli Manning Is Coming," *Fansided*, January 12, 2017, http://nflspinzone.com/2017/01/12/new-york-giants -eli-manning-life-after/.

5. Gary Myers, "Giants, Led by Odell Beckham and Party Boat, Waste Chance for Eli Manning to Win One More Super Bowl," *New York Daily News*, January 9, 2017.

6. Stanton Peele, "The Psychology of Archie Manning and Sons," *Psychology Today*, February 1, 2014, https://www.psychologytoday.com/blog/addiction -in-society/201402/the-psychology-archie-manning-and-sons.

7. Zach Braziller, "Ben McAdoo Throws "Sloppy" Eli Manning Right under the Bus," *New York Post*, September 19, 2017.

8. Ryan Wilson, "Eli Manning on Embracing Coach's Criticism: 'Everybody

Has Gotten Very Sensitive,'" CBS Sports, September 21, 2017, https://www
.cbssports.com/nfl/news/eli-manning-on-embracing-coachs-criticism
-everybody-has-gotten-very-sensitive/.

9. Kyle Porter, "Peyton Manning Gets Mobbed for Autographs at Pebble Beach
Pro-Am," CBS Sports, February 10, 2013, https://www.cbssports.com/golf
/news/watch-peyton-manning-gets-mobbed-for-autographs-at-pebble
-beach-pro-am/.

INDEX